中華五千年文明藝術展

啟功題

CHINA

5,000 YEARS

INNOVATION AND TRANSFORMATION IN THE ARTS

SELECTED BY SHERMAN LEE

GUGGENHEIM MUSEUM

front cover:
Rearing dragon
TANG DYNASTY (618–907)
cat. no. 59

back cover:
Shang Xi
The Xuande Emperor on an Outing
MING DYNASTY (1368–1644)
cat. no. 190 (detail)

frontispiece:
Qi Gong
Exhibition of 5,000 Years of Chinese Art and Culture
1997

previous two pages:
Mythical beast
EASTERN ZHOU, SPRING AND AUTUMN PERIOD (770–476 BCE)
cat. no. 46

Guggenheim Museum Publications
1071 Fifth Avenue
New York, New York 10128

Hardcover editions distributed by
Harry N. Abrams, Inc.
100 Fifth Avenue
New York, New York 10011

ISBN 0-8109-6908-4 (hardcover)
ISBN 0-89207-202-4 (softcover)

Design by Tsang Seymour Design, Inc., New York
Printed in Italy by Mariogros

CHINA: 5,000 YEARS
Curated by Sherman Lee

Solomon R. Guggenheim Museum
February 6–June 3, 1998

Guggenheim Museum Bilbao
Summer 1998

China: 5,000 Years has been organized by the
Guggenheim Museum in collaboration with the
Ministry of Culture of the People's Republic of China
and the National Administration for Cultural
Heritage of the People's Republic of China,
China International Exhibition Agency and
Art Exhibitions China.

Major sponsors of this exhibition are

Significant additional support has been provided by
The Starr Foundation
The W.L.S. Spencer Foundation
and
Mori Building Company Limited

This exhibition has also been made possible in part
by a major grant from the National Endowment for
the Humanities, expanding America's understanding of
who we were, who we are, and who we will be.

This catalogue is supported by a grant from The Li-Ching
Cultural and Educational Foundation.

CHINA
5,000 YEARS

HOWARD ROGERS GENERAL EDITOR

Naomi Noble Richard CONSULTING EDITOR
Sylvia Moss EDITOR

SPONSOR'S STATEMENT

Of all cultures that have existed for thousands of years, China's is one of the oldest. Since the travels of Marco Polo, it has intrigued the Western imagination and has had an immense influence on European art and culture. This fascination with China has thrived right up until the present day, and a journey to "the Middle Kingdom" remains an extraordinarily rich and captivating experience. Since the earliest contacts between China and the West, transportation technology has made considerable contributions to cultural interchange, first through maritime trade and later, on a more extensive scale, through air traffic as well. Lufthansa, which has participated in the realization of this exhibition, undertook its first test flights to China during the 1920s, and in 1927 and 1928, the famous Asian expert Sven Hedin explored the Gobi desert and its climate with Lufthansa's assistance.

These initial adventures developed into commerical flights, when, in 1930, Lufthansa and the Chinese Ministry of Transport signed an agreement for the operation of a European-Asian air-mail company, Eurasia. The company flew its Shanghai-Nanjing-Beijing-Manshuli route once a week, and, although this scheme soon had to be given up, its pioneering flights represented a further step in China's relationship with Europe and the rest of the world.

Today, air connections to China are both comfortable and plentiful. As in the early days of aviation, however, Lufthansa's commitment in China is greater than the transportation of passengers and cargo. Together with Air China, Lufthansa operates a maintenance center for Chinese aviation, cooperates in the training of aviation personnel, and runs air-catering kitchens.

China: 5,000 Years is an expression of the ties between the West and China as it reemerges as an economic and political superpower. We are pleased to offer our support for this exhibition as a Global Partner of the Solomon R. Guggenheim Foundation, with the conviction that works of art build the longest-lasting bridges to mutual understanding.

Frederick W. Reid
President and Chief Operating Officer
Lufthansa German Airlines

Lufthansa

SPONSOR'S STATEMENT

As we begin our association with the Guggenheim Museum, Nokia is especially pleased to play a role in bringing this rich story of five thousand years of Chinese art and culture to people of the Western world. In our contemporary global society, where the written and spoken word may disjoin, art unifies. It projects the essence of a people, their values, and their inspiration.

For Nokia, art embodies the principles of openness, creativity, and lasting value to which we as an institution are committed. For that reason, we are proud not only to sponsor *China: 5,000 Years* but also to support the Finnish Museum for Modern Arts in Helsinki and the Chinese Year of Fine Arts 1998 in Beijing. The thinking that underlies these sponsorships is reflected in our products, which are designed for aesthetic appeal as well as technological achievement.

Because of this, our association with the Guggenheim is a natural step in the continuing evolution of Nokia's corporate culture. We share a common vision of connecting people and enriching lives through technology, art, and design. From its original location in New York to the new museum in Bilbao, the Guggenheim is synonymous with the development and preservation of art, and thus with furthering knowledge and social achievement.

China: 5,000 Years is the culmination of the efforts of a distinguished international team of experts. As the largest exhibition of such art ever to be seen outside China, it presents an extremely broad and unprecedented view of Chinese cultural development in which we all can find inspiration. We hope that you enjoy the exhibition and the great wealth it offers.

Jorma Ollila
President and Chief Executive Officer

SPONSOR'S STATEMENT

On behalf of the thousands of Ford Motor Company employees around the world, I am pleased to salute all of those involved in presenting *China: 5,000 Years*. Their unique collaboration offers the people of the United States and Spain this extraordinary exhibition, which demonstrates the full scope of Chinese artistic development over the last five thousand years.

Our thanks go to the Guggenheim Museum; Qian Qichen, Vice Premier and Foreign Minister of the People's Republic of China; Li Daoyu, Ambassador of the People's Republic of China to the United States; the Ministry of Culture of the People's Republic of China; the National Administration for Cultural Heritage of the People's Republic of China; China International Exhibition Agency; and Art Exhibitions China for organizing this major cultural exchange between the United States and the People's Republic of China.

We at Ford Motor Company believe deeply in shared understanding between nations, and especially in strengthening the relationship between the governments, businesses, and people of the United States and China. We are particularly pleased to serve as a partner in bringing the rich cultural heritage of China to the people of the United States and Spain, and look forward to introducing the people of China to American art when the exchange exhibition *America: 300 Years* is presented in Beijing and Shanghai in late 1998 and 1999.

Alex Trotman
Chairman and Chief Executive Officer

SPONSOR'S STATEMENT

China: 5,000 Years offers Americans the opportunity to appreciate the beauty created over five millennia by one of the world's oldest civilizations. From early Neolithic jade carvings to twentieth-century pieces, the exhibition allows the world its first view of many magnificent works.

The Coca-Cola Company commends the Guggenheim Museum for bringing an extraordinary collection of Chinese artistic treasures to the United States, and for its leadership in fostering mutual understanding between cultures. We welcome the opportunity to demonstrate our commitment to education through the arts, from the global exchange of ideas and information to the promotion of human understanding and diversity.

As a partner of the Guggenheim Museum, we are pleased to help spotlight China's rich cultural heritage, and to encourage a deeper understanding of the profound achievements of generations of Chinese artists.

M. Douglas Ivester
Chairman of the Board and Chief Executive Officer

The Coca-Cola Company

HONORARY CHAIR

HONORARY COMMITTEE

HONORARY COMMITTEE

PEOPLE'S REPUBLIC OF CHINA

Liu Zhongde	Minister, Ministry of Culture of P.R.C.
Li Yuanchao	Vice-Minister, Ministry of Culture of P.R.C.
Zhang Wenbin	Director General, National Administration for Cultural Heritage, P.R.C.
Ma Zishu	Vice-Director, National Administration for Cultural Heritage, P.R.C.
Qi Gong	Member, Standing Committee of the Chinese People's Political Conference of P.R.C.; Director, State Committee for Identifying Cultural Relics
Sun Weixue	Director, Bureau for External Cultural Relations, Ministry of Culture of P.R.C.
Lei Congyun	Director, Art Exhibitions China
Hao Zhan	Director, China International Exhibition Agency
Yu Weichao	Director, National Museum of Chinese History, Beijing
Ma Chengyuan	Director, Shanghai Museum
Tan Bin	Deputy Director, Palace Museum, Beijing
Su Bai	Professor, Beijing University
Ren Jiyu	Director, Beijing Library
Wang Wenqing	Director, Shaanxi Provincial Bureau of Cultural Relics
Yang Huancheng	Director, Henan Provincial Museum, Zhengzhou
Ma Jiayu	Director, Sichuan Provincial Institute of Archaeology and Cultural Relics, Chengdu
Xu Huping	Director, Nanjing Museum, Jiangsu Province
Jia Yang	Deputy Director, Bureau of Culture of Tibetan Autonomous Region
Li Kunsheng	Director, Yunnan Provincial Museum, Kunming
Shu Zhimei	Director, Hubei Provincial Museum, Wuhan
Xia Lu	Director, Shanxi Provincial Museum, Taiyuan
Wang Mianhou	Director, Liaoning Provincial Museum, Shenyang
Xiong Chuanxin	Director, Hunan Provincial Museum, Changsha
Zhang Lizhu	Director, Hebei Provincial Bureau of Cultural Relics
Ji Genzhang	Director, Jiangsu Provincial Bureau of Culture
Bao Xianlun	Director, Zhejiang Provincial Bureau of Cultural Relics
Mai Yinghao	Honorary Director, Museum of the Tomb of the Nanyue King of the Western Han Dynasty, Guangdong Province
Zhang Qingjie	Director, Shanxi Provincial Institute of Archaeology, Taiyuan
Wang Limei	Director, Foreign Affairs Office, National Administration for Cultural Heritage, P.R.C.
Meng Xianmin	Department Director, National Administration for Cultural Heritage, P.R.C.
Zheng Guangrong	Department Director, National Administration for Cultural Heritage, P.R.C.
Yang Yang	Deputy Director, Art Exhibitions China
Yin Jia	Director, Exhibition Department, Art Exhibitions China
Zhang Jianxin	Director, External Affairs Department, Art Exhibitions China
Qian Wei	Assistant Research Fellow, Exhibition Department, Art Exhibitions China

ADVISORY COMMITTEE

GUGGENHEIM MUSEUM

Sherman Lee — Director (retired), Cleveland Museum of Art
Helmut Brinker — Professor, University of Zurich
James Cahill — Professor Emeritus, History of Art, University of California, Berkeley
Elizabeth Childs-Johnson — Visiting Scholar, New York University
Patricia Ebrey — Professor, Department of History, University of Washington
Michael Knight — Curator of Chinese Art, Asian Art Museum of San Francisco
Regina Krahl — Independent Scholar, Affiliated with the Royal Museums of Art and History, Brussels
Jenny So — Curator of Ancient Chinese Art, Freer Gallery of Art and Arthur M. Sackler Gallery, Smithsonian Institution, Washington, D.C.
Peter Sturman — Associate Professor, Department of the History of Art and Architecture, University of California, Santa Barbara
Wu Hung — Harrie A. Vanderstappen Distinguished Service Professor in Chinese Art History, University of Chicago
Zhao Feng — Professor, China National Silk Museum, Hangzhou

ADVISORY COMMITTEE

PEOPLE'S REPUBLIC OF CHINA

Su Bai — Professor, Beijing University
Qi Gong — Member, Standing Committee of the Chinese People's Political Conference of P.R.C.; Director, State Committee for Identifying Cultural Relics
Huang Jinglue — Head, Expert Committee of the National Administration for Cultural Heritage, P.R.C.
Xu Pingfang — Researcher, Former Director, China Social Science of Archaeology Institute, Beijing
Yu Weichao — Director, National Museum of Chinese History, Beijing
Ma Chengyuan — Director, Shanghai Museum
Zhang Zhongpei — Researcher, Palace Museum, Beijing
Wang Qingzheng — Deputy Director, Shanghai Museum
Liu Jiu'an — Researcher, Palace Museum, Beijing

EXHIBITION PROJECT TEAM

GUGGENHEIM MUSEUM

Jane DeBevoise, Manon Slome, Xiaoming Zhang,
Emily Wei, Nicole Lin, Shihong Aldin,
Mary Jane Clark, Tracy Power, Adegboyega Adefope

Exhibition Design Consultant:
Arata Isozaki

EXHIBITION PROJECT TEAM

PEOPLE'S REPUBLIC OF CHINA

National Administration for Cultural Heritage:
Wang Limei, Meng Xianmin, Zheng Guangrong

Art Exhibitions China:
Yang Yang, Yin Jia, Zhang Jianxin, Qian Wei,
Chen Shujie

LENDERS TO THE EXHIBITION

National Museum of Chinese History, Beijing
Palace Museum, Beijing
Liaoning Provincial Museum, Shenyang
Tianjin Municipal History Museum
Hebei Provincial Museum, Shijiazhuang
Hebei Provincial Institute of Cultural Relics, Shijiazhuang
Henan Provincial Museum, Zhengzhou
Henan Provincial Institute of Archaeology and Cultural Relics, Zhengzhou
Zhengzhou Municipal Museum, Henan Province
Guanlin Museum of Stone Sculpture, Luoyang, Henan Province
Luoyang Cultural Relics Work Team, Henan Province
Luoyang Municipal Museum, Henan Province
Nanyang Municipal Museum, Henan Province
Hubei Provincial Museum, Wuhan
Hunan Provincial Museum, Changsha
Administrative Office for Cultural Relics, Anxiang County, Hunan Province
Museum of the Tomb of the Nanyue King of the Western Han Dynasty, Guangdong Province
Shanxi Provincial Museum, Taiyuan
Shanxi Provincial Institute of Archaeology, Taiyuan
Museum of Terra-cotta Warriors and Horses of Qin Shihuangdi, Xi'an, Shaanxi Province
Shaanxi History Museum, Xi'an
Forest of Steles Museum, Xi'an, Shaanxi Province
Institute for the Protection of Cultural Relics and Archaeology, Xi'an, Shaanxi Province
Famen Temple Museum, Shaanxi Province
Baoji Municipal Museum, Shaanxi Province
Zhouyuan Museum, Xi'an, Shaanxi Province
Sichuan Provincial Museum, Chengdu
Sichuan Provincial Institute of Archaeology and Cultural Relics, Chengdu
Administrative Office for Cultural Relics, Xindu County, Sichuan Province
Yunnan Provincial Museum, Kunming
Administrative Office of Norbu Linka, Lhasa, Autonomous Region of Tibet
Shanghai Museum
Nanjing Museum, Jiangsu Province
Suzhou Municipal Museum, Jiangsu Province
Zhenjiang Municipal Museum, Jiangsu Province
Yangzhou Municipal Museum, Jiangsu Province
Zhejiang Provincial Museum, Hangzhou
Zhejiang Provincial Institute of Cultural Relics and Archaeology, Hangzhou
Administrative Office for Cultural Relics, Wenling, Zhejiang Province

NOTES TO READERS

Romanization. Chinese is here transcribed according to the *pinyin* system of romanization adopted by the People's Republic of China and now in general use. Sanskrit names and terms are transcribed using full upper diacriticals but no lower diacriticals. Parenthetic *C:* and *S:* stand for "Chinese" and "Sanskrit," respectively.

Names. All Chinese names are cited in traditional Asian fashion, surname followed by given name.

Dates. Following custom, Chinese emperors from antiquity to the beginning of the Ming dynasty are referred to by the name of their dynasty followed by their posthumous names (e.g., Song Huizong, whose personal name was Zhao Ji). Again following custom, emperors of the Ming and Qing dynasties are referred to by the auspicious name chosen by themselves for each of their reigns (e.g., the Xuande ["Far-Reaching Virtue"] emperor). Note that the reign-era (*nianhao*) never exactly corresponded to the dates of the reign itself, usually being proclaimed some months after the enthronement and continuing in use until the successor, some time after *his* enthronement, proclaimed a new reign-era.

Ceramics. Chinese place-names changed frequently, usually reflecting political changes. Most ceramics are conventionally called by the ancient names of the states, counties, or towns in or near which the principal kilns were located (Cizhou ware, Yue ware), or by the site names of the first characteristic finds (Yangshao ware). Names of other wares refer to their glaze color (e.g., *qingbai*, "bluish white," or *sancai*, "three-colored"). Note that the gray-green, blue-green, or olive-green wares formerly differentiated as Northern and Southern Celadons, Ru ware, and Guan ware are here all termed "green-glazed ware," as an indication that they are all branches of a single stylistic and technological "family."

Introduction

Zhang Wenbin

Director General,
National Administration for
Cultural Heritage, Beijing

China: 5,000 Years, an exhibition nearly

four years in preparation, is a major event

in Sino–American cultural exchanges, one

that will undoubtedly further mutual

understanding between our two

governments and friendship between our

two peoples. On this occasion, both as

Director General of the National

Administration for Cultural Heritage and

in my personal capacity, I am delighted to offer warm and heartfelt congratulations for the exhibition's opening at the world-renowned Solomon R. Guggenheim Museum, and to anticipate its resounding success.

The exhibition *China: 5,000 Years* is aptly named, for the more than two hundred Chinese cultural treasures here assembled range from extraordinary and inspired creations of our prehistoric forebears to objects of luxury and paintings dating from the reigns of the Yongzheng (r. 1723–1735) and Qianlong (r. 1736–1795) emperors of the Qing dynasty. Thirty-nine different cultural institutions throughout China have made these treasures available. Among the exhibits are a jade pig-dragon of the Hongshan culture in Liaoning Province (cat. 2), the extraordinary four-ram bronze *zun* of Shang date from Hunan Province (cat. 23), and a *mise*-glazed octagonal bottle from the Famen Temple in Shaanxi Province (cat. 125), as well as stone carvings from a Song dynasty temple site in Shaanxi Province (cat. 177), and Song, Yuan, Ming, and Qing dynasty paintings from the collections of the Shanghai Museum and the Palace Museum in Beijing. Some of these national treasures of long-standing fame are being exhibited abroad for the first time. I may therefore say without exaggeration that, for quality, size, comprehensiveness, and diversity of sources, *China: 5,000 Years* sets new standards for overseas exhibitions of Chinese cultural relics. This is truly a magnificent show, and those who see it will have reason to rejoice.

As Chinese and American experts agreed, this exhibition at the Guggenheim Museum will focus on the magnificent advances in the civilization of the Chinese people over five millennia, as reflected in culture and art. I strongly agree with this well-conceived approach, and fully support its implementation. Although the appearance and development of every art form are subject to the constraints of natural, social, and historical conditions, art, which expresses as well as nourishes the essence of the human spirit, often epitomizes the starting and end-points of human development. It transcends the limitations of era, country, and ethnicity, brings together all the dignity and pride of the human race, and demonstrates that most precious wisdom and capacity inherently possessed by people. Hence, works of art can reflect the continuity and variation of a cultural tradition, the internal meaning and outward manifestations of an era, and the internal character and spiritual qualities of a people. They do so in the profoundest and most diverse ways, from a wealth of perspectives, and through the freshest and liveliest forms. For this reason, works of art can also easily overcome the constraints of time and space to communicate knowledge and friendship between people of

different ethnicities and cultural traditions, and in so doing to build bridges of understanding and trust. Although the various artistic treasures displayed in *China: 5,000 Years* are but a tiny portion of China's ancient artistic heritage, they are among the most representative and most expressive specimens. My respected teacher, Professor Su Bai of Beijing University, and others have prepared excellent detailed comments and analyses. I am therefore fully confident that through an appreciation of these remarkable works of art, viewers will gain a clear and deep, albeit not comprehensive, impression of the Chinese people over five millennia, and of the breadth and depth of their history and culture.

Among the world's great civilizations, that of China is unique in its *continuity*. The Mesopotamians or the Mayans have no modern heirs, but modern Chinese culture has demonstrably descended in an unbroken line from its ancient roots. Chinese culture is also remarkable in the degree to which cultural differences, born of time and vast distance, interpenetrated and catalyzed the development of a coherent and enduring Chinese culture. Like a mighty and luxuriant tree, China stands tall in the forest of the world's peoples, surviving and thriving through five thousand years of winds and rains, a remarkable history that may not be well known in the West.

In this exhibition one can see about thirty bronzes from the Xia, Shang, and Zhou periods (21st-5th c. BCE). They come from the nine provinces of Hebei, Henan, Shanxi, Shaanxi, Hubei, Hunan, Zhejiang, Sichuan, and Yunnan. The sites where they were unearthed span a distance roughly equal to that between the east and west coasts of the United States and a period of roughly fifteen hundred years. In design, ornamentation, stylization, and casting techniques these bronzes display dissimilarities ranging in degree from variations to pronounced differences. The resulting richness and diversity was occasioned not only by passage of time and change of dynasties but also by differences in region and ethnicity. This richness and diversity testifies to continuous progress in social productivity, social structure, and social consciousness in Bronze Age China. Diversity of form and technique, however, was subsumed in a commonality of function: the bronzes of this period all served as utensils for rituals and ceremonials (such as sacrifices and banquets) and as symbols of the social status of their users.

So too with other types of artworks from other periods of Chinese history; interpenetration and continuity became a basic phenomenon of Chinese cultural development. Such cultural intermingling and merging demonstrate the influence and absorptive power of the orthodox culture, which was primarily that of the majority Han people (as well as of their predecessors, the Huaxia people). It reflects the stability of that culture, as well as the harmonious coexistence of cultural diversity and uniformity, which is its essential quality. To the best of my knowledge, this may be a mode of cultural progression unique to China. It germinated in prehistoric China, took shape in the pre-Qin period, and was continually reinforced in dynastic China. History has already shown that China's vast and wondrous soil affords a great stage for her many nationalities to exercise their native bents and abilities.

A people must have a source of spiritual strength. The great wellspring of spiritual strength and survival for the Chinese people over several millennia has been their sense of dignity, love, confidence, and respect for themselves; their love of country and struggle for unity; their perseverance, self-renewal, and ability to carry on against all adversity. It was precisely the tremendous creativity unleashed by this spirit that has enabled the Chinese people to flourish at an early period of human history, to maintain their place, unceasing and uninterrupted, among the peoples of the world, and in so doing to make an indelible contribution to human culture. A full recognition of this characteristic of Chinese culture will help deepen our understanding of its perseverance and also reinforce our confidence in its future.

The treasures displayed in *China: 5,000 Years* have existed for thousands of years and will continue to exist for uncounted years more, providing strong evidence of China's enormous potential. A dependable foundation for the full realization of this great potential, 5,000 years of cumulative cultural achievements augur well for China's swift ascent in the twenty-first century.

May 1997, Honglou Shatan, Beijing

Introduction and Acknowledgments

Thomas Krens

Director, The Solomon R.
Guggenheim Foundation

China: 5,000 Years explores innovation

and transformation in Chinese art over a

period of five millennia, from neolithic

jades of the third millennium BCE

through the modern era. While the very

length of this continuous cultural

tradition may suggest a profound

conservatism, China has in fact produced

daring, transgressive, and stylistically

and technologically innovative art for a longer period of time, and at a higher level of sophistication, than any other civilization in history. This exhibition, which is designed to confirm that assertion, results from the timely convergence of two distinct factors: a wealth of newly excavated objects and artifacts of stunning beauty and significance, and an increased appreciation in China of cultural achievements of the twentieth century. As a consequence, the juxtaposition of modern Chinese art with its traditional counterpart in an exhibition mounted by a major Western museum has been made possible for the first time ever.

The major exhibitions of art from Taiwan that have been staged in recent years have encouraged a popular perception that works of comparable quality do not exist today in China. It is important to stress, first of all, that significant portions of the former imperial collection never left China but remained in Beijing and elsewhere; the Palace Museum in Beijing, for example, still holds some ten thousand premodern paintings and pieces of calligraphy. Second, major collections remained in private hands, and many of these works subsequently entered public collections in Shanghai (where approximately six thousand scrolls are located), Nanjing (about fifteen hundred scrolls), and other large and small museums throughout the country. Finally, large-scale artworks, such as stone sculpture, which could not be readily removed, remained in numerous religious and secular contexts.

It has been noted that China's cultural legacy, unlike that of Greece or Rome, was preserved beneath rather than on the surface of the ground, due to the long-standing practice of burying artworks with the deceased. The clandestine opening of tombs began as early as the time of Confucius, in the fifth century BCE, and bronzes and jades so gathered formed part of the imperial collection in later centuries. But formal archaeological excavations were virtually unknown in China before the present century, and were not conducted continu-

ously and systematically until after the founding of the People's Republic of China. During the nearly five decades since then, the pace of discovery has quickened from a trickle to a deluge of new finds, a logical outcome of the surging economic development that required the digging of foundations for new factories, houses, office buildings, roads, airports, and power facilities. China has now become the scene of more archaeological activity than anywhere else in the world, and the discoveries have added immensely to our existing knowledge in some areas, while opening entirely new chapters in others. The discovery, conservation, and analysis of these objects and artifacts will, of course, continue, and a definitive cultural history remains to be written. But *China: 5,000 Years*, which draws heavily on these new resources and discusses them in a scholarly context within this exhibition catalogue, has become an active participant in that process.

The traditional section of *China: 5,000 Years* draws its material from the cultural treasures held in museums throughout the People's Republic of China, as well as the discoveries that have come to light in the last fifty years, to present an expanded vision of Chinese culture. Professor Sherman Lee is the chief architect of this enterprise. His lifetime commitment to the art of China, his extraordinary professional career—which included twenty-six years as Director of the Cleveland Museum of Art, where he built one of the great collections of Chinese antiquities—and his reputation as America's leading scholar of Chinese culture have given him a singular platform from which to formulate an exquisite sensitivity toward and understanding of Chinese art history. Professor Lee's insights, which are reflected in his selection of objects for this exhibition, include the dynamic relationships that existed between the early Chinese and the spiritual, natural, and cosmological worlds in which they lived. He also emphasizes an aggressively innovative and transformative impulse— rather than a reliance on tradition—as the enduring achievement of Chinese art, and he gives an unprecedented primacy to three-dimensional work, particularly to Buddhist sculpture.

These, then, are the great formative themes of *China: 5,000 Years*, which emerged as a result of Professor Lee's numerous trips to China over the past four years. During these visits, he traveled throughout the country to provincial museums and archaeological excavations, as well as to the great collections in Beijing and Shanghai. He searched through warehouses of recently excavated material and considered well-known objects currently on display. The selection of objects he made for this exhibition reflects his personal vision, and it has a freshness and a breathtaking elegance that will make scholars and laymen alike feel that they are seeing Chinese art for the first time. Professor Lee's vision has been supported by an impressive array of international scholars, who have provided assistance and consultation on every aspect of the project, including Helmut Brinker, James Cahill, Regina Krahl, Howard Rogers, and Jenny So, who rendered continuous support and advice on all aspects of the exhibition as it was being planned and on the structure and rhythm of the installation at the Guggenheim Museum. On the Chinese side, Zhang Wenbin, Director General of the National Administration for Cultural Heritage, and Wang Limei, Director of the Foreign Affairs Office of the National Administration for Cultural Heritage, structured the lengthy discussions and negotiations with the various museums and archaeological excavations that have lent objects to the exhibition. They also provided invaluable advice, as did the directors of the Palace Museum in Beijing and the Shanghai Museum, Yang Xin, Ma Chengyuan, and Wang Qingzheng, who not only made their collections available, but often suggested improvements to the checklist that went beyond our expectations. In short, the traditional section of *China: 5,000 Years* is a visionary and collaborative enterprise of unprecedented proportion between Chinese, American, and international scholars.

The modern section of *China: 5,000 Years* has no less an engaging history. As China has modernized and gradually become more accessible to the Western world during the past 150 years, so too has its visual culture, but the country's most recent cultural production has been largely ignored by a Western sensibility dominated almost exclusively by a Modernist Western canon. The turbulent political and social context in which twentieth-century Chinese art has developed, however, is no reason to separate it from the larger history of Chinese art from which it derives much of its inspiration, or from the Western traditions that it also reflects. Its particular fascination will not be found in the degree to which it participated in the development of a Euro-American Modernism, but rather in the struggle that is reflected in its attempt to bridge traditional Chinese attitudes with the inevitable consequences of contemporary politics and expanding contact with the West.

The late nineteenth to early twentieth centuries brought a certain cultural cross-fertilization between China and Europe. Just as European artists were influenced by Asian block-printing techniques, perspectival flatness, and decorative tendencies, for example, Chinese artists were drawn to Western approaches, methodologies, and techniques, such as Impressionism, abstraction, realistic portraiture, and oil painting. The late nineteenth century in China saw innovations within the traditional context, which developed under the patronage of Shanghai's new economic elite. Highlights included elaborate works with bird and flower themes, and paintings based on fantastic narratives, which appealed to a new class of collectors in this vibrant industrial port city. Chinese art of the early part of the twentieth century reflected the growing cosmopolitan attitude of Chinese artists, many of whom studied abroad. The 1920s saw a re-emergence of the woodcut as a powerful artistic medium, as art became swept up in the social and political upheavals that were coursing through China. The inherently stark contrast and imminent reproducibility of woodcuts made this a natural medium for communicating the horrific realities of the Japanese invasion, and the numerous prints reflecting the horrors of war from this period recall the graphic work of Francisco de Goya in their shocking impact. Postwar communism brought a socialist-realist format that produced some of the most outstanding examples of realist painting ever seen. Although Chinese socialist realism was not considered by most Western critics, there is no doubt that painterly technique flourished in the Chinese academy at a level of extraordinary sophistication, and this laid the foundation for a rejuvenation of Chinese art during the past two decades through a blending of traditional, academic, and international influences. In short, the art of China in the twentieth century tells a compelling story, which demands to be considered in the context of the long train of Chinese art history, and in the context of an emerging global sensibility.

The Guggenheim has been again fortunate in attracting a first-rate team of scholars to organize this narrative of modern Chinese art, under the leadership and direction of Professor Julia Andrews of The Ohio State University, one of the world's leading scholars of twentieth-century Chinese art. Professor Andrews has been ably assisted in her selection by contributions from Kuiyi Shen, Presidential Fellow, The Ohio State University; Jonathan Spence, Sterling Professor of History, Yale University; Shan Guolin, Chief Curator of

Painting and Calligraphy, Shanghai Museum; Christina Chu, Curator, Xubaizhai, The Hong Kong Museum of Art; Xue Yongnian, Professor of Art History, Central Academy of Fine Arts, Beijing; May-ching Kao, Professor of Fine Arts and Director, Art Museum, The Chinese University of Hong Kong; and Joan Lebold Cohen, critic and author.

While one great achievement of *China: 5,000 Years* is to place the traditional and the modern into adjacent contexts, they remain two distinct stories—one a reexamination of classical, dynastic Chinese art in terms of its innovative and transgressive tendencies; the other an account of modern Chinese art as a reflection of political history and in terms of its attempt to sustain both classical and Western cultural vocabularies. Together they make a third story: five thousand years of continuous cultural history in China that continues to the present day.

The sheer scope of such an exhibition enterprise is, of course, ambitious, and it carries with it many challenges and contradictions. In its very title, *China: 5,000 Years* poses many questions: Can any single exhibition legitimately explore five thousand years of any culture, let alone one as rich as this? Does it make sense to link twentieth-century Chinese culture with forty-nine centuries of "traditional" culture? Is the Guggenheim Museum—with its collections and expertise firmly rooted in twentieth-century Western art—a legitimate organizer of such an event? How does the narrative thread of this exhibition relate to the history of Chinese art as it is understood through the weight of scholarship on Chinese history and art to date, and through the Chinese objects exhibited and studied in museums in Taiwan, Europe, and America? The answers to these questions will inevitably be found in the exhibition itself. The importance of *China: 5,000 Years* will be a function of its ability to present a fresh, incredibly rich, and provocative new chapter to the study of the cultural history of China.

The story of the genesis and development of *China: 5,000 Years* as an exhibition project is itself an extraordinary tale. That it is organized by, and shown in, the Guggenheim Museums in New York derives from a specific sequence of conditions and circumstances favorable to such an enterprise, and from the participation and commitment of a diverse and impressive group of individuals who are committed to China and to fostering international understanding through cultural communication. The initial impulse for the project—its primary motivation—derives from the simple fact that China is a country of deep traditions, extraordinary achievement, startling paradoxes, and enormous

potential. At the close of the twentieth century, China is inhabited by 1.22 billion people, the largest population on earth; it occupies the fourth largest land mass of any country, and is the projected superpower of the twenty-first century. China is also in the midst of historic transitions—from a rural/agrarian- to an urban/manufacturing-based society, and from a communist command economy to a capitalist market-based one. Its sheer size, potential, and history make it a force to be reckoned with. Yet it is also a country whose character, culture, and traditions are still very much unfamiliar in the West.

On both a political and an economic level, China's future demands a special relationship with the United States. The two countries are locked in an embrace that is everywhere in evidence. China sends 17 percent of its exports to the United States, and now holds over $130 billion in foreign-currency reserves in the form of U.S. Treasury bonds; American companies have more than $20 billion invested in China; an estimated fifty thousand Chinese study at American colleges and universities, constituting the single largest body of foreign students in the United States; more than half a million American tourists visited China in 1996; and fifteen million Americans are of Chinese ancestry. His Excellency Jiang Zemin, President of the People's Republic of China, visited the United States last October, and the Honorable Bill Clinton, President of the United States, is planning a state visit to China later this year. The growing need for China and the United States to accommodate one another has created a simultaneous demand for cultural engagement, and this was the major precondition for the motivation, the will, and the opportunities on both sides required to conceive of and organize this exhibition.

On a more local level, another major precondition for the exhibition was the nature of the evolving direction and focus of the Guggenheim Museum itself. During the past ten years, the Guggenheim has experienced a significant transformation. With the renovation of its original Frank Lloyd Wright building, the construction of a new addition, and the establishment of the Guggenheim Museum SoHo in 1992, the Guggenheim Foundation broadened its physical and programming base and established a strong position in New York City, one of the greatest cultural capitals in the world. This local expansion was supplemented by continued improvements and a modest expansion at the Peggy Guggenheim Collection in Venice, and by the dramatic completion and opening of the Guggenheim Museum Bilbao, a building designed by Frank Gehry that many critics are saying will take its place alongside the Frank Lloyd Wright–designed Guggenheim in New York as one of the two greatest buildings of the twentieth century. The Bilbao opening was followed two weeks later by the opening of Deutsche Guggenheim Berlin.

The Guggenheim is becoming a truly international museum not only in terms of buildings and locations, but also through an equally intense commitment to expanding its programming, reflected both in the growth of its permanent collection and in the breadth and depth of its special exhibitions. The original mission of the museum was to collect, preserve, and present the art of the Modern and contemporary periods. Nine superlative curators from three countries have dramatically expanded the scope of programming, with major monographic exhibitions devoted to, among others, Ellsworth Kelly, Roy Lichtenstein, Claes Oldenburg, and Robert Rauschenberg; important historical exhibitions such as *The Great Utopia: The Russian and Soviet Avant-Garde, 1915–1932*, *The Italian Metamorphosis, 1943–1968*, *Picasso and the Age of Iron*, and *Africa: The Art of a Continent*; and smaller, focused exhibitions such as *Max Beckmann in Exile*, *Visions of Paris: Robert Delaunay's Series*, and *Rrose is a Rrose is a Rrose: Gender Performance in Photography*. In the process of developing these projects, the Guggenheim has become a major producer of exhibitions. A measure of its success is reflected in the fact that, during the past five years, Guggenheim-organized exhibitions have been presented in more than eighty museums around the world, from Bilbao to Shanghai, from Los Angeles to Munich, and from Singapore to Vienna.

A fundamental shift in attitude has complemented this extraordinary programmatic growth. The Guggenheim recognizes that culture in the twentieth and twenty-first centuries cannot be treated as a Western-oriented, Euro-American hegemony. Museums in particular cannot maintain a high regard for classical and antique cultures from around the world while remaining skeptical about the contemporary art of non-Western traditions. That a new postmodern, multifaceted, multilingual contemporary global culture is emerging in an increasingly interconnected and Internet-linked world is a fact that cannot be ignored. Africa, Asia, and South America all sustain vibrant contemporary cultures that a global museum must engage. The Guggenheim's aspirations as an international museum are viable only to the degree that a broad-based international program comes into place. The museum buildings—for all their architectural brilliance and geographic diversity—are only a point of departure.

The Guggenheim's interest in non-Western cultures was heralded by *Japanese Art After 1945: Scream Against the Sky*, an exhibition organized in conjunction with the Yokohama Museum of Art and presented to critical acclaim at the Guggenheim Museum SoHo in 1994. For American audiences, the material was fresh and sophisticated, related to European attitudes but not derivative. The art reflected Japanese culture and traditions, in a vocabulary that was simultaneously recognizable and original. Various commentaries on the exhibition noted the "Japaneseness" of the material, and pointed out that this was an art that had been consistently ignored or overlooked by Western museums. For the Guggenheim, the project was exhilarating. The task was to understand the narrative of postwar Japanese art not only as a reflection of its immediate sociohistorical context, but also in relation to the some three thousand years of cultural history that preceded it.

By late 1994, the stars were almost in alignment for *China: 5,000 Years* to become a reality. The skeletal framework of the global Guggenheim—and the exhibition-organizing engine—were largely in place. The concept of a far-reaching exhibition program that included, every few years, an exhibition challenging the conventional direction of the Guggenheim while taking advantage of its scholarly criteria and organizational capacities was approved by the Board of Trustees. All that remained was to connect the source of the vision for *China: 5,000 Years* with the curatorial expertise to bring it to life. That connection was provided by Sherman Lee. More than twenty-five years ago, in 1969, as an undergraduate economics and political-science major at Williams College, I took my first art-history course—on Chinese landscape painting—with Professor Lee. When the opportunity for an exhibition of Chinese art at the Guggenheim arose, there was never any doubt in my mind that Professor Lee was the only person to provide the bold and unique vision to select it. Happily, several weeks after I presented the general thesis of an exhibition of five millennia of Chinese art drawn exclusively from material in China to him, Professor Lee agreed to head the curatorial team for the traditional section.

The next step was to secure the participation and cooperation of the Chinese. In the autumn of 1994, the Honorable Gianni De Michelis, former Foreign Minister of Italy and Guggenheim trustee, helped arrange a meeting with the Honorable Qian Qichen, Vice Premier and Foreign Minister of the People's Republic of China. Our mission was simple: to seek an unprecedented collaboration with the Chinese government by presenting the objectives of *China: 5,000 Years* with reference to its political significance in the context of developing Sino-American relations. As a result of that meeting the following January, the Guggenheim was put in contact with representatives of the Ministry of Culture, National Administration for Cultural Heritage, China International Exhibition Agency, and Art Exhibitions China to begin planning.

To implement this striking and ambitious vision, Sherman Lee, with the able support of Howard Rogers, assembled an outstanding team of advisors who not only wrote essays for this catalogue, but also provided consultation on every aspect of the exhibition, from issues of conservation to the installation plan and educational materials. This team includes the top specialists in their areas of expertise: Helmut Brinker, Professor, University of Zurich; James Cahill, Professor Emeritus, History of Art, University of California, Berkeley; Elizabeth Childs-Johnson, Visiting Scholar, New York University; Patricia Ebrey, Professor, Department of History, University of Washington; Michael Knight, Curator of Chinese Art, Asian Art Museum of San Francisco; Regina Krahl, independent scholar, affiliated with the Royal Museums of Art and History, Brussels; Jenny So, Curator of Ancient Chinese Art, Freer Gallery of Art and Arthur M. Sackler Gallery, Smithsonian Institution, Washington, D.C.; Peter Sturman, Associate Professor, Department of the History of Art and Architecture, University of California, Santa Barbara; Wu Hung, Harrie A. Vanderstappen Distinguished Service Professor in Chinese Art History, University of Chicago; and Zhao Feng, Professor, China National Silk Museum, Hangzhou.

In addition, the National Administration for Cultural Heritage of the People's Republic of China, our partner in the organization of the traditional section of *China: 5,000 Years*, provided scholarly assistance at all levels of the planning and development of the exhibition. Zhang Wenbin assembled an impressive team of support for the project, including the following prominent scholars and high-level museum professionals who contributed essays to this catalogue: Su Bai, Professor, Beijing University; Yu Weichao, Director of the National Museum of Chinese History, Beijing; Ma Chengyuan, Director of the Shanghai Museum; Wang Qingzheng, Deputy Director of the Shanghai Museum; and Liu Jiu'an, Researcher, Palace Museum, Beijing. Yang Yang, Yin Jia, Zhang Jianxin, Qian Wei, and Chen Shujie of Art Exhibitions China; Lu Chenglong and Xu Qixian of the Palace Museum; Wang Changqi and Gao Man of the Institute for the Protection of Cultural Relics and Archaeology, Xi'an; Li Xuefang of the Forest of Steles Museum, Xi'an; and Han Jianwu of the Shaanxi History Museum, Xi'an, also provided important scholarly contributions and research for this exhibition. June Mei skillfully translated these essays.

There are always many, many important people to thank for helping put together an exhibition of this complexity and scope. First of all, the task of assembling such a broad range of material from a wide range of sources demanded a unique organizational structure and support at the highest level. Our most sincere gratitude is extended to President Jiang Zemin; the Honorable Li Peng, Premier of the People's Republic of China; Vice Premier and Foreign Minister Qian Qichen; and the Honorable Liu Zhongde, Minister of Culture of the People's Republic of China, without whose support this project would never have been realized. The Foreign Ministry supported this exhibition through the good offices of the Honorable Li Daoyu, Ambassador of the People's Republic of China to the United States, who provided advice and consultation at important stages of the project. We would like to extend our most sincere thanks and gratitude to the Honorable Qiu Shengyun, Consul General of the People's Republic of China in New York. The complex task of organizing the specifics of the exhibition—in particular, arranging loans from the many lending institutions—fell to the Ministry of Culture of the People's Republic of China and, for the traditional section, the National Administration for Cultural Heritage. At the Ministry of Culture, I would like to extend my personal thanks to Li Yuanchao, Vice-Minister of Culture, and Ding Wei, Deputy Director of the General Bureau of External Cultural Relations, who were steadfast in their support for the project and instrumental in providing direction and focus. With particular respect and friendship, we would like to single out Zhang Wenbin and Wang Limei at the National Administration for Cultural Heritage, without whose professional and steadfast leadership, this complicated and far-reaching exhibition would never have come to fruition. This exhibition would also not be possible without the support of Lei Congyun, Director of Art Exhibitions China, and Yang Yang, Deputy Director of Art Exhibitions China, who oversaw all the logistical and organizational details, in addition to research responsibilities. We are also indebted to the team of specialists who accompanied the artworks from China for their installation in New York: Shan Guolin of the Shanghai Museum; Feng Xiaoqi of the Palace Museum, Beijing; and Chen Shujie of Art Exhibitions China. Our very special thanks go to Hu Chui, photographer at the Palace Museum, who spent many days and even months traveling around China, applying his art to the task of photographing the objects in the exhibition. The beautiful plates in this catalogue are testimony to his uncompromising eye for quality and detail. We will provide our extended thanks to the team at the China International Exhibition Agency in our catalogue dedicated to the modern section of the exhibition, but I would like to take this opportunity to express my particular gratitude to Hao Zhan, Director, and Wan Jiyuan, Li Li, and You Shu.

I would also like to express my gratitude to Gianni De Michelis for his inspiration and generosity, and for nurturing this project at its inception and remaining a strong supporter and advisor. Ji Chaozhu and Simon Jiang also must be thanked for their support.

One of the astonishing aspects of this exhibition is the large number of lenders from all over China who recognized its historic importance and contributed to its success by allowing precious works from their collections to travel to the exhibition venues. A separate page is devoted to a list of our lenders—thirty-nine in total in the traditional section of *China: 5,000 Years*—but I would like to take this opportunity to offer them our deepest gratitude for their enormous generosity and cooperation, without which this exhibition would not have been possible.

In the United States, there were also a large number of people without whom we would not have been able to bring this exhibition to fruition. It has been a privilege and an honor to work with Sherman Lee on this project. A deep debt of gratitude is owed to him, and also to his wife, Ruth, who accompanied Professor Lee on his many visits to China in preparation for this exhibition. I would also like to thank Howard Rogers, who served as consulting curator and as general editor of this catalogue. Having worked closely with Professor Lee over a period of many years, he has a deep appreciation and sensitive understanding of Professor Lee's vision. His own formidable grasp of all aspects of Chinese art is the result of more than thirty years of involvement in the field, including eighteen years as a professor of Chinese art history at Sophia University, Tokyo. Howard Rogers's wife, Mary Ann, herself an expert in Chinese art, was also ever generous in her support. David Sensabaugh, Ann Wardwell, Pat Berger, and Jan Berris also provided important advice.

At the Guggenheim, Jane DeBevoise, Director of the China Exhibition Project, assisted by Manon Slome, Project Assistant Curator, oversaw all aspects of the exhibition planning, coordination, and execution, from checklist and loan negotiation to installation planning and design, as well as catalogue development and execution. With considerable managerial expertise, indefatigable energy, true team leadership, and impressive facility with the Chinese language, Jane DeBevoise ably moved each stage of the project toward completion. Manon Slome coordinated the myriad details of the exhibition planning and design with intelligence and

determination, and, together with Xiaoming Zhang, who impressively managed the English/Chinese dual-language database, and Emily Wei and Nicole Lin, who provided key research and organizational support, formed the hub of the exhibition, holding together the project's many varied spokes. Our thanks are due also to Frances Yuan, Eileen Hsu, and Andrew Leung, who provided research for the didactic material, and to our interns Patty Chang, Shihong Aldin, Jackie Chien, Simon Murphy, and Katherine Cheng for their tireless efforts and their valuable contribution to the complicated administration of this multifaceted project. Suzanne Quigley, Head Registrar for Collections and Exhibitions; Mary Jane Clark, Project Registrar; and Joan Hendricks, Associate Registrar, professionally handled the logistics of the international transportation of the objects. A highly skilled staff of conservators, including Project Conservator Tracy Power of the Asian Art Museum of San Francisco; Gillian McMillan, Senior Conservator (Collections); Carol Stringari, Senior Conservator (Exhibitions); Eleanora Nagy, Assistant Conservator; and Ellen Pratt, Project Conservator, oversaw the care and condition of the precious objects in the exhibition at every stage of the project. The exhibition design is the work of Arata Isozaki and Adegboyega Adefope. The Art Services and Preparations department lent their considerable expertise to the installation of the exhibition. In particular, I wish to thank Karen Meyerhoff, Director of Exhibition and Collection Management and Design; Scott Wixon, Manager of Art Services and Preparations; Peter Read, Manager of Exhibition Fabrication and Design; Jocelyn Brayshaw, Acting Chief Preparator; Liz Jaff, Assistant Paper Preparator; Joseph Adams, Senior Museum Technician; Richard Gombar, Museum Technician; Mary Ann Hoag, Lighting Designer; and Jocelyn Groom, Exhibition Design Coordinator. David Horak also provided invaluable assistance with the installation. Len Steinbach, Director of Information Technology, provided constant support for the many sophisticated technical requirements of a dual-language database. I would also like to thank Marilyn Goodman, Director of Education, and Diane Maas, Education Program Manager, who developed an outstanding education program; Rosemarie Garipoli, Deputy Director for External Affairs, and George McNeely, Director of Institutional Development; Ruth Taylor, Director of Budget and Planning; and Jay A. Levenson, former Deputy Director for Program Administration, who steered the project at its early stages. Patrick Seymour of Tsang Seymour Design, together with Marcia Fardella, Graphic Designer, Susan Lee, Assistant Graphic Designer, and Jessica Ludwig at the Guggenheim, produced the exhibition's many graphic-design elements with sensitivity and expertise.

This catalogue, published by the Guggenheim's Publications Department under the direction of Anthony Calnek, Director of Publications, and designed by Patrick Seymour, has in itself been an impressive project. Coordinated by Howard Rogers, with the perceptive and sensitive editorial support of Naomi Richard and Sylvia Moss, the catalogue reflects an extensive international collaboration between some of the most distinguished scholars in the field and will hopefully be a valuable reference for years to come. We are particularly impressed that great scholars from both China and the West embraced this historic occasion to develop their ideas and communicate their scholarship. We firmly believe that the diversity of material and commentary is one of the great strengths of this project as a whole, and we have made no attempt to bring into conformity the opinions expressed by the authors. The production of this catalogue was handled with great skill by Elizabeth Levy, Managing Editor/Manager of Foreign Editions, and Melissa Secondino, Production Assistant. Along with related exhibition materials, it was also made possible with the assistance of Edward Weisberger, Editor; Jennifer Knox White, Associate Editor; Carol Fitzgerald, Assistant Editor; and Domenick Ammirati, Editorial Assistant, as well as Keith Mayerson and Nicole Columbus.

An exhibition of this scale could never take place without the generous support of our sponsors. First, I would like to thank Lufthansa for the ongoing commitment and leadership support it has shown to the Guggenheim as a Global Partner. In particular, I would like to thank Frederick W. Reid, Lufthansa German Airlines's President and Chief Operating Officer, and Josef Grendel, Lufthansa's Vice President Corporate Communications, for their enlightened generosity. We are also very fortunate to have had the opportunity to work with Nokia. Their international vision and their skill at connecting people and cultures are deeply impressive. For their support, I am particularly indebted to Jorma Ollila, President and Chief Executive Officer; Lauri Kivinen, Senior Vice President Corporate Communications; Jim Bowman, Vice President Corporate Communications, Nokia Americas; and Micaela Tucker-Kinney, Manager, Corporate Communications, Nokia Americas. We are also most grateful to Alex Trotman, Chairman and Chief Executive Officer of Ford Motor Company, for his leadership and commitment to this project. At Ford, we also wish to thank Wayne M. Booker, Vice Chairman; Peter J. Pestillo, Executive Vice President, Corporate Relations; Gary L. Nielsen, Vice President, Ford Motor Company Fund; and Mabel H. Cabot, Director, Corporate Programming, for their creativity and their dedication to this landmark exhibition. Finally, we

would like to thank M. Douglas Ivester, Chairman of the Board and Chief Executive Officer of The Coca-Cola Company, for his leadership in supporting this important project. The collaboration of Douglas N. Daft, President, Middle and Far East Group at The Coca-Cola Company, was also vital to its realization.

Significant additional support for this exhibition was provided at an early stage by The Starr Foundation and The W. L. S. Spencer Foundation. Their generous help allowed us to move the project forward during the critical processes of research and development. Mori Building Company Limited has also assisted substantially in the realization of the exhibition. I would like to thank Minoru Mori, President, for his inspired support. The exhibition has also been made possible in part by a major grant from the National Endowment of the Humanities, who provided us with important early endorsement and encouragement. The generous support of The Li-Cheng Cultural and Educational Foundation has assisted in the publication of the two-volume catalogue accompanying the exhibition.

As I complete these remarks in a Tokyo hotel room, I look at the scroll of calligraphy that hangs in the *tokunoma* alcove of my room. A Japanese friend tells me that it was created by a nineteenth-century Japanese artist whose style was based on that of a seventeenth-century calligrapher named Dong Qichang, whose work is included in *China: 5,000 Years*. The text, "Peach Blossom Spring," by the fourth-century Chinese poet Tao Yuanming, speaks of the peace and contentment that become possible on removal from the temporal world, just as the author himself achieved lasting renown by giving up secular ambition in order to cultivate his soul. My friend then comments that the writing itself seems lacking the confidence expressed by the verbal content, which leads to this final observation: the boundaries between East and West, between past and present, are truly falling. Artists and poets today are no different from their predecessors in their willingness to appropriate or reject what they need—from their own history, from their contemporary context, from outside influences—to formulate a response to their dilemma. *China: 5,000 Years* will appeal to experts and scholars. But by far the largest number of people to see the exhibition will be those with only a limited understanding of the culture of this extraordinary country. They are free to approach this art from their own perspectives, to bring themselves into the encounter and challenge their preconceptions. The process will challenge them to learn and grow, and the two countries will move a little closer as a result. It is in this potential that *China: 5,000 Years* finds its ultimate justification.

Chronology

NEOLITHIC PERIOD CA. 7000–CA. 2000 BCE

YANGSHAO CULTURE (north central China)   {CA. 5000–CA. 3000 BCE}

HONGSHAN CULTURE (northeastern China)   {CA. 3600–CA. 2000 BCE}

LIANGZHU CULTURE (southeastern China)   {CA. 3600–CA. 2000 BCE}

LONGSHAN CULTURE (eastern China)   {CA. 3000–CA. 1700 BCE}

EARLY DYNASTIC CHINA

XIA PERIOD (protohistoric)   {CA. 2100–CA. 1600 BCE}

SHANG PERIOD   {CA. 1600–CA. 1100 BCE}

ZHOU PERIOD   {CA. 1100–256 BCE}

Western Zhou	CA. 1100–771 BCE
Eastern Zhou	770–256 BCE
Spring and Autumn period	770–476 BCE
Warring States period	475–221 BCE

DYNASTIC CHINA

QIN DYNASTY   {221–207 BCE}

HAN DYNASTY   {206 BCE–220 CE}

Western Han	206 BCE–8 CE
Xin (Wang Mang usurpation)	9–23
Eastern Han	25–220

PERIOD OF DISUNITY   {220–589}

Three Kingdoms	220–280
Wei	220–265
Shu Han	221–263
Wu	222–280
Western Jin	265–316
Southern dynasties (Six Dynasties)	
Wu (southernmost of Three Kingdoms)	222–280
Eastern Jin	317–420
Liu Song	420–479
Southern Qi	479–502
Liang	502–557
Chen	557–589
Northern dynasties	
Sixteen Kingdoms	304–439
Northern Wei	386–534
Eastern Wei	534–550
Western Wei	535–557
Northern Qi	550–577
Northern Zhou	557–581
*Sui	581–589

SUI DYNASTY		{589–618}
TANG DYNASTY		{618–907}
FIVE DYNASTIES		{907–960}
LIAO DYNASTY		{916–1125}
SONG DYNASTY		{960–1279}
Northern Song	960–1127	
Southern Song	1127–1279	
JIN DYNASTY		{1115–1234}
YUAN DYNASTY		{1279–1368}
MING DYNASTY		{1368–1644}
Hongwu	1368–1398	
Jianwen	1399–1402	
Yongle	1403–1424	
Hongxi	1425	
Xuande	1426–1435	
Zhengtong	1436–1449	
Jingtai	1450–1456	
Tianshun	1457–1464	
Chenghua	1465–1487	
Hongzhi	1488–1505	
Zhengde	1506–1521	
Jiajing	1522–1566	
Longqing	1567–1572	
Wanli	1573–1620	
Taichang	1620	
Tianqi	1621–1627	
Chongzhen	1628–1644	
QING DYNASTY		{1644–1911}
Shunzhi	1644–1661	
Kangxi	1662–1722	
Yongzheng	1723–1735	
Qianlong	1736–1795	
Jiaqing	1796–1820	
Daoguang	1821–1850	
Xianfeng	1851–1861	
Tongzhi	1862–1874	
Gangxu	1875–1908	
Xuantong	1909–1911	

*Note: Sui dynasty declared in 581; unified the realm by conquest in 589.

Introduction

Sherman Lee

Director (retired),
Cleveland Museum of Art

Vast generalities of time and space are

unavoidable when discussing traditional

Chinese art, for only with their aid

do the main achievements of that long–

lived culture become clearly apparent.

This easier access comes at a cost,

however, since significant regional

diversity is obscured and homogenized

into an undifferentiated whole, and

varying periods of creativity and stagnation are averaged into a neat and continuous timeline, all of which contributes to the popular image of China as a monolithic country, fixed in its boundaries and evolving only slowly over time.

This exhibition seeks to deconstruct that invariant image, to demonstrate artistic diversity rather than unity and to identify periods of heightened activity and creativity in the arts. These pieces, which will delight their audience by aesthetic merit, were carefully chosen to emphasize the themes of innovation and transformation: the conceptual innovations that led artists to shift focus from the supernatural to the human world, then to the natural world, and thereafter to adopt elements from all these worlds as vehicles of self-expression; and the technological inventions and discoveries that occurred as artists sought the most appropriate medium in which to give form to their conceptions.

I.

Early Chinese art manifests in form and decoration a fascinating world of imaginary beasts, demons, chimeras, and grotesques. These may have originated in real creatures, whose forms were then abstracted, commingled, and otherwise transformed into complex animal images. These images are not merely decorative; the major elements must have embodied meanings, whether as totems, clan insignia, or other consequential signifiers. This early, animistic art is essentially static; the designs covering the bronze ritual vessels imply no potential for movement.

By the end of the Zhou dynasty several striking innovations are apparent, foremost among them the appearance of the human world and of potential movement. Recognizable animals are placed in comparatively realistic environments. The animals and landscape are still not interconnected as a scene, but the animals now appear capable of swift and light movement while wind is suggested in the mountains—what had been bound and static before is freed. On lacquers and incised bronze tubes of the late Zhou–Han period even the mountain peaks, cliffs, foliage, and "cloud patterns" pulsate with life. We see here the first signs of an interest in representing real landscape in the arts.

The Qin–Han era, however, is predominantly the world of humankind. Beginning with the life-size and startlingly lifelike Qin military figures, human scale and a human point of view come to dominate much subsequent art. Given the epochal importance of this shift, it seems appropriate that the English name "China" derives from the name of the first of the imperial dynasties, the Qin. And just as the frontiers of the empire are gradually extended, and border regions pacified, so too is nature tamed and contained in urban hunting parks, which figure significantly in the poetry of the period as well as in the art. Animals continue to be important but now within a context defined by purely human concerns.

Among these human concerns are ideas about religion, expressed in Buddhist and Daoist thought and imagery that comes to dominate art in the Six Dynasties–Tang era. As the foreign styles associated with Buddhism are gradually assimilated and Sinified, the human figure continues to dominate its pictorial environment. The fantastical creatures of the past survive as decorative forms rather than as embodiments of awesome powers. At the same time a growing interest in landscape for its own sake becomes apparent alongside the dominant figural tradition.

The landscape art created by the Chinese during the late Tang–Five Dynasties–Song period is one of the great glories of human achievement. Its technical evolution can be traced from the linearity of early incised, inlaid, and painted designs to the more complex spatial representations of the later Tang era; conceptually it is the final stage and beneficiary of the supernatural- and human-centered worlds described above. In this aesthetic culmination, which occurred in China centuries earlier than elsewhere in the world, natural forces which had earlier been describable only as delimited and isolated forms, are fully encompassed by the human mind and described in integrated landscapes that are monumental in scale and freighted with symbolic meanings.

II.

Another way of approaching the art and culture of early China is by considering the continuous series of technical innovations occurring in the various mediums used by early artists. It was William Willetts, in his *Chinese Art* of 1958, who first brought to bear the findings of Joseph Needham's *Science and Civilization in China* in his brilliant study of Chinese art. Willetts's focus on technology created a particularly useful framework for the study of such "decorative" or "useful" or "minor" arts as jades, bronzes, lacquers, textiles, and ceramics as well as sculpture and painting.

Worked jades first appear in the Liangzhu and Hongshan Neolithic cultures, demonstrating at that early period already advanced techniques for shaping this most recalcitrant material. The forms and designs of the earliest jades—the pig-dragons and masks—doubtless held potent meanings for their contemporaries, notwithstanding our inability to interpret them. Eventually these formal and hieratic patterns give way to ever more intricate designs, and many centuries later jade working became and remained a purely decorative art.

Bronze casting, which begins during the Xia and Shang dynasties and flourishes into the Han, follows a similar sequence, in which great early invention and ingenuity in support of meaningful iconography are gradually superseded by technical mediocrity and decorative repetition. The use of ceramic piece-molds, which permit shape and surface decoration to be created simultaneously, is the distinguishing feature of Chinese bronze technology, and had reached a stage of enormous complexity and brilliant virtuosity by the Anyang phase of the Shang dynasty. The vessels cast in these piece-molds testify to the early Chinese interest in and aptitude for representing a world of imaginary and transmogrified creatures, demons, and grotesques. Many of the early Zhou dynasty bronze vessels bear inscriptions that constitute important historical documents, and by the end of the Zhou these same forms were embellished with the precious metals and gemstones that enhanced their new function as visual markers of social and economic status.

Lacquer as a protective and decorative coating is in origin Chinese and is known to have been used very early on, although the first extensive remains date from the Warring States era of the late Zhou dynasty. Painted and incised lacquer designs of that period relate stylistically to contemporaneous textile and bronze designs. In later centuries lacquer-working techniques became more complex; forms and designs were molded using a variety of techniques, then carved and/or inlaid with various precious materials. These manifold techniques as well as cultivation of the lac tree itself spread to Korea, Japan, and Okinawa, and those cultures continue to benefit from this Chinese innovation.

Silk manufacture too was an early Chinese invention, one that had an even more complex development and greater impact on the larger world, spreading to the West during Hellenistic and early Christian times. Paper and printing, appearing in this exhibition in the form of early paintings and block-printed books, are even more famous examples of Chinese inventions that were instrumental in shaping Asian and European culture.

Sculptures is represented in the exhibition in clay, metal, and stone. The first of these mediums comprises mainly tomb figurines, which manifest simultaneous concern with this life and with the afterlife. Proper burials not only served the afterlife needs of the deceased but testified to the moral virtues, social responsibility, and pecuniary

substance of their living relations. Upper-class tombs were abundantly furnished with realistic effigies of all the familiar objects, animals, and humans that constituted the material world—perhaps idealized—of the living. These lively and closely observed tomb figurines, created to accompany and serve the dead, represent the broad and complex world of the living and are material evidence of society over a significant period of time. The burial furniture and figurines manifest artistic creativity, but at the same time their vast numbers attest to virtual mass production, with great technical skill and high standards of quality. The alert and natural figures of animals and humans provide us with a visual image of their world far more vivid than the descriptions by historians of the day.

The coming of Buddhism to China in the mid-first century CE and its enthusiastic acceptance in the succeeding centuries brought with it a great figural style of image making as it had developed in India and had been transformed as it moved eastward. The Chinese adapted it rapidly and creatively in all three mediums, especially in the north; works produced in this development are remarkably varied in nature, with strong provincial styles being created during the fifth and sixth centuries in Shanxi, Shaanxi, Shandong, Yunnan, and Sichuan. By the beginning of the seventh century, in the Sui and early Tang dynasty, a national Chinese style was emerging. Ultimately this became a truly international style, prevalent throughout East Asia.

In general, the Chinese intellectual and cultural elite placed little aesthetic value on the sculptor's art, especially that in stone. But the protean artisan image-makers have left a large body of work that begins in the early Six Dynasties with images imbued with great energy and movement and develops by the Tang dynasty into figures of worldly and splendid elegance. The sensuous and rounded volumes of Tang sculptures correspond to the fashions of female court beauties as revealed in the early scroll paintings, seen in this exhibition in photographic reproductions of contemporaneous wall murals. This is the first exhibition from China to feature stone Buddhist sculptures in significant numbers.

Among Chinese contributions to world culture, it is perhaps porcelain that was most devoutly admired and fervently sought after in the West. The course of development of Chinese ceramics, from the early high-fired stonewares through various types of later white- and green-glazed wares to the pinnacle represented by porcelain, is well represented in this exhibition. The selection was based on the quality of individual pieces as well as on features that would reveal the intriguing development of various types of body and glaze and styles of decoration, each reflecting the technology and the ethos of its time and its particular patrons.

An almost equally long-lived and practical art is calligraphy, which in China had a double nature. Its practical uses are readily apparent in the West. But in China calligraphy was not simply a tool for recording; it was the premier art, the badge of rulers and officials, landowners and literati. In China, unlike the Near Eastern and European empires and kingdoms, writing—calligraphy—was a key or pass to greatness and station. The proper manipulation of ink with brush was the most respected of accomplishments, held to reveal the moral character of the writer. Calligraphy was also a fully aesthetic practice, one with its own tradition, discipline, and criteria of excellence, evolved during four thousand years of continuous development. Even without access to the literary meanings, philosophical assumptions and implications, and long stylistic history, we in the West may still sense the kinesthetic accomplishment of the brush moving across paper or silk.

The use of brush and ink defined the literati class. It underlay both calligraphy and painting, the twin insignia of the civil and civilized life as distinct from its correlative opposite, the military or physical life. It is noteworthy too that, in a society that generally prized group solidarity over solitary genius, individualism in art, the creation of an individual style, came to be held the highest, most admirable achievement. The paintings in this exhibition thus manifest a wide range of individual styles and approaches; they also fall naturally into two groups, the earlier presenting a more descriptive, objective view of nature, the later, from the fourteenth century onward, a more expressive, subjective approach. From the tenth to the thirteenth century artists investigated a wide range of phenomena in the macrocosm of nature. Most if not all of these phenomena were understood as embodiments of qualities that existed in the microcosm of the human world—such things as mountains, water, bamboo, blossoming plums, chrysanthemums, and orchids functioned as emblems for qualities associated with the ideal scholar-gentleman—but reality, although pervaded with moral and metaphysical and auspicious meanings, was still granted an objective existence outside the mind that sought to apprehend it and that endowed it with those meanings.

During the Yuan and later dynasties artists tended to move away from direct engagement with outer reality—even that defined in idealistic terms—and to create more subjective works. Often using a stylistic and technical syllabary derived from art of the past, painters created new pictorial structures united by innovative grammars. At its best, this intensely art-historical later painting drew ever-renewing vitality from the singular vision of each of its practitioners. But as printed books in the exhibition demonstrate, complex styles could be analyzed, broken down into their constituent parts; these in turn were often made the full substance of later paintings. Such a concentration on details and on technical features like brushwork ultimately had an adverse affect on the pictorial tradition. A similar emphasis on technology rather than creativity overtook later Qing dynasty jades, lacquers, porcelains, and textiles, and this tendency constitutes one of the greatest challenges bequeathed by late dynastic artists to their twentieth-century successors.

The reader will by now be aware that this is an exhibition which stresses the art of an ancient culture with particular relation to innovation and creativity. It is not meant to emphasize the historical, sociological, ethnographical, or literary aspects of Chinese culture. But so compelling are the achievements of these artists and artisans that their creations illumine the civilization in which they were produced—its material options and constraints, its social obligations and expectations, its moral compulsions and freedoms, its aesthetic preferences and boundaries. These works appear before us as tangible witnesses to China's cultural history.

Essays

Some Elements in the Intellectual and Religious Context of Chinese Art

Patricia Ebrey

Professor, Department of History,
University of Washington

As with the art of any other great civilization, that of China has been intimately linked to ideas generally classified under the rubric religion and philosophy—ideas about life and death, human nature and human society, the natural world of mountains and streams, plants and animals, and the invisible world of gods, ghosts, spirits, and demons.

Some of the most important of these ideas appeared early and persisted for centuries; most were altered in major ways over time; some died out or were supplanted; others coexisted with opposing but equally entrenched ideas.

The relationship between art and these diverse ideas is just as complex. Religious and philosophical traditions provided the occasions for creating many objects later treasured as art. The finest examples of jade, bronze, silk, and ceramics were frequently made to be used in religious rituals. These traditions also provided a significant share of the imagery of Chinese art: phoenixes, dragons, cicadas, birds, and other creatures of cosmological significance are common decorative motifs; sages, filial sons, Buddhas, bodhisattvas, immortals, demons, and gods are frequent subjects of figure painting and sculpture. Chinese discourses on aesthetics, personal refinement, and the value of the past all influenced which objects would be treasured and preserved. Placing higher value on a sample of handwriting than on a finely crafted chair, for instance, owes much to Confucian and Daoist ideas about self-cultivation. But certainly it is not always the case that the ideas are prior and the art an expression or reflection of them; meanings can be created and conveyed through objects independently of words and texts. Sometimes it is the textual version that is the reflection or rationalization of meanings created by the deployment or decoration of objects. For example, most Chinese explanations of the meaning of objects buried with the dead probably should be interpreted as after-the-fact rationalizations or speculations.

It is common practice for art historians to relate the objects they study to elements in Chinese intellectual and religious culture. In this volume, for instance, Elizabeth Childs-Johnson relates the decoration of early jades and bronzes to shamanism, Wu Hung relates Warring States and Han tomb furnishings to ideas about post-mortem existence, and Helmut Brinker places Buddhist sculpture in

the context of Buddhist teachings. In this chapter I shall take a broader view and try to relate the larger contours of the history of Chinese art to the larger contours of Chinese religious and intellectual history. I will do this by examining four complexes of ideas that have particular bearing on Chinese art—ideas about rulers, mountains, writing, and icons. I selected these four not because they make a nice Chinese-sounding set of "The Four Sacred Things," but because they let me get at some key tensions and contradictions in the layered traditions of Chinese religious and intellectual thought. Other ideas, ones associated for instance with the sage, vital force, the cosmos, paradise, flowers, fate, emotions, and so on, could have been added or substituted. But the four discussed here are diverse enough to show something of the dynamics of a cultural framework in which inconsistent, even contradictory, ideas interacted in fruitful ways. [1] In ordinary social life, the coexistence of ideas in some way opposed to each other gives people room to think for themselves and to maneuver against others for personal advantage; in the sphere of art it gives artists and patrons the freedom to pick and choose elements that suit their moods or purposes as well as to refashion them into something new. When their work is most creative, it provokes the rethinking of basic notions, thus altering the intellectual traditions from which they drew. Although we may feel strongly the urge to look for key principles that bring clarity to the apparent untidiness of Chinese culture, in my view we actually gain a deeper understanding if we resist that urge and strive instead to comprehend a dynamic situation in which opposing ideas, practices, and symbols run up against each other and people feel strongly the truth or beauty of ideas and things not entirely consistent with each other.

THE RULER

Chinese ideas about kingship cannot be ignored by the student of Chinese art. Much of Chinese art was either made for kingly use or influenced by standards of taste set at court. In this exhibition the exquisite objects from the tombs of the royal consort Fu Hao, the marquis of Yi, the king of Zhongshan, and the First Emperor of Qin are the most obvious examples of this. Even art not from royal tombs owes much to the technical advances made by artists and artisans in the employ of rulers who demanded objects of the highest possible quality and who could provide the material resources required. That rulers had resources at their disposal is probably best explained in terms of political and economic history. But the way they chose to use those resources has much to do with conceptions of kingship.

The notion that properly there is only one supreme ruler goes very far back in Chinese history. In the late Shang known from the excavations at Anyang (ca. 1200–1100 BCE), the king referred to himself as "The One Man" or "The Unique One," and seems to have operated on the assumption that he could command the obedience of everyone in the realm. Above him, however, were powerful spirits, especially his own ancestors. He was the intermediary between humankind and these celestial powers, whom he served through sacrifices of animals and even human beings. In the most important cults the king acted as the head priest, making the sacrifices and pronouncing the prayers. He expended much of the wealth at his disposal on the performance of these rites, and the concentration of material resources in his hands was justified on the basis of his priestly powers. That is, he was the one best able to communicate with his powerful ancestors through divination and influence them through sacrifices, and these ancestors were the best able to communicate with the high god Di, and so for the welfare of the entire society it was essential that he have the material resources to perform the rites in the most efficacious possible manner.

Sacrifices to ancestors and other divinities remained central to kingship into the Zhou period (ca. 1100–256 BCE), but the most important divinity of the early Zhou was Heaven. Heaven, perhaps originating in a sky divinity, had by this time come to be conceived as something like the sacred moral power of the cosmos. Just as there was only one Heaven, there could be only one true universal king, the "Son of Heaven," uniquely qualified and obliged to offer sacrifices to Heaven. The early classic Shu jing ("Book of Documents") portrays Heaven as taking a direct interest in the performance of the king. If he neglected his sacred duties and acted tyrannically, Heaven would display its disfavor by sending down ominous portents and natural disasters. If the king failed to heed such warnings, political and social disorder would ensue, signaling that Heaven had withdrawn its mandate.

Thus, the Shu jing portrays the final Shang ruler as a dissolute, sadistic king who had lost Heaven's favor and the Zhou conquerors as just and noble warriors who had gained it. Kingly tendencies toward ostentation were judged harshly. The charges against the last king of the Shang included spending too much on his personal enjoyment, taking resources from the people to build "palaces, towers, pavilions, embankments, ponds, and all other extravagances";[2] kings were not, however, criticized for commissioning lavishly decorated bronze vessels for use in sacrifices or for burial in graves, since that was done for the ancestors.

To the contrary, bronze sacrificial vessels remained an important symbol of lordship. Many early Zhou vessels bear inscriptions showing they were presented by the king to a lord to accompany the granting of a fief. A myth grew up about the "nine tripods" created by the founders of the Xia dynasty. These tripods symbolically united the realm, as they were made of metal from the various regions and decorated with images of animals from all over. They also were attuned to Heaven. When the ruler's virtue was commendable and brilliant, the tripods would be heavy though small, but when the ruler lacked virtue, they would be light even though large. When the Xia dynasty ended, it was believed, the tripods passed like royal regalia to the Shang rulers, then centuries later to the Zhou rulers.[3]

Conceptions of the ruler as the pivotal figure in the cosmos may well draw from very ancient ideas of shaman-priests who intercede with celestial powers, but by mid-Zhou times they were evolving in a text-centered tradition, fashioned by literate court specialists to suit the needs of rulers, nobles, and the ruling class more generally. From the eighth century on the Zhou kings progressively lost actual power and regional lords grew stronger, but these new circumstances did not lead to a new cosmology that eliminated the need for a universal king. Rather it led to a profusion of ideas on how best to recover or recreate a central monarchical institution capable of bringing unity to a politically divided world.

To Confucius (traditional dates 551–479 BCE), the solution lay in getting rulers to act like true kings. He held up as examples Yao and Shun, the sage-kings of antiquity, as well as the more recent founders of the Zhou dynasty, King Wen and King Wu. These true kings were antitheses of the selfish, aggressive, heavy-handed, vainglorious rulers of the states of his day. The true king would honor the ancient ways and rule through ritual (li) and moral force (de). He would not overburden his people to satisfy his own greedy desires for ostentatious display or incessant conquest. "If a ruler himself is upright, all will go well even though he does not issue orders. But if he himself is not upright, even though he gives orders, they will not be obeyed" (*Analects*, 13.6). "Were a true king to appear, within a generation goodness would prevail" (*Analects*, 13.12).

The true king would rule through ritual, but Confucius did not conceive of him as a priest-king. Nor did Confucius ever imply that the gods or ancestors would cause harm to those who failed to perform the sacrifices to them properly; he himself is said to have performed sacrifices "as though" the spirits were present. Later followers like Xunzi (ca. 310–ca. 220 BCE) explicitly denied any link between the performance of rites and the action of spirits or gods. Xunzi argued that Heaven is impartial and human affairs result from human efforts. Praying to Heaven or to gods does not get them to intervene.

Both Confucius' and Xunzi's love of ritual was based at least in part on aesthetic attraction: they responded to the beauty of well-choreographed ceremonies combining instrumental music, song, and dance. But their intellectual argument, addressed to rulers, concerned the nearly magical way in which ritual can create social and political harmony. Confucius told his disciple Yan Hui that "the whole world would respond to the true goodness of one who could for one day restrain himself and return to ritual" (*Analects*, 12.1). Ritual, to Confucius, was not restricted to dealings with ancestors or deities: it was also an aspect of the way the ruler dealt with his subjects. "Lead the people by means of government policies and regulate them through punishments, and they will be evasive and have no sense of shame. Lead them by means of virtue and regulate them through rituals and they will have a sense of shame and moreover have standards" (*Analects*, 2.3).

Xunzi went much further than Confucius in emphasizing the connection between ritual and distinctions of rank. The funerals of rulers had to be on a scale corresponding to their rank in every detail—the numbers of inner and outer coffins, the quality and quantity of burial clothes and food offerings, the length of the interval between death and burial. In ancestral rites, the highest ruler, presiding over the entire realm, had to offer numerous types of food and wine to seven generations of ancestors, but a ruler of a single state should make fewer offerings to only five generations, and so on. Rulers must perform these rituals correctly, not because they need the aid or fear the wrath of the dead, but in order to demonstrate their filial gratitude and respect for tradition, and to show that they accept their place in the political hierarchy.

Confucius and his followers elevated the ruler by placing him firmly at the top of a moral hierarchy in which all—rulers and subjects, nobles and commoners, parents and children—wholeheartedly devote themselves to fulfilling the parts assigned to them; in this ideal world superiors and inferiors look after each other and everything gets done without conflict or the use of force. This view of the ruler exalts him but also burdens him, for when the world is not in perfect harmony the fault is mostly his. Mencius (ca. 370–ca. 300 BCE) once told a king that if a ruler were to appear who was not inclined toward killing people, "The people would flow toward him the way water flows down. No one would be able to stop them" (1A.6). On another occasion he told a king that if he treated his people well by reducing taxes and lightening punishments, they would be so eager to fight for him that even if armed only with sharpened sticks they could defeat the well-equipped soldiers of the powerful states of Qin and Chu, which had been encroaching on the king's territory.

As texts recording the teachings of Confucius and his followers began to circulate in the late Zhou, they helped freeze the Confucian position and also invited counter-arguments. A few thinkers—generally ones labeled Daoist—went further than the Confucians in urging rulers to do less. The *Laozi* said, "The sage manages affairs by doing nothing and spreads the teachings that are not put in words." The more a ruler does, the worse the result: the more laws and regulations, the more thieves and robbers. The sage ruler "ensures that the people know nothing and desire nothing."[4]

More common than calls for nonaction, however, were calls for action. Mozi (ca. 490–ca. 403 BCE) proposed strengthening the ability of rulers to command obedience. He argued that unless one man was elevated above all others, there would be no final authority and everyone would have his own opinion, making any sort of cooperation or social organization impossible. The solution was for everyone to agree with those above—including the ruler, who must conform to Heaven: "What the superior thinks right, all shall think right." The text attributed to Guanzi (traditional dates 683–642 BCE) agreed that the peace and stability of the state depend on elevating the ruler. But Guanzi drew attention to the need for coercion. What secured the ruler's control was his power "to grant life, to kill, to enrich, to impoverish, to ennoble, to debase." Even if the ruler's personal conduct was not superior, given these powers, all would accept his leadership and "not dare to indulge in opinions about the quality of his conduct."[5]

The leading Legalist thinkers would largely have agreed with these sentiments. In the book ascribed to him, Lord Shang (Shang Yang, or Gongsun Yang; d. 338 BCE) urged the ruler not to hesitate to institute changes in his efforts to strengthen his state. The founders of the Xia, Shang, and Zhou had not been afraid to make changes, because "wise people create laws while ignorant ones are controlled by them; the worthy alter the rites while the unworthy are held fast by them." Law to him was the sovereign's will, carefully codified and impartially applied.

Han Feizi (d. 233 BCE), author of the fullest exposition of Legalist thought, argued that the Confucian notion of ruling through virtue rather than force was based on a faulty analogy with the family. "A mother loves her son twice as much as a father does, but a father's orders are ten times more effective than a mother's." Moreover, the common people have about as much understanding of what is good for them as infants who scream when their loving mothers lance their boils. The ruler who taxes the people to fill granaries against times of famine or war should ignore their protests the way the mother ignores the baby's wails. Rulers should even be wary of the advice of their top ministers. Given subordinates' propensities to pursue their own selfish interests, the ruler cannot afford to be candid or warm toward any of them. Rather he should keep them in awed ignorance of his intentions and control them by manipulating competition among them. "When the ruler trusts someone, he falls under that person's control."[6]

By Han Feizi's time ideas about the ruler were also colored by myths about the Yellow Emperor (Huangdi), first of the sage-kings of high antiquity. Han Feizi at one point referred to the Yellow Emperor summoning the ghosts and spirits to the top of Mount Tai, travelling there on a chariot pulled by dragons, with tigers and wolves leading the way, ghosts and spirits following, lizards and snakes below, a phoenix above. In the version of the myth current in Han Feizi's day, the Yellow Emperor was notable above all for his military might. He had overcome the Divine Husbandman (Shennong), who had introduced farming but shied away from the use of arms. By teaching the bears, leopards, and tigers to fight for him, the Yellow Emperor had been able to conquer all those who opposed him. In addition, the Yellow Emperor had associations with rain and with dragons; some texts say he had the face of a dragon and that dragons appeared when he received Heaven's mandate.[7] The later chapters of the Daoist text *Zhuangzi* present the Yellow Emperor sometimes as an arrogant conqueror, dangerous in the excess of his zeal for bringing order to the world, sometimes as a devoted disciple of the master Zhuangzi, listening to teachings on longevity. Often he was identified with the Daoist Sage, a being of immense powers,

physically and mentally free, able to wander freely to the four corners of the universe and to live in perfect unity with everything in the cosmos.[8]

During the fourth and third centuries, as the smaller states (such as Zhongshan, prominent in the exhibition) were eliminated by their larger neighbors, the competition between the surviving states became even more intense. The state of Qin systematically eliminated the hereditary lords of the states it conquered, a policy that led to unprecedented concentration of resources in the hands of a single ruler, the king of Qin. Legalist ideology insists on rationality and efficiency as the means to achieve and exercise authority; there is no implication in the writings of Lord Shang or Han Feizi that the ruler would be wise to spend freely on luxuries in order to impress his subjects with his power. But Legalist ideology does not explicitly urge austerity on the ruler, or indeed set limits of any sort on his actions, and the man to oversee the unification of China by Legalist means, the First Emperor of Qin (Qin Shihuangdi, r. 246–210 BCE) (see cats. 88–92) did not set many limits on himself. Drawing together the resources of All-Under-Heaven made possible enormous construction projects. Although he already had several hundred palaces and scenic towers, in 212 the emperor conscripted seven hundred thousand subjects to build his tomb and a huge new palace complex, large enough to seat ten thousand people. Many of his palaces were connected by elevated walkways and walled roads so that the emperor could move between them undetected.

Although he was rigorous in enforcing such Legalist policies as strict rewards and punishments, the First Emperor of Qin was personally open to non-Legalist ideas as well, including the more grandiose conceptions of rulership conveyed by the myth of the Yellow Emperor and cosmological schemes that proved to him that the Qin ruled through the power of Water and thus was destined to succeed the Zhou, which had ruled through Fire. This cosmological strain of thought drew on very old ideas about the production of the myriad things through the workings of Yin and Yang. Yang, identified with the sun, Heaven, light, the male, the assertive, and the changing, contrasts with Yin, identified with the moon, earth, darkness, female, dampness, receptivity, and continuity. The movement from Yin to Yang and back again corresponds to such phenomena as the daily changes in the position of the sun and moon and the yearly succession of the seasons. The theory of the Five Phases (earth, wood, metal, fire, water) is a much more complex system, which divides and classifies the cosmos in both time and space on the basis of equivalencies, resonances, and influences connecting cosmic principles, astral events, and earthly phenomena, especially government. These theories provided the basis for medicine, divination, and the interpretation of dreams and portents. Moreover, because they required searching for both anomalies and regularities in the skies, the weather, flora, and fauna, they fostered advances in astronomical and calendrical calculation and in natural history.

The collapse of the Qin within a few years of the death of the First Emperor led to the discrediting of Legalism but not of other ideas on which Qin had drawn, such as the Five Phases cosmology or the myth of the Yellow Emperor, all of which in Han times were drawn together into an ideological justification of imperial rule. Dong Zhongshu (ca. 179–ca. 104 BCE) wrote at length on the interconnections among Heaven, earth, and humanity. Among human beings, the ruler was unique in his capacity to link the three. Moreover, using terms that echo Daoist and Legalist conceptions, Dong described him as ruling through nonaction—abstaining from administration—to maintain his exalted status. The *Record of Ritual*, dating from the early Han, draws on earlier texts like the *Lüshi chunqiu* to depict the ideal ruler as one who coordinates the activities of his state with the forces of nature, analyzed in terms of Yin and Yang and the Five Phases. His movements had to be in tune with ritually demarked times and places. In the first month of the year, for instance, the Son of Heaven lives in the apartments on the left side of the Green Bright Hall, rides in a chariot with green pennants drawn by dark green dragon horses, wears green robes and pendants of green jade. Also in that month no trees may be cut down and no people may be summoned for any service, nor may arms be taken up.

Although Confucian scholars claimed to be experts in the traditional texts on ritual, they were not the only ones designing the rituals that would keep the ruler in harmony with the Five Phases. Rituals designed on the basis of ancient texts by Confucian scholars who held secular views of ritual were always in danger of becoming mere social ceremonies, useful for creating and confirming social distinctions, but unable to touch people in powerful ways. As a consequence, Confucian scholars were not able to monopolize the design of court rituals, and many rulers were receptive to men who claimed alternative ways to tap into cosmic powers. In 110 BCE, when Emperor Wu of the Han dynasty journeyed to Mount Tai to perform the *feng* and *shan* sacrifices, he dismissed the Confucian scholars because they "insisted on confining themselves to what was written in the *Odes* and *Documents* and other old books" and objected to sacrificial vessels the emperor had made because they were not the same as the ones used in ancient times.[9] In their place he relied on men who were experts in the lore of the Yellow Emperor, the god Great Unity, and routes to immortality. In later periods as well, Confucian scholars tended to advocate austere textually-based "ancient" rituals while experts in the occult or later Daoist priests choreographed elaborate ritual pageants more satisfying to many emperors.

To sum up, throughout the imperial period, the production of luxury goods to be used in imperial palaces, temples, and tombs took place in a cultural context in which rulers were given all sorts of advice. They were told to demonstrate their rank in everything they did but not to burden the people through excessive extraction; they were told to model themselves on sage-kings whose attributes ranged from the mild and temperate Yao to the all-conquering Yellow Emperor; they were likened to gods but also told to perform highly scripted roles that left them little in the way of personal discretion. Art produced for the court would have resonated with these ideas in various ways. Moreover, art produced for other sites often was shaped by these discourses indirectly. In later centuries Buddhist and Daoist temples were often modeled on palaces, and their deities on kings and queens. Thus, ways of decorating temples and depicting deities participated in the discourse on rulership. Art that was distinctly nonimperial also, of course, drew from this discourse. Scholars who identified with the Confucian critique of imperial extravagance had to choose a more austere style for their own homes and gardens.

MOUNTAINS

Depictions of mountains were very common in Chinese art from the late Warring States period on, and there are many examples in the exhibition (cats. 50, 51 [reverse], 153, 186, 189, 192–95, 200, 204–9, 212).[10] Mountains share some of the aura of kings. Kings sacrifice to mountains. The sage-king Shun, the *Book of Documents* reports, regularly sacrificed to the mountains from afar, and once every five years made a journey to each region of the empire, making burnt offerings to Heaven at the sacred mountains Tai in the east, Heng in the south, Hua in the west, Heng in the north, and Songgao in the center. Mountains were also like rulers, rich in Yang power, towering above the ordinary, linking the lowly to the heavens. The death of a ruler was euphemistically called the collapse of a mountain. "Great and lofty is the mountain/ With its might reaching to Heaven," read the first two lines in a poem in the *Classic of Poetry* (poem 259).

Many ideas about mountains undoubtedly derived from folk traditions about particular local mountains and the deities or creatures that inhabited them. Han Feizi recorded the story of King Zhao (r. 306–251 BCE) of the state of Qin who climbed to the top of Mount Hua and left an inscription there saying, "King Zhao once played a game of *bo* with a heavenly deity here." Mountains were also wild places where fantastic and dangerous creatures lived. The late Zhou and Han *Shanhai jing* ("Classic of Mountains and Seas") describes mountains inhabited by animals like the human-devouring *zhuhai*, with horns like a bull, human eyes, and hog's ears. The deities residing in the mountains are also often hybrid, combining human, bird, snake, sheep, or dragon parts.

In late Zhou local cults of immortality were gaining strength and spreading, and in these cults immortals were often associated with mountains. Magicians advised the First Emperor of Qin that immortals dwelled in exquisite palaces of gold and silver in the mountains of an island in the Eastern Sea, and he sent out teams of young people to search for them. In Han times Emperor Wu was told that the Yellow Emperor had attained immortality by visiting these islands. The *Huainanzi,* a Daoist-tinged compilation sponsored by a Han prince during the mid-second century BCE, describes the magic realm of the Kunlun Mountains in the far west, where immortality could be attained. Sometimes this mythical mountain was associated with the cult of a goddess called the Queen Mother of the West (Xiwangmu). In her paradise trees of deathlessness grew and rivers of deathlessness flowed. Mythical birds and beasts kept her company, including the three-legged crow, dancing toad, nine-tailed fox, and elixir-producing rabbit.

Mountains also have a special significance in the "science" of earth forms, or geomancy, which dates back at least to Han times and flourished in subsequent centuries. The earth is viewed as an organism with energy flowing through its veins, much the way blood flows through the body. Mountains are full of such energy in their "dragon veins," and studying the configuration of a mountain or mountain range to determine where these channels of energy are located makes it possible for one skilled in geomancy to site a house or grave to best advantage.

By the end of the Six Dynasties (220–589) the earlier image of the mountain as a wild realm of fearsome powers coexisted with a more benign image of the mountain as the favored dwelling place of immortals, who lived in palatial luxury in brightly painted halls set among gardens and populated by elegantly dressed "jade maidens." The connection between rulers and mountains survives, but in a tamer, more civilized form that emphasizes material comfort and leisure rather than awesome

power. In time private gardens, and probably also imperial gardens, came to be designed as embodiments of the paradises of the immortals in the remote mountains.

In the late Han individual seekers after immortality started to visit mountains to search for herbs, to receive divine revelations, or to acquire magical powers. Ge Hong (ca. 280–ca. 343) proposed that those seeking immortality should go to mountains, where they could pursue their quest without distraction. But he urged them to choose "big mountains" ruled by gods, rather than little mountains infested by demons or minor spirits of trees or stones.[11] The tradition of seeking insight in mountains would continue through the rest of Chinese history, simultaneously promoting and being reinforced by the practice of establishing Buddhist and Daoist monasteries in remote mountain locations. In the Shangqing (also called Maoshan) school of Daoism of the fourth century and later, adepts could also visit mountains without leaving home by visualizing their visits to the abodes of the immortals. Because of the assumed correspondences between the macrocosm and the microcosm, the exploration of a mountain or even a single rock could lead to an understanding of the entire cosmos.

The holy aura of mountains also attracted "mountain men," men who wished to withdraw from society even if they were not seeking immortality or salvation. Confucian scholars disgusted by the corruption of the government or lamenting the fall of the dynasty they had served could retreat to the mountains to avoid further political entanglement. Others could retreat there to seek spiritual freedom and escape from social obligations. These hermits and recluses were generally conceived as men of wisdom and conviction, uninterested in material things, content to eat and dress roughly and live in caves or huts. They are thus almost exact opposites of the immortals dwelling in diaphanous robes in palatial luxury.

Mountains and rulers were frequently likened to each other. The image of the mountain enhanced the image of the ruler by stressing his imposing majesty, connections to Heaven, and links to the realms of the immortals. At the same time, mountains had an anti-monarchical side, from their association with recluses who refused to have anything to do with the ruler and the world of government with its hierarchies and rules.

WRITING
In China, writing has been imbued with religious and philosophical significance from early times.[12] The divinatory texts that have survived from Shang

times record statements addressed to ancestors or spirits. The earliest transmitted texts from the Zhou period came to be considered the holy texts of the Confucian tradition, classics to be read with reverence or, better yet, memorized. Even though these texts did not convey the words of gods, they contained the teachings of the sages. In later centuries, after the use of paper became common, paper with writing on it was considered sacred, and well into the twentieth century old men would collect and burn scrap paper, that being the way to dispose of it with proper respect. Writing was also, of course, considered an art—to many, calligraphy was the highest of all the arts.

The power of written texts can be fully tapped only by those learned in the written traditions, able to interpret the preserved texts and add to the repertoire by writing books themselves. Because the Chinese language was written in a logographic script—one graph for each word—reading and writing were skills that took many years to master, and from Shang times on those who had mastered the thousands of symbols used to make records were technical experts in demand at court. In Confucius' day learned men served at court as advisers, teachers, strategists, and clerks. They knew the rules for rituals and ceremonies, such as sacrifices to ancestors and reception of envoys; they knew about the Heavens and could advise on setting the calendar; they kept records and advised on precedents. But they depended on rulers for employment, and as states were destroyed, these learned men frequently found themselves in the uncomfortable position of having to locate a new lord in need of their services.

Confucius urged his followers to master the literary traditions of their day, and the *Analects* reported that Confucius often discoursed on "poetry, history, and the performance of ceremonies" (7.17). Yet he did not want men of education to think of themselves as narrow experts, but rather as persons whose moral sensibilities had been cultivated by studying the words of the sages. Their aim should be to become "gentlemen," men of integrity and honor who deserved to be respected as much for their moral cultivation as for their mastery of tradition. The true gentleman, in Confucius's vision, is not moved by profit like the petty man, but rather aspires to things lofty. He concentrates on improving himself and is indifferent to recognition or reward. "The gentleman feels bad when his capabilities fall short of the task. He does not feel bad when people fail to recognize him" (15.18). If he can retain his self-respect even though no ruler employs him, he is not dependent on the ruler, and can develop ideas and take stands independent of the ruler.

The Confucian claim to the moral autonomy of the educated came to have much greater historical significance after men trained in Confucian texts gained a hold on government posts, giving them some degree of social and political independence as well. During the course of the Han, it became widely accepted that officials should be men trained in the Confucian classics and respected for their character. Ambitious young men sought out teachers with whom to study the classics, for learning could lead to power and prestige. All over the country teachers attracted large numbers of students and disciples, and the enrollment at the imperial academy increased from a few dozen students to more than thirty thousand in the mid-second century CE.

Confucian officials, trained to view their obligation to the ruler in moral terms, made forthright critics of imperial policies. During the Han many Confucian scholars and officials opposed activist policies such as government monopolies, questioning their morality and their effect on people's livelihoods. Scholars regularly objected to imperial extravagance, urging emperors to reduce their spending on palace ladies, entertainment, hunting parks, stables, and rituals. Thus, the coupling of Confucianism and the Chinese bureaucracy created a sort of balance of power between the emperor and the Confucian-educated officials who staffed the government but did not consider themselves mere servants of the emperor. Because the court set the standards that the literati had to fulfill to gain entry into officialdom, it circumscribed their autonomy, their capacity to set their own standards, but it never eliminated it. By the end of the Han those with Confucian educations had become self-conscious of their common identity. In the succeeding centuries the strength and coherence of this elite of educated gentlemen proved as important as political centralization or economic integration as a basis for the unity of Chinese civilization.

The impact of these developments on Chinese culture was profound. The importance placed on texts and learning fostered some of China's most renowned advances, such as the invention of paper in the Han period and printing in the Tang period. The obligation of the gentleman to devote himself both to learning the tradition and to refining and cultivating his own character legitimated artistic activities of many sorts, above all, perhaps, poetry-writing and calligraphy, but also painting and connoisseurship of ancient objects. A highly self-referential style in painting and calligraphy, one that required firm grounding in what had come before, accorded well not only with the Confucian commitment to learning but also with the literati approach to other intellectual pursuits, such as making extensive use of allusions in poetry and writing commentaries on the classics.

Although it is common to associate learning in China with the Confucian literati, Confucian-trained scholars were never the only significant group of learned men who owed their standing to mastery of a body of texts. In Han times the astrologers, diviners, and experts in unseen forces transmitted their knowledge both orally and through texts. Buddhism had entered China as a religion with a vast body of scriptures, and monks gained standing, both within the Buddhist community and outside it, by mastering a body of texts and adding to the understanding of them through writing commentaries. In the fourth and fifth centuries religious Daoism acquired a large body of revealed texts, and although these texts were not publicly distributed the way the Confucian classics or Buddhist sutras were, priestly powers were closely tied to knowledge of them. Words, including written prayers and charms and oral incantations and hymns, were as much a part of Daoist rituals as the odor of incense, the sounds of flutes and drums, and the colors of robes and banners.

But the story does not end there. The supremacy of the written word and of those learned in the written word did not go unchallenged in China. To the contrary, from very early times important philosophical and religious thinkers disputed the priority given words, texts, the educated, and the kind of knowledge that gets created and promoted through words and texts. They pointed to the limits of language and to forms of knowing that could not be communicated through language. To put this another way, some thinkers have always resisted the way writing fixes, limits, and binds meanings, and have tried to preserve or recover the reality that exists prior to or beyond writing. These sets of ideas have been as powerful in Chinese art as the pro-text ideas, perhaps particularly because visual symbols are not words.

The earliest formulation of this challenge to words is found in the early Daoist classics. "The Way that can be told is not the invariant Way" is the opening line of the *Laozi*. Words and writing are assertive and thus destructive. It would be better, the *Laozi* asserts, if people knew less, if they gave up tools and abandoned writing. They would be satisfied with their own lives and not envy their neighbors. Zhuangzi argued that the labeling of experience with words and its division into distinct categories was a falsification from the start, since reality could never be conveyed in this way. Zhuangzi placed the knowledge of the craftsman above the knowledge found in books. In one parable he had a wheelwright audaciously tell a duke that books

were useless since all they contained were the dregs of men long gone. When the duke demanded either an explanation or his life, the wheelwright replied:

> I see things in terms of my own work. When I chisel at a wheel, if I go slowly, the chisel slides and does not stay put; if I hurry, it jams and doesn't move properly. When it is neither too slow nor too fast, I can feel it in my hand and respond to it from my heart. My mouth cannot describe it in words, but there is something there. I cannot teach it to my son, and my son cannot learn it from me. So I have gone on for seventy years, growing old chiseling wheels. The men of old died in possession of what they could not transmit. So it follows that what you are reading are their dregs.[13]

Truly skilled craftsmen do not analyze or reason or even keep in mind the rules they once learned; they respond to situations spontaneously.

Whereas Confucians, who saw truth in books, recognized an obligation to bring this truth to the attention of the ruler, Zhuangzi, who did not see truth in books, felt no need to serve in government. He told of receiving an envoy from the king of Chu, bearing an offer to give him charge of the entire realm. In response he asked the envoy whether a tortoise that had been held sacred for three thousand years would prefer to be dead with its bones venerated or alive with its tail dragging in the mud. On getting the expected response, he told the envoy to go away; he wished to drag his tail in the mud.

Although the social standing of the educated in China owes much to Confucian ideas of the worth of written traditions and men educated in them, it would be a mistake to infer that the educated elite always thought exclusively in pro-text terms. In particular, Daoist ideas that questioned the role of words and texts appealed deeply to many educated men. These ideas also colored the development of Buddhism in China. The most Sinified school of Buddhism, the Chan school (known as Zen in Japan), rejected the authority of the sutras and claimed the superiority of mind-to-mind transmission of Buddhist truth through a series of patriarchs, the most important of whom were the First Patriarch Bodhidharma, an Indian monk who came to China in the early sixth century, and the Sixth Patriarch Huineng, a Chinese monk who died in the early eighth century. The illiteracy of Huineng at the time of his enlightenment was taken as proof of the Chan claim that enlightenment could be achieved suddenly through insight into one's own true nature, even by people who knew nothing of textual traditions. Chan masters tried to get their followers to free their minds from the traps of discursive thought by taking language to the limits. They would assign them baffling anecdotes or questions to ponder and respond to their efforts with cryptic utterances, shouts, or even blows.

Tension between the world of the book and the world that cannot be contained by the book cut across many different traditions. In China, as elsewhere, people felt a strong urge to impose order on experience by specifying, categorizing, evaluating, and judging via words and their inscription in texts, but their attempts could never totally succeed because of all that could not be contained by texts, the disrupting forces and uncontrollable potency of rulers, mountains, divinities, oral revelations, dreams, emotions, and so on. The Confucian literati normally took their stand on the side of texts and order, but the distinction here goes beyond simple divisions of literati versus rulers, or Confucians versus Buddhists and Daoists. Buddhists, Daoists, and rulers all drew on texts and their ordering potential, and Confucian scholars to varying degrees drew on the magical power of rituals and the visual and emotional power of images, not to mention retreating to mountains or practicing meditative techniques that could lead to insights without use of books.

The art of calligraphy, paradoxically perhaps, drew from both the reverence for writing and the deep belief in powers and forces that cannot be fully conveyed in words. Examples of writing were thought to reflect the writer's character and feelings, not just the thoughts he was trying to convey. The strength, balance, and flow of the strokes were believed to convey the calligrapher's moral and psychological make-up as well as his momentary emotions. The flow of energy within the person was found manifest in the movement of his hand and brush and the resulting traces of ink.

ICONS

The ideas discussed so far are indigenous ideas, developed in the huge subcontinent we loosely label China. But some key elements in Chinese religious traditions entered from outside, particularly as part of or in the company of Buddhism, and these elements also provided part of the context of Chinese art.

Representations of human beings appear occasionally in early Chinese art. Some Neolithic pots have human faces depicted on them (cat. 114), as do a few Shang-period bronzes; some late Zhou bronzes are decorated with small images of human beings engaged in warfare, hunting, rituals, or agriculture; sometimes the base of a lamp or tray was made in the form of a human servant (cat. 47). From the Han period there are many portrayals of human figures on the walls of temples or tombs; some of these appear to be generic figures, others are labeled as specific figures from history or mythology (cats. 103, 104).

There is little evidence, however, that these depictions of human beings were idols or icons, made to represent gods or spirits during sacrifices or other rituals. Pre-Buddhist Chinese shrines were not centered on statues or paintings of deities. Chinese sacrificial ceremonies could be performed either in the open, with a temporary altar, or in temples, but in either case objects other than paintings or statues were used to represent the spirits or gods. The central object for the *she* sacrifices to the earth, for instance, was a small earthen mound; for sacrifices to ancestral spirits, a tablet inscribed with the name of the dead was sufficient.

With the introduction of Buddhism, however, the use of images to depict divinities and spirits expanded radically (see essays by Helmut Brinker and Su Bai in this volume). Buddhists used images both to teach Buddhist doctrine and to provide a focus for devotional activities. Within a few centuries of the introduction of Buddhism, not only did the altars in Buddhist temples house images of Buddhas and bodhisattvas, but Daoist and folk temples held images of their gods, and ancestral temples also often came to contain images of the ancestors.

The reverencing of icons was not a practice that the historical Buddha Śākyamuni taught his disciples in India. But by the time Buddhism arrived in China as a religion of foreign merchants and missionaries, the use of icons was well established. The *Scripture on the Production of Buddha Images* (*Zuo fo xingxiang jing*), one of the earliest sutras translated into Chinese, records the conversation between the Buddha and King Udayana concerning the rewards received in later lives by those who produce images of the Buddha.[14] Even the most eminent monks taught followers devotional practices centered on images. The learned monk and translator Daoan (312–385) would set up a holy image and light incense whenever he gave a lecture. The equally eminent monk Huiyuan (334–417) in 402 assembled a group of monks and lay people in front of an image of the Pure Land, the Western Paradise of the Buddha Amitābha. With such prompting, the production of Buddhist images expanded greatly. By 524, according to one observer, there were over a thousand Buddhist statues in the city of Luoyang. Each year, on the seventh day of the fourth month, all these were brought to the Jingming Temple, where the emperor would come in person to scatter flowers on them as part of the Great Blessing ceremony.

Both Confucians and Daoists denounced many Buddhist ideas and practices as immoral or unsuited to China. For instance, they portrayed the great sums spent on construction of temples, statues, and ceremonies as a drain on the economy that impoverished the people and thus indirectly the state. At the same time, they borrowed extensively from the repertoire of ideas and practices that Buddhists had introduced into China, including the use of images on altars. Probably the adoption of icons should be attributed to their visual effectiveness. Icons work differently from words and texts, because images of the human form are potent in arousing emotions. Moreover, the meanings they can convey are not fixed, but mediated by the response of the viewer—different people can give an image different meanings at different times—an attribute that makes images good objects for meditation.

Although most of the icons that survive from Tang and Song times are of Buddhist divinities, not local or Daoist gods, ancestors, or Confucian sages, there is abundant textual evidence that by Tang and Song times temples of all sorts represented their central objects of worship with images. These statues and paintings must have constituted a large share of the art that the average person had occasion to see. Temples to Confucius and to Confucian sages and teachers regularly had statues in them. The imperial ancestral cult was expanded to accommodate halls with statues of emperors. And Buddhist monasteries added halls with images of their former abbots, treating them as ancestors.[15]

DIVERSITY AND CREATIVITY: THE CASE OF THE SONG DYNASTY

I have already suggested some of the ways the diverse ideas sketched here were linked to the equally diverse objects we now view as China's art treasures. The best way to extend my analysis of the ways creativity played out in a cultural context that encompassed the coexistence of numerous unintegrated ideas is to look at the conjunction of such ideas in a single time period. The Song dynasty (960–1279) offers a good case.

The Song was without doubt a time when new ideas and practices appeared in profusion. Science and technology were making rapid progress, with advances in abstract disciplines like mathematics and in such practical matters as the technology of iron and steel, ceramics, ballistics, and textiles. New gods appeared, and existing cults spread. In Buddhism, Tiantai teachings underwent a revival. In Daoism, Celestial Heart and Thunder Rites

teachings gained prominence. Among Confucians, polymaths like Shen Gua (1031–1095) contributed to everything from mathematics to geography, archaeology, music, printing, medicine, divination, military strategy, and agricultural technology. Other Confucian scholars like Cheng Yi (1033–1107) were drawn to metaphysical speculation about the nature and workings of the cosmos.[16]

Certain trends and issues crosscut many traditions. For instance, concern both with texts and with what cannot be conveyed in texts enlivened intellectual life in many circles. Many highly educated Confucian scholars were attracted to forms of spirituality that did not rely on texts, including meditation and visionary experiences, and they were ready to make use of Buddhist and Daoist traditions toward these ends.[17] At a less elevated level, many literati were captivated by cases of spirit-writing, in which spirits created texts by possessing objects or people. Zhu Xi (1130–1200), the towering figure in Confucianism, took a strong line against Buddhist and Daoist practices, advocating the "investigation of things" through careful reading of the Four Books and the classics more generally; he also, however, advocated "quiet sitting," a form of meditation. In a comparable way, Chan Buddhism, notwithstanding its emphasis on transmission outside texts, was expanded to accommodate highly literate Chan monks who excelled in poetry and other literary arts. The impact of this lively interest both in words and in what goes beyond words is evident in Chan painting, which seems to extend the idea of communicating through nondiscursive means to painting that is suggestive much more than descriptive.

I would also argue that the fundamental conflict between the claims of rulers and of the educated to moral authority helped rather than hindered artistic creativity. The Song was a time when the moral autonomy of those with Confucian educations was strongly reasserted and became a matter of political struggle between the court and the Confucian literati. The size of the educated class grew so large in Song times that there was always a large supply of highly educated men who could not find employment in government service, but this did not make them more subservient to the court. To the contrary, literati residing in their home communities found a variety of ways to assert their moral autonomy. For instance, they frequently erected shrines to honor scholar-heroes of the past who had been persecuted or unfairly neglected. Leading literati like Su Shi (1037–1101), who took an interest in painting, calligraphy, and poetry writing, helped validate aesthetic and scholarly pursuits in and of themselves, even if they did not lead to serving the ruler. Others, like Cheng Yi and

Zhu Xi, rejected the scholar-aesthete model on the grounds that cultural activity should convey moral principles, not just entertain or express personal feelings. But they too strongly asserted the moral autonomy of the learned by insisting that the goal of learning was attaining sagehood, not office.

Art comes into this story because both the court and literati circles used art to bolster their own authority and legitimacy, and the resulting competition, collaboration, appropriation, and specialization seems only to have promoted creativity. [18] The tremendous flourishing of landscape painting and calligraphy in Song times should not be seen simply as automatic outgrowths of the long-established cultural value placed on mountains and writing, but rather as the product of the conjunction of many elements, including the competition and collaboration between the court and circles of literati ambivalent about their relationship to the court.

The creation of a canon of masterpieces that set the standards in calligraphy involved an interplay of imperial sponsorship and literati connoisseurship. In 992 the court had ordered the printing of a book of rubbings that reproduced copies of famous pieces of calligraphy, especially early ones by Wang Xizhi (307?–365?) and Wang Xianzhi (344–386). But comparing these pieces and determining their relative quality was largely the work of private scholars such as Mi Fu (1052–1107/8). [19]

Court and literati taste often diverged, of course. Su Shi, who enjoyed social occasions at which educated men would compose poems, paint pictures, or inspect antiques, offered a theoretical justification for the superiority of "scholar's painting" over professional painting. He valued spontaneous creation over laborious technique, asserted the moral superiority of creating a work without thought of financial reward, and viewed painting as a form of self-expression much like poetry. Capturing the outward form of an object was not nearly as valuable as conveying its inner principle. [20]

Some of the monuments of landscape painting were created at court for imperial patrons, but court painters viewed themselves not as artisans but as scholar-officials, with all the moral independence claimed for that status. Guo Xi (ca. 1001–ca. 1090), for instance, was a learned man who wrote on the theory of painting and participated in literati circles, and in his writings he took a romantic view of art as self-expression. Yet his employment at court would have required him to work on projects not entirely of his own choosing. To complicate matters further, Guo Xi is also known to have been a Daoist devotee, and his specialization in landscapes may owe something to his understandings of Daoist ideas about the correspondences of the microcosm and macrocosm: a single depiction of a mountain and a river can represent the entire cosmos.

The emperor who took the greatest interest in art, Huizong (r. 1100–1126), did not care for Guo Xi's paintings and had them put in storage. Moreover, he did not share Su Shi's rejection of technique. In his paintings he took considerable pains to convey the outer form of objects, and he trained court artists to observe nature with minute attention. Some of this difference in artistic taste may relate to Huizong's ambivalence toward the Confucian scholars of his day. Intellectually, Huizong was attracted to subjects like music, poetry, calligraphy, and medicine, interests many literati like Su Shi and Shen Gua shared. As a prince, he had shared a passion for art collecting with his uncle, the painter Wang Shen (see cat. 184), who in turn was on good terms with Su Shi. As emperor, he invited Su Shi's friend, the renowned painter and calligrapher Mi Fu and later his son Mi Youren (d. 1165) to come to court as curators/professors. Yet politics estranged Huizong from the circle of Su Shi, since for most of his reign he excluded from his court those involved with the opposition to Wang Anshi, who had been prime minister during the reign of his father, Shenzong (r. 1067–1085). Even the books written by the leaders of the opposition, such as Su Shi, were banned and could not be reprinted.

Huizong took a strong interest in Daoism, which can be seen in such paintings as the one he made to commemorate the appearance of white cranes over the main gate of the palace during a festival in 1112. Such a painting certainly glorified Huizong, as the appearance of the cranes was interpreted as a portent that cosmic powers approved of his rule. But the painting itself was probably seen only by a relatively small number of people in the palace. Much more important for impressing the general population with the grandeur of his rule would have been his many construction projects. Over the course of his reign he had many temples, palaces, government buildings, and gardens constructed, often on grand scale. To Huizong, however, the religious impulse behind these projects may have been stronger than the desire to impress his subjects. Through his gardens, in particular, he attempted to recreate the cosmos, with all of its myriad plants and animals, mountains and waters. [21]

Although Confucian scholars might condemn the grandiosity of Huizong's construction projects, it was much more difficult for them to decry his attempts to collect and catalogue cultural treasures. Huizong had a passion for antiques, especially Shang- and Zhou-period bronze vessels and musical instruments, which he had collected and had scholars catalogue for him. His catalogue of calligraphy gave pride of place to the same calligraphers esteemed for centuries by the literati.

After Huizong and his son Qinzong had been captured by the Jurchens and a new Song court established at Hangzhou (in 1138), the new emperor, Gaozong (r. 1127–1162), made concerted efforts to gain the support of the literati. He directed his court artists to produce works on historical or classical subjects that served to associate his court with China's cultural heritage.[22] Gaozong himself was a highly accomplished calligrapher and often made gifts of pieces of his calligraphy to favored officials. He brought Mi Youren back to court and had him serve as the curator of the palace painting collection and court painter. Art, thus, had become a site for earning the support and respect of the literati.

There is a strong tendency in Chinese thought to rank unity or oneness above disunity, to assume the superiority of consensus over disagreement, of uniformity over diversity. We need to understand this frame of mind, but we do not need to subscribe to it. Even if Huizong and Zhu Xi would have each agreed that the world would be a better place if all thought as he did, much of the vitality and creativity in Chinese culture derives from the fact that such unification of thought was beyond the capacity of either of them.

NOTES

1. The existence of opposed tendencies in Chinese thought has long been recognized. See the classic article by Benjamin Schwartz, "Some Polarities in Chinese Thought," in *Confucianism in Action*, ed. David S. Nivison and Arthur F. Wright (Stanford: Stanford University Press, 1959). Here, because my focus is on connections to art, I have selected a rather different set of ideas than Schwartz did. Moreover, I do not see a larger system that comprehends all of the polarities, but a much messier situation in which inconsistencies and even incoherence are not only possible but an accepted part of the way things are.

2. See James Legge, trans., *The Chinese Classics III: The Shoo King* (Hong Kong: University of Hong Kong Press, 1960; reprint of Oxford University Press ed.), pp. 283–85.

3. See K.C. Chang, *Art, Myth, and Ritual: The Path to Political Authority in Ancient China* (Cambridge: Harvard University Press, 1983), pp. 95–97; Wu Hung, *Monumentality in Early Chinese Art and Architecture* (Stanford: Stanford University Press, 1995), pp. 4–12.

4. See A.C. Graham, *Disputers of the Tao* (La Salle, Ill.: Open Court, 1989), pp. 232–34.

5. On Mozi's and Guanzi's political thought, see Kung-chuan Hsiao, *A History of Chinese Political Thought*, trans. F.W. Mote (Princeton: Princeton University Press, 1979), pp. 235–43, 322–26.

6. Translation from Patricia Buckley Ebrey, ed., *Chinese Civilization: A Sourcebook,* 2nd ed. (New York: Free Press, 1993), pp. 33–37.

7. See Mark Edward Lewis, *Sanctioned Violence in Early China* (Albany: State University of New York Press, 1990), pp. 174–212.

8. See Isabelle Robinet, *Daoism: Growth of a Religion*, trans. Phyllis Brooks (Stanford: Stanford University Press, 1997), pp. 30–32, 46.

9. Burton Watson, trans., *The Records of the Grand Historian of China* (New York: Columbia University Press, 1961), p. 57.

10. On Chinese ideas about the sacred powers of mountains and their expression in Chinese art, see Kiyohiko Munakata, *Sacred Mountains in Chinese Art* (Urbana: University of Illinois Press, 1990); Lothar Ledderhose, "The Earthly Paradise: Religious Elements in Chinese Landscape Art," in *Theories of the Arts in China*, ed. Susan Bush and Christian Murck (Princeton: Princeton University Press, 1983), pp. 165–83; and John Hay, *Kernels of Energy, Bones of Earth: The Rock in Chinese Art* (New York: China House Gallery, 1985).

11. Robinet, p. 95.

12. On this topic, see also K.C. Chang, *Art, Myth, and Ritual*, pp. 81–94; Derk Bodde, *Chinese Thought, Society, and Science: The Intellectual and Social Background of Science and Technology in Pre-Modern China* (Honolulu: University of Hawaii Press, 1991), pp. 26–31.

13. Translation from Ebrey, ed., *Chinese Civilization: A Sourcebook,* p. 31.

14. See Robert H. Sharf, "The Scripture on the Production of Buddha Images," in *Religions of China in Practice*, ed. Donald S. Lopez, Jr. (Princeton: Princeton University Press, 1996), pp. 261–67.

15. See Patricia Ebrey, "Portrait Sculptures in Imperial Ancestral Rites in Song China," *T'oung Pao* 83 (1997), pp. 42–92, and T. Griffith Foulk and Robert H. Sharf, "On the Ritual Use of Ch'an Portraiture in Medieval China," *Cahiers d'Extrême-Asie* 7 (1993–94), pp. 149–219.

16. For an overview of the religious and philosophical situation in Song times, see Peter N. Gregory and Patricia Buckley Ebrey, "The Religious and Historical Landscape," in *Religion and Society in T'ang and Sung China*, ed. Ebrey and Gregory (Honolulu: University of Hawaii Press, 1993), pp. 1–44.

17. For a good example, see Robert M. Gimello, "Chang Shang-ying on Wu-t'ai Shan," in *Pilgrims and Sacred Sites in China*, ed. Susan Naquin and Chün-fang Yü (Berkeley: University of California Press, 1992), pp. 89–149.

18. For recent overviews of Song court art, see Craig Clunas, *Art in China* (Oxford: Oxford University Press, 1997), pp. 53–63, and Wen C. Fong, *Beyond Representation: Chinese Painting and Calligraphy 8th–14th Century* (New York: Metropolitan Museum of Art, 1992), pp. 173–245.

19. See Lothar Ledderose, *Mi Fu and the Classical Tradition of Chinese Calligraphy* (Princeton: Princeton University Press, 1979) and Peter Charles Sturman, *Mi Fu: Style and the Art of Calligraphy in Northern Song China* (New Haven: Yale University Press, 1997).

20. See Susan Bush and Hsio-yen Shih, *Early Chinese Texts on Painting* (Cambridge: Harvard Yenching Institute, 1985), pp. 196–234, passim.

21. See James M. Hargett, "Huizong's Magic Marchmount: The Genyue Pleasure Park of Kaifeng," *Monument Serica* 38 (1988–89), pp. 1–48.

22. See Julia K. Murray, *Ma Hezhi and the Illustration of the Book of Odes* (New York: Cambridge University Press, 1993).

Five Thousand Years of Chinese Culture

Yu Weichao

Director, National Museum of
Chinese History

Recent years have seen a growing attempt to understand the Chinese artistic tradition—like the world's other artistic traditions—by relating it to its cultural context. In so short an essay, however, one can only sketch the outline of a conceptual framework for this topic, which spans the entire Eurasian land mass over more than four millennia.

I.

At least since the seventh century CE, three major artistic traditions have coexisted in the world: the East Asian tradition centered in China, the Western tradition centered in Europe (and, after the eighteenth century, in the United States), and the Islamic tradition. All three have long historical roots, and these roots are neither unitary nor linear. Their later evolutions have been shaped primarily by the evolutions of their vastly different cultural systems—the East Asian based on Confucianism, the Western on the commingling of Classical thought and Christianity, and the Islamic on the teachings of Islam.

The definition of "culture" here is that used in contemporary anthropological research, namely, "Culture consists of patterns, explicit and implicit, of and for behavior acquired and transmitted by symbols, constituting the distinctive achievement of human groups, including their embodiment in artefacts. . . . Culture systems may, on the one hand, be considered as products of action, on the other as conditioning elements of further action."[1] In short, "culture" consists of those predominant concepts that determine the rules of behavior of members of society and form the "cultural phenomena" of their groupings. From this perspective, it is the "culture" of any country or people that truly gives shape to its artistic expression.

Because for a long historical period artists were considered mere craftsmen, their works expressed not the maker's subjective aspirations but the collective or individual values of society's dominant groups, whence came their patrons. Subsequently there emerged some artists who did not depend on patronage for their livelihood, and whose works therefore could express their own interests and perceptions. Because these were generally members of the upper classes, however, their works too mostly reflect the consciousness of the social elites to which they belonged. Not until the modern era have art works come increasingly to express the individual characters of their makers, and to show a concomitant proliferation of styles. Within every artistic tradition, this pattern in the history of art has caused the works of different periods to be strongly stamped with hallmarks of their eras.

Societies everywhere follow essentially similar processes of historical development, but at disparate paces and with disparate cultural content. This underlying similitude of developmental paths produces considerable similarities among the art works of different countries and peoples at the same stage of social development; at the same time, the overlying disparities in cultural characteristics make for entirely different artistic traditions. Among the three major world artistic traditions, two were based on religious concepts—Christianity and Islam. Only in China and East Asia did a secular ethos and system of secularly derived moral values—Confucianism—come to constitute the foundation of society. This created a distinct aesthetic, which, in conjunction with differences in the conditions of life, gave rise to an artistic tradition different from the other two both in content and in forms of expression.

At a time when Christianity and Islam were widely accepted in Europe and the Middle East, Buddhism had an enormous following in China. Why, then, did Buddhist concepts not become a major basis of Chinese culture (although they did dominate certain cultures, such as the Tibetan)? The answer must be that, for a fairly lengthy period, Christianity and Islam were state religions in Europe and the Middle East; government and religion were integrated. In China, on the other hand, although the embrace of Throne and creed was sometimes close, it was always limited in time, space, and degree. Additionally, Buddhism was never supreme in the culture of the Han ethnic majority, even during its apogee, from the Northern and Southern Dynasties era through the Sui and Tang. Furthermore, Chinese Buddhism absorbed many Confucian moral and ethical concepts. In other words, among the three major cultures, the Chinese was by far the most secular.

It was in the Middle East that cultural systems coalescing government with religion originated some five thousand years ago. In ancient Egypt, for instance, the Pharaoh was also the monarch, uniting in his person state and creed. In Europe, by contrast, almost till the end of the Classical age, state and religion were mutually supportive but structurally and functionally separate institutions. Not till the fourth century CE did Rome adopt Christianity as the official religion, a policy soon followed by Rome's successor kingdoms in Europe and continued (although not unchallenged) into the era of the modern nation-states. In this regard, the Classical civilization of Europe, including its Cretan and Mycenean precursors, must be considered an interlude between the cultures of Mesopotamia and ancient Egypt and that of medieval Europe. As for Islam, it has since its beginning been accepted as a state religion in the Middle East.

The formation of the Chinese cultural tradition proceeded along different lines. Since its beginnings during the Xia, Shang, and Zhou eras, government and religion were separate, except under King Xin of the late Shang, who at one point assumed the power to offer sacrifices. The separation of government and religion simultaneously reflected and promoted a strong sense of secularism in the Chinese cultural tradition, but this secularism did not become pronounced until the reign of Emperor Wu of the Western Han (r. 141–87 BCE), when Confucianism was established as the orthodox state ideology.

II.

China's land area is very extensive, and a complex regionalism characterized the primitive cultures of the Neolithic era. Over time, of course, the various cultures changed and influenced each other, thus narrowing the differences between them. But even after entering the age of civilization, regional disparities continued to exist because of variations in the natural environment and in cultural origins. In this essay Chinese culture is taken to mean only the mainstream culture.[2]

Approximately five thousand years ago, from the Liao River in the northeast through the central and lower Yellow River basin and southward to the central and lower Yangzi River basin, civilization began to dawn. About four thousand years ago the three early dynasties, Xia, Shang, and Zhou, emerged successively in the central Yellow River basin, and China entered the age of civilization. What is generally known as Chinese culture originated during this period, defined and reinforced, from this time forward, by the traits listed below.

First, the polity that emerged was multiethnic, centered around the Huaxia people (later called the Han people) and associated with other somewhat closely related peoples. Even when one particular ethnic group seized political control from another, the state always remained multiethnic. In fact, its specific structure became ever more tight knit. A multiethnic state in which the Han people formed the majority group emerged during Qin and Han.

Second, government took the form of an autocracy, centered around the ruler as Son of Heaven. Heaven, however, was not a personalized deity, nor were the emperors god-kings or even priest-kings. Rather, Heaven represented an idea of willed cosmic order and propriety which the emperor was expected, by means of moral example, prescribed ceremonial, and effective governance, to reify on earth.

Third, a basically uniform writing system was adopted, which promoted cultural interchange and consensus among regions and peoples.

Fourth, hierarchical systems of rites were established, to set norms for the conduct of the different social classes. Of the systems created during the three early dynasties, that begun during the Zhou was the most comprehensive. Since it was originally created to stabilize the Zhou class system,

the period-specific aspects of these rites disappeared with the demise of the Zhou, but the rites themselves did not disappear. They continued to influence social behavior in subsequent dynasties, and became a part of a longstanding tradition of ritual conduct for individuals as well as the state.

A fundamental component of culture is beliefs. The exact beliefs prevalent during the three early dynasties are still unclear but are thought to have been forms of shamanism, meaning in large part the superstitious worship of heaven and earth, with shamans as intermediaries between humankind and the supernatural.[3] From the late Neolithic Liangzhu culture of the Yangzi delta (ca. 3600–ca. 2000 BCE) through the Shang and Zhou periods, precious jade objects were used as offerings to heaven and earth—jade *bi* disks to heaven and jade *cong* tubes to earth. The mysterious and mesmerizing patterns on ritual bronzes of the Shang and Zhou would seem to make them instruments of shamanism, so that Professor Zhang Guangzhi (K.C. Chang) has used the term "shamanistic culture" to explain them.[4] Shamanism, a pre-religious structure of magical beliefs, was common to most early cultures. But the use of jades for sacrifices to heaven and earth, and the use of ritual bronzes in the worship of ancestors and mountain and river gods, was unique to the magical beliefs of China during the three early dynasties. Like the Zhou rituals, at least some of these practices survived into the Ming and Qing dynasties as ceremonials protective of state and society and as evidence of Heaven-pleasing righteousness in the practitioners.

The (to us) mysterious images on ritual bronzes of the three early dynasties could not have been cast solely for the purpose of evoking awe. According to the entry for "the third year of Duke Xuan" in the *Zuo zhuan* (a historical narrative of the early Eastern Zhou period, probably compiled toward the end of Eastern Zhou), "There was virtue in the time of the Xia, so the Nine Provinces submitted to the Xia, and offered bronzes which they made in tribute. Those living afar also offered drawings depicting local spirits and demons. Then the Xia cast a large *ding* on which were portrayed all the spirits and demons, so that the people might know of them. Thus, when they travelled to the mountains, rivers, and forests around the land, they would not be molested by the many spirits and demons. To handle affairs from all over in this manner was to act according to the mandate of Heaven."[5]

During the three early dynasties people were just beginning to emerge from a state of barbarism. They attributed all good and ill to supernatural forces that were amenable to prayer and propitiation, hence the popularity of shamanism.

Given this cultural background, it was natural that images of various spirits and deities became the principal subject of the arts of the three dynasties.[6]

III.

By the Han dynasty, and particularly after the reign of Emperior Wu, the magical cosmos of the three early dynasties had changed into a secular cosmos conceived in strongly Confucian terms.

During the three early dynasties the primary objects of worship were heaven and earth, mountains, rivers, and ancestors. Similarly, moral precepts stressed the duties of venerating heaven and earth, worshiping all the spirits,[7] and honoring one's ancestors. Magical beliefs and social morality were basically one.

During the Eastern Zhou, and particularly after the late Spring and Autumn period, the teachings of Confucian and other secularly inclined philosophers flourished, gradually coming to dominate the ideological sector; at the same time, secular works of art began to increase.

Confucius, from whom the Confucian school of thought is considered to take its origin, propounded a coherent system of social ethics and morality. During the reign of Emperor Wu of the Western Han, other schools of socio-political thought were proscribed and Confucianism alone reigned supreme. Thenceforth, although individual rulers might espouse or even promote Buddhism or Daoism, Confucian ideas held sway over China for some two thousand years. Also during the reign of Emperor Wu the philosopher and political adviser Dong Zhongshu (ca. 174–ca. 104 BCE) distilled Confucian teachings on ethics and morality into the formula "three human relationships and five constant virtues" (sangang wuchang),[8] which remained normative throughout the next two millennia. Dong also proposed that "Heaven and man are one," a theory of "resonance (or mutual interaction) between heaven and man," which linked the shamanistic worship of Heaven with secular ethics and morality. In other words, Heaven is possessed of supreme power and beneficent will, humans are possessed of the potential for virtuous or evil actions; the "oneness" or "resonance" or mutual interactivity of Heaven and humankind posits that human actions affect Heaven's will, which in turn affects all mundane events, including human fortunes.

In the ancient world the theory of "Heaven and man are one" was unique to Chinese culture,[9] and from the reign of Emperor Wu it dominated Han philosophy. The theory generated a vast body of omen lore: the appearance of rare animals or plants or meteorological phenomena, or the discovery of ancient treasures were regarded as symbols of Heaven's approbation and humans' resulting good fortune. The devotees of religious Daoism, which began to take shape during late Western Han, aimed at transcending all bodily constraints, including aging, death, and their earthbound condition. This begot an obsession with the occult, including alchemy, numerology, divination, and quasi-magical dietary-respiratory-gymnastic regimens—all intended to permit adepts to attain corporeal immortality. At about the same time Buddhism also arrived and was accepted in China, conflated to a certain extent with early religious Daoism.

A common subject of Han art was the coexistence and congruence of secular activities and the heavenly world. This was most intensely and completely manifested in the pictorial programs that covered the walls of Eastern Han tombs. These included pictures of the heavenly world and astronomical phenomena, as well as many immortals and divinities; drawings of auspicious symbols that represented the idea of "resonance between Heaven and man"; and depictions of the everyday life of the deceased. Since the simple burials of the poor have not survived, what we see are the concerns and the appurtenances of the upper classes: mansions, banquets and entertainments, carriage processions and outriders, along with the farming, animal husbandry, and handicrafts that supported the estate.[10] Most strikingly, abundant images of everyday life have joined the spirits, deities, and shamans who form the principal subjects of surviving pre-Han art.

Reflecting the enlarging secularism of the Han world-view, Han tomb furnishings—pottery models, stone sculptures, murals, as well as possessions cherished in life—reflect less of a sense of mystery and more of a simple secular feeling than pre-Han tomb accoutrements. Even art works with religious themes had a strong humanistic tone. This was an extremely important change in the course of Chinese art; for a very long time hereafter many purely religious works of art sought to stir the feelings of believers and art lovers alike through their expression of humanity.

IV.

Throughout human history certain universal social processes have promoted the spread of religious beliefs in medieval eras. Beginning about the end of the third century, in the period of disunion following the fall of the Han dynasty, religious belief became widespread, permeating Chinese culture. In China, from the Northern and Southern Dynasties period through the Sui and Tang, Buddhism reached its apogee. Society was still governed, however, according to Confucian ethical and moral precepts. Moreover, the ardent Buddhism of these centuries was many times punctuated by government-sponsored anti-Buddhist campaigns, motivated by political necessity or by a given ruler's pro-Daoist leanings in the perennial competition between Buddhism and Daoism. Clearly, despite its popularity, Buddhism remained ideologically subordinate.

Furthermore, during the late Han and Three Kingdoms periods, as Buddhism began to flourish, it did so in part by acculturation, that is, by taking on, in part, the teachings of Confucius and Mencius. For example, the *Shijiamuni lihuo*, the first Buddhist text written (and not just cited) in China, proposes the essential "unity of the three creeds"—Buddhism, Daoism, and Confucianism.[11] In the third and fourth centuries certain Buddhist metaphysical doctrines (*xuantan yili*) were held to be related to contemporary neo-Daoist metaphysical teachings (*xuan xue*), which were themselves tinged with Confucian theories. Cultural influences did not flow in one direction only. Based on the theory that every human mind contains and can discover within itself the Buddha-mind, the Chan Buddhist patriarch Huineng (638–713) propounded the doctrine of "sudden enlightenment" (*dunwu*). In later centuries, long after the heyday of Buddhism, this concept of sudden, unmediated perception or realization became a key element of Chinese philosophy and aesthetic theory. Its influence on the intellectual life of China was profound, pervasive, and lasting, but it exerted that influence not as a precept of Buddhist faith but as an element of secular Neo-Confucianism.[12] This Sinification of Buddhist precepts was another manifestation of the predominance of Confucian thought in Chinese society even when Buddhism was at its peak.

Where social thinking consists mainly of religious doctrines, all aspects of social culture will be permeated by religious overtones; where Confucian ethics and morality form the content of social thought, secularity will predominate. Chinese culture from the period of disunity through the Sui and Tang was clearly of the second type.

Buddhist sculpture and painting of this era, adorning temples and cave-temples, was indeed highly sophisticated, but no more so than art works of secular content. Noted artists of the time, such as Gu Kaizhi (ca. 344–ca. 406) of the Eastern Jin, portrayed religious and mundane subjects alike. New artistic heights were achieved both by the Buddhist volumetric sculptures of Yungang and Longmen in the north, which show influence from Gandharan and Guptan art, and by the Six Dynasties tomb carvings near Nanjing in the south, which continued the Eastern Han tradition of relief carving, mostly non-Buddhist in content, on the interior walls of tombs. Murals in later aristocratic tombs—like that of Lou Rui (531–570) of Northern Qi; or of Princess Yongtai and the princes Yide and Zhanghuai of Tang, all buried in 706—reflect metropolitan style and court standards of workmanship and are secular in content. As one would expect, the contemporaneous murals in the Buddhist cave-temples at Dunhuang, in far western Gansu, show a great mixture of stylistic influences and a more provincial level of workmanship.

When court sculptors were set to work to produce Buddhist sculptures for the ruling houses, the results equaled any contemporaneous secular works. Court sculptors of the Northern Wei imbued the colossal Buddha at Yungang with solemn dignity and the reliefs in the Binyang Cave at Longmen with devout majesty. Court sculptors of the Tang empress Wu Zetian (r. 684–704), a wily ruler and passionate Buddhist, imbued the colossal Buddha and eight attendant divinities at the Fengxian Temple of Longmen with benevolence, gentleness, earnestness, and power. All these figures embody Chinese sculpture at the top of its bent, and reflect the cultural efflorescence of the capitals to which they were adjacent. They combine sublimity with a worldly magnificence that attests to the secular coloration acquired by Chinese Buddhism. Arguably, the finest Chinese Buddhist sculptures of this period were also the finest art works of their time anywhere in the world.

Mainstream ideas, the cultural basis of both religious and secular art, evolved gradually during the Southern Dynasties, Sui, and Tang from the intermingling of Buddhism and Confucianism to the integration of Buddhism, Daoism, and Confucianism. This trend continued until after the Northern Song, when a renewed and enriched Confucianism achieved the social and political importance held by its precursor during the Han, and Buddhist art went into a rapid decline.

V.

Song Neo-Confucianism, and its continuations during the Ming and Qing, was by no means a monolithic set of teachings. The philosophers assembled under this rubric ranged considerably in their opinions and disputed their differences vehemently. But the common core of Neo-Confucianism was a primary concern with problems of ethics and epistemology and a wholly secular approach to both these sets of questions. Vastly oversimplifying, we might say that Neo-Confucians sought to understand the metaphysical essence of the universe (the *Dao*) and to bring the human mind/heart (*xin*, which of itself "has no substance; it takes its reactions to the rights and wrongs of everything in Heaven and earth for its substance"[13]) into harmony with it.

The literati, as the culture-bearing elite of later dynastic China were called, scorned sculpture as mere artisanry but valued the kinds of paintings that they considered metaphors of the *Dao* (primarily landscapes) or of the enlightened, cultivated *xin* (paintings of various subjects, primarily in ink monochrome, that were expressive in intent and amateur in rendition). Of course, during the millennium from the founding of the Song to the overthrow of the Qing, the styles (and to some extent the subjects) of literati-approved painting evolved greatly, but without losing touch with their secular, Neo-Confucian origins.

Only in the recent past, with the introduction of Western knowledge and fundamental changes in the political system and economic structure of society, Chinese culture has received massive shocks and Chinese art has been in constant turmoil. Of course, there are close links between political systems, economic structures, and cultures, but cultural traditions also have a degree of autonomy. New culture and new art, which reflect new yearnings, must evolve out of the foundation of the original cultural traditions. Contemporary intellectuals must not forsake the search for a new culture and a new direction for art. In order for us to correctly assess China's traditonal culture and develop contemporary Chinese culture and arts, and in order for modern Chinese to understand their own values, it is necessary to review the course of China's culture over the last five thousand years, to think about the traditions existing within this course, and to understand the foundations of China's culture and its arts. The above ruminations are part of such a quest. As to their validity, I await the comments of my readers.

Translated, from the Chinese, by June Mei.

NOTES

1. A.L. Kroeber and C. Kluckhohn, "Culture: A Critical Review of Concepts and Definitions," Harvard University, *Papers of the Peabody Museum of American Archaeology and Ethnology*, 47:1 (1952), p. 181.

2. "Su Bingqi on the China Dream of Archaeology," *Mingbao yuekan*, 1997:7.

3. Mircea Eliade, *Shamanism—Archaic Techniques of Ecstasy*, trans. Willard R. Trask (Princeton: Princeton University Press, 1972).

4. Zhang Guangzhi, *Six Lectures on Archaeology* (Wenwu Publishing House, 1986), pp. 47–52.

5. Part 1 of the *Jiaosizhi* in the *Han shu* addresses the subject of supernatural beings and defines the term *wu* as referring to spirits and demons.

6. Yu Weichao, "Changes in World Views as Seen in Archaeological Art Materials from the Pre-Qin, Qin, and Han Eras," in *Collected Essays Celebrating Su Bingqi's Fifty Years in Archaeology* (Beijing: Wenwu Publishing House, 1989), pp. 113–15.

7. During Western Han, all famous mountains and rivers were considered to be or to house numinous spirits. Hence, part 1 of the *Jiaosizhi* in the *Han shu* says, "[During the Western Zhou,] the Son of Heaven made sacrifices to all the famous mountains and rivers in the land, and to mollify all the spirits, but there are no written records of the rituals."

8. The three relationships—all hierarchical but also encompassing mutual responsibility—are sovereign-subject, father-son, husband-wife; the five virtues are human kindness, righteousness, propriety, knowledge, sincerity; together, *sangang wuchang* might be understood as "the whole duty of humankind." (Definition supplied by Stephen Allee, Freer/Sackler Galleries, Smithsonian Institution.)

9. Qian Mu, "The Contribution That Traditional Chinese Culture Can Make to the Future of the Human Race," in *Chinese Culture Past, Present, and Future — Essays Celebrating Eighty Years of the Zhonghua Shuju* (Zhonghua shuju, 1992).

10. Xin Lixiang, *Studies of Han Dynasty Painted Stones* (Tokyo: Doshisha, 1996).

11. Ren Jiyu, ed., *History of Chinese Buddhism* (Chinese Academy of Social Sciences Publishing House, 1981), vol. 1, chaps. 3–5.

12. Chinese Buddhist Association, ed., *Chinese Buddhism*, vol. 1, articles on "Buddhism of the Northern and Southern Dynasties," and "The Chan Sect" (Shanghai: Oriental Publishing Center), pp. 29–30, 319–25.

13. *Chuanxilu*, part 2, of *Complete Works of Wang Wencheng, Sibu Congkan* edition, vol. 3, p. 31a.

Jade as Material and Epoch

Elizabeth Childs-Johnson

Visiting Scholar, New York University

Jade, "the fairest of stones," is described
in the revered and earliest of Chinese
dictionaries as embodying five virtues:
"Benevolence is typified by its luster that
is bright and warm; integrity by its
translucency; wisdom by its sonorous ring
when struck; courage by its hardness;
and steadfastness by its durability."[1] As far
back as the late Neolithic period, this

obdurate stone, known as nephrite jade, could be worked into what are for Chinese tradition technical masterpieces of ritual and aesthetic function. *Yu* jade was, in fact, the preeminent medium of the late Neolithic period, exploited earlier than bronze as a political and religious power symbol which may now be associated with China's earliest civilization.[2] Late Neolithic prehistoric cultures—Hongshan, Liangzhu, and Longshan—have been identified archaeologically as three successive jade-working cultures of circa 3600-2000 BCE, predating the historic Xia, Shang, and Zhou periods. Each culture boasts a major jade art that is idiosyncratic yet telling in the formation of later Chinese values and cultural expression.

In this exhibition, jades are drawn not only from the jade-working cultures of Neolithic date, but also from other periods of great innovation such as the Western and Eastern Zhou, when jade was first used for head and body covers in burial and for elaborate pectorals hanging down the front of aristocratic robes, and from later periods, Han through Tang, when jade was worked into a variety of exquisite ornamental forms.

JADE AS MATERIAL
Nephrite, like jadeite, is considered "true jade" by specialists today. Unlike the emerald green and harder jadeite, nephrite varies in color from translucent white to various shades of green and brown and is the only jade that was used during the Neolithic and early dynastic periods.

Based on a recent identification, nephrite can now be documented as originating in Neolithic China. A specimen taken from an outcropping of rock at Zhaomeiling in Liyang, Jiangsu Province, has been confirmed as having mineral qualities similar to Liangzhu-period nephrite.[3] It is likely that local deposits of nephrite were found elsewhere in the lower reaches of the Yangzi River. The nephrite found in tombs of the far northeast (Hongshan culture) is also thought to have been mined locally.

Mineralogically, nephrite is a rock composed of densely intergrown, randomly oriented, interfelted fibers of the minerals tremolite and actinolite. These minerals are calcium-magnesium-iron silicates, $Ca_2 (Mg,Fe^{2+})_5 Si_8 O_{22} (OH)_2$, and belong to the amphibole mineral group.[4] The difference between actinolite and tremolite is in the quantity of magnesium and iron. In actinolite, iron appears in greater quantities, 10 to 50 percent; in tremolite, iron occupies under 10 percent of the total. Iron content affects the color of nephrite by darkening it, creating gray to green hues. In its purest form, the nephrite is translucent white (see, for example, cats. 17, 20).

Minerals sometimes mistaken for jade—referred to as "false jades" or as "pseudo-jades"—include agate, bowenite, fluorite, talc, and serpentine. The major scientific means of distinguishing tremolites and actinolites from other minerals is by their specific gravity. Nephrites have a higher specific gravity and greater hardness than pseudo- and false jade minerals.[5]

Jade is one of the most difficult stones to fashion: on Mohs's scale of hardness for minerals (ranking from 1 to 10) jade measures 6–6.5; thus, it requires a harder stone such as quartzite (7–7.5) or diamond (10) to abrade or "carve" it. Several scholars have theorized about how early jade—the translucent nephrite as opposed to emerald green jadeite— was worked in ancient China.[6] Each has described a technique that involves various stages of working with abrasives, from initially slicing off a chunk or slab of jade from a rock outcropping to boring holes and modeling linear motifs and openwork designs on the final jade piece. It is likely that a straight-edged hand or gut-string saw was the tool used to cut, slice, and pare the jade into a workable form.

Other tools involved probably included the awl and tubular drill, which may have been of bamboo. Since a flint (*suishi*) awl has been excavated from a Liangzhu tomb, it is possible that this was the type of tool used to carve the minute detail decorating *cong* (prismatic tubes) and related ornaments.[7] Other specialists have argued that shark teeth excavated from Liangzhu tombs were used or that only a tool with a diamond point was sufficiently hard to carve such refined detail.[8] That the Liangzhu craftsmen working jade used a bamboo or comparable drill with quartzite as an abrasive to make holes in ritual jades such as *bi* (disks) and *cong* (prismatic tubes) is convincing, since the remaining elliptical marks, particularly marked in the centers of *cong*, identify that type of tool. These holes are created from two sides by a bamboo drill whose point loses sharpness and thus width at the very center so that a ridge is formed. Quartzite crystals have been found on the surface of many Liangzhu and Hongshan jades, thus confirming that quartzite was the abrasive used with water when working the surface. On Neolithic jades, abraded decorative motifs often appear chipped; on later jades, metal-tipped tools were used so that these decorative motifs appear as clean, crisp lines.

In recent experiments on jades at the Freer and Arthur M. Sackler galleries in Washington, D.C., Wen Guang and Janet Douglas have shown that certain jades of dark green and brown color, dating to the Longshan and successive cultures and deriving from north and northwest China, are mineralogically iron- and manganese-rich nephrites.[9] These jades possess small amounts of manganese oxide that can be measured by X-ray fluorescence and related tools that measure mineral composition and the microstructure of minerals.[10] The dagger-ax (*ge*; cat. 11) from the Shaanxi Provincial Museum falls into this category of manganese oxide–rich nephrite. Wen Guang has explained that the dark green and brown to almost black coloration of tall *cong* (see, for example, cat. 5) appears to derive from jades that have been collected over time. This phenomenon may be attributable to *panmo*, the repeated handling of jade that causes discoloration over time, especially through oxidation of the iron content. The so-called chicken-bone white (*jigubai*) or chalky white surface patches, particularly common on Liangzhu jades (see cat. 3) but also on others (cats. 2, 12), appears to be caused primarily by heating to a temperature above 900° C rather than by alteration during a long burial.[11] The jade mineral does not decompose, but its density decreases and its microstructure becomes looser so that the jade may become brittle and less translucent.

Jade as a precious stone has an eminent history in China and for this reason is intimately linked with the beginnings of Chinese ritual and Chinese civilization. As one archaeologist has pointed out, all characters, or graphs, written with the jade graph *yu* are associated with spiritual power or beauty.[12] For example, the word *bao* ("precious") incorporates the jade graph. So does the word *gui* (a kind of jasper stone or an adjective meaning "extraordinary" or "admirable").

Jade's sacrosanct position in the history of Chinese tradition is probably best told not through later anecdotal descriptions, but rather through excavated finds and the earliest literary reference to ritual (*li*) in Shang period bone inscriptions.[13] The character *li* incorporates the jade graph *yu*, suggesting by its inclusion that jade was the earliest material as art to be used in religious worship. The function of jade as a preservative and symbol of immortality is also well known through Han alchemical practice and the life-preserving quality that is signified in the burial jade body suits of the Warring States and Han periods.

JADE AS RITUAL IMPLEMENT AND INSIGNIA
The working of jade is well illustrated by numerous finds from the three successive late Neolithic cultures that occupied coastal northern through southern China, from Liaoning down as far as Fujian. As Willetts once noted, Yuan Kang in *The Lost Records of Yue* (*Yue jueshu*), a Warring States text, wrote that after the Stone (Neolithic) and before the Bronze and Iron ages, man used jade for weapons; this "Jade Age" was a period contemporary with the legendary Five Emperors

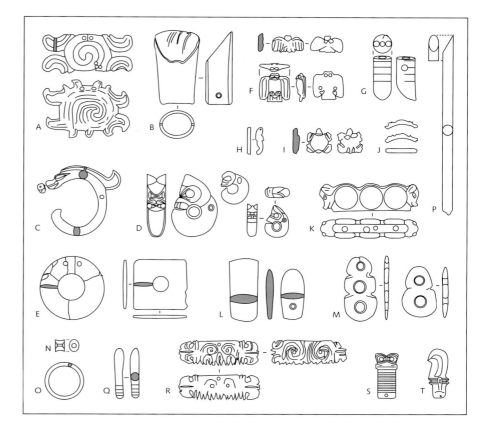

Fig. 1. Jade types of the Hongshan culture: A. Hooked cloud; B. Horse-hoof shape; C. Dragon; D. Pig-dragon; E. Disk; F. Cat-headed bird; G. Cicada; H. Fish; I. Turtle; J. Double dragon-head arch; K. Three-ring ornament with pig-head protomes; L. Ax ; M. Three-hole flat ornament; N. Bead; O. Bracelet; P. Pencil-shaped stick; Q. Bauble; R. Animal face with tusk-like extensions; S. Animal-face handle; T. Hook-shaped handle. Neolithic period, Hongshan culture (ca. 3600–ca. 2000 BCE).

and prior to the historic Xia.[14] Archaeological evidence documents this reference: jade was the primary medium exploited by the elite to symbolize their power to rule. Whether or not we use the label "Jade Age," the use of jade over an approximate sixteen-hundred-year period (ca. 3600-2400 BCE) may be traced largely to coastal parts of China, an area of great cultural innovation at this time.[15] Elite tribal groups forming what anthropologists now describe as China's earliest city-states are associated with these jade-working cultures—the Liangzhu in China's southeastern provinces of Zhejiang and Jiangsu and in Shanghai; and slightly later Shandong Longshan cultures of northeast China; but also possibly by the slightly earlier Hongshan, of far northeast China, primarily, Liaoning and Inner Mongolia provinces.

Jade types from Hongshan tombs (see fig. 1) are striking in their seemingly non-Chinese taste for sculpturally sensuous form. Two jades in this exhibition— an ornament in the form of hooked clouds with profile bird (cat. 1) and an ornament in the form of a curling so-called pig-dragon (*zhulong*;

cat. 2)—are quintessentially Hongshan Chinese. Both works are directly tied to fertility-cult interests.[16] Small jade figures as well as clay figures of various sizes representing nude females with large hips and buttocks have been found on outdoor stone-lined altars, in the Goddess Temple foundation, and within aristocratic cist tombs at Niuheliang; their discovery suggests the presence of a cult centered on a form of mother goddess. The only items seen in tombs of the elite are jades, however. Most are pierced with holes for suspension or attachment to cloth, suggesting a function similar to that of an amulet worn by a specialized religious, ruling elite.

Most of the excavated Hongshan burials with jades derive from select areas, as at Niuheliang, which on the basis of present evidence was once a center for religious worship. The hooked cloud shape of jade (see, for example, cat. 1) has been found on the chest area of several corpses in the elite cemetery at Niuheliang, suggesting that this type of ornament decorated the chest as a pectoral. The shape, with hooks at four corners framing a bird's head in profile, represents the prototype of the age-old bone and bronze script symbol for cloud with emerging bird or dragon head,[17] evidently a reference to the heavenly bird in later Chinese myth.

The pig-dragon (cat. 2) also suggests a potent symbol in its emphatic disposition which begins in a boar-like head flaunting tusks and beady eyes and ends in a short thick body curl. This fetal posture emphasizing birth and nascent power is imitated in the shape of the pictograph for *qiu*, the earliest form for writing dragon in Chinese script.[18] In all later Chinese history, dragons bring rain and beneficence. During the Neolithic period the Chinese domesticated the boar. As symbols of wealth, boar (or pig) skulls are commonly found in elite tombs.[19] That the image of dragon with boar tusks and other fertility deities presided as symbols of control in this northern Hongshan culture is also made clear by the remains of dragon and fertility goddess sculptures, which decorated the wall of what, at Niuheliang, excavators describe as a mother goddess temple. In addition to their association with fertility, the pig-dragon jades are remarkable for their sensitive and painstaking modeling: they appear as though they were sculpted, wet clay rather than flat and linear, calligraphically defined jades that are traditionally associated with Chinese aesthetics.

The Liangzhu culture, of overlapping and slightly later date, reflects a more advanced social stage in the new and more complex layout of religio-administrative centers, as well as an increased complexity of jade types and their functions. In burials, jade not only decorates the dress of elite

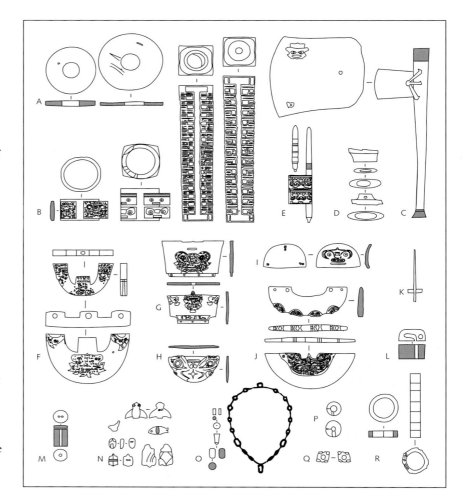

Fig. 2. Jade types of the Liangzhu culture: A. Disk (bi); B. Short and tall prismatic tubes (cong); C. Ax head and reconstructed ax with parts; D. End attachments to the staff of an ax; E. Arrow and spear heads; F. Three-pronged headdress ornament; G. Trapezoid-shaped headdress ornament of a talisman; H. Lower body / shoe ornament; I. D-shaped headdress ornament; J. Arc-shaped ornaments (huang); K. Spindle whorl; L. Belt buckle; M. Staff knob; N. Bird, fish, cicada, tortoise, and frog ornaments; O. Necklace ornament; P. Slit earrings; Q. Ornament; R. Plain and decorated bracelets. Neolithic period, Liangzhu culture (ca. 3600–ca. 2000 BCE).

leaders, but now appears worked into shapes of ritual implements and weapons (fig. 2).[20] Liangzhu jade owners wielded power over more sophisticated and complex religious rites and political and military matters as well.

The new appearance of specific ritual implements such as *cong* and *bi*, and of broad axes (*yue*) in large numbers complements the more complex scenario of ritual and socio-political administration that anthropologists currently describe as characterizing China's earliest city-state. They propose that the Liangzhu culture encompassed a time span of roughly 3600/3300–2000 BCE and that it included four major phases.[21] Fully mature jade types representing Liangzhu periods III–IV of circa 3000–2400 BCE are represented in the exhibition by three *cong* (cats. 3, 4, 5).

The *cong* is the most idiosyncratic of all jades. It may be defined by its shape: a tube that is prismatic on the outside and circular and open from top to bottom inside. The Neolithic jade *cong* is decorated with animal and/or semihuman masks on the prismatically shaped corners of its outer square. In later ritual texts the *cong* is also defined as a symbol of the earth.

Liangzhu jades derive almost entirely from burials, evidently of a ruling, religious elite. These differ from Hongshan burials not only in their larger and more complex jade assemblage, but in their design; they were part of a man-made earthen mound with raised outdoor altar (figs. 3-4). Apparently, such raised earthen mounds with jade-filled burials functioned initially as outdoor ritual altars and subsequently as burial grounds called *jitan mudi* ("joint sacrificial and burial centers") and were locally described as *tuzhu jinzita* ("earth-constructed pyramids").[22]

Recently, it has been proposed that Sidun, in Jiangsu Province, and possibly twenty other related burial-ground mounds were part of larger city-states that were cosmologically designed in the form of the *cong*, the ritual jade implement (figs. 2B, 4A:2, 5).[23] At present, however, only Sidun, Zhaolingshan, and Mojiaoshan appear to possess adequate features that qualify them as candidates for this ideal plan (fig. 4A).[24] The proposed plan encompasses a central earthen altar and four axially located burial grounds as well as many residences and defensive moats: the Sidun mound complex measures 900,000 square meters in area, and the mound proper is over 100 meters wide and over 20 meters high.[25] This design conjures up the look of today's surviving Angkor Wat in Cambodia, Tikal in Guatemala, and the religious structure called "Bright Hall" (*mingtang*) with circular moat (*piyong*) mentioned in later Chinese ritual texts.[26] In any case, what emerges in the archaeological data is a new and extremely sophisticated phase of settlement: a city-state with spiritual center, outlying towns, a defensive system, and competitive arts serving both religious and political needs. This archaeological evidence of the Liangzhu culture defines the heart of the so-called Jade Age, not only in the sophisticated architectural design of a spiritual center but because over 90 percent of the ruling elite's burial goods were jades.

For protohistoric Chinese the *cong* was evidently more than a talisman; it appears to have been a mechanism of ritual and spiritual control. Positioned in four directions, it symbolized the power to petition or exorcize spiritual and demonic forces in a universe that was conceived as prismatically square. It is no accident that the shamanic *fangxiang*, or *wu*, the major exorcizer of

Fig. 3. Mound remains of the earthen outdoor altar at Yaoshan, Yuhang county, Zhejiang Province. Neolithic period, Liangzhu culture (ca. 3600-ca. 2000 BCE).

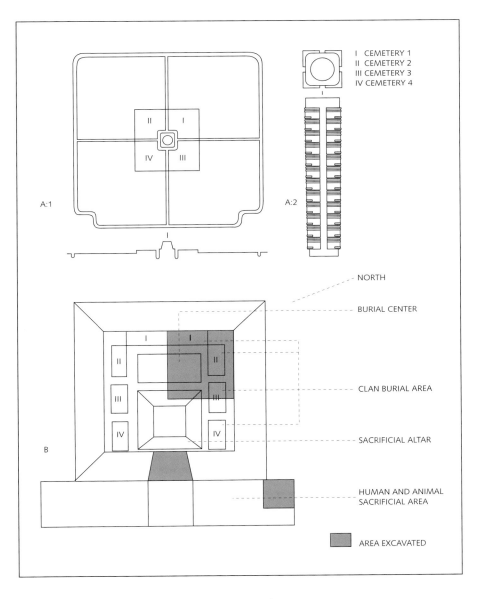

Fig. 4. Reconstruction of (A:1) outdoor altar at Sidun, Jiangsu Province, with (A:2) drawing of jade cong, *and (B) outdoor altar at Zhaolingshan, Jiangsu Province. Neolithic period, Liangzhu culture (ca. 3600–ca. 2000 BCE).*

demonic influences in Han dynasty religious practice, had vision in four directions. The character for *wu* ("shaman")—although not known textually until Eastern Zhou times—is related in origin to the Shang character for *fang* ("direction").[27] As is evident, one of the variations for *fang* in Shang bone inscriptions is like the Greek cross, the same shape as the *cong*. And it may also be no accident that in the ancient myth of China's origins the eight cosmic pillars that upheld the universe when the mythic Pan Gu created the world were axially oriented.[28]

The other popular ritual implement, the circular *bi*, is also probably significant in its association with the heavens, the circular vault or dome mentioned later in *Huainanzi* and the *Chuci* ("Songs of the South")[29] The few representations of birds and clouds that decorate *bi* (fig. 6) are in keeping with what must be a symbol of skyward power in which clouds and birds are associated in all later Chinese lore.

The *cong* (cat. 3) that comes from the largest tomb, No. 12, at Fanshan, in Zhejiang Province, is a marvel of craftsmanship. Twenty-four tiny representations of simple and complex mask types decorate all the flat surfaces of this vessel's exterior, straddling all corners and intervening passages (fig. 5A). Two alternating image types—the semihuman mask with horizontally striated headdress and the

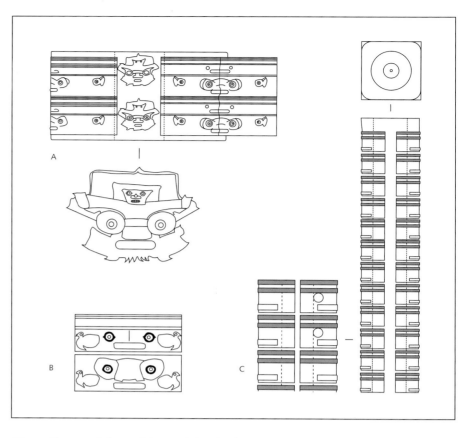

Fig. 5. Shape and decor of three exhibited jade prismatic tubes (cong): A. Cong (cat. 3) from tomb No. 12, Fanshan, Zhejiang Province; B. Cong (cat. 4) from Fuquanshan tomb No. 9, Qingpu county, Shanghai; C. Cong (cat. 5) from tomb No. 3, Wujin county, Jiangsu Province. Neolithic period, Liangzhu culture (ca. 3600–ca. 2000 BCE).

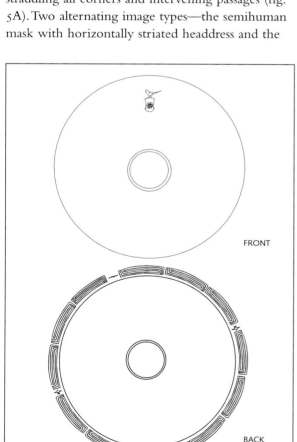

Fig. 6A. The bird and cloud motif on a jade disk (bi) from the Freer Gallery of Art, Smithsonian Institution, Washington, D.C. (17.348). Neolithic period, Liangzhu culture (ca. 3600–ca. 2000 BCE).

Fig. 6B. Jade disk (bi). Neolithic period, Liangzhu culture (ca. 3600–ca. 2000 BCE). Freer Gallery of Art, Smithsonian Institution, Washington, D.C. (17.348).

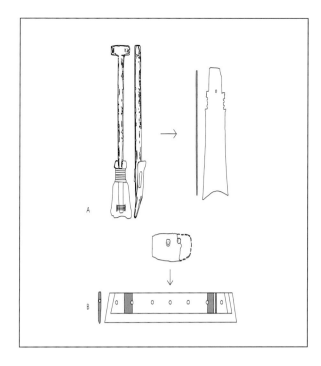

*Fig. 7. Evolution of the (A) jade blade (*zhang*) and (B) knife (*dao*) from agricultural tools. Neolithic period (ca. 7000–ca. 2000 BCE).*

schematic interpretation of the mask aligning the four corners of this tall *cong* is the semihuman mask, simplified to an abstract design of eye, mouth, and headdress.

Jade usage takes a new turn during the last phase of the Neolithic and first phase of China's ancient historical period, which begins with the Xia (ca. 2100–ca. 1600 BCE). The new jade types that appear during the Longshan and Xia (Erlitou culture) periods—the last flowering of the "Jade Age"—include the blade (*zhang*) and the knife (*dao*). Usually plain in decor, they function as insignia. Both the blade and the knife are based on agricultural tool types.[32] The blade, which is swordlike in shape and flares out at one end, originates in the hoe and is known mostly in bone or ivory as early as 5000 BCE at Hemudu, in Zhejiang Province (fig. 7A).[33] The knife derives from the harvesting knife (fig. 7B). The recarved jade knife (*dao*; cat. 6) from the Shanghai Museum may be attributed to the Shandong Longshan Neolithic. Representational imagery still decorates the front of the jade knife.

The blades (*zhang*; cats. 7, 8) reflect two styles. The first is a classic Xia blade (*zhang*; cat. 7), seen in excavated examples from Erlitou (fig. 8A). The handle is typically rendered with a delicate, dentiled outline and paper-thin relief strips running from top to bottom on the front side only. This geometrically textured area contrasts with the blade, which flares out and is slightly concave. The blade (cat. 8) from Sanxingdui, Guanghan, in Sichuan Province, is a manneristically distorted regional version of the classic Xia type. For example, the blade's mouth does not flare; it comes to a point like a dagger-ax that then is bifurcated. Comparable blades excavated from the same two hoards at Sanxingdui are equally eccentric (fig. 8B). They either violate classical form through the addition of an extraneous, small profile bird placed at the bifurcated mouth or destroy the beauty of the paper-thin strips through harsh, repetitive incised lines across the handle. The latter examples represent the end of a classical Longshan and Erlitou period tradition of working jade blade insignia.

animal mask with layered eyelids and nasal ridge—decorate each prismatic surface. These semihuman and animal-mask images are also represented more complexly on the interstices. The latter, more elaborate version portrays the semihuman with feathered headdress, trapezoidal face, and winged arms embracing the animal mask, which has tusks and framing limbs ending in claws (fig. 5). Both Mou Yongkang and Wu Ruzuo have identified these masked deities as sun gods.[30] When depicted as two different images, they should be interpreted as a sun god and his vehicle, the embodiment of animal power. Working these minuscule motifs must have required great delicacy and painstaking labor in digging and working away the surface with a tiny flint or diamond awl. Although it has altered in color to a chalky white, the *cong* retains its brilliant luster, which through burnishing seems to have intentionally captured the rays of the sun. This *cong* has been nicknamed the "king of *cong*," after the vessel's large size and superbly worked imagery.[31]

The *cong* from tomb Number 9 at Fuquanshan, near Shanghai, is marked by a translucent gleaming yellow-brown to green color (cat. 4). Miniature masks and flanking birds fill four sides of this *cong*, which is more circular than square (fig. 5B). Body parts, only one millimeter wide, of both the masked images and birds are filled with tiny whorling cloud scrolls. On the *cong* from tomb Number 3 at Sidun, Jiangsu Province (cat. 5; fig. 5C) thirteen levels of mask images represent a standard variation of the tall *cong* type that is tempting to associate with the stacked arrangement of repeated images on a native American totem pole of the Northwest. The more

It is apparent that at this point in time more sophisticated tools, probably metal tools in the form of disks and drills (the modern lathe called the *chatou*), were used with abrasives to carve the insignia and their decor. The appearance of multiple, small lengthwise scratches on a jade's surface indicates burnishing with metal-tipped tools.

During the Shang period (ca. 1600–ca. 1100 BCE), certain jades— particularly, weapons in the form of

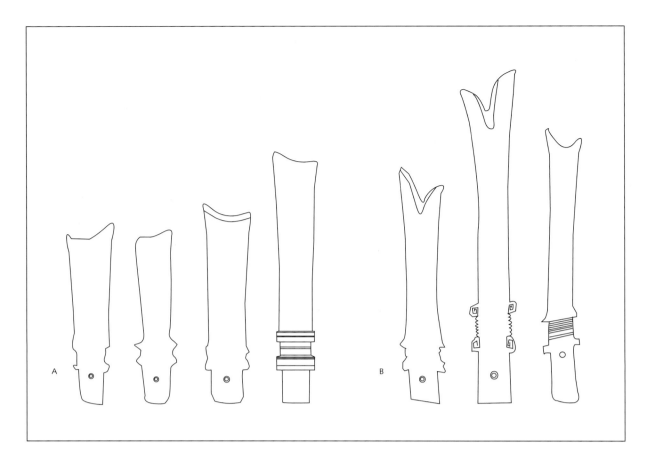

Fig. 8. Representative jade blades (zhang) from (A) Erlitou and (B) Sanxingdui. Xia/Shang periods (ca. 1800–ca. 1500 BCE).

dagger-axes (*ge*) or broad axes (*yue*)—continue to reflect the Xia taste for large-scale insignia. Jade types that eventually replace the insignia are the flat or round small figurines, designed more for decorative than ritual purposes. The small animal and human figures popular during the Shang are represented in the exhibition by four pieces excavated intact from the celebrated tomb belonging to the Shang queen popularly referred to as Fu Hao,[34] but correctly identified by the name Fu Zi.[35] Three of the jades represent variations of the bird motif—one naturalistic version from the side (cat. 10[3]), another with headdress and human-like legs tucked in profile (cat. 10[4]), and a third bird with ram's horns (cat. 10[1]). A fourth small jade (cat. 10[2]) of light translucent green represents a human whose hands rest on his knees in servile attitude. All four jades have holes for attachment and were probably worn suspended as charms or decorative baubles. In the excavation report, jade figurines from this rich tomb amounted to over three hundred out of a total of six to seven hundred jades.[36]

JADE AS LIFE PRESERVATIVE AND ORNAMENT
The Western Zhou period (ca. 1100–771 BCE) is represented here by two jade works. A jade dagger-ax (*ge*; cat. 11) from Xi'an, Shaanxi Province, is a Western Zhou version of this weapon made popular during the Shang period. The Zhou date is

apparent in the grooving and downward point of the blade's tip, as found on dagger-axes of Western Zhou date excavated from Sanmenxia, Henan Province, and Tianma, Shanxi Province.[37] The major artistic innovation in the jade medium during the Western Zhou period is seen in the rich assemblage of jade pieces creating a burial mask (cat. 12; fig. 10) and extended chest and body pectoral with additional, flanking jade insignia of dagger-axes and *bi* (fig. 10), excavated at Sanmenxia in 1990.[38] This earliest of jade face masks, dating to the ninth century BCE, clearly anticipates the creation of a complete jade body suit by the Western Han period (206 BCE–8 CE) in provinces as far afield as Hebei, Shandong, Guangdong, Jiangsu, and Hubei.[39]

Sanmenxia has long been known as a Western Zhou cemetery site of the Guo state—an enfiefment that was probably of very early Western Zhou date.[40] In the 1950s over two hundred tombs were excavated at this site, and in the last fifteen years new finds, including tomb Number 2001, to which the jade mask (cat. 12; fig. 10) belongs, were reported. This burial find is of high interest for what it says about Western Zhou burial rites and ritual reform, which required sets of vessels and jades that by their number and quality were designed to signify status. For example, tomb Number 2001 included not only bronze sets of *gui* (grain), *ding* (meat), and *li* (steamer) vessels (six to eight per set of identical form but different size), but sets of chimes and bells, as well as other unusual art works such as an unprecedently early belt with gold decorative attachments and an iron sword with jade fitting.

This rich tomb also documents that there was a specified manner of decorating the corpse with jade. The burial mask (cat. 12), for example, is composed of fourteen jade pieces, and the pectoral running from the corpse's neck to its knees is composed of seven *huang* (arc-shaped) jades that are interconnected with agate and faience beads (fig. 10). Flanking the corpse were two jade dagger-ax-like blades at chest level, two pair of *bi*, and two handle attachments at foot level. Additional stone cowries (*han*) were placed in the corpse's mouth, and round post-shaped jades (*wo*) were placed in the corpse's hand. Two further sets of eight small jade inlays were found on the feet. The excavators explain that these jades lay on top of what appear to have been over ten layers of red and yellow decorated silk cloth.[41] The jade face mask was sewn to a silk cover, while the pectoral of jades formed a necklace that lay on the corpse's chest. The practice of decorating a corpse with jade necklaces may be traced back to the Liangzhu period, when multiple strands of jade beads were commonly placed on both male and female corpses.

The fourteen jades of the Sanmenxia burial mask (cat. 12) mark pairs of eyebrows, eyes, temples, ears, and cheeks and individually mark the forehead, nose, mouth, and neck. This type of jade face mask with elaborate jade pectoral and mouth and hand plugs may be compared with various others identified recently not only elsewhere in Henan, but also in Shaanxi, Shanxi, and Hebei, dating to the Western Zhou and later Eastern Zhou periods.[42] The latter burials derive from cemeteries identifying Zhou enfiefments belonging to the ancient states of Jin (Qucun, Tianma, Shaanxi), Ying (Pingdingshan, Henan), Guo (Fengxi, Xi'an, Shaanxi), Jing (Zhangjiapo, Shaanxi), Yu (Baoji, Xi'an, Shaanxi) and Yan (Liulihe, Fangshan, Hebei). Evidently, the practice of burying the elite with jade face masks and pectorals was standardized at this point in Western Zhou history.

In addition, jade was used to plug the orifices of the corpse. These jade investments protected the corpse from disintegrating while allowing the spirit (*hun*) to continue living, as described in various texts of Eastern Zhou and Han date.[43] In the *Yi Li* ("Ceremonial Rites"), there is reference to the *mingmu* (the spirit mask that covers the head), with the commentary that the invoker of the spirit wore this jade covering at funerals in order to summon up the departed spirit which relatives and friends sought to keep from drifting far away.[44] After the invocation rite, the jade face mask would then be buried with the corpse. (In archaeological literature, this face mask is commonly described as a "sewn jade face guard" [*zhuiyu mianzhao*].) The interest in invoking the spirit is well known as the objective of the shaman that inspired the poem "Summons of

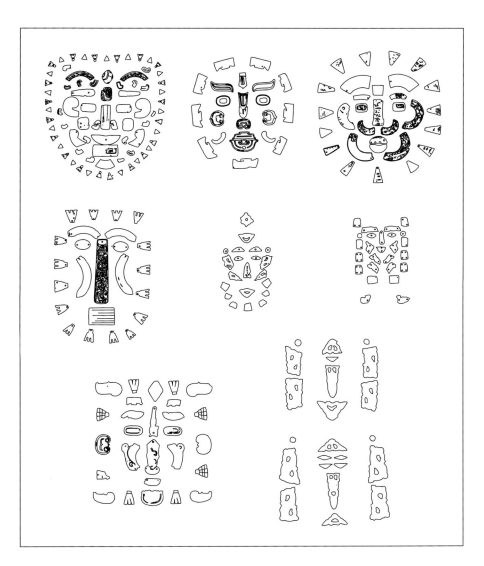

Fig. 9. *Jade face masks from the Spring and Autumn period: From tomb Nos. 92–93, Jin cemetery, Qucun, Tianma, Shanxi Province; From tomb No. 651, Shaogou, Luoyang, Henan Province; From tomb Nos. 637, 1316, 1723, 2717, 2209, at Zhongzhoulu, Luoyang, Henan Province. Eastern Zhou, Spring and Autumn period (770–476 BCE).*

the Soul" in the *Chuci* ("Songs of the South"). Thus, the purpose of these jade masks is not only aesthetic but profoundly religious.

The rich and decorative sway of jade that peaked as a revived art during the Eastern Zhou (770-256 BCE) is amply illustrated by its widespread use in pectoral and girdle ornament decorating the robes of the literati. The exhibited jades (cats. 13–16) representing small plaques, dragon pendants, disks, and rings fall into this category of decorative object. Competitiveness in the arts was at a premium during the Warring States period. This was the time of "The Hundred Schools," when roving philosophers plied their trade in trying to win the support of an overlord. Confucius allegedly worked the literati crowd of Lu in Shandong. By the seventh century BCE, the central Zhou state was reduced to puppet status and was at

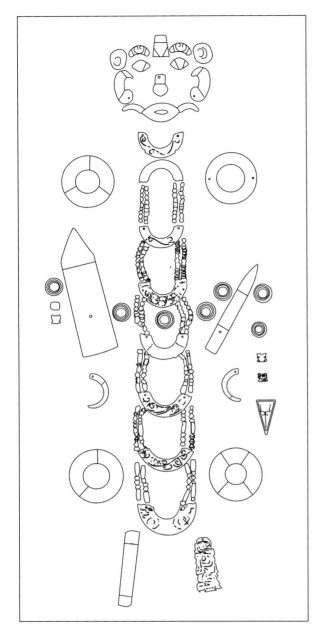

Fig. 10. Jade mask and pectoral from tomb No. 2001, Shangcunling, Sanmenxia, Henan Province. Western Zhou period (ca. 1100–771 BCE).

Fig. 11. Jade ornamental plaque from tomb No. 1 at Xiasi, Xichuan, Henan Province. Eastern Zhou, Spring and Autumn period (770–476 BCE).

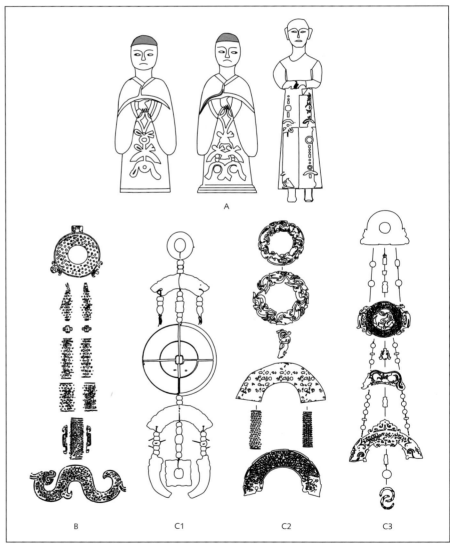

Fig. 12. Variations of Eastern Zhou and Han jade pectoral and girdle ornaments: A. Decorative painted wooden figurines from Chu tombs at Xinyang, Henan Province, and Jiangling, Hubei Province; B. From tomb No. 58, group Yi, Lu state, Shandong Province; C:1–3. From burials accompanying the tomb of the King of Nanyue, Guangdong Province. Eastern Zhou–Western Han periods (770 BCE–8 CE).

the mercy of the most powerful states of the day, known then as the Five Hegemonies (Wu Ba).

By the beginning of the fifth century BCE, internecine warfare was intensive. China was divided into seven powerful states, and there were numerous smaller ones that came and went, such as Peng in southern Henan at Xujialing, which was consumed by Chu. We read in poems from the *Chuci* ("Songs of the South") about various types of art whose specialty belonged to one of the competitive states. For example, the state of Qin was esteemed for its basketware, Qi for its silk cords, Zheng for its silk banners, and Jin apparently for its finely made belt buckles (*xibi*) that "glittered like bright suns."[45] Although Jin is credited with creating exquisite belt buckles—presumably of jade—the artistic domain of jade was not limited to this northwestern state. Jade girdles and pectorals

Fig. 13. Jade pectoral of Concubine A (right) from tomb of the King of Nanyue, Guangzhou, Guangdong Province. Western Han dynasty (206 BCE– 8 CE). The Museum of the Western Han Tomb of the Nanyue King, Guangzhou.

for suspension or attachment, it appears to have decorated a pectoral or girdle rather than a belt buckle. Although small, its shape and decoration are representative of the Eastern Zhou interest in richly textured surfaces and in the revival of Shang imagery that appears in all mediums of this period. An Eastern Zhou interpretation of the Shang animal mask is seen in the round eyes and body extensions in the form of C-curls which vary in textural effects from feathers, granulation, hooks with volutes, and scales, to claws.

A pair of dragon (*long*) pendants (cat. 14) from Pingliangtai, Huaiyangshi, Henan Province, of Warring States date is another ubiquitous form in Eastern Zhou art.[48] In fact, during this phase of artistic activity, the dragon is the most popular ornament; and the most popular design at this time is the dragon type from Pingliangtai, with its head thrown back, its body in S-shape, and its claws rendered as curls. This pair of dragon pendants may also be joined to form the heraldic centralized motif of a pectoral. During this phase, the sensuous effect of the sinuous dragon body is enhanced by raised curls.

The Warring States jade ring (*huan*) with S-pattern (cat. 15) from Xujialing in Xichuan county, Hubei Province, and the Han *bi* with grain pattern (cat. 16) from Zhouzhi county, Shaanxi Province, are also probably pendant parts of pectorals that were worn by aristocrats when they were alive (see figs. 12, 13). The green jade *bi* is covered with the so-called grain pattern, the small-scale nodules that rise symmetrically out of tightly coiled C-hooks, a motif that appeared on late Zhou bronze vessels (see, for example, cat. 44). Shapes of sacred ritual design of Neolithic origin, such as the *bi*, were revived along with the animal mask as another popular ornament enriching Western and Eastern Han period art. The most elaborate designs, texturally varied concoctions, and elegantly inventive assemblages hung down the front of both male and female aristocrats. Variations of girdles and pectorals, clanging and swaying, glittering and ringing signified dignity and rank—a sonorous and well-dressed elite.

were ubiquitous in China throughout the Western and Eastern Zhou periods; they represent what one wore while alive and apparently took along into the next world. There is, however, some question about which jade necklaces were worn in life and which appear to have been made for burial. The jades initially used to create jade face masks from the late Western Zhou as represented by the jade face mask (cat. 12), and eventually body covers, apparently were often created out of reused or lesser quality jade.[46]

An early example of one these decorative Eastern Zhou pectoral jades is the small plaque (cat. 13; fig. 11) excavated in 1987 from Xiasi, Xichuan county, in Henan Province. This jade (only 7.1 centimeters high) apparently came from tomb Number 1, which belonged to the wife of the Chu Prince Shuzhi Sun Peng, chief minister of Chu from 551 to 548 BCE.[47] There is no archaeological data that may be used to describe the piece's function, however. Since the plaque has two holes

Jade continued to grow as an art from Han to Tang times. In contrast to the Shang versions of small animal carvings, those from the Han and later periods tend to be more naturalistic. The winged horse (cat. 17) and so-called *bixie* (a winged lion with horns, cat. 18) illustrate the new naturalism, seen in images of both mythical and non-mythical animals of Han date (206 BCE-220 CE). Although stereotyped through such conventions as the arched neck and suspended tail to signify liveliness and movement, these animal shapes of hardstone jade begin to turn and twist in space.

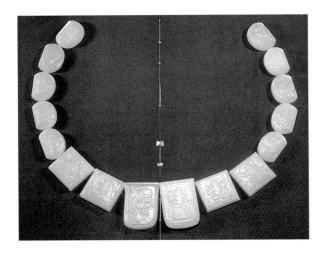

Fig. 14A. Jade belt decorated with Persian tribute bearers, from cache at Hejia village, Xi'an, Shaanxi Province. Tang dynasty (618–907). Shaanxi Provincial Museum, Xi'an.

The climax of the Eastern Zhou and Han periods is represented by a white jade vessel (*zun*; cat. 19) belonging to Liu Hong, Duke of Xuancheng and Commander Guarding the South, from Huangshantou, Anxiang county, Hunan Province.[49] Dating to the Western Jin (265–316), this vessel is a remarkable jade facsimile of a bronze original (see, for example, cat. 51), a popular type in Han times. The immortal mountain theme is signified by animal heads emerging from cloud motifs and by immortals, winged humans, seated or running pell-mell alongside dragons and other supernatural creatures, including the Goddess of the West herself, wearing the distinctive mortarboard-style headdress. It has its source in the Daoist cult of immortality symbolizing the mountain Kunlun, which was the domain of the Goddess of the West (Xiwangmu) (see cats. 19, 49, 50, 51). This scene in relief complements the Hongshan Neolithic sculpted ornament. Both are emblematic: the Hongshan jade (cat. 1) represents a bird amid clouds, most likely signifying the skyward realm of heaven; and the relief on the Western Jin vessel (cat. 19) represents the heavenly abode of Mount Kunlun, where immortality was granted by an empowered goddess.

Jade continued to be valued for its immortal power and beauty during the Tang dynasty (618–907). The translucent Xinjiang white jade belt excavated from a cache at the village of Hejia, in Xi'an, Shaanxi Province (cat. 20; fig. 14B) is one superb example. Discovered in 1970, this cache has become famous for its gold and silver vessels, amounting to about 270 out of some 1000 objects, which are unprecedented for their variety, workmanship, and quality of preservation.[50] The royal hoard has been identified as belonging to a prince of Bin, whose mansion in ancient Chang'an (present-day Xi'an) was consumed by flames in the mid-eighth century during the rebellion of general An Lushan. Like the

Fig. 14B. Jade belt plaques from cache at Hejia village, Xi'an, Shaanxi Province: 1. (top) lion plaque (detail, cat. 20) and 2. (bottom) Persian tribute-bearer plaque. Tang dynasty (618–907).

decor of so many of the solid silver and gold vessels of this hoard, the major decorative motifs of the belt represent Central Asian and Persian subjects. The belt is composed of sixteen pieces: fourteen that are square and two that are D-shaped. On the back of each piece are loops where the piece was sewn to a leather backing. Each jade piece was worked into a relief image of a lion: poses vary from standing, sitting, sniffing, to pawing the air—all different and all indicative of a very lively animal (fig. 14B:1). This motif is one of three that appear to be popular on jade belts of eighth-century Tang date. The other themes are also exotic, featuring Persians playing musical instruments or Persians bringing tribute offerings (figs. 14A, B:2). The lion is also well known as foreign to Tang and earlier China, and is probably of Central Asian origin.[51]

The art of working jade is special to China. The fact that this hardstone, nephrite, could be worked at all as early as the Neolithic period is indicative of the singular reverence the Chinese have paid to the stone. Over time nephrite was abraded into almost any shape—from a prismatic tube to a relief representing the paradise landscape of a goddess—reflecting the sophisticated level to which this art could be perfected. It is understandable, then, that the Chinese identified jade philosophically with the celestial sphere, immutable and indestructible, the material embodying the vital energy of nature.

SOURCES FOR FIGURES

Fig. 1. After Elizabeth Childs-Johnson, "Jades of the Hongshan Culture," Arts Asiatiques 56 (1991), fig. 1, p. 83.

Fig. 2. After Elizabeth Childs-Johnson, unpublished paper.

Fig. 3. After Liangzhu wenhua yuqi (Beijing: Wenwu chubanshe, 1989), pl. 1.

Fig. 4. After Zhongguo wenwu bao (December 31, 1995), fig. 1, p. 3; and Xu Huping, ed., Dongfang wenming zhiguang [Nanjing: Nanjing bowuyuan, 1996], fig. 12, p. 191.

Fig. 5. After Wenwu, no. 2 (1988), figs. 19–20, p. 12; Gems of the Liangzhu Culture: From the Shanghai Museum Exhibition (Hongkong: Urban Council, 1992), no. 89, p. 224; Wenwu, no. 2 (1984), fig. 9, p. 119.

Fig. 6A. After Deng Shuping, Gugong xueshu jikan 10 (1992), figs. 1–2.

Fig. 7. After Elizabeth Childs-Johnson, "Symbolic Jades of the Erlitou Period," Archives of Asian Art 48 (1995), fig. 2, p. 66.

Fig. 8. After Elizabeth Childs-Johnson, "Symbolic Jades of the Erlitou Period," Archives of Asian Art 48 (1995), fig. 25, p. 85; fig. 1, p. 65.

Fig. 9. After Huaxia kaogu, no. 3 (1992), fig 2:3–4, p. 107; Zhongguo yuqi quanji, vol. 2 (Shijiazhuang: Hebei meishu chubanshe, 1993), pl. 296.

Fig. 10. After Wenwu, no. 1 (1994), figs. 18, 38–39; Wenwu, no. 7 (1995), figs. 10–11, 17–19, 49; Wenwu, no. 8 (1994), figs. 3, 7; Zhongguo yuqi quanji, vol. 3 (Shijiazhuang: Hebei meishu chubanshe, 1993), figs. 1, 7–9, 11–17.

Fig. 11. After Xichuan Xiasi Chunqiu chumu (Beijing: Wenwu chubanshe, 1991), fig. 82:1, p. 100.

Fig. 12. After Zhongguo yuqi quanji, vol 3 (Shijiazhuang: Hebei meishu chubanshe, 1993), figs. 23, 25–27; Jades from the Tomb of the King of Nanyue (Hongkong: Woods Publishing, 1991), figs. 8, 10, pp. 28, 30.

Fig. 13. After Jades from the Tomb of the King of Nanyue (Hongkong: Woods Publishing, 1991), pl. 133.

Fig. 14A. After Zhongguo meishu quanji, vol. 9 (Shijiazhuang: Hebei meishu chubanshe, 1993), pl. 219, pp. 120–21.

Fig. 14B. After Zhongguo meishu quanji, vol. 9 (Shijiazhuang: Hebei meishu chubanshe, 1993), fig. 225, p. 79.

NOTES

1. Shuowen jiezi gulin, ed. Ding Fubao (Shanghai: Yixue shuju, 1930); see also the translation in S. Howard Hansford, Chinese Jade Carving (London: Humphries, 1950), p. 31, cited in William Willetts, Chinese Art, vol. 1 (New York: George Braziller, 1958), pp. 53–62.

2. Elizabeth Childs-Johnson, "The 'Jade Age' and Incipient Civilization: The Archaeological and Artistic Evidence for Jade as a Power Symbol during the Late Neolithic of ca. 3600–2000 BCE" (paper presented at "Stones from Heaven," Ancient Chinese Jade Symposium, Los Angeles County Museum of Natural History, 24 March 1996); and Elizabeth Childs-Johnson, Ritual and Power: Jades of Ancient China (New York: China Institute, 1988).

3. Wen Guang and Jing Zhichun, "A Geoarchaeological Study of Chinese Archaic Jade," 18th Percival David Foundation Colloquy on Art and Archaeology in Asia—Chinese Jades (London: University of London, 1995), pp. 116–18.

4. Most of this text on the technical and mineralogical properties of jade is from Wen and Jing, "A Geoarchaeological Study," p. 3.

5. See ibid., p. 3; and Wen Guang, "Bian yu" ("Distinguishing Jade"), Wenwu, no. 7 (1992), pp. 75–80.

6. Wu Tanghai, Renshi guyu ("Understanding Ancient Jade") (Taibei: Zhonghua minguo ziran wenhua xuehui, 1994); Hayashi Minao, "Liangzhu wenhua yuqi wenshi de diaoke jishu" ("The Art of Working Liangzhu Jade Decor"), in Xu Huping, ed., Dongfang wenming zhiguang—Liangzhu wenhua faxian 60-zhounian jinian wenji ("The Light of Oriental Civilization—Collected Essays in Commemoration of the 60th Anniversary of the Discovery of Liangzhu Culture") (Nanjing: Nanjing bowuyuan, 1996), pp. 338–47; Zhang Minghua, "Liangzhu guyu cong lun" ("Discussion of the Ancient Jade Cong of Liangzhu"), Dongnan wenhua, no. 2 (1992), pp. 112–19; and S. Howard Hansford, Chinese Carved Jade (London: Faber and Faber, 1968).

7. Wang Zunguo, "Liangzhu wenhua 'Yu jian cang' shuluo" ("Analysis of the 'Jade Shroud' of the Liangzhu Culture"), Wenwu, no. 2 (1984), p. 33.

8. For the argument that shark teeth were used, see Zhang Minghua, "Liangzhu guyu de kewen gongju shi shemma" ("What Are the Tools Used to Work Early Jade of the Liangzhu Culture?"), Zhongguo wenwu bao (6 December, 1990), p. 1; Zhang Minghua, "Liangzhu guyu conglun" ("Discussion of Liangzhu Jade"), Dongnan wenhua, no. 1 (1993), pp. 112–14; and for the argument on the diamond point, see Hayashi Minao, "Liangzhu wenhua yuqi," p. 338.

9. Janet Douglas, personal communication with the author, 7 December, 1996.

10. The mineral composition and microstructure of jade can also be measured by FTIR (Fouriers transform infrared absorption spectrometry) and by SEM (scanning electron microscopy).

11. Wen Guang and Jing Zhichun, "Mineralogical Inquiries into Chinese Neolithic Jade," The Journal of Chinese Jade 1 (1996); and Hansford, Chinese Carved Jade, p. 39.

12. Zhejiang sheng wenwu kaogu yanjiu suo et al., ed., Liangzhu wenhua yuqi ("Jades of the Liangzhu Culture") (Beijing: Wenwu chubanshe, 1990), p. 11.

13. For two examples of the bone graph li ("rite/ritual"), see Li Xiaoding, Jiaguwenzi jishi ("Explanation and Commentary on Oracle Bone Graphs"), vol. 1 (Nangang: Zhongyang yanjiu yuan lishi yuyan suo zhuankan 50), p. 49.

14. Willetts, Chinese Art, p. 90; Yuan Kang, Yue jue shu, ed. Qian Peiming, vol. 13 (Beijing: Zhonghua chubanshe, 1985), p. 58; or Yue jue shu, Sibu congkan ed., vol. 62, p. 93b.

15. See Childs-Johnson, "The 'Jade Age,'" pp. 1–3.

16. Elizabeth Childs-Johnson, "Jades of the Hongshan Culture, the Dragon and Fertility Cult Worship," Arts Asiatiques 56 (1991), pp. 82–95.

17. See, for example, the bone graph for "cloud" (yun) in Li, Jiaguwenzi, vol. 11, p. 3459.

18. Childs-Johnson, "Jades of the Hongshan Culture," p. 95.

19. See, for example, Dawenkou (Beijing: Wenwu chubanshe, 1974), figs. 6, 8.

20. For the division of Liangzhu jades into categories of weapons, costume ornament, and implements for ritual use, see Childs-Johnson, Ritual and Power, pp. 19–22; and Zhejiang wenwu chu, ed., Liangzhu guyu ("Ancient Jade of Liangzhu") (Hangzhou: Zhejiang wenwu chubanshe, 1996), pp. 16–24.

21. Bian Fengshi, "Liangzhu wenhua de fenqi yu niandai" ("The Periodization and Chronology of the Liangzhu Culture"), Zhongyuan wenwu, no. 3 (1992), pp. 79–97; and Song Jian, "Lun Liangzhu wenming de xingshuai guocheng" ("Concerning the Formation of the City-State of the Liangzhu Civilization") (paper presented at Liangzhu wenhua guoji taolunhui

[International conference on Lianzhu culture], Yuhang, Zhejiang, 1–4 November 1996). For an English summary of Song's paper, see Elizabeth Childs-Johnson, "The International Symposium on Liangzhu Culture," *Early China News* 9 (1996), p. 28.

22. As used by Li Wenming and Wu Rongqing, "Zhongguo wuqiannianqian de 'tuzhu jinzita'—Jiangsu Kunshanshi Zhaolingshan yizhi ji qi chutu wenwu" ("The Five-Thousand-Year-Old Earthen Pyramid of China—The Remains and Relics Unearthed at Zhaolingshan, Kunshanshi, Jiangsu"), *Longyu wenwu yishu* (1993) 17, pp. 24–32.

23. Che Guangjin, "Yu cong yu Sidun yizhi" ("The Remains of Sidun and the Jade Cong"), *Zhongguo wenwu bao* (31 December 1995), p. 3; reprinted in Xu, ed., *Dongfang wenming*, pp. 371–73.

24. Ji Jianfang, in "Liangzhu wenhua mucang yanjiu" ("Research on Burials of the Liangzhu Culture"), in Xu, ed., *Dongfang wenming*, fig. 12, p. 191, proposes a slightly different design which he describes as a patriarchal clan cemetery mound at Zhaolingshan (see fig. 4B in this essay). Zhang Zhiheng, "Liangzhu wenhua juluo qun de tezheng" ("Special Characteristics of Settlement Groups of Liangzhu Culture"), *Zhongguo wenwu bao* (7 April 1996), p. 3, reviews evidence for a similar structure at Mojiaoshan, although this site also possesses significant remains of columned foundations.

25. Che, "Yu cong yu Sidun yizhi," p. 3.

26. For an example of the ideal structure of the *mingtang* and *piyong* based on the square and circle, see Nelson Wu (Wu Nosun), *Chinese and Indian Architecture* (New York: George Braziller, 1963), pp. 40–41, pls. 129–30; and Nancy Steinhardt, *Traditional Chinese Architecture* (New York: China Institute, 1984), pp. 70–77, pls. 3.1–3.4

27. Fan Yuzhou, "Yinxu buci zhong de 'wu' yu 'wu di'"

("'Wu' and 'wu di' in Yinxu Inscriptions"), *Nanfang wenwu*, no. 2 (1994), pp. 115–19.

28. See, for example, a reference to this myth in the *Huainanzi*, in John Major, *Heaven and Earth in Early Han Thought: Chapters Three, Four, and Five of the Huainanzi* (Albany: State University of New York Press, 1993), p. 49; and in David Hawkes, *Ch'u Tz'u: The Songs of the South* (Oxford: Clarendon Press, 1959), p. 47.

29. Major, *Heaven and Earth*, pp. 38–39.

30. Mou Yongkang, "Dongfang shiqian shiqi taiyang chongbai de kaogu xue guancha" ("Archaeological Investigation of Sun Worship in the East During the Neolithic"), *Gugong xueshu jikan* 12 (1995), p. 4; Mou Yongkang, "Liangzhu yuqi shang shen chongbai de tansuo" ("Discussion of Deity Worship of Liangzhu Jades"), *Qingzhu Su Bingqi kaogu wushiwu nian lunwenji* ("Collected Essays Celebrating Fifty-five Years of Su Bing's Archaeological Research") (Beijing: Wenwu chubanshe, 1989), p. 186; and Wu Ruzuo, "Luolun Changjiang, Huanghe liang liuyu shiqian shiqi de taiyangshen congbai" ("Discussion of Sun God Worship Along the Two River Valleys of the Yellow River During the Neolithic"), *Huaxia kaogu*, no. 2 (1996), pp. 75–85.

31. Zhejiang sheng wenwu, ed., *Liangzhu wenhua yuqi*, p. 184.

32. Elizabeth Childs-Johnson, "Symbolic Jades of the Erlitou Period: A Xia Royal Tradition," *Archives of Asian Art* 48 (1995), pp. 64–90.

33. See, for example, Lin Huadong, *Hemudu wenhua chutan* ("Preliminary Discussion of the Hemudu Culture") (Hangzhou: Zhejiang renmin chubanshe, 1992), pp. 159–66, and fig. 6–3, p. 161, pl. 4, top.

34. For example, see Chang Ping-ch'uan, "A Brief Description of the Fu Hao Oracle Bone Inscriptions," in K. C. Chang, ed., *Studies of*

Shang Archaeology (New Haven: Yale University Press, 1986), pp. 121–40.

35. For example, see Chang Cheng-lang, "A Brief Discussion of Fu Tzu," in Chang, ed., *Studies of Shang Archaeology*, pp. 103–20.

36. *Yinxu Fu Hao mu* ("The Burial of Fu Hao at Yinxu) (Beijing: Wenwu chubanshe, 1980), pp. 114–15. For an English translation of the original site report, see Elizabeth Childs-Johnson, *Excavation of Tomb No. 5 at Yinxu, Anyang*, Chinese Sociology and Anthropology Series, vol. 15, no. 3 (Armonk, N.Y.: M. E. Sharpe, 1983), p. 83.

37. Kaogu yanjiu suo, ed., *Shangcunling Guoguo mudi* ("The Cemetery of the Guo State at Shangcunling") (Beijing: Kexue chubanshe, 1959), pl. 21:8–10.

38. For the site report on this tomb, see Kaogu yanjiu suo, ed., "Sanmenxia Shangcunling Guoguo mudi M2001 fajue jianbao" ("A Brief Excavation Report of Tomb No. 2001 at the Cemetery of the Guo State at Shangcunling, Sanmenxia"), *Huaxia kaogu*, no. 3 (1992), pp. 104–13.

39. For a very recent discovery of an early Western Han jade burial suit, see the report on the burial of Liu He at the Han imperial burial center near Xuzhou, Jiangsu Province, in *Zhongguo wenwu bao* (20 October 1996), p. 1.

40. See Kaogu yanjiu suo, ed., *Shangcunling Guoguo mudi*, pp. 48–54, and pp. 83–85 (English summary).

41. According to the site report, numerous other jades such as *bi, gui, ge, cong*, handle-shaped pieces, tigers, deer, dogs, ox heads, horse heads, birds, turtles, and fish lay on top of the coffin cover; Kaogu yanjiu suo, ed., "Sanmenxia Shangcunling Guoguo," p. 105.

42. This is identified in part by Zhang Changshou, "Xi Zhou de cangyu—1983–1986 nian Fengxi fajue ciliao zhi ba" ("Burial Jades of the Western Zhou—Excavated Material at

Fengxi, from 1983 to 1989"), *Wenwu*, no. 9 (1993), pp. 55–59. For other examples, see jade masks illustrated in *Luoyang Zhongzhoulu*, (Beijing: Kexue chubanshe, 1959); see also Kaogu yanjiu suo, ed., "Tianma—Qucun yizhi Beizhao Jinhou mudi disanzi yu disizi fajue" (The Third and Fourth Excavations of the Cemetery of the Marquis of Jin at Tianmu—Qucun Remains"), *Wenwu*, no. 8 (1994), pp. 4–33. For the recently excavated jade face mask of Western Han date from Changqingxian, Shandong, see *Zhongguo wenwubao* (10 October 1996), p. 1.

43. J. J. M. de Groot, *The Religious System of China* (reprint, Taibei: Chengwen, 1969), chap. 3, pp. 269–74.

44. *Yili* ("The Classic of Rites"), Sibu congkan ed., vol. 12.

45. Hawkes, *Ch'u Tz'u*, pp. 105–9.

46. Jade from other, earlier contexts was often reused to make face masks—for example, for those buried in the Jin state cemetery at Beizhao, Tianma-Qucun, Shanxi Province; see *Wenwu*, no. 1 (1994), p. 27. "Pseudo-jade" was used to create burial suits for some occupants of the Nanyue tombs (tomb No. 2); see Wen Guang "Xi Han Nanyue wangmu yuqi di zhi kaogu xue yanjiu" ("Geological and Archaeological Research on Jades from the Royal Tomb of the King of Nanyue"), *Gugong xuexu jikan* 11, no. 1 (1993), pp. 9–30; and Wen Guang, "Yu yu min guyu" ("True and Pseudo-Jade"), *Gugong wenwu yuekan* 11, no. 4 (1993), pp. 126–37.

47. See Henan sheng wenwu yanjiu suo, ed., *Xichuan Xiasi Chunqiu Chumu* ("The Chu Tombs of the Spring and Autumn Period at Xiasi, Xichuan") (Beijing: Wenwu chubanshe, 1991), p. 98, and fig. 82:1, p. 100. For the identification of the female belonging to tomb No. 1 from which the jade derives, see p. 324; for the jade, see also *Zhongguo meishu quanji, 9: Yuqi*

("The Complete Arts of China, 9: Jade") (Shijiazhuang: Hebei meishu chubanshe, 1993), pl. 108, and p. 40. This jade is probably unfinished since there is a lack of corresponding detail on one of the upper sides; one side of the piece lacks the corresponding filler detail of the claw and scale motifs. This piece may be compared with one similar in size and shape from the Cunguoji burial at Lianjiaxian, Shandong; ibid., pl. 103.

48. Representative examples of this popular jade dragon type are illustrated in *Zhongguo yuqi quanji 3: Chunqiu Zhanguo* ("The Complete Set of Chinese Jade 3: Spring and Autumn and Warring States Periods") (Shijiazhuang: Hebei meishu chubanshe, 1993), pls. 36–40, 132–33, 209, 213–15.

49. For the site report on Huangshantou, Anxiang, Hunan Province, see "Hunan Anxiang Xi Jin Liuhong Mu" ("The Tomb of Liuhong of the Western Jin at Anxiang, Hunan") *Wenwu*, no. 11 (1993), pp. 1–12.

50. For the site report on Hejiacun, Xi'an, Shaanxi Province, see "Xi'an Nanjiao Hejiacun faxian Tangdai jiaocang wenwu" ("The Cultural Relics from the Cache of the Tang Dynasty Discovered at Hejiacun, Nanjiao, Xi'an"), *Wenwu*, no. 1 (1972), pp. 30–42.

51. For an explanation of the origin of the lion in China, see Laurence Sickman and Alexander Soper, *The Art and Architecture of China*, (reprint, Harmondsworth: Penguin Books, 1984), pp. 61–62.

Ritual Bronzes— Epitome of Ancient Chinese Civilization

Ma Chengyuan

Director, The Shanghai Museum

All the major civilizations of the ancient world passed through a developmental phase that we call the Bronze Age. In ancient China bronze vessels were essential symbols of monarchic rule and of aristocratic status, and this special significance brought about the exceptional development of Chinese bronze workmanship. The magnificence of China's bronzes is unmatched by those of any other Bronze Age civilization.

BRONZES OF THE XIA DYNASTY (21ST–16TH CENTURIES BCE)

The first hereditary monarchy in Chinese history, known as the Xia dynasty, was also the beginning of the age of Chinese culture. Historical records, which note that bronze casting was already quite highly developed by the time of the Xia, are borne out by the archaeological evidence of the Erlitou culture. The Erlitou site at Yanshi, Henan Province, which predates the Erligang site of the Shang at Zhengzhou, was discovered during the 1950s. Found in the third level of the tumulus at Erlitou were a tomb and bronze vessels, weapons, and jades that had been buried with the deceased.[1] The bronzes of the Erlitou culture at Yanshi comprised primarily *jue*, but also *jia*, *he*, and cooking vessels. In shape, these vessels were exceedingly similar to pottery vessels of the same period or earlier. The bronze *jue* from the Shanghai Museum (cat. 21) closely resembles the pottery *jue* found at the Erlitou site, and is obviously primitive in its casting and design. Xia bronzes also include some relatively finely worked pieces.

Some of the more distinctive Xia bronzes are turquoise-inlaid ornamental plaques of unknown use. But apart from these and a very few vessels that bear simple geometric decorations, the vast majority of Xia bronzes are plain and undecorated. In this, they differ greatly from the Shang Erligang period bronzes from Zhengzhou, which are generally decorated with zoomorphic patterns. One of the items unearthed at Erlitou is a round bronze ornament decorated with an inlaid turquoise cross within concentric circles, a decoration unique to the Erlitou culture. A bronze ax (*yue*) with similar inlaid turquoise crosses in a circle is in the collection of the Shanghai Museum, and its date can be ascertained through a comparison with the objects from Erlitou. This *yue*, which is very large and heavy, is the most magnificent of extant Xia bronzes; it was not a functional weapon but a symbol of military authority. From it, we may anticipate the discovery of similarly large and impressive Xia bronzes. Functional bronze weapons found at the Erlitou site include dagger-axes (*ge*) and battle-axes (*qi*). The Xia bronzes discovered to date were cast in the latter part of the Xia dynasty.

Palace foundations and groups of tombs have been found at sites of the Erlitou type located along the Yellow River in Henan Province; similar culture sites are also located north of the Yellow River in southern Shanxi. The remains of a rather large early Shang city, which is later than the Erlitou site, has been discovered east of Yanshi. According to historical records, this region became part of the

Xia domains after the dynasty was founded. Of course, the picture of Xia bronzes is far from complete. Much more archaeological excavation of Xia cultural sites remains to be done.

SHANG DYNASTY BRONZES (16TH–11TH CENTURIES BCE)

The development of Shang bronzes can be divided into early, middle, and late periods.

Early Shang bronzes, from the beginning of the Erligang period, have been found mainly at Zhengzhou, Henan Province, and date approximately to the sixteenth century BCE. New vessel shapes such as the *gong*, *zun*, and *li* appeared during this period. The strong primitive inclination to imitate pottery, which is found in Xia bronzes, is absent in those of Erligang. Among bronzes of this period zoomorphic masks (*taotie*) are the most commonly seen decorative motif, and animal forms were used extensively as well.

Mid-Shang saw further variations in the types of bronzes. Shapes were gradually perfected. Decoration expanded to cover much of the surfaces of the vessels, and also greatly increased in both the line density and complexity of composition. Further development produced decorative patterns rendered in strong relief, and bronzes began to be ornamented with animal heads done in high relief. Casting technology extended to the casting of large vessels, as revealed by the number of large *zun* and other vessels discovered. A large square *ding*, a meter tall, has also been unearthed at the site of the Shang city in Zhengzhou. Bronzes of the middle period include the dragon-and-tiger *zun*[2] discovered at Funan, Anhui Province; a jar with movable loop handles[3] found with a group of bronzes at Zhengzhou, Henan Province; and bronzes from some of the sumptuous Shang tombs at Panlong city in Huangpi county, Hubei Province.[4] All of these vessels are markedly more mature than the early Shang bronzes of the Erligang period at Zhengzhou. At the same time they differ noticeably from the late Shang bronzes, marking the period from the fifteenth through the fourteenth, or perhaps into the thirteenth, century BCE as one of transition.

The late Shang was the greatest period in the development of Chinese bronzes, showing the largest variety of shapes and decorative schema, and the bronzes from the "Yin ruins" at Anyang, Henan Province, offer the most representative and complete view of the period. Along with the increase in types of objects there developed set rules governing the proper combinations of vessels, and the shapes of pieces reached a fully mature stage. New to this period were vessels in the shape of birds and animals. In these vessels artistry and practicality were superbly integrated, as exemplified by the *Fuhaoxia zun* in this exhibition (cat. 24).

It is noteworthy that the bronzes with the most distinctive animal designs are often found far from Anyang, in peripheral areas of the Shang domain. For instance, the pig *zun* and elephant *zun* in this exhibition (cats. 27, 25) were unearthed in Hunan. Moreover, Shang bronzes from places other than Anyang, particularly those from Hunan and Jiangxi provinces, which lie south of the Yangzi River, do not merely differ in their form from those at Anyang but are often conspicuously more ornate. This kind and degree of difference merits our attention. Why were these most lavish Shang bronzes not unearthed in the area that was the political and economic center of the Shang dynasty, but rather in places so distant as to be regarded as barren wilderness in that era? Their exquisite craftsmanship indicates that these pieces could not have been cast in such places, and the names of individuals and clans cast on some of the bronzes show that they were possessions of some of the great clans of central China. Archaeological data gathered during their excavation shows that— unlike the bronzes found at Anyang—the vast majority of them were not burial furnishings, nor are there any signs that they were ever used in sets for rituals. They were generally buried at various sites atop mountains or along the banks of rivers. It is highly possible that these choice samples of Shang bronzes were specially imported into the peripheral regions, where they were regarded as expressions of respect and admiration for Shang culture. In 1963 an animal mask *you* was unearthed in Ningxiang, Hunan Province. Inside this vessel were over a thousand solid and tubular jade beads.[5] This exhibition features the *Ge you*, from a royal tomb in Ningxiang, Hunan Province, which also contained over three hundred jade beads, jade pieces, and tubular jade beads (cat. 26). An animal mask *pou* found in Hunan contained over two hundred small bronze ax heads. From this, we can see that in this outlying region Shang bronzes were preserved as a form of wealth. Perhaps future archaeological discoveries will elucidate the formation and nature of this cultural phenomenon.

The most common decorative motif found on late Shang bronzes is the zoomorphic mask formerly known as the *taotie* pattern. This was generally executed in clearly layered relief against a dense and fine-lined intaglio spiral pattern. In particular, the eyes of the mask were made large and prominent, enhancing the mysterious, solemn, and intimidating aspect of the image. On late Shang bronzes small birds or small dragons often flank the mask, with bird patterns the more frequent. This type of design composition has ancient historical origins. Late Neolithic jade *cong* from the Liangzhu culture,

which existed in what is now Jiangsu, Zhejiang, and Shanghai, were often carved with images of deities represented by their two eyes. Often, a bird in flight was placed on each side of the deity, with the birds' heads turned away from the central image.[6] The heads of the birds accompanying the zoomorphic masks on late Shang bronzes are the same as those on the Liangzhu culture jades, indicating that this type of decoration was an adoption and continuation of the traditions of Liangzhu culture. Oracle bone inscriptions describe the phoenix as the Wind God and also the envoy of the Celestial Emperor,[7] entrusted with the mission of relaying information between Heaven and humans. An animal mask flanked by bird patterns may have been an image of deity. The decorative motifs on Shang bronzes always invoke the Celestial Emperor and various spirits; they were not merely more or less stylized animals. Rather, they expressed a strong religious desire for communion between Heaven and humans and for blessings from the Celestial Emperor and various spirits. The birds flanking the zoomorphic masks may represent the phoenix as emissary in these transactions. The great flourishing of decorative art on Shang bronzes manifests religious aspiration.

The casting of Shang bronzes was done in pottery section molds. Specially prepared clay was made into the number of external and internal mold sections required by a particular shape. Patterns and inscriptions were carved or incised into the external mold sections. After being thoroughly dried and fired, the mold sections were fitted together and reinforced to form a complete mold, which was fitted with a cover containing a pouring hole for the bronze to enter and one or more holes through which air bubbles would be expelled. Molten bronze was poured between the inner and outer molds. After the bronze had cooled, the mold was broken and the bronze removed and given a final finishing and polishing. Shang workmanship in the making of pottery molds was extremely fine, and set the highest standards in the ancient world for the casting of bronze pieces in pottery molds. Pottery molds were used exclusively to cast bronzes through the Eastern Zhou, after which additional methods were introduced.

WESTERN ZHOU BRONZES
(11TH CENTURY–771 BCE)
Early Western Zhou (ca. 1050–ca. 975) bronze making was to a large extent a continuation of late Shang practices. Late Shang and early Western Zhou are often considered as a single and supreme period in the evolution of Chinese bronze making. Withal, the Zhou people differed significantly from the Shang people in their political organization, religion, and cultural concepts, differences concretely manifested as time

went on by a great diminution in the absolute numbers and types of wine vessels and a corresponding increase in bronze vessels for food. The establishment of rites that stressed food rather than drink led directly to considerable development of such existing types of bronze food vessels as the *ding*, the *yan*, and the *gui*. The large round *ding* of the Western Zhou greatly outnumbered those of the Shang; the *yan* was used more extensively than during the Shang; square-based *gui*, such as the *Li gui* and *Da Feng gui* from the time of King Wu, were entirely new to this era. The Zhou attached great importance to ancestor worship, in strong contrast to the Shang worship of gods and spirits. Religious connotations are less apparent in bronze decorations of the Western Zhou. Apart from zoomorphic masks, the most gorgeously executed bronze motif of the Western Zhou, particularly during the time of kings Kang and Zhao (perhaps early 10th c.), was the phoenix pattern. Phoenix patterns, beautifully accomplished in limitless variety, became a feature of this period, imparting an aura of wealth and luxury to the bronzes. Their vogue, however, was brief; beginning in middle Western Zhou, such sumptuous phoenix patterns were seldom to be found on bronzes. But, like the last burst of twilight, they brought the peak period of Chinese bronze making to a magnificent close.

Early Western Zhou bronzes show another important change from Shang: the appearance of long inscriptions inside the vessels. Many of these inscriptions recorded major events of the time, events often not mentioned in surviving historical texts. For instance, the inscription on the *He zun* featured in this exhibition (cat. 32) records and precisely dates the building of the Western Zhou capital, Chengzhou (in the area around present-day Luoyang, Henan Province) by King Cheng, successor of the Zhou conqueror: "It was at the time when the king began the building of Cheng-zhou. . . . This happened in [King Cheng's] fifth year."[8] These inscriptions are our most direct and most reliable historical sources for the study of ancient Chinese history.

From the reign of King Mu of the Western Zhou, the types, shapes, and decorations of the bronzes changed significantly, reflecting new customs and uses. Bronze wine vessels, including the *jia*, *gong*, *zun*, and *you*, essentially faded from use, and although some new shapes such as the *ling* appeared to take their place, the proportion of wine vessels was much smaller than before. Beginning in the middle period (ca. 975–875) of the Western Zhou, many new types of food vessels such as the *fu* and *shu* appeared, and older types of food vessels such as the *dou* and *pu* were used more extensively than before. New variants of some commonly used

vessels like the *gui* emerged. Zoomorphic masks, for centuries the chief decorative motif of bronzes, gradually changed in appearance. Major parts of the mask, such as the relatively well-formed ears, eyebrows, mouth, fangs, and claws, were simplified or sometimes omitted altogether. The eyes, which had been the paramount feature, lost their former power, sometimes being reduced to two small, socket-less circles, and at other times only faintly suggested by a stylized outline. These changes drained the masks of their former solemnity, ferocity, and mystery.

The middle period of the Western Zhou also saw a noticeable reduction in the use of dragon and bird patterns for bronze decoration and, as with the zoomorphic masks, modifications in the design of these traditional motifs. These modifications transformed the dragons and birds into what were formerly known as "curved zigzag patterns"—what we now call "modified animal patterns," "intertwined animal eye patterns," "coiled animal body patterns," etcetera. These patterns were generally composed as continuous bidirectional horizontal bands of decoration around the bronzes, imparting a sense of simplicity and sprightliness. The most distinctive pattern of this period was the wave pattern (formerly known as the "curved band pattern"), whose regular, rhythmic undulations create a powerful sense of motion.

Bronzes of the late Western Zhou period (ca. 875–771) show basic continuity with those of the middle period. An ever-greater proportion of the food vessels consists of *fu* and *shu*. At the same time both the prescribed uses and the appearance of common food vessels such as the *ding* and *gui* became increasingly formulaic. Of two principal *ding* variants, one was flat-bottomed with a relatively shallow belly, the other round-bottomed and deep-bellied. The principal form of *gui* had a contracted mouth with cover, swelling belly, two symmetrically placed animal-shaped lug handles spanning the belly, and three evenly spaced zoomorphs serving as feet under a ring base. The decorative combinations were also more fixed: for example, a flat-bottomed, shallow *ding* would generally have a modified animal pattern around the lip and a wave pattern around the belly, whereas a *ding* with deep belly and rounded bottom was usually more simply decorated, sometimes with only a few parallel lines under the lip, sometimes with an overlapping fish-scale pattern in a band around the lip. This trend toward formularization suggests a certain stagnation in bronze making at this time; nevertheless, some items produced for royal use were still very well made. During the late Western Zhou the greatest innovation in bronze decoration was the interlaced dragon pattern. This consisted of a central dragon flanked on both sides by several subsidiary dragons.

The dragon bodies were interlaced, that is, not merely overlapped but passed under-and-over one another, creating a sense of undulant motion that was further developed during Eastern Zhou. Late Western Zhou dragon interlace generally appears on square *hu*. The famous *Song hu*, and the *Jin Hou hu* recently unearthed from the tomb of the Marquis of Jin in Quwo, Shanxi Province, both bear this type of pattern.

EASTERN ZHOU BRONZES: THE SPRING AND AUTUMN AND WARRING STATES PERIODS (770–221 BCE)

Aristocratic tombs of the early Spring and Autumn era have revealed very few bronzes that were relatively well crafted. The Zhou kings had lost the western part of their domain and relocated their court to their eastern capital near present-day Luoyang. In the smaller states that made up the Zhou realm, bronze making was rather crude. In the larger states, however, signs of progress were already appearing.

By the mid-Spring and Autumn era Zhou kingly authority had declined and the various fiefdoms were expanding their power and their borders and beginning to come into collision. But as the authority of the Zhou ruling house dwindled and the political and military struggles between the states intensified, ideas and political institutions evolved apace. Unsettled times stimulated major advances in the forces of social production, begetting countless new forms of workmanship. The earlier forging of iron weapons and implements led to mastery of the art of casting iron. Bronzes became an indispensable symbol of power, status, and legitimacy for the new elites in the aristocratic states, spurring bronze making to an unprecedented period of innovation and development. To meet rapidly escalating military needs, the casting of bronze weapons was also carried to new heights. Even some small states possessed significant quantities of bronzes, and with the breakdown of centralized patronage along with centralized authority, regional traits of bronzes of this period became quite distinct.

New vessels appeared, and old types were rendered with fresh shapes and unusual designs, which made for an entirely new look. Included in this exhibition is the square lotus-and-crane *hu* (cat. 45) found in Xinzheng, Henan Province, in 1923. Openwork petals rise from the lid, on which stands a crane raising its wings as if about to fly. Lug handles on two sides of the *hu* take the form of crested dragons looking backward, and winged dragons mark the four corners of the square belly. Two powerful slinking animals support the vessel, which is decorated overall with an interlaced double-bodied dragon pattern. The effect is opulent

and dazzling: the stolid and heavy bronze style that had prevailed since the late Western Zhou has here been wholly replaced by the innovative spirit first apparent in the mid-Spring and Autumn era.

Regional characteristics of bronzes of the late Spring and Autumn era are best exemplified by works from the kingdoms of Qin in the west, Jin in the north, Qi in the east, and Chu in the south. In the 1920s a group of unusually designed and exquisitely decorated Jin bronzes were unearthed at Liyu village in Hunyuan, Shanxi Province. These, together with the bronzes recently found in tomb number 251 at Jinsheng village in Taiyuan, can be considered representative of Jin style bronzes (cats. 43, 44),[9] whereas those from the Chu tomb at Xiasi, Xiquan county, in Henan Province are typical of the Chu style.[10] In both shape and decoration the recently discovered *he* of King Fuchai of Wu is an example of how features of the Jin and Chu bronzes were absorbed and integrated elsewhere.[11]

Improvements in casting techniques using pottery section molds, the spread of the complementary processes of casting-on and precasting, and the considerable maturing of the lost-wax casting technique all reflect significant advances in the bronze technology of this period. A major revolution in the art of bronze making during the Spring and Autumn and Warring States periods was the use of stamps to create the surface designs in the molds. Besides increasing the number of bronzes that could be produced, it also assured the uniform quality of the decorative patterns on the pieces. This advanced technique is seen most frequently among the extant bronzes of the Jin state. Excavation of the site of the Jin bronze workshop at Houma in Shanxi Province has fully revealed the advanced bronze casting technology of the time.[12] Advances such as the use of stamps in mold-making changed the nature of creating surface decoration: only the maker of the stamp required artistry; the workers who impressed the design from the stamp onto the mold needed only simple technical skill. Subsequently new arts of surface decorating appeared, using inlaid gold, silver, and copper to create a varicolored surface. The gold, silver, and copper would be hammered into sheets or threads, and the threads might be coiled into tight spirals, then inlaid into the grooves cast in the bronze to receive them. On some bronzes, copper, gold, silver, and turquoise were inlaid in combination to form a sumptuous, brocade-like design.

It was during the late Spring and Autumn period that human activity began to be used as a decorative motif, a clear manifestation of the unprecedentedly strong social humanism of the time. Subjects like battles, hunting, banquets, rituals, musical performances, and mulberry-leaf picking might be depicted in inlaid copper or chiseled into the surfaces of bronzes. Inlay and incising were also used to portray fantastic creatures such as human-headed animals or bird-headed humans.

On bronzes of the Spring and Autumn and Warring States periods the most popular decorative motifs were variations of dragon patterns—an abrupt change from the ubiquitous zoomorphic masks of Shang and Western Zhou, which doubtless signals a change in society's beliefs. The dragons might be interlaced, or coiled, or stylized into a dragon-like pattern. However the dragons were rendered, they commonly encircle the vessels in continuous designs, in strong contrast to the separate units characteristic of earlier bronze decor. Elaborate and delicately linear detail characterizes these dragons. Late variants of the dragon patterns omitted the heads, leaving only the interlaced bodies. The impulse toward variation and increasingly fine detail eventually turned bronze decorations into geometric designs. That was the final stage of bronze decoration, succeeded by the appearance of large quantities of plain, undecorated bronzes after the mid-Warring States period.

BRONZES OF THE QIN AND HAN PERIODS (221 BCE–220 CE)

The vast majority of bronzes of the Qin and Han periods were practical vessels without ritual significance, objects of daily use, often with inscriptions indicating their weight or capacity. Most vessels had little or no decoration. Some bronzes, however, from aristocratic and royal tombs of the Western Han, display exquisite workmanship.[13] In particular, the surface decorative techniques of gilding, gold-and-silver inlay, and painting had reached very high standards. Implements for daily use, cast in human or animal forms, became notable achievements of Han bronze making. These include the Changxin Palace lamp, as well as the lamp in the shape of a goose holding a fish (cat. 53).

Han period bronzes made by peoples living around the periphery of the empire are markedly different from those of central China. The most notable ones come from the bronze culture of the Yi people in the western parts of Yunnan. Since the 1950s a large number of bronze artifacts have been recovered from an ancient tomb at Shizhaishan, Jinning, Yunnan. Among them is a gold seal marked "Seal of the King of Dian," which confirms the ethnic origin of the bronze culture at this site.[14] Shizhaishan bronzes show very advanced use of lost-wax casting, gold-and-silver inlay, gilding, and inlaid gemstones. Both linear and fully modeled depictions of people, animals, structures, etcetera, richly varied and lifelike, adorn these bronzes. They

are composed in scenes of sacrificial offerings, music and dance, production, trade, war, and hunting, offering a vivid picture of Dian society of the time. During this same period the Xiongnu of the northern grasslands, the Donghu tribe of the Xianbei people in the northeast, and the Yue in the south were also creating bronze cultures, each with its own style. Together, they complete the current picture of developments in ancient Chinese bronze making.

Translated, from the Chinese, by June Mei.

NOTES

1. Erlitou work team of the Institute of Archaeology, Chinese Academy of Sciences, "Brief Report on the Excavations of Sections 3 and 8 of the Erlitou Site at Yanshi, Henan," *Kaogu*, 1975:5.

2. Ge Jieping, "Bronzes of the Shang Era Found at Funan, Anhui Province," *Wenwu*, 1959:1.

3. Henan Provincial Institute of Cultural Artifacts and the Zhengzhou Municipal Museum, "Newly Discovered Buried Shang Dynasty Bronzes from Zhengzhou," *Wenwu*, 1983:3.

4. Hubei Provincial Museum, "Erligang Period Shang Bronzes from Panlong City," *Wenwu*, 1976:2.

5. Gao Zhixi, "Shang Bronzes and Sites Discovered at Huangcai, Ningxiang, Hunan," *Kaogu*, 1963:12.

6. Shanghai Municipal Commission for the Preservation of Cultural Artifacts, "Tombs of the Liangzhu Culture at Fuquanshan, Shanghai," *Wenwu*, 1984:2.

7. An oracle bone inscription reads, "The Emperor sent the Phoenix." See Guo Moruo, *Puci tongzuan*, p. 398.

8. Ma Chengyuan, "A Tentative Interpretation of the *He Zun* Inscription," *Wenwu*, 1976:1.

9. Shanxi Provincial Institute of Archaeology and Taiyuan Municipal Commission for the Preservation of Cultural Artifacts, "Brief Report on the Excavation of a Large Spring and Autumn Era Tomb (no. 251) and Horse-and-Chariot Pit at Jinsheng Village, Taiyuan," *Wenwu*, 1989:9.

10. Henan Provincial Institute of Cultural Artifacts, et al., "A Chu Tomb of the Spring and Autumn Era at Xiasi, Xiquan" (Wenwu Publishing House, 1991).

11. Chen Peifen, "King Fuchai of Wu," *Bulletin of the Shanghai Museum*, no. 7.

12. Shanxi Provincial Institute of Cultural Artifacts, *The Bronze Casting Site at Houma* (Wenwu Publishing House, 1993).

13. *Report on the Excavation of a Han Tomb at Mancheng* (Wenwu Publishing House, 1980).

14. Yunnan Provincial Museum, *Report on the Excavation of a Group of Ancient Tombs at Shizhaishan, Jinning, Yunnan* (Wenwu Publishing House, 1959).

Innovation in Ancient Chinese Metalwork

Jenny So

Curator of Ancient Chinese Art,
Freer Gallery of Art and Arthur M.
Sackler Gallery, Smithsonian Institution,
Washington, D.C.

ERLITOU PERIOD

By the early second millennium BCE ancient China's artists and craftsmen had already been creating ceramics and working jades for over two thousand years. Their mastery of these two materials is evident in the outstanding workmanship, elegant shapes, and sophisticated designs that characterize the

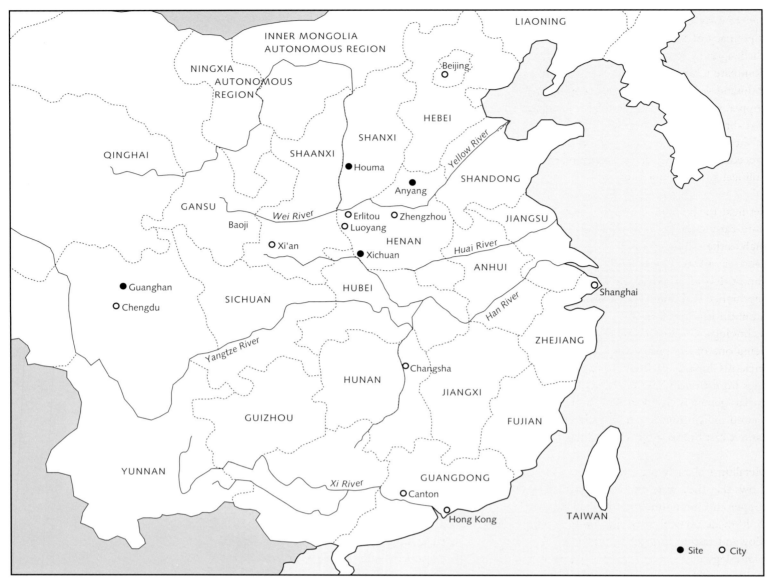

Map 1. *Map of China showing major ancient and modern cities and sites.*

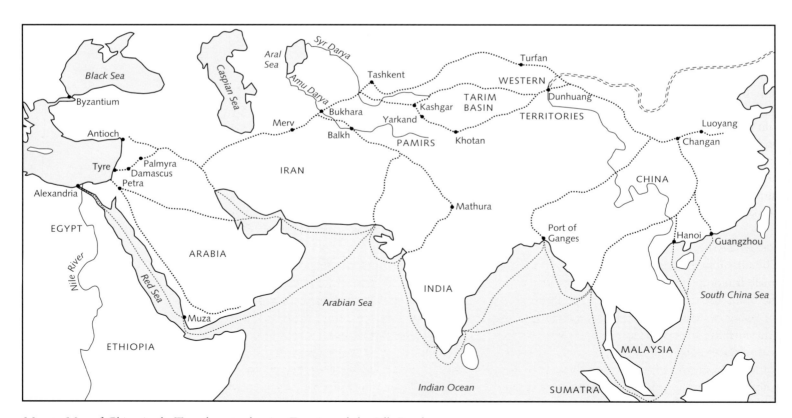

Map 2. *Map of China in the Tang dynasty showing Eurasia and the Silk Road.*

best of early Chinese ceramics and jades. But the supremacy of these two mediums was soon to be challenged by a new material that would eventually dominate China's artistic scene for the next thousand years: cast bronze, an alloy mainly of copper, with smaller amounts of tin and/or lead. Cast-bronze objects became symbols of the power of the ruling elite, replacing the ritual jades of the preceding Neolithic era as ceremonial regalia in political and religious rites.

Set next to the refined ceramics and jades of the time, early attempts at bronze casting in China, such as the wine cup (*jue*; cat. 21) made circa 1700–circa 1600 BCE, appear unusually crude and almost devoid of artistic merit. But the *jue's* modest appearance and undecorated surface should not diminish its significance in the history of this new technology. The vessel has the unusual distinction of being one of the earliest bronze vessels made in ancient China, as it closely resembles similar wine cups from Erlitou, Yanshi, Henan Province, where burials generally dated to the second quarter of the second millennium BCE have yielded some of the earliest cast bronze objects (see Map 1).[1]

Metallurgical analysis of the Erlitou wine cups shows that they were cast from a deliberate alloy of copper and tin, poured in a molten state into a mold made up of four or more fitted sections. The alloy and casting (instead of cold-working) technology evident on these vessels, as well as the mold-assembly methods, were major innovations in material use and manufacturing technique for China of the early second millennium BCE. But these first bronzes were also firmly linked to China's older, established ceramic industry. The eccentric shape of the wine cup, certainly not easily cast in bronze, was based on cups commonly made in pottery during the early second millennium BCE (fig. 1). The potter's experience in maintaining high kiln temperatures must have contributed to the bronze maker's ability to smelt, refine, and mix his ores for casting. Excavations at Erlitou habitation sites also yielded fragments of clay casting molds, further demonstrating that the early bronze casters worked closely with potters of the time.[2]

ZHENGZHOU PERIOD

The unassuming beginning exemplified by the small drinking cup (cat. 21) does not prepare us for the bronze caster's astonishing progress in the following centuries. By 1500–1400 BCE the undecorated early vessels had given way to vessels with surfaces enhanced by varied scrolled designs (cat. 22). Bronze makers must have been quick to realize the decorative potential offered by a casting technique that utilized section molds (fig. 2): it gave access to the interior surface of the mold, allowing designs to be executed with relative ease in the soft

Fig. 1. Ceramic wine cup (jue). Early second millennium BCE. Erlitou, Zhengzhou, Henan Province.

clay.[3] It is possible to incise designs into the hard surface of cold bronze, but such a technique could not have created the flowing rhythm of the many scroll designs on the early bronzes. The raised linear designs on the *fang ding* (cat. 22) embody the decorative possibilities of section-mold casting technique at their simplest: lines incised on the interiors of mold sections become raised lines (thread relief) on the cast vessel. Continuous refinement of this unique advantage offered by section molds enabled the bronze workers to create vessels with ever more ornate surfaces from circa 1300 to circa 1100 BCE (cats. 23–26).[4]

More amazing, perhaps, than the advance in decorative technique is the existence, as early as the mid-second millennium BCE, of foundries that could handle such monumental castings as the *fang ding* (cat. 22). Nor was this rectangular cauldron, which weighs about 40 kilograms and is 82 centimeters high, entirely unique in its time; it was found, in a shallow pit at Qian village, Pinglu county, Shanxi Province, with two round *ding* vessels, each about 70 centimeters high.[5] Farther east, in the vicinity of Zhengzhou, Henan Province, believed to be the site of one of the earliest capitals of the Shang dynasty,[6] three separate discoveries have unearthed eight other square or rectangular cauldrons, closely comparable to the present example in size and decoration, together with additional large round *ding* vessels.[7] The largest of these *fang ding* is 100 centimeters high and weighs 82.4 kilograms.

Differences in alloy composition and mold assembly among these *fang ding* suggest that the bronze casters were still learning and experimenting, especially with large castings. Scientific analyses of two of the Zhengzhou vessels show a fairly consistent range in the percentage of copper in the alloy, but wide fluctuations in the percentage of lead, which contributes to the viscosity—hence, ease in pouring—of the alloy.[8] Casting seams left on the vessels also suggest that different mold assemblies and casting procedures were used to make vessels of the same shape and decoration. On one Zhengzhou vessel, as in the Pinglu example (cat. 22), the four central sections of each side, the legs, and the flat bottom appear to have been precast. These were inserted into the molds for the four corner sections, and then the rest of the vessel was poured around the precast parts. Large areas of metal overflow on the four faces of the Pinglu vessel where these joints occur testify to problems in the casting. On several of the Zhengzhou vessels, one single mold section was used for each of the four sides, producing a more polished casting less marked by casting seams (compare the reconstruction in fig. 2).

ANYANG PERIOD

Sometime around 1300 BCE the Shang kings relocated their capital to the vicinity of present-day Anyang in northern Henan Province. The two centuries or so between the manufacture of the *fang ding* (cat. 22) and the bronzes associated with the court at Anyang (cats. 23–26), saw huge strides in the bronze caster's craft. By about 1200 BCE not only were China's bronze casters able to create dense, multilayered decoration on a vessel's surface, they were also able to produce vessels with complex shapes that must have challenged the ingenuity of the section-mold makers of the time. Whereas decorating the bronze surface allowed bronze casters to develop two-dimensional designs, the inherent three-dimensional form of the vessels presented opportunities to create sculpturally. For example, a fairly ordinary abstract shape—a four-sided vessel (cat. 23)—became, with the addition of a ram at each of the vessel's four corners, an inspired organic form that still fulfilled its function as a container. The rams' heads emerge as fully three-dimensional sculptures, while their chests and front legs appear in relief, rendered with astonishing realism amid a dense sea of spiral and scroll patterns. The shallow well of the large basin (cat. 29) becomes a viable pool for the coiled dragon whose three-dimensional head rises most convincingly from its two-dimensional snakelike body. These vessels are made more remarkable by their unusual size—the basin is the largest example of its kind—and by the likelihood that they were made not in the capital region of Anyang but in workshops in the remote southern and southeastern

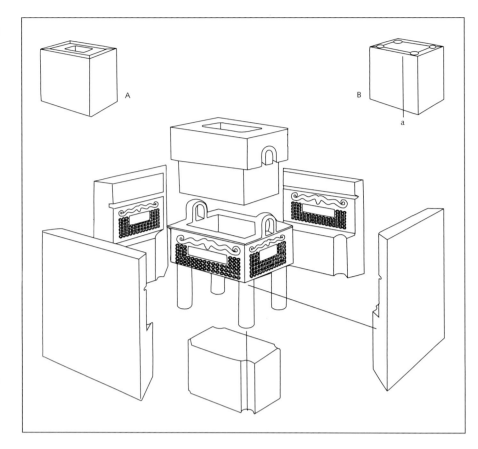

Fig. 2. Reconstruction of section-mold assembly for casting.

fringes of the Shang domain, along the Yangzi River basin.[9]

Conceptually different from vessels incorporating animal forms are two creations (cats. 27, 25) that are wholly sculptural. An accidental find in Hunan Province, south of the Yangzi River, the boar (cat. 27) is exceptional not just for its size but for its realism; its cloven hoofs, boarish snout, and tusks are all carefully observed and convincingly depicted. Even the fine scale-pattern and the large spiraling motifs on its haunches evoke the animal's hide and musculature. Unlike most bronzes of the time, the boar is not a container, and we can only surmise its function. Cylindrical channels running crosswise through the boar's front and back haunches suggest that it might have been carried, by means of poles inserted through the channels, perhaps at ceremonial processions.[10] If so, the choice of animal would have been related to the religious or ritual requirements of the local (southern) patrons for whom it was made. The elephant (cat. 25), one of only two known (the other is in the Freer Gallery of Art, Smithsonian Institution), served a better-attested function as a wine or water container.[11] Though a vessel, it too is animal-shaped; its elaborate surface motifs, however, are utterly nondescriptive of elephants. The small hare-like creature perched on top of the elephant's trunk serves no function but presents an incongruous—therefore witty—juxtaposition.

Two oddly shaped vessels (cats. 28, 24) are anomalous both as vessels and as animals. Neither accurately represents a real animal or can be linked to a specific shape in the standard vessel repertoire. The silhouette of catalogue 28 suggests a snake or a crocodile; in fact, both snakes and crocodiles appear as decorative motifs on its surface. It is likely that the creators of this vessel, excavated in the brackish semidesert region of northern Shanxi Province, in the middle reaches of the Yellow River basin, were actually familiar with these creatures.[12] The bird-shaped vessel (cat. 24) is one of a pair recovered from the late thirteenth-century BCE tomb of the Shang royal consort Fu Hao at Anyang, Henan Province.[13] It is not based on any recognizable bird, although its large hooked beak suggests that of a parrot. The ambiguity of its shape carries over onto its decoration, where visual puns and double meanings tease the eye and the imagination. Two dragons diving onto the bird's forehead double as horns; the large spirals of its wings are also coiled serpents; an owl, with distinctive eyes and beak, appears as part of the tail feathers. The small three-dimensional figures of a bird and dragon, which also serve as handles for the lid on the back of its head, seem to peer playfully between the horns.

Bronze casting expanded greatly in geographical range, in productivity, and in creativity during the last centuries of the second millennium BCE, as demonstrated both by the artifacts themselves and by their archaeological locations. The magnificent four-ram *zun* (cat. 23) and the bronze boar (cat. 27) were found south of the Yangzi River in Hunan Province; so were the elephant-shaped vessel (cat. 25) and the bail-handled covered container (*you*; cat. 26).[14] The large basin (cat. 29) came from the lower Yangzi River basin in southeastern China, the serpentine vessel (cat. 28) from a site just south of the Great Wall in northwestern China. In the quality of their workmanship some of these vessels are virtually indistinguishable from the best products of the capital region of Anyang. Some, like the elephant or the *you*, may have come from the area of Anyang; others may have been made by regional workshops according to local tastes or ritual needs (cats. 27–29).

Other artifacts from the Yangzi River valley, like the drum (*gu*; cat. 34) which was a chance find in Chongyang county, Hubei Province, further attest to locally distinctive bronze-casting traditions in the peripheral regions. It is one of only two bronze drums known, both distinctly southern in style. Bronze drums may have played a special part in the rites and rituals of the south.[15] No bronze drums have yet been recovered along the Yellow River basin, although drums made from humbler materials such as earthenware and wood were in use there.[16] The loose design of spirals on the present drum suggests a relatively early date of manufacture (ca. 1500–1300 BCE); if correct, this means that local bronze-casting workshops were in operation in the south at about the same time as their northern counterparts in the Shang heartland along the Yellow River basin.

Dramatic evidence of the geographical extent of southern bronze casting and the skills of the casters has been afforded by recent discovery of two sacrificial pits, containing bronzes dated to the late second millennium BCE, at Sanxingdui, Guanghan county, Sichuan Province in southwestern China.[17] The Sanxingdui pits and Fu Hao's tomb at Anyang are closely contemporary but about eight hundred miles apart, and the bronzes from the two sites differ strikingly in type, form, and size (fig. 3). The impressive bronze mask (cat. 30), the largest of three recovered at Guanghan, has no parallel elsewhere in China. Its function and context of use are unclear, its form and size unprecedented, and the meaning of its extraordinary projecting pupils is a mystery. That they had special meaning for the society that created them is evident from the extra effort required to produce them. Projecting a startling distance from the face, the pupils appear to have been precast, then inserted into the mold for the rest of the face, which was cast around them in a second pour of metal. In the use of precast elements, as well as in its monumental size, this casting is reminiscent of similarly ambitious products of northern workshops, such as the large *fang ding* (cat. 22) discussed above. The rectangular slot at the center of the forehead may have held an extension, perhaps resembling the long scrolled projection fitted on one of the other two masks.[18] Clearly the people who commissioned the bizarre bronzes at Guanghan and buried them together with a rich assortment of bronze, jade, and ivory objects in two large pits (not tombs) were masters of a bronze-casting technology closely comparable to that of their counterparts farther north in the Yellow River basin. Although the bronze casters of the lower Yellow River basin may have been the first to explore, develop, and eventually achieve high standards in bronze casting, it was the distant workshops that seem to have tested the limits of the technology by attempting eccentric shapes, unorthodox decoration, and gigantic castings.

WESTERN ZHOU PERIOD

It was precisely one of these distant centers of power, one located in the middle and upper Yellow River basin, that eventually overcame the Shang kings at Anyang about 1100 BCE. The conquerors, whose homeland spanned present-day Gansu and Shaanxi provinces, established the Zhou dynasty, locating its capital in the easternmost part of their realm, near present-day Xi'an.[19] Not only did the Zhou adopt Shang rituals and customs and

bovine horns on the lid; coiled serpents on the shoulders; beasts with large coiled bodies below; and realistic recumbent buffalo on the foot; all rendered in varying relief against a fine spiral ground.

Similar features can also be seen within the Zhou realm, on bronzes excavated near Baoji county, Shaanxi Province, datable to the first hundred or more years of Zhou rule (ca. 1100–ca. 950 BCE). Comparable energy and power are exuded by the massive hooked flanges and bold *taotie* with outward-spiraling horns on the vessel for liquids (*zun*; cat. 32),[22] the intimidating bovine horns on the base of the food container (*gui*; cat. 35),[23] and the exuberant arrays of real and imaginary creatures on both the *gui* and the rectangular *gong* (cat. 36).[24] Zhou bronze casters exploited the hooked flanges on the *zun* (cat. 32) for maximum effect by deliberately extending them beyond the rim—the overhangs were separately cast and attached to the existing flanges by additional pours of metal. The massiveness of this vessel is not purely visual: unusually heavy for a vessel of its size, it weighs 14.78 kilograms. The same complexity of manufacture characterizes the above-mentioned *gui* and *gong*: on the *gui*, intricate mold assembly for the projecting bovine horns, precast, multianimal handles, and a small bell attached to the underside of its base; on the *gong*, the three-dimensional, down-curving horns of the creature that forms the lid. The new aesthetic requirements of early Zhou patrons continued to push bronze casters to the limits of their skills, and with surpassing results.

Fig.3. Bronze standing figure. Late second millennium BCE. Sanxingdui, Guanghan, Sichuan Province.

continue to require the bronze casters' services, their patronage infused new life into a tradition by then over five hundred years old. The Zhou brought with them a liberating flamboyance most certainly influenced by the eccentric creations from the south, southwest, and southeast.[20] Vessels in this exhibition dating from the early part of Zhou rule (ca. 1100–ca. 1000 BCE) illustrate some of these distinctive Zhou features (cats. 31, 32, 35, 41).

The container for liquids (*lei*; cat. 31), found far from the Zhou realm in a cache in Zhuwajie, Peng county, Sichuan Province, is an outstanding example of Zhou's invigorating effect on bronze design.[21] Vessels of equally imposing size were made by the Shang casters, but the bold elephant-trunk handles and the ferociously hooked flanges running from lid to foot create a bristling silhouette that is assertively different from the monumental *lei* vessels of the Shang. Its surface decoration augments this effect with a host of new motifs: *taotie* (semiabstract zoomorphic motifs) with almost freestanding

Besides introducing new aesthetics and motifs, the Zhou conquest also appears to have brought a change in ritual practices that presented a different set of problems to the Zhou bronze caster.[25] The *gong* (cat. 36), dating from the early tenth century BCE, formed a set with two other vessels, each different in shape but identical in design and bearing the same forty-character inscription inside.[26] The rectangular container (*fang yi*; cat. 41) from the late tenth century BCE is also part of a set of three vessels different in shape but identical in surface decoration and inscription.[27] Zhou nobles, prompted perhaps by religious customs or ritual requirements at court, seem to have been the first group to require sets of vessels with matching designs, shapes, or dedicatory inscriptions. By the early ninth century BCE, when the large container for liquid (*hu*; cat. 39) and its mate were made, large sets of bronze vessels, often carrying matching dedicatory inscriptions and comprising a narrow range of shapes and designs, had become the norm.[28] This development, which required that the bronze caster produce virtual duplicates (often in decoration and sometimes in shape), presented new demands on an industry that, up to then, had only been making one-of-a-kind bronzes.

The increase in sets of vessels with long inscriptions associating them to certain noble families or clans is symptomatic of a political development during the ninth and eighth centuries BCE: the declining power of the Zhou kings and the increasing autonomy of the nobles in their respective domains surrounding the Zhou court. To appear appropriately equipped with the trappings of authority, ambitious dukes and princes began commissioning sets of bronze vessels to display as symbols of power at important rituals and state occasions. The spouted pitcher (*he*; cat. 38) and the food container (*gui*; cat. 39) unearthed at the city of Pingdingshan, central Henan Province, signify this new demand.[29] Both vessels carry inscriptions linking them with the small state of Ying, which fell to rivals sometime in the fifth century BCE. The wealth of bronzes associated with the Ying state at this site has been matched by the rich finds associated with various other principalities, attesting to an overall sharp rise in demand. The bronze-casting industry had to improve production methods, not simply to make duplicate vessels but also to increase output as required by its expanding clientele.[30]

EASTERN ZHOU PERIOD

In 770 BCE the Zhou kings lost their western capital at Xi'an to marauding nomads and fled to their eastern capital near present-day Luoyang, Henan Province. Their shrunken power accelerated the fracturing of the realm into powerful aristocratic states, with concomitant explosive rise in the demand on the bronze industry. This political decentralization must have been responsible in part for the radical changes that took place in workshop organization and production methods of the bronze-casting industry by the seventh and sixth centuries BCE. A large sixth–fifth–century bronze foundry site, under excavation at the city of Houma, southern Shanxi Province, since the 1950s, has yielded workshop debris that hints at techniques capable of meeting all requirements—sets of ritual vessels matching in shape and/or decoration, vastly increased scale of production, foreign exotica, and everyday needs—without sacrificing the high-level workmanship that court and noble patrons had come to expect.[31]

Foundry debris at Houma suggested a production process organized according to specialization and division of labor. The multistep processes of shaping, decorating, and assembling the clay molds, as well as the manufacture of different types of bronzes (both ritual and utilitarian), probably took place in separate areas of the workshop compound, with different groups of workers contributing specific skills toward the final product. Most compelling of all the finds at Houma were the thousands of pieces of decorated clay foundry debris, suggesting the ways in which surface

Fig. 4. Clay model of decorative design for casting. Late 6th–early 5th century BCE. Niucun, Houma, Shanxi Province.

decoration and appendages such as handles, lids, and other decorative accents were made. It seems that some kind of master pattern system was used, so that the same decor units could be variously combined into vessels of diverse shapes, sizes, and designs. A complex multistep decor replication process required taking repeated clay negatives from a single positive model, which served as a master unit (fig. 4). This process made possible identical repeated patterns on a vessel (fig. 4), or identical handles, legs, or decorative appendages on a single vessel. For sets of bronzes in graduated sizes, a series of similarly graduated master units could produce appropriately sized but otherwise identical handles or accents (fig. 5).[32] With a wide variety of master patterns at the workshop's disposal, the decor possibilities were virtually unlimited.

The four-sided vessel (*fang hu*; cat. 43) was likely a product of the Houma workshops. It forms a set with three other identical vessels, recovered from the rich tomb of a noble of the Jin state at Jinsheng village, outside Taiyuan, the capital of Shanxi Province (see also cat. 44).[33] As a measure of the bronze caster's facility in replicating vessel shapes and decoration in a variety of sizes and designs, the tomb that yielded these four *hu* also contained matching sets, but in graduated sizes, of seven and six tripod vessels (*ding*); a set of eight matching stemmed and covered food containers (*dou*); four basins (*jian*); and two sets of bells (*bo*), five in one set and fourteen in the other (fig. 6). Detailed studies of a *hu* in the Freer Gallery of Art, Smithsonian Institution, demonstrated that the continuously interlacing dragon and twisted-rope designs on such vessels were actually replicated from just four or five master pattern units, each repeated as necessary to compose a given register of decoration (fig. 7).[34] Similarly repeated pattern units form the designs on the interior and exterior of the rectangular basin (*pan*; cat. 48). The first-rate workmanship possible on bronzes decorated by

Fig. 5. Drawing of clay molds in graduated sizes for casting bosses on bronze bells of graduated sizes. Late 6th–early 5th century BCE. Niucun, Houma, Shanxi Province. (Drawings by Li Xiating [Shanxi Institute of Archaeology]).

such a process of replication is illustrated by the Freer *hu* and the Palace Museum basin. The densely multilayered and interlacing designs that typify this production method may have been developed in conjunction with it, the better to camouflage the joins between pattern units, as well as the minor adjustments for fit that may become necessary as the units are repeated on vessels of different curvatures, circumferences, and shapes.

The sixth- and fifth-century BCE workshops that produced these bronzes had progressed well beyond the twelfth- and eleventh-century Shang foundries that made individual bronzes, each from its own set of hand-carved clay molds. A section-mold maker at an Anyang foundry would probably have had to have a fair idea of the shape, size, and decoration of his finished vessel. A model or mold maker at the Houma foundry would probably have been familiar with only that element of the vessel for which he was responsible—a lid or a handle or a foot or a unit of decoration—but not with the completed object. In the late sixth- to early fifth-century bronze foundry at Houma one can see perhaps the source of the streamlined division of labor and mass-production techniques associated with the renowned Ming and Qing dynasty porcelain workshops operating at Jingdezhen, Jiangxi Province, nearly two thousand years later (see essays by Wang Qingzheng and Regina Krahl in this volume).

Cultural diversity and increased contact among the divers cultures, along with social and political mobility, proved to be major invigorating forces for the bronze industry through the end of the first millennium BCE. Sculptural bronzes and animal appendages on bronze vessels continued to be major provincial features (cats. 33, 37, 38, 55–58). The spouted vessel (*he*; cat. 38),[35] from a tenth-century BCE context in the city of Pingdingshan, central Henan Province, quaintly borrowed the

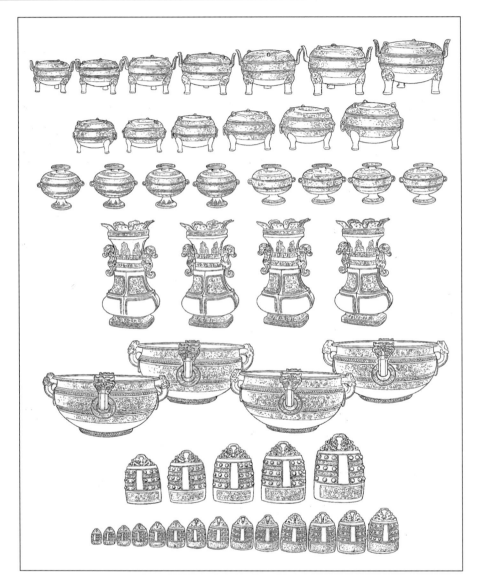

Fig. 6. Drawing of sets of bronze vessels (4 hu, 6 and 7 ding, 8 dou, 4 jian, 5 and 14 bo) from Jinshengcun, Taiyuan, Shanxi Province. Late 6th–early 5th century BCE. (Drawings by Li Xiating [Shanxi Institute of Archaeology]).

duck-shaped spout characteristic of ceramic *he* vessels from the southeastern coastal provinces of Jiangsu and Zhejiang, while retaining the more traditional Zhou shape, handle, and legs (fig. 8). The endearingly awkward elephant-shaped vessel (cat. 37) from Rujiazhuang, Baoji county, Shaanxi Province, is a tenth-century BCE local descendant of the boar- and elephant-shaped bronzes of a few centuries earlier (cats. 27, 25).[36] On the

*Fig. 7. Container for liquids (*hu*). Early 5th century* BCE. *Bronze. Freer Gallery of Art, Smithsonian Institution, Washington, D.C. (57.22).*

*Fig. 8. Covered spouted server (*he*). 11th–10th century* BCE. *Bronze. Freer Gallery of Art, Smithsonian Institution, Washington, D.C. (33.2).*

Rujiazhuang elephant the elaborate surface decoration of the earlier vessels has dwindled to a large spiral above each leg, no doubt intended to suggest rippling musculature but appearing essentially ornamental. The animal's head, however, is rendered with considerable realism.

The bronze bell (*bo*; cat. 33) represents a group of bells with similar decoration that date from the late tenth century BCE and are now in various Chinese and Western collections.[37] Like bronze drums (cat. 34), bronze bells are closely identified with the Yangzi River basin, having a continuous history of use and production there since the late second millennium BCE.[38] By the tenth century BCE, however, they had penetrated the Zhou court, where sets of large bronze bells began to appear as important components of ritual regalia. Despite the integration of the bells into mainstream Zhou tradition, many of their southern characteristics persisted, particularly the use of animal decoration, such as the four tigers climbing down the sides of the bell, or the bird at the top of the flange in the center.

Other peripheral regions also contributed to metropolitan bronze designs, as exemplified in an unusual lopsided vessel (cat. 44). Part of the large group of bronzes unearthed from the same Jin noble's tomb that contained catalogue 43, this flask with asymmetrical profile and bird-shaped lid

illustrates the ancient Jin state's contact with nomadic peoples living in the area north of today's Great Wall.[39] Its peculiar shape was probably inspired by the animal-skin flasks carried by hunters and herders who lived along ancient China's northern and western borders, an antecedent more clearly illustrated by a plain bronze example recovered in northern Hebei Province (fig. 9).[40] Its surface decoration, however, was drawn from the standard late sixth-century BCE Chinese decorative repertoire, and its workmanship is typical of Jin state bronzes. Such bronze vessels were probably made in Jin or similar workshops as exotica for their noble patrons, and occasionally to be presented as gifts to leaders of northern tribes.

One of these northern tribes, known in Chinese historical texts as the Di, actually settled south of the Great Wall in the fourth century BCE, founding the small and short-lived state of Zhongshan just south of Beijing. The multiarmed lamp in the shape of a tree (cat. 54), together with a rich assortment of bronzes that reflect the tribe's northern heritage, came from the tomb of a Zhongshan king who died at the end of the fourth century BCE.[41] In this lamp eight monkeys, perceptively—even affectionately— portrayed, scamper about and hang from the tree branches, as two bare-chested fellows below appear to be cajoling the monkeys, ready to catch whatever may be flung to them. Two centuries later the elaborate fittings on the

Fig. 9. Flask. 6th century BCE. *Lijiazhuang, Xingtang county, Hebei Province.*

canopied carriages of Western Han princes reveal the continuing Chinese fascination with these border tribes: a mounted hunter executing a Parthian shot at a leaping tiger behind him, and topknotted foreigners riding elephants and camels (cat. 49; see also cat. 51).[42] This exotic iconography is further enhanced by lavish inlays of gold, silver, and turquoise, colors that might have approximated the brightly appliquéd felts and other fabrics worn by the northern peoples.[43]

The bronze casters of south China, whose repertoire of masks, drums, and bells, and preference for sculptural ornament on vessels, contrast so strikingly with the bronze conventions of the heartland, attained new heights during the late first millennium BCE. Three exceptional bronzes (cats. 45, 46, 52) can be associated with the state of Chu, the most powerful ruling house to emerge south of the Yangzi River in the second half of the millennium. Chu's exoticism differs from that of the north, featuring intricate baroque forms and fantastic, serpentine imagery.[44] The sinuous creatures with elaborate horns that support the large, early sixth-century BCE vessel (cat. 45) are close relatives of the pair of slightly later, malachite-encrusted beasts, one of which is represented here (cat. 46).[45] The rhythms generated by the sinuous body, animated pose, lolling tongue, and spiraling horns of the fabulous animal amplify the more subtle rhythms produced by the interlaced pattern and sculptural appendages on the earlier vessel (cat. 45). A kneeling humanoid, biting one snake as

he grips two more in his hands (cat. 52), is one of two such corner fittings that supported a lacquer screen found in a tomb at Guangzhou, Guangdong Province, just north of Hong Kong. This fabulous creature demonstrates Chu's far-reaching geographical and temporal influence on the bronze maker's art.

Successful production of these intertwining and curvilinear forms posed a new challenge to bronze casters trained in section-mold casting techniques. Although the main body of the *hu* vessel and of the fabulous inlaid beast were still cast using mold sections, like myriad bronzes before them, the gyrating, spiraling horns of the appended creatures on the *hu* were made with a little-used technique: lost-wax casting. Compared with the millennium-old section-mold casting technique, lost-wax casting is an easier way to cast complex three-dimensional shapes and decorations. The technique starts with a wax model of the shape to be made; because wax is soft and pliable, this shape can be as intricate as desired (fig. 10). After the model is encased in clay, the whole assembly is heated so that the wax melts away through vents left for this purpose, leaving a cavity inside that exactly duplicates the model. Molten bronze is then poured into this cavity. When the bronze has cooled, the clay mold is broken open to reveal the final product in cast bronze. This technique appeared in China sometime during the sixth century BCE, used primarily to cast complex decorative appendages on Chu bronzes (like the horns on cats. 45 and 46); it may have been prompted by the special demands of Chu aesthetics.[46]

WESTERN HAN PERIOD

By the late second century BCE, when the screen support (cat. 52) was made, lost-wax casting was widely used in both metropolitan and regional workshops to produce large, intricately shaped or sculptural bronzes (cats. 50, 53, 55–58). The exquisite gold-inlaid incense burner (cat. 50) belonging to the Western Han prince Liu Sheng is a handsome product of metropolitan workshops.[47] The frank realism and exotic imagery of the bronzes from the Dian kingdom in Yunnan Province, in southwestern China, illustrate the foreign heritage of its people and the huge distances that separated them, culturally and artistically as well as geographically, from the Han court (cats. 55–58).[48] The Dian peoples wore fitted trousers and short tunics typical of horse-riding tribes of Central Asia and seemed to delight in animated (perhaps even rowdy) dancing (cat. 56).[49] Bulls appear to have held a significant place in Dian ritual and sacrifice (cat. 57); and the brutality of war was apparently acknowledged, perhaps even gloried in (cat. 55). These Dian bronzes were all made with the lost-wax casting technique. In subsequent

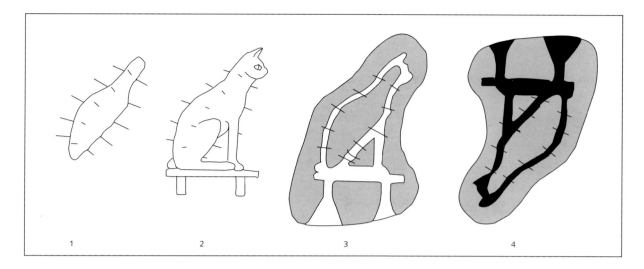

Fig. 10. Reconstruction of mold assembly for lost-wax casting.

centuries systematic refinement of this latest technical innovation allowed bronze casters to produce the myriad Buddhist and secular gilt bronzes of the Tang dynasty (cats. 160, 169) as well as such spectacular creations as flying dragons (cat. 59).

Lost-wax casting constituted a major technical innovation of the first millennium BCE, but by no means the only one. Continued intermingling of new ideas from different parts of China stimulated a variety of new decorative techniques. One of these was the use of color. Whereas the decoration of bronze surfaces had previously been monochromatic, accomplished solely with patterning, the bronzes might now be inlaid with gold, silver, and semiprecious stones (cats. 46, 49, 50), gilded with mercury amalgam (cats. 51, 52, 56), or simply painted with pigments, among other devices (cat. 53). These colorfully decorated bronzes kept the industry healthy and productive well into the first centuries CE, despite rising competition from the lustrous jades, colorful lacquers, and embroidered silks that had begun to capture the hearts and budgets of wealthy elite patrons.[50]

Local and peripheral traditions were not the sole sources of challenge and inspiration for bronze casters of the first millennium BCE. Deliberate archaism resurrected orthodox Shang and Zhou styles. Although the four-sided wine vessel (*fang hu*; cat. 43) dates from the early fifth century BCE, its shape, paneled design, and petaled crown represent deliberate echoes of a vessel type popular during the ninth and eighth centuries BCE.[51] Echoes of past traditions continued to figure in bronze designs of the late first millennium BCE, contributing to their already complex artistic character and meaning.[52]

A third driving force behind the creativity of the first millennium BCE had little connection either

with the somber rituals of the Shang and Zhou courts, with longstanding artistic traditions, or with particular local customs. The miniature carriage, a box on wheels (cat. 42) dating from the eighth century BCE, is an early hint of this new force.[53] This remarkable object is ingeniously designed with fifteen moving parts: six turning wheels; four hinged openings (on top and at one end); a sliding door bolt; and four pivoting birds. The one-legged doorkeeper might have been chosen specifically for his handicap, for he could not easily make off with the treasures he is guarding. The carriage's clever design, movable parts, and miniature size all suggest that this was a toy. Perhaps it and other miniatures found in the same context were indeed toys, the idle elite's playthings or collectibles—perhaps even containers for precious memorabilia.

Demand for similar utilitarian or luxurious secular items flourished by the end of the first millennium BCE (cats. 49, 51, 52, 56). The crowning achievements in this category must be the bronze lamps made in the last centuries BCE (cats. 53, 54). Never meant as funerary paraphernalia or as ritual implements, bronze lamps were strictly functional furnishings in affluent households. Some, like the multiarmed lamp (cat. 54), performed their function simply by supplying effective lighting through a delightful shape; others, like the lamp in the shape of a goose (cat. 53), are dazzlingly ingenious, even ecologically minded designs. As the wick burns inside the cylinder on the goose's back, the vertical panels that form the cylinder may be slid back and forth so as to throw the light anywhere within 360 degrees. The smoke from the burning oil rises up into the fish-shaped cover and thence to the neck of the goose; from there it descends into the goose's hollow body, which has been filled with water to absorb the smoke. This keeps the room free of smoke and smell.[54] Han dynasty householders were clearly as mindful of the air they breathed as we are today.

TANG PERIOD

Even surpassing the extravagant luxury goods of the Han court were those made for the ruling class of the Tang dynasty (618–907). Both the Han and Tang courts shared the blessings of a stable, unified realm whose expansive territory reached far into Central Asia, bringing trade and tribute from the westernmost end of the Silk Road to the Tang capital (see Map 2). The Tang court was grand, cosmopolitan, and sophisticated, and the luxury goods of the Tang ruling elite reflected these qualities. Exotic goods, peoples, and customs poured into the capital at Chang'an (modern Xi'an), endowing Tang society with a rich multiculturalism unsurpassed before or since.[55] Bronze, the preeminent luxury material of the previous two thousand years, was no longer the choicest substance, even at times being used for funerary goods like its more common ceramic counterparts. Gilt bronze continued, however, to hold a special place in Buddhist contexts (cats. 160, 169), and the magnificent gilt-bronze dragon (cat. 59) is exceptional in any context.[56] This dragon, which is over 34 centimeters long, has an awesome presence; with its hind legs and tail flung high in the air and its front legs held taut, it seems as if it had just touched down. The function of this remarkable object remains a mystery, since the circumstances of its discovery provide no clue to its use or context. As an emblem of the power of the Tang empire, both at home and abroad, this flying dragon is unmatched.

Instead of bronze, the preeminent status metals throughout the Tang period were gold and silver (cats. 60–65). Among the peoples of ancient Central and West Asia glittering precious metals had long held pride of place, and their prestige at the Tang court was a direct result of prolonged contact with these peoples along the Silk Road.[57] Two caches recovered in recent years in Xi'an illustrate the best of this new medium in Tang times. The treasures sealed in the foundation of the Famen Temple pagoda in 874 reveal the exalted status of gold and silver in religious and imperial rituals (cats. 64, 65).[58] The rich assortment of tea utensils from the trove illustrate that tea drinking and its associated rituals and ceremonies had noble connotations in Tang imperial, literati, and Buddhist circles (fig. 11). The rarified custom of storing processed tea in the form of hardened cakes is revealed by the openwork basket (cat. 64) used to keep the cakes dry until they were ground for brewing. Among the tea utensils, articles like the salt caddy (cat. 65) confirm practices previously known only from texts, such as adding salt and spices to tea to reduce its bitterness.

The three gilded silver plates (cats. 60–62) were part of a cache of 270 gold and silver objects, foreign coins, and jades (cat. 20) stuffed into two large pottery urns and buried at Hejia village, south of Xi'an, perhaps by a noble family fleeing the Tang capital to escape the rebel An Lushan in 755.[59] The

Fig. 11. Group of gilded silver tea utensils and Buddhist ritual objects. 9th century CE. Famen Temple, Xi'an, Shaanxi Province.

animals highlighted inside these plates came from a variety of cultural backgrounds: the fabulous, single-horned winged horse (cat. 60) recalls the similar creature of West Asian myths; the bear (cat. 61) belongs to the northern forests; and the foxes (cat. 62) may have been inspired by Chinese folk tales. These repoussé motifs and hammered shapes came to China with foreign silversmiths and their wares, but they left a lasting influence on China's native lacquer and ceramic industries. Their metallic shapes and relief decoration were adopted on Tang and Song lacquers and glazed ceramics (cats. 133, 138).

During the two thousand years from the creation of the first crudely made cast-bronze vessels of the early second millennium BCE to the exquisite bronze and silver objects of the Tang dynasty, China's metalworkers invented, developed, and perfected the casting of bronzes using section molds, exploited as necessary new casting (lost-wax) and decorative techniques (inlaying, gilding), and eventually also acquired and mastered the foreign techniques of cold-working silver and gold. A multitude of forces—political, cultural, social, and religious—contributed to these changes and developments over time. The cornucopia of beautiful objects they produced remains as evidence of their remarkable achievements.

SOURCES FOR FIGURES
Fig. 1. After Cream of the Pottery from Erlitou *(Beijing: Social Sciences Press, 1995), no. 161.*

Fig. 2. After W. Thomas Chase, Ancient Chinese Bronze Art: Casting the Precious Vessel *(New York: China House Gallery, 1981), fig. 1.*

Fig.3. After Zhongguo wenwu jinghua *(Beijing: Wenwu chubanshe, 1990), no. 30.*

Fig. 4. After Houma zhutong yizhi *(Beijing: Wenwu chubanshe, 1993), pl. 153:3.*

Fig. 9. After Hebei sheng chutu wenwu xuanji *(Beijing: Wenwu chubanshe, 1980), no. 159.*

Fig. 10. After Henry Hodges, Artifacts *(London: 1976), p. 72, fig. 10.*

Fig. 11. After Xi'an: Legacies of Ancient Chinese Civilization *(Beijing: Morning Glory Press, 1992), p. 176.*

NOTES
1. *Kaogu*, no. 5 (1975), pl. 9, p. 2; and Henan sheng wenwu yanjiusuo, ed., *Henan kaogu sishinian (1952–1992)* (Zhengzhou: Henan renmin chubanshe, 1994), p. 176. For calibrated carbon-14 dates ranging between 1900 and 1500 BCE obtained from wood remains at the site, see *Kaogu*, no. 10 (1983), pp. 923–28; and Institute of Archaeology, ed., *Radiocarbon Dates in Chinese Archaeology (1965–1991)* (Beijing: Wenwu chubanshe, 1991).

2. Henan sheng wenwu, *Henan kaogu sishinian*, p. 174.

3. Much of the discussion here and in subsequent sections regarding the relationship between early bronze casting and the pottery industry is treated in greater detail in Robert Bagley, *Shang Ritual Bronzes in the Arthur M. Sackler Collections*, Ancient Chinese Bronzes from the Arthur M. Sackler Collections, vol. 1 (Washington, D.C. and Cambridge, Mass.: Arthur M. Sackler Foundation and Arthur M. Sackler Museum, Harvard University Press, 1987); and Robert Bagley, "Shang Ritual Bronzes: Casting Technique and Vessel Design," *Archives of Asian Art* 43 (1990), pp. 6–20.

4. A detailed periodization, based on increasing ornateness of surface decoration, was first proposed by Max Loehr in "The Bronze Styles of the Anyang Period," *Archives of the Chinese Art Society of America* 7 (1953), pp. 42–53; it was further developed by Bagley in *Shang Ritual Bronzes in the Sackler Collections*, secs. 1.3–1.8, 1.10, 2.1–2.5.

5. *Wenwu jikan*, no. 1 (1992), pp. 18–19.

6. Henan sheng wenwu yanjiusuo, ed., *Zhengzhou Shang kaogu xin faxian yu yanjiu (1985–1992)* (Zhengzhou: Zhongzhou guji chubanshe, 1993); discussions regarding the historical significance of the site are summarized in Henan sheng wenwu, *Henan kaogu sishininan*, pp. 201–4.

7. Of these eight fang ding, two are published in *Wenwu*, no. 6 (1975), pp. 64–68, the larger of which is also illustrated in Wen Fong, ed., *The Great Bronze Age of China* (New York: Metropolitan Museum of Art, 1980), no. 11; two more, identical in size and recovered in 1982, are published in *Wenwu*, no. 3 (1983), pp. 49–59; and the remaining four (83, 75, 64, and 59 cm. high, respectively), found in 1996, are published in *Zhongguo wenwubao*, 21 April 1996. All, including the present example (cat. 22), were discovered in caches, not burials.

8. One vessel showed only 0.1 percent lead, while another contained 17 percent lead; see *Wenwu*, no. 3 (1983), p. 59.

9. For cat. 29, see *Zhongguo wenwu jinghua* (Beijing: Wenwu chubanshe, 1993), no. 70; for cat. 23, a chance find in 1938 at Yueshangpu, Ningxiang county, Hunan Province, see *Kaogu*, no. 12 (1963), p. 648. For a detailed discussion, including arguments for its likely local manufacture, see Fong, ed., *Great Bronze Age*, no. 20, chap. 3.

10. *Hunan kaogu jikan*, no. 1 (1982), pp. 19–20.

11. For cat. 25, see *Wenwu*, no. 7 (1976), pp. 49–50; both examples are discussed in Fong, ed., *Great Bronze Age*, no. 24.

12. *Wenwu*, no. 7 (1960), pp. 50–52; the find is also discussed in connection with Fong, ed., *Great Bronze Age*, no. 21.

13. The excavation is reported in full in *Yinxu Fu Hao mu* (Beijing: Wenwu chubanshe, 1980); this vessel, the tomb, and some of the other bronzes are also discussed in detail in Fong, ed., *Great Bronze Age*, pp. 177–81, nos. 28–33; and in Jessica Rawson, *Mysteries of Ancient China* (London: British Museum Press, 1996), pp. 90–105.

14. *Wenwu*, no. 1 (1972), pp. 6–7; also discussed in Fong, ed., *Great Bronze Age*, no. 25.

15. *Wenwu*, no. 4 (1978), p. 94; also in Fong, ed., *Great Bronze Age*, no. 18. The other, in the Sen'oku Hakkokan, Kyoto, is discussed in Fong, ed., *Great Bronze Age*, no. 18.

16. For earthenware drums, see Rawson, ed., *Mysteries of Ancient China*, no. 8; for evidence of wooden drums, see *Kaogu*, no. 1 (1983), pl. 6:5, pp. 37–39. A pictographic inscription on a *fang lei* from Luoyang, Henan Province, shows two hands, each holding up a club to a drum on a stand: see Luoyang Cultural Relics Team, ed., *Luoyang chutu wenwu jisui* (Beijing: Zhaohua chubanshe, 1990), no. 3, indicating that the type, in bronze or another material, was certainly not unknown along the Yellow River basin.

17. See Robert Bagley, "A Shang City in Sichuan Province," *Orientations* (November 1990), pp. 52–67. Selected bronzes from the Guanghan cache are also discussed in Rawson, ed., *Mysteries of Ancient China*, nos. 22–32. A general discussion of southern bronzes is in Robert Bagley, "Changjiang Bronzes and Shang Archaeology," *Proceedings, International Colloquium on Chinese Art History, 1991,*

Antiquities, Pt. 1 (Taipei: National Palace Museum, 1992), pp. 209–55.

18. Rawson, ed., *Mysteries of Ancient China*, no. 25.

19. Fong, ed., *Great Bronze Age*, chap. 5.

20. Jessica Rawson, *Western Zhou Ritual Bronzes from the Arthur M. Sackler Collections*, Ancient Chinese Bronzes from the Arthur M. Sackler Collections, vols. IIA, IIB (New York and Cambridge: Arthur M. Sackler Foundation and Arthur M. Sackler Museum, Harvard University, 1990), sect. 2.3.

21. This *lei* was found with three other similar vessels and fifteen bronze weapons inside a large pottery urn without signs of an accompanying burial: see *Kaogu*, no. 6 (1981), pp. 496–99; also published in *Zhongguo wenwu jinghua* (Beijing: Wenwu chubanshe, 1990), no. 47. An earlier cache, likewise with no signs of accompanying burial, found in 1959, contained five similar *lei*, two other bronze vessels, and thirteen weapons; see *Wenwu*, no. 11 (1961), pp. 28–31.

22. Found in 1963 in Baoji county, Shaanxi Province; *Wenwu*, no. 1 (1966), p. 4; *Wenwu*, no. 1 (1976), pp. 60, 66, 93; see also Fong, ed., *Great Bronze Age*, no. 42.

23. A detailed report of the tomb that yielded this vessel is in Lu Liancheng and Hu Zhisheng, *Baoji Yu Guo mudi*, 2 vols. (Beijing: Wenwu chubanshe, 1988); see also *Zhongguo wenwu jinghua* (Beijing: Wenwu chubanshe, 1993), no. 74.

24. The *gong* is part of a cache of 103 bronzes discovered in 1976 at Zhuangbai, Fufeng county, Shaanxi Province. See *Wenwu*, no. 3 (1978), pp. 1–24, 42; see also Fong, ed., *Great Bronze Age*, no. 45.

25. For a discussion of the "ritual revolution" during the Zhou period, see Rawson, *Western Zhou Ritual Bronzes*, chap. 4; and Jessica Rawson and Emma C. Bunker, *Ancient Chinese and Ordos Bronzes*

(Hong Kong: The Oriental Society of Hong Kong, 1990), pp. 32–38.

26. The other two vessels in the set—a *zun* and a *fang yi*—are illustrated in *Shaanxi chutu Shang Zhou qingtongqi: 2* (Beijing: Wenwu chubanshe, 1980), nos. 15–16.

27. This set and three additional bronzes formed part of a cache discovered at Qijiacun, Fufeng county, Shaanxi Province, in 1964; see *Shaanxi chutu Shang*, nos. 120–25.

28. The pair is published in *Shaanxi chutu Shang*, nos. 31–32. Part of a cache of 103 bronzes unearthed in 1976 at Zhuangbai, Fufeng county, Shaanxi Province, the name "Xing" mentioned in the inscription of this *hu* also occurs on 32 other bronzes from the hoard; see *Wenwu*, no. 3 (1978), pp. 1–24; and *Shaanxi chutu Shang*, nos. 27–43.

29. The finds at Pingdingshan, made over a period in the late 1980s, have yet to be systematically published. For the *he*, see *Zhongguo wenwu jinghua*, no. 49; for the *gui*, see *Zhongguo wenwu jinghua*, no. 79; both are also published in the brief report on the excavations in *Zhongguo wenwubao*, 1 September 1996.

30. For examples of bronzes associated with various states, see Rawson, *Western Zhou Ritual Bronzes*, chap. 4; Jenny F. So, *Eastern Zhou Ritual Bronzes from the Arthur M. Sackler Collections*, Ancient Chinese Bronzes from the Arthur M. Sackler Collections, vol. 3 (New York and Washington, D.C.: Arthur M. Sackler Foundation and Arthur M. Sackler Gallery, Smithsonian Institution, 1995), chaps. 2–3; and Jay Xu, "The Cemetery of the Western Zhou Lords of Jin," *Artibus Asiae* 56, nos. 3/4 (1996), pp. 193–231.

31. See So, *Eastern Zhou Ritual Bronzes*, app. 1:4G for an account of the site and its excavation nearly forty years ago; also Li Xiating and Liang Ziming, *The Art of the Houma Foundry* (bilingual), with introduction and English text

by Jay Xu, ed. Robert Bagley (Princeton: Princeton University Press, 1996).

32. More detailed discussions of these new foundry techniques are in So, *Eastern Zhou Ritual Bronzes*, chap. 4.2; and Robert Bagley, "Replication Techniques in Eastern Chou Bronze Casting," in Steven Lubar and W. David Kingery, eds., *History from Things: Essays on Material Culture* (Washington, D.C. and London: Smithsonian Institution, 1993), pp. 234–41.

33. *Wenwu*, no. 9 (1989), cpl. 2:1; see also no. 213.1; So, *Eastern Zhou Ritual Bronzes*, chap. 4.2 and app. 1:4G for a detailed discussion of the tomb.

34. See Barbara W. Keyser, "Decor Replication in Two Late Chou Bronze *Chien*," *Ars Orientalis* 11 (1979), pp. 127–62; and Robert Bagley, "What the Bronzes from Hunyuan Tell Us about the Foundry at Houma," *Orientations* (July 1995), pp. 20–36.

35. *Zhongguo wenwu jinghua*, no. 49; for a similar type from Jiangsu Province, see *Wenwu*, no. 5 (1984), pl.: left.

36. Lu Liancheng and Hu Zhisheng, *Baoji Yu Guo mudi*, 2 vols. (Beijing: Wenwu chubanshe, 1988), cpl. 18; the same tomb also yielded two bird-shaped vessels (ibid., cpl. 19).

37. *Wenwu*, no. 5 (1966), p. 70; similar bells in the Shanghai Museum, the Sen'oku Hakkokan, Kyoto, and the Arthur M. Sackler Gallery, Smithsonian Institution, are discussed in Fong, ed., *Great Bronze Age*, no. 58; Rawson, *Western Zhou Ritual Bronzes*, no. 129; and Lothar von Falkenhausen and Thomas D. Rossing, "Acoustical and Musical Studies on the Sackler Bells," in So, *Eastern Zhou Ritual Bronzes*, p. 440.

38. For Shang dynasty prototypes, see Bagley, *Shang Ritual Bronzes in the Sackler Collections*, no. 104; also Lothar von Falkenhausen, *Suspended Music: Chime-bells in the Culture of Bronze Age China* (Berkeley and Los Angeles: University of California Press, 1993); and Falkenhausen and Rossing, "Acoustical and Musical Studies."

39. *Wenwu*, no. 9 (1989), pl. 2:2.

40. For a detailed discussion of the type, see So, *Eastern Zhou Ritual Bronzes*, nos. 39–40; and Jenny F. So and Emma C. Bunker, *Traders and Raiders on China's Northern Frontier* (Washington, D.C. and Seattle: Arthur M. Sackler Gallery, Smithsonian Institution and University of Washington Press, 1995), no. 20, chap. 3.

41. So, *Eastern Zhou Ritual Bronzes*, chap. 6.2, app. 1:6D.

42. For cat. 28, see Wu Hung, "A Sampan Shan Chariot Ornament and the Xiangrui Design in Western Han Art," *Archives of Asian Art* 37 (1984), pp. 38–59.

43. This is discussed in Emma C. Bunker, "Sources of Foreign Elements in the Culture of Eastern Zhou," in George Kuwayama, ed., *The Great Bronze Age of China: A Symposium* (Los Angeles: Los Angeles County Museum of Art, 1983).

44. This is discussed in greater detail in Jenny F. So, "*Hu* Vessels from Xinzheng: Toward a Definition of Chu Style," in Kuwayama, *Symposium*, pp. 64–71.

45. For cat. 6, see Fong, ed., *Great Bronze Age*, no. 67; So, *Eastern Zhou Ritual Bronzes*, chap. 3.2, app. 1:3D; for cat. 11, see *Zhongguo wenwu jinghua*, no. 83, where the pair is shown; and Rawson, ed., *Mysteries of Ancient China*, no. 61.

46. For a discussion of lost-wax casting, see Bagley, *Shang Ritual Bronzes in the Sackler Collections*, chap. 2.6; and So, *Eastern Zhou Ritual Bronzes*, pp. 35, 53–54.

47. Fong, ed., *Great Bronze Age*, no. 95.

48. Fong, ed., *Great Bronze Age*, no. 97; the find is reported in *Yunnan Jinning Shizhaishan gumuqun fajue baogao*, 2 vols. (Beijing: Wenwu chubanshe, 1959).

49. So and Bunker, *Traders and Raiders*, pp. 23, 34–35; also nos. 1, 3, 11.

50. For these later trends and developments, see So, *Eastern Zhou Ritual Bronzes*, chaps. 3.2, 4–6; and Fong, ed., *Great Bronze Age*, chaps. 8–9.

51. For a prototype, see an example in the Asian Art Museum of San Francisco: René-Yvon Lefebvre d'Argencé, *Bronze Vessels of Ancient China in the Avery Brundage Collection* (San Francisco: Asian Art Museum, 1977), pl. 43: top left.

52. For examples of such "archaisms," see So, *Eastern Zhou Ritual Bronzes*, nos. 1, 5, 62, 80; Jenny F. So, "The Many Faces of the Past in Eastern Zhou Bronzes" (paper presented at the "Mysteries of Ancient China" conference, British Museum, London, 6–8 December 1996); and Li and Liang, *Art of the Houma Foundry*, pp. 13–14 (English summary on p. 83).

53. *Shaanxi chutu Shang*, no. 52; and *Sanjin kaogu*, no. 1 (1994), pp. 139–53, pl. 7.

54. For cat. 9, see *Zhongguo kaogu wenwu zhi mei (6): Zhanguo Xianyu lingmu qizhen, Hebei Pingshan Zhongshan guowang mu* (Beijing: Wenwu chubanshe, 1994), cpl. 56 and drawings on pp. 156–57 for a wide range of examples; one of these is discussed in Fong, ed., *Great Bronze Age*, no. 94.

55. For a study of exotics in Tang society, see Edward H. Schafer, *The Golden Peaches of Samarkand: A Study of Tang Exotics* (Berkeley and Los Angeles: University of California Press, 1963).

56. *Wenbo*, no. 5 (1987), pp. 79–80, pl. 4: top. This is one of two identical dragons recovered in a chance find in the southern suburb of Xi'an. Its mate is damaged beyond repair.

57. For discussions of gold and silver as foreign materials in ancient China, see Emma C. Bunker, "Gold in the Ancient Chinese World: A Cultural Puzzle," *Artibus Asiae* 53, nos. 1/2 (1993), pp. 27–50; and Emma C. Bunker, "The Enigmatic Role of Silver in China," *Orientations* (November 1994), pp. 73–74.

58. Reported in *Kaogu yu wenwu*, no. 2 (1988), pp. 94–106; and *Wenwu*, no. 10 (1988), pp. 1–43.

59. See *Wenwu*, no. 1 (1972), pp. 30–42; and *Kaogu*, no. 6 (1980), pp. 536–41.

So Fine a Luster:

Chinese Lacquerwares

Michael Knight

Curator of Chinese Art, Asian Art
Museum of San Francisco

The objects grouped together as lacquers

(*qiqi*) share the common feature of being

coated with a durable substance derived

from the sap of the tree *rhus verniciflua,* a

native of China. The Chinese have long

valued the durability of this material and

admired its inherent beauty. Its sumptu-

ous surfaces and broad range of applica-

tions have made it a favorite of members

of the court, the aristocracy, religious groups, and wealthy merchants. Lacquers have also served as valued objects of trade. And yet lacquer, for all its lustrousness and durability, has never been translated into symbol, a curious omission in China, where so many other materials have acquired symbolic connotations.

In the writings of the scholar-gentry, many forms of lacquer were associated with excessive wealth and extravagance, with the women's quarters, and with the imperial court; therefore only select types of the medium are found in objects made for the scholar class.[1] The primary exception is furniture. For most furniture, a single coat or a few thin coats were applied to protect a softwood core. Only the most expensive pieces of lacquered furniture, such as the examples from the imperial workshops, were covered with multiple layers and decorated in techniques discussed below.[2] This attitude has also affected the study of the material, which, until recent decades, has been viewed primarily as a minor decorative art. For certain periods in Chinese history, however, and for the social classes who patronized it, lacquer was a medium of great value and significance.

Lacquer production is a long process, beginning with gathering the sap of the lacquer tree by making small slits in the bark and collecting the secretion. The raw sap is a thick, creamy substance filled with impurities; initial steps in preparing the material include filtering through cloth of varying fineness until the desired purity is achieved and allowing excess water to evaporate. Once purified, the clear, viscous, amber liquid is ready to be applied to a core. These cores have traditionally been wood or fabric, but sometimes are made from other materials such as leather, ceramic, or even bronze.[3]

Raw lacquer contains very high concentrations of urushiol.[4] Under the right conditions, including high humidity and temperatures between 60 and 85 degrees Fahrenheit, urushiol undergoes a chemical change and forms a natural polymer having many of the properties of modern plastics: it is impervious to water and to many chemicals, and stable throughout a range of temperatures; depending on the material used for the core, the lacquered object can also be extremely lightweight.

In its raw state urushiol is very caustic, therefore only a limited number of stable pigments can be used to color it. The most common colors for lacquer are red, black, brown, and yellow. Certain of these colors, such as red, had their own significance in Chinese culture, and considerable effort was expended in mining and refining them.

Cinnabar, the pigment used to color red lacquer, is a crystalline form of mercuric sulfide. Deposits of this mineral are found in many parts of China, and its ubiquity along with its stability makes it an ideal pigment for use in lacquer. Red was also an auspicious color for the Chinese, and cinnabar was sprinkled in tombs as early as the Neolithic period (ca. 7000–ca. 2000 BCE). Cinnabar was also thought to have magical powers and was one of the main ingredients in "elixirs of immortality" concocted during the Qin and Han dynasties (221 BCE–220 CE). Once suspended in the matrix of the lacquer polymer, this substance becomes a stable pigment.

During much of the Bronze Age in China cinnabar red lacquer was applied to the interiors of wood coffins and vessels, a further indication of its special significance.

Carbon was the primary pigment for black in early lacquers; because it is not entirely stable in urushiol, it often yielded a dull and brownish hue. The desire for a pure and glossy black surface led later lacquer artists to employ pickled iron, often mixed with arsenic. Yellow was accomplished through the use of orpiment. Brown, in a range of tones, is the natural color of lacquered wood; other more opaque browns can be obtained through the addition of carbon.

To enlarge the available palette, methods were developed to add pigments to the surface of lacquer. Among these was suspending pigments in oils from the tong tree and painting them onto the lacquered surface. Inlays of sheets of precious metals, shells, mother-of-pearl, colored stones, glass, and a broad range of other materials as well as the suspension of powdered metals in lacquer were also important decorative techniques.

There are five principal applications for lacquer: as a protective coating; as a paint to apply two-dimensional decoration; as an adhesive; as a resin that, in combination with other mediums, creates a product of superior strength and durability; and as a medium for carving. These applications are not mutually exclusive, and it is common to find two or more present in any given object.

The earliest use of lacquer must have been as a protective coating, and this remained one of its primary functions. Thick and viscous, lacquer is difficult to paint with. Nevertheless, Chinese lacquer artisans achieved remarkable results, and some of the earliest surviving evidence of Chinese attempts at painting are in this medium.

Use as an adhesive was another early and enduring application of lacquer. Because it is sticky when wet, adheres to most materials, and cures to create a durable bond, lacquer is ideal for this purpose. By exploiting these qualities, artisans working in lacquer are able to inlay or adhere a range of materials to surfaces, thus vastly expanding the decorative potential of their medium.

Like modern fiberglass resin, wet lacquer is absorbed by wood and fabrics; when it has cured, it creates a material that is much stronger than either of the two substances separately. Fabric can be soaked in lacquer and molded, creating a vessel or sculpture that will retain the molded shape. Applied to a wood core, lacquer will form a lightweight, strong, and, if desired, elaborately shaped vessel or object of considerable strength and durability.

A sophisticated understanding of the medium was required before carved lacquers could be created. In order to undergo the chemical change required for curing, lacquer must be applied in very thin coats. The thick coverings necessary for carving are achieved by applying multiple coats. The most complex carved lacquers might have a thin wood core reinforced with a layer of lacquer-impregnated cloth; over that, base coats created by adding combinations of ash, rice paste, wood powder, or fine clay to lacquer; and multiple finish coats of refined lacquer. Each coat has special qualities of sealing, filling, leveling, and finishing, and must be applied in the proper conditions and in proper sequence. Since each coat must cure and be mechanically smoothed before another is added, the thickest applications can require as much as a year from the initial coat to the final finish.[5]

EARLY CHINA (CA. 3000 BCE–220 CE)
In the past, much of the study of early Chinese art has been focused on the nonperishable materials of bronze, jade, and ceramics. In part this was due to the interest of Chinese antiquarians, who were most interested in those materials mentioned in their Classics—bronzes (particularly those with inscriptions) and jades. Early Western studies of bronzes and jades followed similar lines, with a greater emphasis on surface decoration and form. Their advanced technologies and intrinsic beauty have long made Chinese ceramics a focus of Western scholarship. Rarely did objects of lacquered wood or other perishable substances survive to enter a museum or a private collection and allow a glance into their early development.

During the past few decades, however, archaeology has provided a more complete record of these perishable materials. Lacquered objects have been found in considerable numbers in tombs dating as early as 3000 BCE and have provided indications of some of the developments in use and style in a medium employed primarily as a paint. Combined with a number of textiles dating between the late

fourth and early second century BCE, these lacquers have provided a far broader understanding of artistic endeavors in two-dimensional mediums during this period of China's history.

In early China lacquer trees, and therefore the production centers of lacquers, were most common along the Changjiang (Yangzi River) from Sichuan to Zhejiang provinces. Unlike bronze foundries and ceramic kilns, which required substantial industrial equipment and left many traces where they were set up, lacquer required only areas for refining the raw material and brushes and other perishable tools for its application. No sites of early lacquer production have been located.

A cup excavated in 1978 from a site of the Neolithic Weizhi culture at Yuyaohe, Zhejiang Province, is the earliest known Chinese lacquered vessel.[6] Made of a wood core coated with red lacquer, it dates between 5000 and 3000 BCE. The application of colored lacquer to a wooden base attests to an advanced technique; it is likely that lacquer had been in use for some time before this cup was created. The remains of early Bronze Age lacquers found in Shang dynasty sites in Anyang, Henan Province, and elsewhere indicate that lacquer technology advanced rapidly during this period. Most Shang dynasty lacquers have a red ground with designs of *taotie* (abstract zoomorphic masks), *leiwen* ("thunder patterns," which take the form of squared spirals), and other motifs derived from bronze decor of the time.

The use of lacquer as an adhesive was also known during the Shang dynasty, as attested by surviving objects inlaid with the shell of fresh-water clams, turquoise, ivory, and sheets of gold foil. Western Zhou (ca. 1100–771 BCE) lacquers from north China show that lacquer continued to be used extensively as an adhesive during this period as well.[7]

Two major artistic developments from the sixth to the third century BCE were the creation of a painterly style and of a representational art; lacquers are among the major surviving examples of both. Lacquered vessels with smooth, curved surfaces devoid of relief or other three-dimensional patterns, and large lacquered wood objects with flat surfaces, such as tomb chambers and coffins, relied exclusively upon contrasts in lacquer colors for decoration.

The majority of surviving lacquers dating from the Spring and Autumn (770–476 BCE) and Warring States (475–221 BCE) periods come from what was then the kingdom of Chu. Located along the central Changjiang basin, Chu enjoyed a favorable climate, advanced agricultural techniques, an abundance of natural resources, and a network of commerce and trade. It was a wealthy state, and this wealth supported a flourishing of arts and crafts in a pronounced regional style. Happily, the realm of Chu coincided with the area of distribution of *rhus verniciflua*, making it possible for the artists of Chu to paint in lacquer. The flexibility of painting (as compared, say, to casting in bronze) gave the artists of Chu greater freedom to express the unique nature of their culture; many of their lacquerwares are powerful and evocative, others approach the bizarre.

Changsha in Hunan Province has long been associated with early lacquers. From at least the ninth century BCE to the time of the fall of the state in 221 BCE, Changsha was an important Chu city. It was located at the very southern reaches of the state's territory, far from the capitals along the banks of the Changjiang. Excavated materials and contemporary texts confirm its importance to Chu as a center of trade with regions even farther south. Many of the Chu tombs found there belong to members of the lower aristocracy and perhaps even of the merchant class.

Changsha remained an influential political center in southern China during the Western Han dynasty (206 BCE–8 CE) and served as the capital for a state that, while under Han rule, retained a great deal of autonomy and local leadership. In 1972 a series of tombs belonging to the ruling family of the state centered at Changsha was excavated at the suburb of Mawangdui. The arts found in them reveal a continuity with earlier Chu materials combined with an awareness of Han philosophical and religious practices.

The Han period residents of Changsha used lacquer in a very wide variety of forms. The vast majority, if not all, of these objects have wood cores. By far the largest existing pieces are three lacquered coffins (fig. 1) that formed a nested set. Their very scale, together with the descriptions found in contemporary or slightly earlier texts such as the *Chuci* ("Songs of the South"), hint at the extensive use of lacquer in architecture as well.[8]

Only a small number of bronze vessels in traditional shapes were found in the Mawangdui tombs; rather, sets of these vessels were created in lacquer (cat. 66).[9] This clearly reflects changing attitudes toward these two materials and the rising status of lacquer. Early Western Han writings indicate that a lacquer vessel might cost ten times as much as a comparable piece in bronze.

Also found in the tombs at Mawangdui were lacquer boxes in great variety, including picnic sets (cat. 67), toiletries boxes (cat. 68), and document boxes, among others. Nested containers (cat. 67)

Fig. 1. *Set of lacquered wood coffins from Mawangdui tomb No. 1.*

and matched sets of vessels were enormously popular, and great precision was required to create outer boxes that would exactly fit their contents.

During the Western Han dynasty the Chinese lived at floor level: all seated activities customarily took place on platforms or on mat-covered platforms; large-scale raised chairs and tables and other furniture of corresponding scale were not yet in vogue. The impact of this custom on the preparation and presentation of food is quite apparent in the lacquers found in the Mawangdui tombs. Food for the deceased had been laid out in a variety of dishes (fig. 2) assembled on large trays (cats. 69, 70). The large rectangular tray (cat. 70) could well have served as a small portable table. Low screens found in the Mawangdui tombs (fig. 3) are the ideal height to have deflected drafts and preserved privacy for the floor-sitting occupants of Han interiors.

Swirling abstract patterns compose most of the designs on the lacquers from the Mawangdui tombs. The sources for these designs can be found in the curvilinear designs on lacquers and inlaid bronzes of the late Warring States period. By the Western Han dynasty, however, these patterns had come to resemble clouds and served religious as well as decorative purposes. On the surface of one of the coffins from Mawangdui tomb Number 1 (fig. 4), these clouds are occupied by a multitude of strange and wonderful beasts. Beliefs in paradises inhabited by immortals became increasingly widespread during the early Western Han. The *Chuci* ("Songs of the South"), a collection largely of late Warring States date, describes these paradises; many of them exist in the sky among just such clouds and are occupied by just such fantastic creatures as are depicted on this coffin.[10]

Magical clouds were also thought to be omens of good fortune and, as such, played an important role in *xiangrui*, a constellation of beliefs that was well developed by the Western Han. In simple terms, the Han Chinese believed that, by surrounding oneself with auspicious omens and designs, one could attract good fortune and, perhaps more important, ward off bad fortune. Thus cloud patterns are common on eating utensils, burial goods, textiles, and any number of other objects of the time.

Most of the lacquers at Mawangdui were decorated in the traditional palette of red and black, using relatively few coats of lacquer. Some of the more finely finished works (cats. 66, 69, 70) are decorated with alternating bands of solid red and patterned black, with cloud patterns appearing in red on the black bands. The narrow borders also hold abstract patterns executed in red on black, but these tend to be simple and rather broadly conceived, clearly distinguishable from the cloud patterns that serve as the main decor in the black bands.

Among the exceptions to the red-and-black color scheme are one of the coffins (fig. 4) and a small number of boxes (cat. 68). These share a black lacquer ground on which raised lines of lacquer outline multicolored cloud patterns. The palette of the clouds includes ochers, reds, gray-greens, and yellows.

Also found in limited numbers at Mawangdui are boxes and other objects with decoration created by incising (*zhuihua*), a relatively new technique; the earliest excavated examples known to date come from the Warring States period. The decoration was created by scratching the surface of the outermost lacquer layer with a sharp burin. Although the incisions are not deep enough to reveal underlying layers, they create very fine, crisp, linear patterns. *Zhuihua* might be seen as the beginnings of the carved lacquer tradition, which reached full maturity over a millennium later. Most of the designs on this group of lacquers consist of *xiangrui* patterns and depictions of immortal paradises or hunting scenes. The covered box (cat. 71) is a typical example. In many cases the incised decoration is found on the inside surfaces of the piece, while the exterior is decorated in more traditional techniques.

Inscriptions on lacquers of the third and second century BCE include makers' names, numbers, and other information from which we may deduce that many lacquers of this period were produced near Chengdu in Sichuan Province. Similar inscribed lacquers as well as records in historical documents confirm the contemporaneous production of lacquers in Shandong, Henan, Guangdong, and Guangxi provinces.[11] These areas continued to be important centers of lacquer production for most of China's history.

Fig. 2. *Lacquered wood tray, vessels, and utensils from Mawangdui tomb No. 1.*

Fig. 3. *Lacquered wood screen from Mawangdui tomb No. 1.*

THE LATE TANG TO SONG DYNASTY (9TH CENTURY–1279)

Very few lacquers dating from the Eastern Han dynasty (25–220 CE) to the end of the Tang dynasty (618–907) have survived in China. Only indirect evidence from materials found in Japan and from scattered Chinese border sites indicates that lacquer technology continued to develop and that new processes were introduced for the production of luxury goods, vessels, and furniture. During this period various sects of Buddhism became important institutional patrons for the lacquer arts; their demands for lightweight sculpture, implements for worship, and specialized storage containers contributed to such innovations as dry-lacquer (*tuotai*) sculpture.

Tang power extended far into Central Asia, and the Tang hereditary elite, from the north of China, had both blood and political ties to the cultures of that region. Foreign luxury goods, all the more desirable for being exotic, provided stiff competition for native luxuries such as lacquerwares. The artisans working in lacquer responded with a wide range of

Fig. 4. Lacquered wood coffin from Mawangdui tomb No. 1.

new effects: cutwork designs of precious metal leaf or foil might be applied to the surface of the lacquerware, covered with several layers of lacquer, then the whole rubbed just till the gleaming metal emerged flush with the surrounding lacquer, a technique called *pingtuo*; or patterns might be created in the lacquerware by inlaying thin sheets of mother-of-pearl or other iridescent shells. Both these techniques are found on mirror backs, mirror cases, musical instruments, and a variety of other objects.

During the middle and late Tang dynasty a series of events occurred that profoundly affected lacquer production and attitudes toward it and a variety of other materials. The An Lushan rebellion of 755 vastly diminished the political and economic power of the Tang hereditary elite. During the remainder of the Tang dynasty other societal groups emerged as the principal arbiters of taste. They often showed a preference for native materials, including lacquer in more traditional forms.

As the political fortunes of the Tang ruling clans declined, China's borders contracted and the Central Asian trade routes were interrupted by foreign conquest. This encouraged the resurgence of native traditions in the arts, which continued through the Five Dynasties period (907–960) and on into the Song dynasty (960–1279). An increased emphasis on the tenets of Confucianism, a rise in Daoism and certain forms of Buddhism, and the development of strong regional patronage for a

variety of arts marked this long period of time.

During this period tea became a national obsession. The need for vessels and implements to prepare, present, and drink this beverage, along with those for the foods that came to be associated with it, also had a broad-ranging impact on such mediums as ceramics and lacquers.

The artistic movements brought about by these changes in attitude and patronage were fully realized during the Song dynasty. Influenced by Confucian principles and inspired by conscious archaism, the people of the Song took renewed interest in the arts and philosophies of the Han dynasty and earlier. Cut off by hostile neighbors from the foreign influences that had been so strong during the earlier centuries of the Tang dynasty, Song dynasty artists innovated within traditional Chinese mediums. Among these was lacquer.

Song dynasty innovations in lacquer included making lighter and stronger cores, rendering details of the decoration in relief by means of a moldable paste made by adding materials such as fine clay or ash to liquid lacquer, and applying sufficient numbers of layers to allow deep carving in the lacquer. Many of the pieces created during this period were elegant utilitarian vessels and domestic furniture. Others were specially designed to serve in Buddhist ritual practices.

The lacquer cup stand (fig. 5) illustrates many of these patronage and artistic issues. Designed for the display or presentation of a cup, it is a prime example of the group of objects that were created for the service of tea. Its pleasing shape and decoration in subtle shades of brownish red lacquer are typical of the ceramics and other wares that were designed for tea enthusiasts.

Among other motives, the need for elegant, portable, yet sturdy implements for serving tea and displaying tea wares inspired considerable experimentation with new core forms during the Song dynasty. X-rays of a six-petaled dish in the Los Angeles County Museum of Art, a pair of five-lobed dishes on loan to the Asian Art Museum of San Francisco, and a five-lobed dish in the Freer Gallery of Art reveal that their cores consist of single or multiple pieces of wood for the center, to which woven wood sides are joined. This allowed enough thickness in the sides to carve decoration and made a light yet strong object.[12] In basic body type and thickness the cup stand (fig. 5) is similar to this group.

Because they have long been removed from their original context, the use and patrons for this type of lacquer are subject to conjecture. In shape the cup stand in figure 5 relates to ceramics such as Ding ware, which was made for the imperial court during the Northern Song. Chan Buddhism influenced many of the arts of the Song dynasty, and lacquer was no exception. It is likely that this piece was created for the Chan-influenced tea ceremony that became prevalent in China during the Song dynasty, perhaps to hold a small tea bowl. The costly materials establish that the patrons were among the wealthy elite of the time.

Lacquered wood also proved to be the perfect medium for creating elaborate and decorative storage boxes for sutras and other Buddhist paraphernalia. A vertical box (cat. 72) and a sutra container in the form of nested boxes (cat. 73), all quite large, have been found at the site of the Huiguang Pagoda, built in 1043 at Ruian, Zhejiang Province. They have been identified as products of Wenzhou in the same province, one of the most famous centers for lacquer production during the Song dynasty. The vertical box (cat. 72), identified as a reliquary, is decorated on all four sides with Buddhist scenes. The pair of nested boxes (cat. 73), also ornate, held Buddhist scriptures. Although all three are relatively simple shapes, they represent some new departures in decoration and decorative technique.

The overall base color of both the reliquary and the outer sutra box is light brown, with a band of red on the top section of the reliquary. Applied to the surface of both are extensive areas of floral decoration, auspicious animals, and Buddhist figures created from raised areas of molded or embossed lacquer. Portions of the molded floral designs were

Fig. 5. Lacquered wood cup stand. Northern Song dynasty (960–1127). H. 6.5 cm, cup diam. 8.4 cm, saucer diam. 14.2 cm. Unearthed at Hanyang, Shilipu, Wuhan county, Hubei Province. Hubei Provincial Museum, Wuhan.

originally highlighted by applications of gold dust suspended in lacquer. In addition, seed pearls were inlaid into the lacquer to emphasize certain aspects of the design. The beginnings of the raised lacquer technique can be seen in the box from Mawangdui (cat. 68). We also know from materials preserved in the Shōsō-in, in Japan, that both relief and inlaid designs were popular during the Tang dynasty.[13] On the Northern Song reliquary and sutra boxes these techniques are used in a very sophisticated manner to frame the areas of pictorial design and to create major decorative motifs in relief.

On each vertical side of the reliquary floral scrolls frame a scene of Guanyin, the Buddhist deity of mercy and attendant to Amitābha Buddha. These scenes are painted in lacquer pigmented with powdered gold. On the outer sutra box are images of Buddhist deities seated on lotus blossoms and a series of auspicious animals and birds, all in molded lacquer. The inner sutra box is elaborately decorated with scrolling floral designs painted in gold lacquer.

THE YUAN AND MING DYNASTIES (1279–1644)

Profound changes occurred during the brief Mongol-ruled Yuan dynasty (1279–1368) that had a deep impact on Chinese society and the arts. Forced from their traditional role in the Confucian bureaucracy, many of the educated elite turned to the arts as a vocation and refuge. Patronage patterns also changed dramatically during this period. Although Chan and other forms of Buddhism remained strong supporters of the arts, the Yuan court did not patronize the arts in the same fashion as had the Song. Instead, the wealthy landed gentry, particularly those in the south, became the primary patrons of a broad range of artistic activities.

Many of the better-known literati artists became long-term house guests of these wealthy gentry, offering paintings in return for hospitality. The gentry also supported such endeavors as the immensely popular plays and novels of the time. Not surprisingly, the larger-than-life heroes and villains of these works, whether fictional or semihistorical, were the subject of many of the art objects commissioned by the wealthy. Some appear as topics of lacquer decoration.

Several lacquer techniques initiated during the Song dynasty were fully developed during the Yuan dynasty. Following Song precedents, the cores of many Yuan dynasty plates were made in several sections, out of very thin wood. In Yuan examples, the pieces that made up the well of the plate were laid with their grain perpendicular to the grain of the pieces making up the cavetto and rim.[14] This technique strengthened the very thin, lightweight core so that it did not check or shrink as easily as the thicker, single-piece cores of the Warring States period and Han dynasty. These complex cores were susceptible to warpage, however, a problem found in many of the large plates of the Yuan dynasty.

Carved lacquer (*diaoqi*) was one of the more impressive developments in the medium during the late Song and on into the Yuan and Ming dynasties. Although a complex and time-consuming process, this technique offered a broader range of visual effects than the molded and applied lacquer decoration seen in the Buddhist reliquary and sutra boxes discussed above (cats. 72, 73). By the end of the Yuan dynasty carving in lacquer had almost entirely replaced molded and applied decoration.

One of the most complex of the core types described above, cloaked to a considerable depth by multiple coats of lacquer, would be employed as the blank for a piece of carved lacquer. In most cases, the first several finish coats would be followed by two or three coats of a contrasting color of lacquer, which would serve as a depth guide for the carver, preventing him from carving through the finish coats into the core itself.

An extravagant amount of time and energy was required before the blank was even ready for carving. The finest carved lacquers of the Ming and Qing could have as many as two hundred coats of lacquer, each requiring a day or more to cure and to be buffed before another could be applied.[15] The cost in human terms for carved lacquer must also have been very high. Breathing the dust created

while carving through layers of cinnabar red (mercuric sulfide) and orpiment (arsenic) must have devastated the artisans' health. But we know very little about the personal lives or working conditions of the artisan class.

Many of the carved lacquers of the Yuan dynasty are large platters or plates. Many of these, like many of the Yuan dynasty blue-and-white porcelains, were too large for traditional Chinese use; furthermore, deeply carved designs rendered them less than ideal for any practical purpose. Most of them must have been meant for display. The large porcelains were often made for foreign markets, and this may also have been true for the lacquers. Flowers-and-birds or overall abstract cloud-like designs were the usual motifs. In general, these pieces are dark brown or black, although examples also exist in red.

Figural scenes are relatively rare on the carved lacquers of the Yuan dynasty. The covered box (cat. 74) is a superb example of this type. Even rarer are dated examples, and this one bears a date corresponding to 1351.[16] Almost no other dated Yuan dynasty lacquers have survived. The scene on this box, like those on many of the underglaze decorated porcelains of the period, is drawn from a contemporary novel or play. Patrons of such lacquers must have included the wealthy gentry, the same people who would have sponsored the novels and plays and purchased the porcelains and other objects decorated with scenes from them. Not only are the designs different from those on the lacquers intended for the tea ceremony or for Buddhist uses, but the color of figural lacquers is almost always cinnabar red rather than black or brown.

The popularity of deeply carved lacquer continued in the Ming dynasty (1368–1644). Beginning with the reign of the Yongle emperor (1403–1424), boxes and other objects in deeply carved cinnabar lacquer began to be produced under imperial patronage. The covered box illustrated here (cat. 75) exemplifies fifteenth-century developments in carved lacquers either made at imperial workshops in the capital or commissioned by the court. Such lacquers served both as utilitarian items in the court and as luxury gifts bestowed by the emperor or his emissaries on special occasions.

The subject of the scene on this box is similar to that on the Yuan dynasty box discussed above (cat. 74). It has a strong narrative content, with a main figure standing on an open terrace. His servant stands directly behind him, while another scholar busies himself in an open building. Pictorial space on this Ming box is more developed than on the Yuan dynasty piece: the number of elements has increased considerably, and their relationships are more rational. Other developments are the extensive use of diaper patterns as background or to indicate sky or water and the replacement of the abstract patterns on the sides of the Yuan box with various auspicious flowers. On a majority of fifteenth-century covered boxes the sides are similarly decorated.

By the Ming dynasty the full range of decorative techniques was employed in the creation of lacquers: painted lacquer, lacquer overpainted with other materials; carved lacquer (*diaoqi*); "engraved gold" (*qiangjin*), a design consisting of incised outlines inlaid with gold dust over wet lacquer; incised and in-filled lacquer (*tianqi* or *diaotian*), a further development of *qiangjin*, in which the area within the gold-filled outline was painted with a contrasting-colored lacquer; and inlaid lacquer. Throughout the Ming dynasty the number of imperial commissions for lacquer varied with fluctuations in taste, economic conditions, and doubtless other factors. The reign of the Jiajing emperor (1522–1566) was a period of high production for all court-related arts, including lacquer. Dynastic power was in decline during the reign of this emperor, who abdicated almost all his authority to court eunuchs. The Jiajing emperor's fascination with Daoism distracted him further from affairs of state, but was a major influence on the arts commissioned by his court. This emperor spent great amounts of shrinking imperial funds on art. Production at imperially supervised factories and workshops was high, but quality often was not.

A final burst of imperially commissioned artistic activity marked the reign of the Wanli emperor (1573–1620). Like the Jiajing emperor, the Wanli emperor ignored the need to strengthen a government that had been weakened by decades of corruption and poor leadership and instead squandered time and resources on artistic production. By the final years of his reign the Ming court no longer had the financial resources to commission works of art in great numbers or of superior quality. By that time, however, other segments of the population had become significant patrons of the lacquer arts, chiefly members of the wealthy merchant class. Their particular social station and tastes created demands for a variety of lacquer types, often tending toward the highly ornate. Many of the spectacular examples of mother-of-pearl inlaid lacquers of the late Ming and early Qing were intended for them.

THE QING DYNASTY (1644–1911)
Under the Manchu rule of the Qing dynasty, imperial support for the lacquer arts resumed during the reign of the Kangxi emperor (1662–1722) and reached a peak during the reign of the Qianlong emperor (1736–1795). Examples in the full range of techniques and of the highest quality were produced during this period. As with many court-supported arts, production of lacquer declined during the nineteenth century. Lacquer production for the merchant class and for a growing export market continued, and was the main source of support for the medium into the twentieth century.

SOURCES FOR FIGURES
Fig. 1. After Changsha Mawangdui yihao Hanmu ("Han tomb No. 1 at Mawangdui, Changsha") (Beijing: Wenwu chubanshe, 1973), vol. 2, pl. 26.

Fig. 2. After Changsha Mawangdui yihao Hanmu ("Han tomb No. 1 at Mawangdui, Changsha") (Beijing: Wenwu chubanshe, 1973), vol. 2, pl. 160.

Fig. 3. After Changsha Mawangdui yihao Hanmu ("Han tomb No. 1 at Mawangdui, Changsha") (Beijing: Wenwu chubanshe, 1973), vol. 2, pl. 192.

Fig. 4. After Changsha Mawangdui yihao Hanmu ("Han tomb No. 1 at Mawangdui, Changsha") (Beijing: Wenwu chubanshe, 1973), vol. 2, pl. 27.

Fig. 5. After Elizabeth Childs-Johnson, "Jades of the Hongshan Culture," Arts Asiatiques 56.

NOTES
1. The main criterion for the scholar's appreciation of lacquer was antiquity. See Craig Clunas, *Superfluous Things: Material Culture and Social Status in Early Modern China* (Cambridge: Polity Press, 1991), pp. 11, 136–37.

2. The most expensive piece of furniture in the inventory of the material confiscated from the late Ming official Yan Song was a lacquered bed. Clunas, *Superfluous Things*, p. 131.

3. Lacquered leather was used for armor throughout much of East Asia. Although the two materials are not entirely suited for use together, lacquer has been used to decorate bronze sculpture and ritual objects from the Bronze Age to recent times.

4. Urushiol is the material in the *rhus* family (which includes sumac and poison ivy) that causes dermatitis. Special care is required in handling this material in all stages prior to curing.

5. The complexity of these applications are well described by Shogyo Ohba in "The Kyushitsu Technique Demonstrated on a Natsume," in N.S. Bromelle and Perry Smith, eds., *Urushi: Proceedings of the Urushi Study Group, 10–27 June, 1987, Tokyo* (Marina Del Rey: The Getty Conservation Institute, 1988), pp. 91–94.

5. *Wenwu*, no. 4 (1982), p. 70.

6. *Kaogu*, no. 5 (1984), pp. 405–17.

7. David Hawkes, trans., *The Songs of the South: An Anthology of Ancient Chinese Poems by Qu Yuan and Other Poets* (Harmondsworth: Penguin Books, 1985).

8. For a full description of the materials in tomb Number 1 at Mawangdui, see *Changsha Mawangdui yihao Hanmu* (Beijing: Wenwu chubanshe, 1973).

9. Hawkes, *The Songs of the South.*

10. Wang Shixiang, *Zhongguo gudai qiqi* (Beijing: Wenwu chubanshe, 1987), pp. 12–13.

11. Billie Milam and Helene Gillette, "X-Ray Radiography in the Study of Oriental Lacquerware Substructures," in Brommelle and Smith, eds., *Urushi*, pp. 199–226.

12. For examples, see Shōsō-in Bureau of the Imperial Household (Konaichō zōhan Shōsō-in Jimusho hen), eds., *Treasures of the Shōsō-in*, vol. 1 (*Shōsō-in Homotsu I*), North I (*Kitakura I*) (Japan: Mainichi Shinbun, 1974), pp. 40–43, 45–47, 74–81, 138–39.

13. For X-rays of this type of core, see Milam and Gillette, "X-Ray Radiography," pp. 210–11.

14. Sir Harry Garner, *Chinese Lacquer* (London and Boston: Faber and Faber, 1979), p. 23.

15. Wang, *Zhongguo gudai qiqi*, pl. 42, p. 206.

Art of Silk and Art on Silk in China

Zhao Feng

Professor, China National Silk Museum, Hangzhou

Sericulture and silk production are Chinese inventions whose profound impact on culture and civilization extended far beyond China's borders. To most people, silk, however attractive, is merely the stuff of household draperies and clothing; they give no thought to the crucial functions of silk in Chinese art. But silk art, as an independent genre, from its origin was closely related to the other traditional arts of China. The interrelationship is at least threefold: the processes of sericulture and silk production have been illustrated throughout Chinese history in other art objects; the designs developed for patterned silks have influenced and been influenced by other mediums in Chinese art; and silk, used as a ground for painting and calligraphy, interacts materially with the brush to affect the appearance of the created work of art.

The life cycle of the silkworm is extraordinary. *Bombyx mori* begins as the minute egg of a small moth, from which emerges a tiny larva, or caterpillar. This is the silkworm, which by voracious feeding on mulberry leaves grows from about one millimeter to about seven centimeters; its ceaseless feeding is interrupted by four day-long dormancies, after each of which it molts, then continues eating. After some forty days, each worm is placed into an individual compartment, where it spins the cocoon within which it metamorphoses into a chrysalis, or pupa, and finally into a new moth. To emerge, the moth secretes an enzyme that softens and breaks the fibers of the cocoon. To preserve most of the cocoon intact for silk reeling, the pupa is killed before its final metamorphosis into a moth.

From the number of very early renderings of silkworms and their life cycle, we may speculate that such a sequence of metamorphoses, with its alternations between stillness and motion, reminded the early Chinese vividly of the human life cycle, perhaps with the motionless chrysalis within the cocoon representing death and the emerging moth seen as an allegory of rebirth.

Whatever the ancient interpretation, archaeologists have discovered many representations of caterpillar, chrysalis, and moth in many Neolithic sites in north and south China. A carved ivory from Hemudu, Zhejiang Province (5000–4000 BCE), shows four pairs of silkworm patterns; a black pottery shard from Meiyan, Jiangsu Province

(ca. 3000–2500 BCE) is carved with a silkworm pattern; and Xihuang village in Shanxi and Nanyangzhuang in Hebei have both revealed chrysalis-shaped ceramics. A stone carving from a Hongshan site (ca. 3600–ca. 2000 BCE) at Houwa, Liaoning Province, has a pair of small wings on the form of a chrysalis: we are being shown the metamorphosis of chrysalis into mature moth. Numerous Liangzhu culture (ca. 3600–ca. 2000 BCE) sites in southern China have disclosed similar carvings in jade. By their sheer numbers, these survivals suggest the lively importance of the silkworm to Neolithic Chinese. The most important find is the small half cocoon from Xiying village, Shanxi (ca. 3500–ca. 3000 BCE); it is reasonable to assume that the cocoon had been cut open in order to observe the final metamorphosis and emergence of the moth—a form of augury that we might term seriomancy.

Images of the *fusang* tree appear frequently in ancient art. Most texts explain the *fusang* tree as a giant mulberry tree that connects earth with Heaven, or as the Tree of the Sun. In Chinese legend there were once ten suns, one of which, carried by the *jingwu* bird, traverses the sky from east to west every day, then rests on the *fusang* tree all night. Therefore mulberry groves, the true habitats of the *fusang* tree on earth, were places from which people could ascend to Heaven to communicate with the gods, and thus places of prayer.

The *fusang* pattern probably appeared on Neolithic art objects, but the first verifiable image is the bronze *fusang* tree excavated from a Shang ritual site at Sanxingdui, Sichuan (ca. 1600–ca. 1100 BCE). A lacquer box with a design of a *fusang* tree, unearthed from a tomb of the Warring States period (475–221 BCE) in Hubei Province, shows the archer Yi shooting at the *jingwu* bird. The motif derives from a legend in which all ten suns appeared together in the sky one day, threatening to incinerate the earth; the hero Yi saved the world by shooting nine of them out of the sky. On objects dating from the Warring States period through the Han dynasty (206 BCE–220 CE), *fusang* trees appear more frequently than before. We find it, albeit very small and much changed in shape, on the silk gauze embroidered with dragons and phoenixes found in the Chu state tomb at Mashan, Jiangling county, Hubei Province. On the famous silk painted banner from Mawangdui tomb Number 1 (ca. 168 BCE), at Changsha, Hunan Province, we also find a *fusang* tree with nine small suns and one large one. Relief carvings in stone tombs, especially, show *fusang* trees, sometimes with *jingwu* birds, sometimes with a horse tethered to the trunk, sometimes with a leaf-gathering basket or even with female leaf pickers. In that last depiction it very closely resembles a mulberry tree.

Contemporary with Han stone reliefs bearing *fusang* designs are a number of reliefs illustrating silk production. According to archaeological reports, at least seventeen such reliefs exist, nine from Shandong, six from Jiangsu, one from Anhui, and one from Sichuan, including a stone relief depicting silk production now on display at the National Museum of Chinese History in Beijing.

Sericulture and silk production became increasingly prominent art motifs in the Song (960–1279), reflecting the great importance of sericulture in the economy of that time. The best-known example is perhaps the *Gengzhitu* ("Pictures of Tilling and Weaving") of 1145, text and pictures by Lou Shou, administrator of Yuhang county near Hangzhou, then capital of the Southern Song (1127–1279). In part two of this work twenty-four illustrations depict and describe the whole process of sericulture and silk weaving: hatching; gathering newly hatched larvae; silkworm feeding and raising; first, second, and third moltings; arrangement of feeding trays; gathering mulberry leaves; last molting; picking mature silkworms; cocooning; warming the cocoons; gathering the cocoons; selecting the cocoons; storing the cocoons; reeling the silk; silk moths laying eggs; making offerings to the gods of sericulture; winding; warping; wefting; patterning; cloth cutting. The earliest known version of *Pictures of Sericulture and Weaving*, in the Heilongjiang Provincial Museum, bears an inscription attributed to Empress Wu (ca. 1127–1162). A later version, attributed to Chen Qi of the Yuan dynasty (1279–1368), now in the Freer Gallery of Art in Washington, was widely influential. But the most frequently reproduced version is that of the court painter Jiao Bingzhen (act. ca. 1680–1720), whose illustrations accompany didactic verses attributed to the Kangxi emperor (r. 1662–1722). Jiao's illustrations contain Western stylistic elements, learned from the Western missionaries with whom he had contact at the imperial court. Close copies

of Jiao's illustrations appeared throughout the Qing period (1644–1911), in the most various mediums— wood carvings, stone reliefs, painted porcelains, molded ink sticks, and woodblock-printed book illustrations. Furthermore, the *Pictures of Cotton Production* by Fang Guanchen (ca. 1765) and the twelve pictures of sericulture done in relief carving on stone in the Guangyuan Temple in Sichuan Province are undoubtedly derived from the earlier works by Lou Shou and Jiao Bingzhen.

FOREGROUND AND BACKGROUND DESIGNS ON BRONZES, JADES, AND OTHER MEDIUMS

A major evolutionary change is apparent in the decoration of early Chinese art, especially jades and bronzes. In the Neolithic and the earlier Bronze Age the zoomorphic patterns on jades and bronzes were simply rendered against relatively plain backgrounds. Increasing complexity became the rule during the middle and later Bronze Age, with the principal zoomorphic motifs set against geometric background figures such as S or T shapes or squared spirals. What inspired this change? The creation of design, of course, was the main reason. Silks featuring animal motifs embroidered on a damask ground woven with small geometric figures were the prototypes for the later bronze art.

From fragments of mats unearthed from Neolithic sites at Hemudu, Banpo, Qianshanyang, and Caoxishan, we know that patterns made from woven bamboo and braided *ge*-hemp threads were being executed long before patterns woven on the loom. Some traces of the earliest woven patterns on silk can be seen in the form of "ghost" impressions left by cloth or mats that were used to wrap jade and bronze objects of the Shang dynasty (ca. 1600–ca. 1100 BCE). Although the cloth or mat wrapping have long since disintegrated, the patterns that remain include a lozenge pattern from silk tabby on a bronze ax excavated at Anyang and now in the Museum of Far Eastern Antiquities, Stockholm, noted by Vivi Sylwan; the S-shaped pattern from silk tabby on a jade knife now in the Palace Museum, Beijing, which was noted by Chen Juanjuan, and an S-shaped damask pattern on a bronze ritual vessel found at Anyang. Some carved jades and stone sculptures also manifest textile patterns, including T-shaped diaper patterns. Furthermore, we also find traces of silk embroidery on some of the woven figured silks in which the excavated bronzes have been found wrapped; although the complete pattern of most of these has been lost, the embroidered patterns on the fragments seem to be large-scale mythical animals on a damask ground with small geometric figures. Some jade figures from Shang sites show background patterns similar to those found on bronzes of the same period. Patterned silks of that time have two "layers" of design, the woven ground pattern and over it the embroidered principal motif. This style is consistent with ritual usage in all the arts of the time, because the small geometric figures suggest clouds, which would facilitate communication between the officiant at the ceremony and the gods.

Silks with similar embroidered foreground and woven background patterns were made into the Han dynasty. The potpourri bag (cat. 76) from Mawangdui tomb Number 1 in Hunan Province contains examples of both types: a looped warp-faced compound tabby and an embroidered complex gauze. In one section of the potpourri we find a polychrome compound tabby, known as *jin*, with large woven geometric patterns forming the background and various smaller looped patterns forming the foreground. Another section of the potpourri is made of patterned gauze with embroidered cloud designs. Catalogue 77 is another example of silk gauze with woven lozenge patterns.

Similar silks may have been made as early as the Shang dynasty. We know that the style persisted in later periods in a variant known as "brocade windows," a principal motif framed by a circle or roundel against a geometric or similarly figured woven ground. Such designs were also widely used in architecture, as is evident from architectural texts of the Song and from stamped bricks and carved wood of the Ming and Qing dynasties.

STAMPED DESIGNS, SILK PRINTING, AND BLOCK PRINTING

Paper, printing, gunpowder, and the compass are four Chinese inventions that greatly influenced the course of world civilization and the development of the various cultures. Joseph Needham has listed twenty-six great inventions of Chinese science and technology, one for each letter of the alphabet, including the horizontal treadle loom and pattern loom, silk reeling, the spinning and doubling wheel, paper making, and printing. Everyone recognizes the importance of paper and printing, but few people are aware of the significance of silk in the invention of paper making and printing.

It is generally thought that printing originated in the use of stamps. Many stamps were in use in the Qin (221–207 BCE) and Han dynasties, but most of them were employed as seals to make impressions on clay rather than as printing devices to make ink graphs on silk or paper. The first trace of a stamped graph on a textile is found on a piece of warp-faced compound silk tabby from a Warring States period tomb near Changsha, Hunan Province. The graph seems to be a mark of the weaver or the owner of the bolt of silk. Later finds include two famous printed silks from Mawangdui tomb Number 1, one in fine tabby, printed in three colors (two of them

appear to be gold and silver), and a thin tabby printed with a floral pattern in six colors. On both, painting was added to enhance the design. The printing blocks can be identified as small bronze stamps, usually paired, of which examples about four and six centimeters wide were found in the tomb of the king of Nanyue in Guangzhou. Such stamped designs on silk were the prototypes for block printing on paper.

Over time, the stamps became bigger, evolving into printing blocks to be used on silk or on paper; both types of printing developed contemporaneously in China. Some examples are three pieces of stamp-resist dyed silk bearing a portrait of Śākyamuni Buddha and a number of printed Buddhist scriptures, discovered in the underground treasury of the wooden pagoda in Yingxian, Shanxi. Apart from tie dying, the Chinese generally created designs on fabric by means of printing blocks and the closely related stencil technique. For block printing, the pigment was spread on the relief portions of the carved block, and then the block was applied to the silk. In block-brush printing, the piece of silk was laid on the block and rubbed with a stone to receive an impression of the design on the block; this blind impression was then colored with a pigment-laden brush. Stencil printing, often used in north China to make New Year's pictures, creates the design by applying colors to the cloth through the holes in a stencil. All of these later techniques were derived from elementary stamped designs on silk.

SILK TAPESTRY, EMBROIDERY, AND CHINESE PAINTING

Silk, both woven and spun, was once the principal material for Chinese calligraphy and painting. Woven silk is usually unscoured tabby; many Chinese documents and paintings were written or drawn on this type of silk. Spun silk, sometimes known as cocoon paper, is formed directly by the silkworm spinning a flat sheet instead of a cocoon. Spun silk was used as a painting ground or even for clothes in south China. The renowned calligrapher Wang Xizhi's celebrated *Lanting xu* ("Preface to the Orchid Pavilion") of 353 was written using three treasures of the calligrapher: an ivory brush pot, a mousehair brush, and cocoon paper, a splendid medium still used by modern-day painters and calligraphers. Once invented, paper replaced silk to a considerable extent for painting. But in Chinese the character for "paper," *zhi*, refers to a kind of paper-like silk, a sheet of short, scoured silk fibers. By using vegetable fiber instead of silkworm fiber to make such a thin sheet, the Chinese invented true paper.

During the Song dynasty, and especially the reign of Emperor Huizong (r. 1100–1126), the arts of painting and calligraphy were greatly in favor at court. And due to the emperor's interest and favor, silks were exquisitely woven and embroidered to mimic contemporaneous paintings, especially flower-and-bird paintings. Silk art tapestry (*kesi*) developed at that time to answer the demand for fabric designs as naturalistic in style as the works of favorite painters. The resulting woven paintings were regarded not as patterned fabrics but as works of art.

Silk tapestry is a kind of tabby, whose distinguishing technical feature is the use of discontinuous weft threads instead of weft threads that run the whole width of the fabric, as they do in ordinary woven silks. In *kesi*, the weft is introduced only at the point where its particular color is required in the design, which allows the weaver enormous freedom in the shape of the design elements.

Zhuang Chou, a scholar of Northern Song, pointed out this feature in his book *Jilei pian*: "At Dingzhou they weave *kesi*. But they do not employ big looms, and they use natural-colored silk. They string the warps on wood and thorns. As desired, they make figures of flowers, plants, birds and animals, using small spools. When they weave the wefts, they first reserve their places [for spools of each color], then they take variously colored silk threads and interlace them into the warps. Along the weft direction, [the individual masses of color] combine to form a finished pattern, as if they were not connected. When the completed *kesi* is held up to the light, [due to the slits between adjoining colors] it gives the appearance of engraving; hence the Chinese name *kesi*, meaning 'carved silk.' A woman's robe of *kesi* takes a whole year to complete; but although they execute 'a hundred-flowers' or other motifs on it, it is still possible to make them all different, because in working with the small spools, the weft threads do not pass all the way across the fabric."

Examples of wool tapestry are known from as early as the second century BCE in western China; silk tapestry (*kesi*) dating from the late Tang period (618–907) has been found in eastern Central Asia and Mongolia. During the Song dynasty the techniques of *kesi* were adopted in China proper to ornament objects of daily use: a shoe "upper" with a phoenix pattern and a coverlet with a dragon design (cat. 81) were unearthed in a Liao dynasty (916–1125) tomb, and robes and other garments are mentioned in written records of the period. *Kesi* was also used as mountings of important paintings, some of which have survived. Silk embroidery might also be used for the same purposes as *kesi*. Increasingly, however, from the Song on, *kesi* and embroidery were devoted to making copies of paintings, meticulously exact in every detail of composition, form, and color. Such works are exemplified by the album leaf of *Camellias* by the famous weaver Zhu Kerou (cat. 82), or the anonymous *Garden Rocks with High Mallow and Begonia*, after a painting by Cui Bai (act. ca. 1060–1085) (cat. 83), and many others of the flower-and-bird genre. During the Yuan dynasty *kesi* and embroidery also served to make Buddhist icons, such as the *King of Bright Wisdom Budong* (cat. 85), the *Heavenly King of the West* (cat. 84), and *Śākyamuni Buddha* (cat. 86).

In southern China, the principal area of sericulture and silk production during the Ming and Qing dynasties, *kesi* and silk embroidery continued to be heavily influenced by literati painting, which flourished in the Jiangnan region, heart of the Ming dynasty textile industry. Women of aristocratic households, most famously the women of the Gu family of Shanghai and Ni Renji in Zhejiang, became expert at mimicking paintings in many varieties of embroidery, usually with finishing touches added with brush and pigments. This practice of enhancing *kesi* or embroidery with paint was prevalent during the Ming and Qing dynasties, as seen in the Qing dynasty *kesi* tapestry of Li Bai's *"Evening in the Peach and Plum Garden"* (cat. 87).

In summary, silk, in addition to all its "practical" uses, has served as a ground for painting and calligraphy, as a medium in which paintings were superbly imitated in weaving or needlework, and as an inspiration for the invention of paper.

Realities of Life after Death: Constructing a Posthumous World in Funerary Art

Wu Hung

Harrie A. Vanderstappen Distinguished
Service Professor in Chinese Art History,
University of Chicago

"Realities of life after death," from the perspective of art history, means *representations* of life inside a tomb. In China the emergence of such representations coincided with a powerful artistic movement that reinvented Chinese art: during the Eastern Zhou period (770-256 BCE), sacrificial bronzes—the privileged form of traditional ritual art of the Xia, Shang,

Fig. 1. Diagram of tomb No. 7, Niujiapo, Changzi,
Shanxi Province. Eastern Zhou period.

Fig. 2. Unfired clay tomb figurines. Warring States period.
Nülangshan, Zhangqiu, Shandong Province.

and Zhou dynasties—gradually declined, and the
center of ancestral worship shifted from the lineage
temple to the family graveyard, generating new
rites and ritual paraphernalia. Increasingly, tombs
were furnished not only with sacrificed humans
and animals and articles taken directly from the
world of the living, but also with replicas and
representations made specifically for burial. The
variety of forms manufactured for the afterlife were

known collectively as "spirit articles" (*mingqi*).
Among these forms were grave figurines (*muyong*),
which increasingly became a regular component of
tomb furnishings during the middle and late
Eastern Zhou period, from the sixth to third
century BCE.[1]

This was a change with profound implications for
art: the human bodies staffing the tomb were no

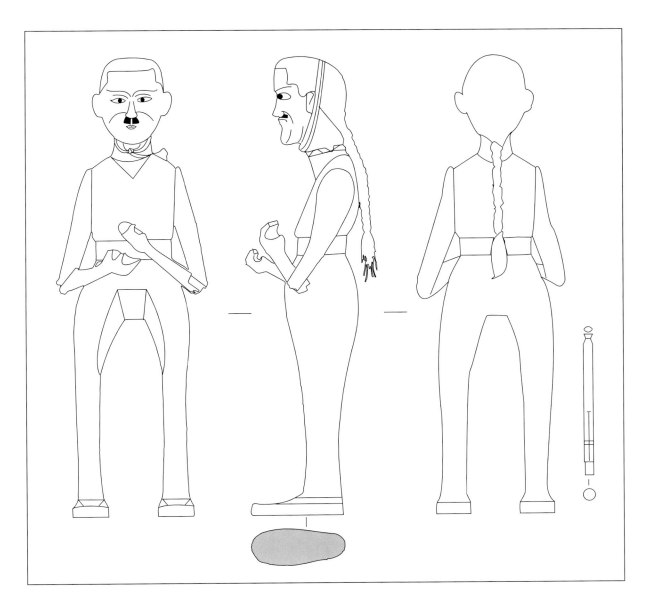

Fig. 3. Wooden tomb figurine. Warring States period.
Tomb No. 2, Baoshan, Hubei Province.

longer provided by nature but had to be created, instead, through artistic observation and production. From this time on, the artifacts contained in a tomb comprised not only *things*—vessels and other kinds of grave goods—but also *figures* or *characters* essential for imagining and constructing a posthumous world.

Four kinds of archaeological evidence allow us to hypothesize that grave figurines were first used as substitutes for the human sacrifices found in earlier and contemporary tombs. First, figurines were often placed next to or around the deceased, an arrangement following the burial pattern of human sacrifices. Second, we know that figurines and human sacrifices were used in combination to furnish tombs: for example, Niujiapo tomb Number 7, in Changzi, Shanxi Province, contained three human victims along the east and south walls and four figurines near the west and north walls (fig. 1). Together, these seven "figures" surrounded and protected the dead person in the middle.[2] Third, figurines were sometimes identified by inscriptions as "dead servants" (*wangtong* or *mingtong*) who would serve their master in the underworld.[3] And fourth, the increasing popularity

Fig. 4. Underground army of Qin Shihuangdi. Qin dynasty. Lishan necropolis, Lintong Xian, Shaanxi Province.

Fig. 5. Scale drawings of a Warring States figurine from Zhangqiu, Shandong Province (right), and a warrior figure from the Lishan necropolis of Qin Shihuangdi.

of tomb figurines was concurrent with the decline and final extinction of human sacrifices.

Archaeology also enables us to develop this "substitution" theory further. It is possible that figurines substituted for some but not all kinds of human sacrifices. Scholars have distinguished two main types of human victims in early China: "companions in death" (renxun) and "human offerings" (rensheng).[4] "Companions in death" included relatives, consorts, subordinates, guards, and servants, who followed the deceased to the afterlife. "Human offerings," on the other hand, were considered a particular kind of "sacrificial animal" (sheng) and always suffered a violent death.

Fig. 6. Clay tomb figurines. Ca. 141 BCE. Yangling, necropolis of Emperor Jing of the Western Han dynasty, Xianyang, Shaanxi Province.

Most early figurines represented guardians, servants, and entertainers; and they clearly stood for human companions, not sacrificial offerings.[5] Moreover, it seems that during this transitional period, the burial of a prestigious nobleman could still have demanded real human victims, whereas for the burial of a lower-ranking person figurines were sometimes used instead. In a fifth-century BCE tomb at Langjiazhuang, in Shandong Province, for example, the deceased was accompanied by seventeen female "companions in death."[6] All these women had individual graves and personal belongings. Two were accompanied by their own human victims, and six of the women by pottery figurines. A similar arrangement was found in another Qi-state tomb, excavated recently at Zhangqiu and dating from the mid-Warring States period.[7] Here the main burial was surrounded by five smaller grave pits of young women; of these, pit Number 1 contained a group of thirty-eight pottery figurines (fig. 2).

Warring States (475–221 BCE) figurines are of two principal types, one generally found in the north and the other in the south. All figurines from the Chu region in the south are made of wood, whereas most examples from the northern states are of clay. The differences between the northern and

Fig. 7. Diagram of tomb No. 1, Mawangdui, Changsha, Hunan Province. After 168 BCE.

Fig. 9. Decoration on front and left panel of third coffin (from the outside), tomb No. 1, Mawangdui, Changsha, Hunan Province. After 168 BCE.

Fig. 8. Decoration on front panel of second coffin (from the outside), tomb No. 1, Mawangdui, Changsha, Hunan Province. After 168 BCE.

southern figurines, however, go far beyond their materials to include their manner of representation and grouping.

Most Chu figurines have brightly painted clothes and facial features, and some of the figurines attest to an intense effort to mimic live human beings. Two extraordinary specimens from Baoshan tomb Number 2, for example, are each more than a meter tall (fig. 3). Their ears, arms, hands, and feet were carved separately and then attached. Their mustaches and braids were made of real hair, and silk robes originally covered their bodies. In Chu

tombs such figurines were usually not clustered together in a group, apart from other tomb contents. Instead, one or more figurines were installed with each type of tomb furnishing—some with horses and chariots, others with kitchenwares, yet others with writing equipment—in separate chambers of the tomb. In this way, the figurines resemble individual puppets in a series of stage sets that represent the various sections of a household.

Northern figurines, on the other hand, were often grouped together in an extensive representation of a single social setting. For example, in the Zhangqiu tomb, arranged in a single tableau, were thirty-eight clay sculptures: twenty-six human figures (including dancers, musicians, and audience members); five musical instruments; and eight birds (fig. 2). The role of such a "set" as a self-contained tableau is reinforced by its miniature form. Almost all northern figurines of the Warring States period are hand-modeled from soft clay; their size—they are often merely seven to ten centimeters tall—allowed only rudimentary representation of faces and costumes.[8]

We wonder why such tiny figures were given wide currency in funerary art. The answer must be found in the specific artistic goals of the miniature. It has been suggested that miniature representations most consciously create an interior space and time in a fictional world. Unlike realism, which attempts to map art upon life, the metaphoric world of the miniature skews the temporal and spatial relations of the everyday world. Buried in a tomb, "the miniature," in Susan Stewart's words, "finds its 'use value' transformed into the infinite time of reverie."[9] The tiny Warring States figurines thus not only "substituted" for human beings but also extended life in perpetuity.

These early figurines provided antecedents for the famous terra-cotta army of Qin Shihuangdi, the First Emperor of Qin (cats. 88–92; fig. 4). Ladislav Kesner has argued that these Qin dynasty figures, instead of replicating real Qin soldiers or abstract figurative types, have "the goal of creating a reality of a different order, a self-conscious representation."[10] This goal, as well as the figures' clay substance and decorative method, reveals their debt to the northern tradition of pre-Qin figurines. But instead of forming a miniature universe, the project signified the First Emperor's desire for the *gigantic*. Here the concept of the gigantic can be understood in two senses: it refers to the scale of a Qin figure compared with a Warring States clay figurine (fig. 5); and it also refers to the scale of the army relative to a human observer. A visitor to the site is surrounded by the army, engulfed by it, encompassed within its shadow (fig. 4).[11]

Miniature figurines regained their popularity during the early Han period (206 BCE–220 CE).[12] Like the northern miniatures of the Warring States period, these construct a fictional interior space, but the Han figurines demonstrate a stronger effort to mimic life forms and an intense interest in the human body. The naked figures from the mausoleums of Emperor Jing (r. 156–141 BCE) and other Han royalty show sensitively observed and modeled torsos and faces (fig. 6). Although these clay sculptures basically followed the northern tradition, they also integrated features of southern figurines: their naked bodies were originally clothed, and their wooden arms, which have completely decomposed, could have been manipulated into various positions. Typical southern figurines of the second century BCE, still made of wood, are exemplified by those from the famous Mawangdui tomb Number 1, whose discovery in 1972 near Changsha, in Hunan Province, was one of the most spectacular archaeological finds in Chinese history.[13] The tomb's undisturbed condition further enables us to explore the belief in the afterlife, an ideological system that must have underlain the structure and furnishing of this burial.[14]

The Mawangdui tomb belonged to an aristocrat, Lady Dai, who died shortly after 168 BCE: it yielded more than a thousand objects, figurines, clothes, and documents in perfect condition; even the woman's corpse had miraculously survived.[15] Following the typical structure of a "vertical pit" grave, the tomb consisted of a cluster of wooden

Fig. 10. Painted silk banner from tomb No. 1, Mawangdui, Changsha, Hunan Province. After 168 BCE.

structures constructed at the bottom of a deep shaft. The outer wooden encasement (*guo*) was divided into five rectangular compartments, or chambers (fig. 7). The middle chamber, called *guan*, contained the woman's body inside nested painted coffins. Numerous household articles and food were stored in the four surrounding compartments, identifying these chambers as a replica of the deceased's former residence.

Most of the wooden figurines were found within the four peripheral chambers of the *guo*. Some of them, including a group of five musicians (cat. 94), were in the northern chamber, which imitated the "retiring hall" (*qin*) in a traditional household. Silk curtains were hung on its four walls and a bamboo mat covered its floor. Eating and drinking vessels and a low table were displayed in the middle. The western section of the *qin* was equipped with bedroom articles and furniture, including cosmetic boxes, an embroidered pillow, incense containers, and a painted screen; in the eastern part of the *qin*, clothed figurines represented Lady Dai's personal

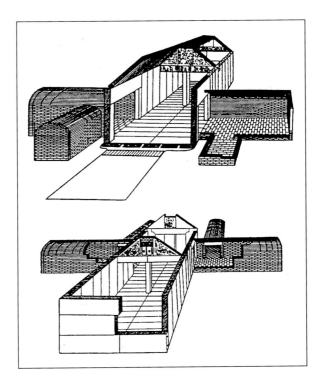

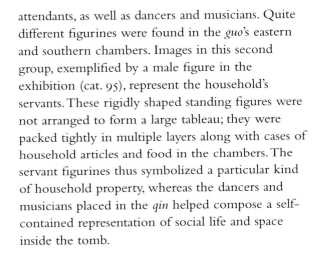

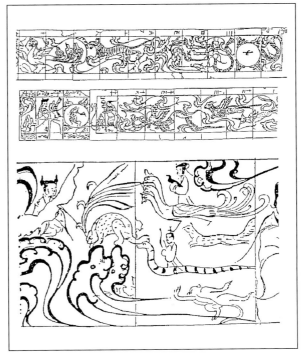

Fig. 11. Cross sections of tomb No. 1, Shaogou, Luoyang, Henan Province. Late Western Han dynasty.

Fig. 12. Drawing of heavenly realm, ceiling mural and detail from tomb of Bo Qianqiu, Luoyang, Henan Province. Late Western Han dynasty.

attendants, as well as dancers and musicians. Quite different figurines were found in the *guo*'s eastern and southern chambers. Images in this second group, exemplified by a male figure in the exhibition (cat. 95), represent the household's servants. These rigidly shaped standing figures were not arranged to form a large tableau; they were packed tightly in multiple layers along with cases of household articles and food in the chambers. The servant figurines thus symbolized a particular kind of household property, whereas the dancers and musicians placed in the *qin* helped compose a self-contained representation of social life and space inside the tomb.

In the Mawangdui tomb the *guo* forms the outermost of three encasements. Within the *guo*, the central compartment is made up of a nest of three outer coffins (fig. 7); these enclose the innermost compartment, which is the coffin containing the woman's body. A painted silk banner overlies this innermost coffin. All three outer coffins are lacquered differently, signifying their different ritual symbolism and forming a coherent pictorial program. The outermost coffin, solid black, separates the dead from the living (as well as from the four outer compartments of the *guo*, which imitate the world of the living). The second, also black, is decorated on all four sides with human, semihuman, and animal figures amid swirling cloud patterns symbolizing *qi* ("universal energy"); the deceased woman appears on the lower edge of the front panel, half entered into this mysterious world inhabited by strange beasts and spirits (fig. 8). The

innermost of the three outer coffins, lacquered a shining red, is painted with a divine mountain centered on the front panel and on one side, flanked by auspicious animals and a heavenly being (fig. 9). Inside this third coffin is the "inner unit" of the burial, which preserved the woman's body both physically and symbolically: while the corpse was carefully wrapped in layers of cloth and tightly sealed in the innermost coffin, the likeness of the dead was preserved on the painted silk banner (fig. 10).

What we find in the Mawangdui tomb, therefore, is a profound impulse to synthesize divergent beliefs and desires into a single mortuary setting and hence into a single reality after death. Instead of establishing logical connections between these beliefs, however, this synthesis was accomplished by multiplying the layers of nested boxes inside the tomb. The result is an essentially "polycentric" tomb, in which are represented four different realms of the dead: the Universe (as shown in the silk banner), the underworld (as shown on the patterned black coffin), the immortal paradise (as shown on the patterned red coffin), and the underground household (as symbolized by the four peripheral chambers and their contents). The relationship between these realms is by no means clear. It seems that in their eagerness to express their filial piety and to please the dead, the tomb builders provided *all* the answers they knew to questions about the afterlife.

But this polycentrism is exactly what makes ancient

Chinese funerary art intriguing. Although the Chinese ancestral cult never produced a systematic theological interpretation of the afterlife, tomb decoration during the four hundred years from the second century BCE to the second century CE became increasingly systematic: by unifying the multiple layers of the Mawangdui tomb into a single pictorial program, tomb designers were able to give the afterlife a more coherent, though not necessarily standardized, image. Such effort was greatly advanced by the emerging fashion for tomb murals, which implies a crucial change in mortuary structure: "horizontal burials," which flourished in the first century BCE, more faithfully imitated an actual dwelling (fig. 11). Built of large and small bricks, a tomb of this type often had a main chamber, with a gate separating it from the outside, and a number of side chambers for storing coffins and funerary goods. Murals painted in prescribed locations transformed the tomb into a symbolic structure and ritual space.

One of the earliest known examples of painted burials, the Western Han (206 BCE–8 CE) tomb of Bo Qianqiu near Luoyang, Henan Province, has been dated to the mid-first century BCE.[16] The demon-queller Fangxiang and accompanying White Tiger and Blue Dragon are portrayed on the back wall; the opposite wall bears the image of a huge bird with a human head, possibly an auspicious symbol or an immortal, above a magic mountain. The painting on the central beam of the ceiling is the most complex. Two groups of images frame this horizontal composition: the male deity Fuxi with the sun, and the female deity Nüwa with the moon (fig. 12); together, they symbolize the opposite yet complementary universal forces of *yang* (the male principle) and *yin* (the female principle). Heavenly beasts, birds, and immortals fill this cosmic structure. Most interestingly, a scene close to the *yang* group at the far right illustrates the journey of the deceased couple to the lands of immortality: the wife rides on a three-headed phoenix and the husband on a snake-like creature; they are traveling to the abode of the Queen Mother of the West (Xiwangmu), a goddess in Han popular religion who is shown here seated on wave-like clouds.

The themes and images of these murals are not unfamiliar: paintings in the Mawangdui tombs expressed the same desire for underground protection, immortality, and divine blessing. But instead of being associated with individual objects, as in the earlier burials, in the Bo Qianqiu tomb these themes and images were reorganized into an architectural space: the ceiling provided a logical location for images of celestial bodies and the heavenly journey; the murals on the front and back walls complemented each other with their respective subjects of divine blessing and demon

Fig. 13. "Three Gentlemen Killed by Two Peaches," mural from tomb No. 1, Shaogou, Luoyang, Henan Province. Late Western Han dynasty.

Fig. 14. Funerary procession over a river. Relief carving, west wall of main chamber of tomb at Cangshan, Shandong Province. Mid-second century CE.

Fig. 15. Funerary procession to the inn. Relief carving, east wall of main chamber of tomb at Cangshan, Shandong Province. Mid-second century CE.

quelling. Thus, the significance of these wall paintings lay not only in the pictures themselves, but also in their transformation of the tomb's architecture into a coherent symbolic universe for the dead.

A nearby tomb at Shaogou (tomb No. 61; fig. 11) was built at about the same time, but its wall paintings signified another trend in tomb decoration: the illustration of traditional stories and morality tales.[17] For example, at Shaogou one composition on the inner side of the partition lintel depicts the story of "Three Gentlemen Killed by Two Peaches," exemplifying the ethic of loyalty and mutual friendship (fig. 13). A second composition depicts the visit of Confucius and Laozi to the child prodigy Xiang Tuo, encouraging Confucian

Fig. 17. Entertainment in the afterlife. Relief carving, inside face of facade-lintel of tomb at Cangshan, Shandong Province. Mid-second century CE.

Fig. 16. Banquet in the afterlife. Relief carving, niche in east wall of main chamber of tomb at Cangshan, Shandong Province. Mid-second century CE.

Fig. 18. Driving outdoors in the afterlife. Relief carving, outside face of facade-lintel of tomb at Cangshan, Shandong Province. Mid-second century CE.

learning. These and other such images entered the stock of funerary painting themes, persisting through Eastern Han. The world of the dead was therefore continually enriched. At the same time that new pictorial motifs were invented and integrated into tomb decoration, new art mediums were employed; burials embellished with stone bas-reliefs or pictorial tiles became fashionable in the first and second century CE (cats. 103–04). An Eastern Han tomb often combined two-dimensional pictorial images with sculptured spirit articles—often vivid miniature representations of servants, dancers, storytellers, musicians, buildings, wells, pigpens, livestock, and household furnishings and equipment of all kinds (cats. 96–102).

Scholars have tried to explore the symbolic "program" constituted by the various forms of funerary art found in a tomb. A long inscription excavated recently in an Eastern Han tomb of the mid-second century CE in Cangshan, Shandong Province, describes the pictorial carving inside the tomb in a coherent narrative.[18] The writer begins his description with the rear chamber, which held the physical remains of the dead person. The images carved in this chamber are all mythical: directional animals and heavenly beasts transform the solid stone room into a microcosm, while intertwining dragons guard the entrance of the burial chamber to keep the corpse safe. The front chamber is decorated with two horizontal reliefs on the lintels. The first relief, on the west wall (fig. 14), shows a chariot procession of local officials crossing a bridge over a river that symbolizes death; below them, the

wives of the deceased are taking a boat across the river, since female (yin) had to be separated from male (yang) and water embodies the yin principle.

The funerary procession continues on the east wall, its members limited now to the close family of the deceased. The wives get into special carriages for women and escort the hearse outside the city (fig. 15). Arriving at an inn, they are greeted by an official. With its half-open door, this inn symbolizes the tomb: entering it symbolizes the burial of the deceased and the beginning of his underworld life. This is why, in the next scene, the deceased is no longer represented by a hearse but appears in human form as the honored guest at an elaborate banquet. This "portrait," engraved in a special niche, announces his rebirth: having regained his human desires, he is now living in his underground home. The scenes that follow represent the fulfillment of all his desires in the afterlife. He is accompanied by the fairies called Jade Maidens (fig. 16); he is entertained by musicians and dancers (fig. 17); and he takes a grand outdoor tour (fig. 18). These last two scenes, engraved respectively on the inside and outside faces of the tomb's facade-lintel, represent the two major diversions that the tomb occupant would forever enjoy.

The Cangshan tomb inscription provides a specific vision of the reality of life after death, focusing on the soul's transformation and underground pleasure; pictures in some other Eastern Han tombs emphasize the social status and moral worth of the deceased. Each pictorial program reflects the beliefs and tastes of the patrons who commissioned it. But generally speaking, these different tomb designs were all variations of a homogeneous funerary art tradition in ancient China; and the three major categories of images found in the tombs correspond to the three major conceptual elements for constructing the afterlife.

The first element is a cosmological model: pictures of heavenly bodies and clouds, often appearing on the ceiling, transform the underground chamber into a miniature universe. A posthumous paradise is the second element: various symbols of immortality in a tomb reflect the desire to transport the deceased to an eternal land after death. The final element is an idealized secular world. The world of the dead person is depicted as an extension and idealization of his former life: death would permit him to enjoy all that he had most valued during his lifetime. The deceased (or his posthumous soul) would live in elaborate halls served by numerous attendants and feast on delicacies while delighting in colorful entertainments. In death, too, an ideal society would be realized, a society regulated by the highest social and moral values of Confucian teachings. The elaborate banquet scenes, carriage processions, and Confucian morality tales illustrated in funerary art enact such earthly desires.

First established in Han funerary art, these three elements—the cosmological model, the posthumous paradise, and the idealized secular world—continued to inspire tomb designers and builders of later ages to create new architectural, sculptural, and pictorial forms such as those so vividly exemplified by the Tang funerary horses (cat. 106) and Yuan tomb tiles (cat. 112) in this exhibition.

SOURCES FOR FIGURES
Fig. 1. After Kaogu xuebao, *1984.4, fig. 2.*

Fig. 2. After Wenwu, *1993.3, pl. 2.*

Fig. 3. After Hubei Provincial Jingsha Railroad Archaeological Team, Baoshan Chu mu (Beijing: Wenwu chubanshe, 1992), p. 169.

Fig. 4. After Zhongguo Kaogu wenwu zhimei, vol. 7 (Beijing: Wenwu chubanshe, 1994), pl. 11.

Fig. 6. After Archaeological Team of Han Mausoleums of Archaeological Institute of Shaanxi Province,

Zhongguo Han Yangling caiyong *(Xi'an: Shaanxi lüyou chubanshe, 1992), p. 50.*

Fig. 7. After Hunan Provincial Museum and Archaeological Institute, CASS, Changsha Mawangdui yihao Hanmu (Beijing: Wenwu chubanshe, 1973), fig. 36.

Fig. 8. After Hunan Provincial Museum and Archaeological Institute, CASS, Changsha Mawangdui yihao Hanmu (Beijing: Wenwu chubanshe, 1973), fig. 18.

Fig. 9. After Hunan Provincial Museum and Archaeological Institute, CASS, Changsha Mawangdui yihao Hanmu (Beijing: Wenwu chubanshe, 1973), figs. 23, 25.

Fig. 10. After Hunan Provincial Museum and Archaeological Institute, CASS, Changsha Mawangdui yihao Hanmu (Beijing: Wenwu chubanshe, 1973), fig. 38.

Fig. 11. After Kaogu xuebao, *1964.2, p. 110.*

Fig. 12. After Wenwu, *1977.6, pp. 10–11.*

Fig. 13. After Kaogu xuebao, *1962.2, pl. 1.*

Fig. 14. After Wu Hung, Monumentality in Early Chinese Art and Architecture (Stanford: Stanford University Press, 1995), fig. 4.49.

Fig. 15. After Wu Hung, Monumentality in Early Chinese Art and Architecture (Stanford: Stanford University Press, 1995), fig. 4.50

Fig. 16. After Wu Hung, Monumentality in Early Chinese Art and Architecture (Stanford: Stanford University Press, 1995), fig. 4.51.

Fig. 17. After Wu Hung, Monumentality in Early Chinese Art and Architecture (Stanford: Stanford University Press, 1995), fig. 4.53.

Fig. 18. After Wu Hung, Monumentality in Early Chinese Art and Architecture (Stanford: Stanford University Press, 1995), fig. 4.52.

NOTES
1. Among the 84 tombs discovered at Deshan in Changde, Hunan Province, none dating from the early Warring States and only 2 dating from the middle Warring States period contained figurines (7 in all). By contrast, 5 tombs of the late Warring States period contained a total of 23 figurines. See *Kaogu*, no. 9 (1963), pp. 461–73.

2. *Kaogu xuebao*, no. 4 (1984), pp. 504–7.

3. *Jiangling Wangshan Shazhong chumu* ("Chu Tombs at Wangshan and Shazhong in Jiangling") (Beijing: Wenwu chubanshe, 1996), p. 278. Similar inscriptions have also been found in Chu tombs at Xinyang and in Mawangdui tomb No. 3 of the Western Han.

4. See Huang Zhanyue, *Zhongguo gudai de rensheng he renxun* ("Human offerings and companions in death in ancient China") (Beijing: Wenwu chubanshe, 1990), pp. 1–12.

5. Not all early figurines represent "companions in death." The features of a small number of examples implied specific ritual or magical functions. Changtaiguan tomb No. 1, for example, contained a room at the rear center directly behind the coffin chamber, in which a long-tongued "tomb guardian beast" (*zhenmushou*) is surrounded by four human-shaped figurines at the four corners. Unlike other figurines in the tomb, the four figures have no robes and their bodies are crudely carved. Most intriguingly, one of them has a bamboo needle piercing the chest. It is possible that these are human sacrifices dedicated to a deity represented by the statue in the center. See *Xinyang Chu mu* ("Tombs of the State of Chu at Xinyang") (Beijing: Wenwu chubanshe, 1986), pp. 18–20.

6. In addition to these 17 "companions in death," 9 other human victims in the tomb, both men and women, had suffered violent deaths, either decapitation or live burial.

These were clearly "human offerings." *Kaogu xuebao*, no. 1 (1977).

7. *Wenwu*, no. 3 (1993), pp. 1–7. Li Rixun, "Shandong Zhangqiu Nülangshan Zhanguo damu yueqi zongkao" ("A Systematic Examination of the Musical Instruments in a Large Warring States Tomb at Nülangshan in Zhangqiu, Shandong Province"), *Zhongguo wenwu shijie* ("The World of Chinese Art"), no. 127 (March 1996), pp. 86–107.

8. In addition to examples from Qi tombs, figurines of similar sizes have also been found at Fenshuiling in Shanxi and at Huixian and Luoyang in Henan. See *Kaogu xuebao*, no. 1 (1957), p. 116; *Huixian fajue baogao* ("A Report of Archaeological Excavations at Huixian") (Beijing: Kexue chubanshe, 1956), p. 45; *Kaogu*, no. 12 (1959), p. 656; *Kaogu*, no. 7 (1960), p. 71; and *Kaogu*, no. 10 (1962), p. 516.

9. Susan Stewart, *On Longing: Narratives of the Miniature, the Gigantic, the Souvenir, the Collection* (Durham: Duke University Press, 1993), p. 65.

10. Ladislav Kesner, "Likeness of No One: (Re)presenting the First Emperor's Army," *Art Bulletin* 77, no. 1 (March 1995), p. 126.

11. Again citing Stewart, "Whereas the miniature represents closure, interiority, [and] the domestic . . . the gigantic represents infinity, exteriority, [and] the public. . ." (*On Longing*, p. 70). It is in this sense that we can link the army with the concept of monumentality and the First Emperor's political ambitions. See Wu Hung, *Monumentality in Early Chinese Art and Architecture* (Stanford: Stanford University Press, 1995), pp. 115–17.

12. From 20 to 50 centimeters tall, early Han figurines are much larger than pre-Qin northern figurines. I call them "miniatures" partly because they reflect the effort to reduce the scale of funerary sculptures. The memory of creating hundreds of life-size Qin

warriors must have been quite vivid in the Chang'an area during the early second century BCE, so that this "re-miniaturization" must have been a conscious effort.

13. The most complete report of this excavation is the Hunan Provincial Museum and Archaeological Institute, CASS, *Changsha Mawangdui yihao Hanmu* ("The Mawangdui Tomb No. 1 in Changsha"), 2 vols. (Beijing: Wenwu chubanshe, 1973). For an English summary, see David Buck, "The Han Dynasty Tomb at Mawangdui," *World Archaeology* 7, no. 1 (1975), pp. 30–45.

14. For a detailed discussion of the architectural structure of the Mawangdui tomb and its ritual function and symbolism, see Wu Hung, "Art in Ritual Context: Rethinking Mawangdui," *Early China* 17 (1992), pp. 111–44.

15. According to archaeological evidence, Mawangdui tomb No. 1 was constructed after Mawangdui tomb No. 3, which belonged to Lady Dai's son (d. 168 BCE). See Hunan Provincial Museum and Archaeological Institute, CASS, "Mawangdui ersanhao Han-mu fajue de zhuyao shouhuo" ("The Main Achievements from the Excavation of Mawangdui Tomb Nos. 2 and 3"), *Kaogu,* no. 1 (1975), p. 47. Li Cang, Lady Dai's husband, died in 186 BCE.

16. Paintings have been found on the walls of a second-century BCE tomb in Guangzhou, which belonged to a king of Southern Yue. But these include only decorative patterns, thus differing from the pictorial compositions in first-century BCE tombs near Luoyang. The excavation of the Bo Qianqiu tomb is reported in *Wenwu,* no. 6 (1977), pp. 1–12. Discussions of the tomb murals include Chen Shaofeng and Gong Dazhong, "Luoyang Xi Han Bo Qianqiu mu bihua yishu" ("The Murals in the Western Han Tomb of Bo Qianqiu in Luoyang"), *Wenwu,* no. 6 (1977), pp. 13–16; and Sun Zuoyun, "Luoyang Qian Han Bo Qianqiu mu bihua kaoshi" ("An Interpretation of the Murals in Bo Qianqiu's Tomb of the Former Han in Luoyang"), *Wenwu,* no. 6 (1977), pp. 17–22.

17. The tomb's excavation is reported in *Kaogu xuebao,* no. 2 (1964), pp. 107–25. General introductions to the tomb include Jonathan Chaves, "A Han Painted Tomb at Luoyang," *Artibus Asiae* 30 (1968), pp. 5–27; and Jan Fontein and Wu Tung, *Han and Tang Murals* (Boston: Museum of Fine Arts, 1976), p. 22.

18. For a detailed discussion of this inscription and the carvings, see Wu Hung, "Beyond the Great Boundary: Funerary Narrative in Early Chinese Art," in John Hay, ed., *Boundaries in China* (London: Reaktion Books, 1994), pp. 81–104.

The Development of Chinese Ceramics: A Brief Survey

Wang Qingzheng

Deputy Director,
The Shanghai Museum

Pottery is common to the entire human race, but porcelain was a Chinese invention.

Although pottery making might have been unknown during the early Neolithic era, the mature Neolithic era was everywhere characterized by the appearance of pottery. The date when pottery first appeared in China remains to

be determined, but it is certain that it was already widely produced some six to seven thousand years ago.

The successful firing of pottery signified the ability of humans to transmute natural substances for their own advantage. In studying the techniques of pottery making during the Neolithic period, we need to examine the choice of clays, the practice of washing the clay, the mixture of materials, the evolution of vessel shapes, firing temperatures, and the relation between firing conditions and color of the fired vessel.

On pottery produced by the Yangshao culture of the Yellow River basin, the decorative impulse found expression primarily in painted designs, whereas in the Yangzi basin, during both the Hemudu culture and the slightly later Majiabang through Liangzhu cultures, incised decorations were prominent. Whether the origins of the incised decorations of the Longshan culture can be traced to southern influences is a question worth pondering. A typology of the incised decorations on Neolithic pottery reveals clearly that these were the origins of the later bronze decoration (figs. 1, 2).

The appearance of white pottery marks a technical advance, the discovery of the potential of kaolin clay, which by virtue of its extremely high Al_2O_3 content fires to a white body. But since the technology of the time did not allow firing temperatures high enough to sinter the kaolin, these vessels, though white-bodied, are nevertheless "pottery." White pottery has been found in both Yangshao and Majiayao culture sites. The Shang dynasty double-eared white jar in this exhibition (cat. 117) was decorated with patterns taken from the bronze repertory; it was made solely for aristocratic appreciation. This type of white pottery comes mainly from the Shang ruins at Anyang in Henan Province, and it exemplifies the great skill in pottery carving achieved during the last phase of the Shang period.

Fig. 1. Pottery shard with incised design. Longshan culture (2400–2000 BCE). Shanghai Museum.

Fig. 2. Pottery shard with incised design. Liangzhu culture (ca. 3600–ca. 2000 BCE). Unearthed at Tinglin site, Jinshan, Shanghai. Shanghai Museum.

Some three thousand years ago, during the late Shang dynasty, a type of green-glazed ware, different from pottery, appeared. Known as "protoporcelain," it was made from clay with an iron content under 3 percent, glazed, and then fired at approximately 1200°C. (By contrast, the clay used in pottery had an iron content over 3 percent, the early pottery was all unglazed, and it was usually fired at temperatures under 1000°C.) Probably 1200°C was the highest temperature achievable anywhere at that time (not just in China); even bronze casting—the defining technology of the Shang—only required temperatures under 1100°C. Protoporcelain was highly regarded from the late Shang dynasty, some three thousand years ago, through the Warring States era, which ended in the late third century BCE. Its characteristic thin greenish glazes had iron oxides as their colorant. The green-glazed *zun* (cat. 118) in this exhibition is a typical piece of Shang protoporcelain.

Protoporcelain has been found only in certain regions and appears to have been used only by upper classes. It did not take the place of pottery; everyday utensils and tomb furniture were still made mainly of pottery.

The Han pottery sculptures in this exhibition amply illustrate the widespread popularity of pottery burial objects. These lifelike pottery figures demonstrate the superb artistry of Han pottery sculpting, and at the same time they illuminate, in differing degrees, various social phenomena. For example, most earlier scholarship conjectured that China's oral literature owed its burgeoning mainly to the practice of reciting and singing Buddhist texts during the Tang and Five Dynasties. But the reciting/singing pottery figures exhibited here (cats. 96, 97) show that the tradition of oral literature was already strong during the Han.

The high-temperature glaze applied to the protoporcelains mentioned above was fired at 1200°C. High-temperature glazes were first used in China, but low-temperature pottery glazes, fired at roughly 700–900°C, were in use even earlier in the Middle East. Low-temperature lead glazes were probably not used in China before the fourth century BCE, and they were not in widespread use until the Han dynasty. Lead-glazed pottery burial objects were very popular during the Han, with a limited palette of colors created by the addition of different colorants to the glazes. The principal colors used in the Han were rust browns (some with a reddish tint) with iron as the colorant, and a green for which copper was the colorant. The reddish-glazed pottery dog (cat. 101) in this exhibition is lifelike and appealing, and the green-glazed waterside pavilion (cat. 100) affords a vivid example of Han architecture.

Mature porcelain appeared initially in the mid-Eastern Han, and continued to be made during the Three Kingdoms, with early green-glazed ware reaching its apogee during the Western Jin. The best wares of this era had glazes of a consistent greenish gray or a slightly yellowish green, with a rather lustrous surface. Beauty of shape and ornamentation was prized in vessels. Animal forms were widely used, and vessels of all types were decorated with stamped, incised, or applied patterns. Openwork and modeling were also very highly developed.

Green glazes were developed much later in northern China than in the south. To date, not a single kiln making green-glazed porcelain during the Western Jin period has been found north of the Yangzi River. It is believed that green-glazed porcelains gradually appeared north of the Yellow River around the sixth century CE. The Northern Qi incised jar with six lugs and the chicken-headed

Fig. 3. White-glazed box, inscribed with character ying. *Tang dynasty (618–907). Xing ware; h. 7.2 cm, diam. at mouth 15.7 cm. Shanghai Museum.*

ewer with dragon handle (cats. 121, 122) have the exuberant forms unique to the north, and are typical of green-glazed porcelain produced in the north.

Tang polychrome-glazed pottery ware developed out of Han lead-glazed pottery. The more extensive Tang palette comprised primarily green (from copper oxide), blue (cobalt oxide), and a range of ferruginous hues from cream through yellow and amber to dark brown (ferric oxide); it also included a near-black, purple, and white. The famous Tang three-color (*sancai*) wares were generally decorated with overlapping splashes of different-colored glazes, which were allowed to flow together in the kiln. This created a richly mottled, harmonious, resplendent effect. At the same time, various techniques such as molding, incising, appliqué, and hand modeling were used to create decoration. Yellow-and-green as well as blue lead-glazed pieces were found in the tomb of Zheng Rentai (664 CE) at Liquan county in Shaanxi Province, proving that polychromes were being manufactured by the early Tang, and they were produced on an even greater scale by the reign of Empress Wu (r. 684–704). The polychrome braying camel with monster-mask saddle (cat. 107) is a representative work of this period.

In the history of Chinese porcelain making potters of the Tang dynasty accomplished the transition from the production of green-glazed wares alone to an equally significant production of white porcelain as well; they also advanced the development of black, brown, multicolored, and painted porcelains.

The Tang expression "green-glazed ware in the south and white-glazed ware in the north" refers to the regional predominance of these two types: white porcelain, as typified by the Xing ware of Neiqiu in Hebei Province, and green-glazed ware, as typified by the Yue ware of eastern Zhejiang. Among northern white porcelains, Ding ware from Quyang in Hebei Province later displaced Xing ware (fig. 3).

This exhibition includes a variety of green-glazed wares, among them *mise* (or *bise*) ware, denoting a hue once "reserved" to the use of local rulers in Zhejiang Province. Two such pieces, discovered in 1987 in the underground chamber of the Famen Temple in Fufeng county, and an octagonal bottle from the collection of the Palace Museum in Beijing (cats. 123–25), are representative of Yue ware of the Tang dynasty.[1]

Although green-glazed ware has a long history in China, prior to the Tang dynasty porcelains were merely utilitarian, not objets d'art for the elite. It was not until the successful firing of *mise* Yue ware during the Tang that such ceramics began to be admired by the gentry. For the last millennium, however, scholars have failed to agree on the identity of *mise* Yue ware, on the actual dates of its production, and on the location of the kilns. In 1995, an international symposium on *mise* Yue ware was held in Shanghai. Participants discussed the porcelains found in 1987 in the underground palace of the Famen Temple pagoda, the efforts in recent years to locate and classify the Yue ware kilns in Zhejiang, and both Yue wares and presumably *mise* Yue wares from various sites.[2] A rough consensus was reached. Regarding the definition of the term *mise*: the most common glaze color of Tang dynasty Yue ware is a yellowish green, like mugwort; the Yue wares found at the Famen Temple site, however, are a much different and rarer hue of green. Therefore we may assume, provisionally, that *mise* refers specifically to the hue of these Famen Temple green-glazed wares.

Two pieces of white porcelain, marked with the character *guan*, were unearthed in 1985 at Huoshaobi in Xi'an, Shaanxi Province (cats. 126, 127). They are probably late Tang Ding ware. Many pieces of white porcelain unearthed in recent years from late Tang, Five Dynasties, and Northern Song sites have been marked with the character *guan*, and the majority of these are Ding ware. The same character also appears on Yaozhou ware and Yue ware (fig. 4). This *guan* cannot denote the fabled Guan ware, because many superb pieces of Ding, Yue, and Yaozhou ware are not marked *guan*; moreover, not all the pieces so marked are outstanding. During the Tang dynasty a "Yinguanshu" Office served the court.[3] One of its

Fig. 4. Celadon jar with two lugs, inscribed with character guan. *Five Dynasties (907–960). Yue ware; h. 28.6 cm, diam. at mouth 9.5 cm. Unearthed in 1970 from a Five Dynasties tomb in Banqiao, Lin'an, Zhejiang Province. Zhejiang Provincial Museum.*

functions was to supply the imperial court with pottery utensils, as well as to provide burial objects for the court to bestow on deceased officials at their funerals. Burial objects could be made of wood as well as pottery. Many of the pieces of white porcelain marked with the word *guan* have been unearthed from the tombs of high officials and aristocrats. Hence Ding pieces inscribed *guan* might very well have been ordered from the Ding kilns by the Yinguanshu to serve as burial objects. Reinforcing this hypothesis, we know that during the Tang, Five Dynasties, and Northern Song many pieces of porcelain were marked with the name of the agency that had ordered them.

Although the Five Dynasties lasted altogether only fifty brief years, they have an important place in the history of ceramics. During these years Ding ware,

Fig. 5. Five-footed brush washer. Southern Song dynasty (1127–1279). Ge ware; h. 9.2 cm, diam. at mouth 8.8 cm. Shanghai Museum.

Fig. 6. Footed brush washer. Northern Song dynasty (960–1127). Jun ware; h. 9 cm, diam. at mouth 24.3 cm. Shanghai Museum.

in the north, developed toward its apex in the Northern Song. In the south, Yue ware reached its peak. In the northwest, potters of the Yaozhou kilns in Shaanxi, building on the successes of Yue ware, worked toward the creation of a truer green glaze; these Five Dynasties potters accomplished the transition from the varied green glazes of the Tang to the more uniform blue-green of the Northern Song. It was also during the Five Dynasties that the

production of white- and green-glazed porcelains at Jingdezhen in Jiangxi laid the foundation for major development of Yingqing ("shadow blue" glaze, also called Qingbai) during the Northern Song.

In the history of Chinese ceramics many wares reached their florescence during the Song dynasty, whose so-called "five great wares" were Ru, Guan, Ge, Ding, and Jun.

There surely must be some significance in the fact that of these five wares, the organizers of this exhibition chose to display only Ru, Guan, and Ding wares, and not Ge or Jun wares. In fact, the site and period of production of Ge ware remain major topics for exploration in the history of Chinese ceramics. Although an international symposium on Ge ware was held in Shanghai in October 1992,[4] no answers were to be had (fig. 5). As for Jun ware (fig. 6), it exists in some quantity in the United States and Europe. The Art Institute of Chicago, in particular, owns a collection of Northern Song Jun ware unequaled in China except in the Beijing Palace Museum and the Taibei Palace Museum. In the first half of the twentieth century some European and American collectors and scholars had regarded these specimens of Northern Song Jun ware as Yuan or Ming products. But excavation of the site of the Northern Song kilns at Diaotai in Yu county, Henan Province,[5] completely verified the existence of Northern Song Jun ware.

For the past thousand years Ru ware has been

Fig. 7. Brush washer. Northern Song dynasty (960–1127). Ru ware; h. 2.9 cm, diam. at mouth 17.1 cm, diam. at base 9.1 cm. Shanghai Museum.

renowned for its ash-colored body, its sky blue glaze with fine crackling, and for being wholly glazed and fired on tiny sesame seed-shaped spurs (fig. 7). Of all the great Chinese porcelain wares, Ru ware has survived in the smallest numbers and is perhaps the most prized. For a long time, the location of the Ru kilns could not be confirmed, but in the winter of 1986 two studies made by staff from the Shanghai Museum verified the site of the Northern Song Ru kilns at Qingliangsi in Baofeng county, Henan Province.[6] The kilns were then excavated by archaeologists from Henan Province. Ru ware was produced only for an extremely brief time, and in very limited quantities. Some pieces found at the kiln site lack the above-mentioned defining characteristics; these clearly are not Ru ware.

Song dynasty Guan ware is an even more controversial subject in the history of Chinese ceramics. Historical documents indicate that there were three types of Guan ware, one made in the Northern Song capital of Bianliang (present-day Kaifeng, in Henan Province), one at the Xiuneisi ("Palace Works Bureau") of the Southern Song capital at Hangzhou, and one at the Jiaotanxia kilns of Southern Song Hangzhou. To date, only the Jiaotanxia site, at Wuguishan in Hangzhou Municipality, Zhejiang Province, has been verified. The Northern Song Guan kilns and those of the

Southern Song Xiuneisi have yet to be confirmed, and among existing pieces there is no way to distinguish those made at the Northern Song Guan kilns from those made at the Southern Song Xiuneisi. Some scholars of Chinese ceramics have recently questioned whether the Northern Song and Xiuneisi Guan kilns in fact even existed.[7] In 1997 an ancient kiln site was discovered at Fenghuangshan in Hangzhou Municipality, Zhejiang Province, but further scientific excavation is needed before it can be determined if this is indeed the Xiuneisi kiln.

However exquisite and acclaimed, the "five great wares" of Ru, Guan, Ge, Ding, and Jun do not encompass the total achievement of Chinese ceramics during the Northern and Southern Song, Liao, and Jin dynasties. Yaozhou wares of the north and Longquan wares of the south, both green-glazed, were enormously significant both in the quantity produced for use by society and in the quality of individual pieces.

Only in the past few decades has Yaozhou ware achieved wide recognition. Prior to the 1950s little was known about ancient green-glazed wares from northern China, and except for Ru ware and Jun ware, all pieces produced during the Northern Song and Jin dynasties were called northern Longquan or northern Chuzhou ware. Since 1984 large-scale scientific excavations of the Yaozhou kilns have fully revealed their nature. Although the Yaozhou kilns of the Northern Song also produced white-glazed, black-glazed, and brown-glazed porcelain, green-glazed porcelains were, of course, their principal output. These were decorated by carving, incising, molding, appliquéing, and modeling, and the powerfully carved pieces are particularly noteworthy.

Longquan wares of the Song were of two types—thick-bodied with thin glaze, and thin-bodied with thick glaze. The first had a slightly yellow-hued green glaze, highly transparent, and sometimes carved or incised designs; the other was the world-famous powder-green or "plum"-green (*meizi*) Longquan ware. The thick-bodied, thin-glazed Longquan with relatively rough carving or incising was made mostly from the mid-to-late Northern Song until the early Southern Song, whereas the thin-bodied, thick-glazed powder-green celadon was popular during the late twelfth and early thirteenth centuries. The peak period for powder-green and *meizi*-green celadons was the thirteenth century. The jar with everted mouth and molded bowstring pattern in this exhibition is a classic example of powder-green Longquan ware (cat. 134).

Cizhou ware derives its name from what is now Ci county in Hebei Province (formerly a part of

Cizhou), and kilns that made typical Cizhou ware have been located at Guantai township and Yezi village in Ci county. In fact, a network of many kilns, from Henan westward into Shanxi and eastward into Shandong, were producing similar wares. Mostly they made white and black stonewares, but also polychrome- and green-glazed pieces, and during the Jin dynasty they even created underglaze painted porcelains. Most of their output was sold to the mass market. Cizhou ware was decorated in a variety of ways, most often with underglaze black or brown designs painted on a white slip-covered ground. More laboriously, designs might be carved or incised through the white slip to the buff-colored body fabric, then clear-glazed—another way of creating two-tone decoration. Sometimes an allover pattern of small circles, called pearl-dotting or ring-matting, would be stamped on the ground. Green-painted and polychromed Cizhou pieces have also been found.

During the Ming and Qing dynasties Jingdezhen was the Chinese porcelain capital, supplying vast orders to the imperial court, the domestic market, and an avid foreign trade. (It should be remembered that the technique of making porcelain was unknown in the West until the eighteenth century.) Long known for its many superb wares, the most immediate and consequential cause of its ascendancy was the development there in the mid-fourteenth century of underglaze blue and underglaze red porcelain. Blue-and-white, red-and-white, and all the polychrome variants descended from these, swept the public taste, ousting monochrome green-glazed ware from its millennia-long supremacy.

Porcelain manufacture in Jingdezhen entered its peak period during the Yongle and Xuande eras of the Ming dynasty in the first half of the fifteenth century.

During the preceding Yuan dynasty Jingdezhen was already producing blue-and-white porcelains and selling them by the batch to other East Asian countries and in the Middle East, but they were relatively insignificant in the domestic market. In records from the late Yuan and early Ming, there is no endorsement of blue-and-white, nor did the gentry consider blue-and-white to be aesthetically important. Beginning in the Yongle era, however, blue-and-white began to make its way into the palaces and houses of the social elite. Relative to the Yuan dynasty, there was major progress in the production of both body and glaze. Potters in the imperial kilns during the Yongle and Xuande periods perfected blue-and-white wares beyond anything seen during the Yuan dynasty, achieving a finely textured and pure white body, bright and lustrous glaze, and rich, well-controlled blue color.

Zheng He's seven expeditions to the southwest further promoted trade links with central and west Asia, and brought back cobalt ore for "Somali" blue. This imported blue colorant had a high iron and low manganese content. The low manganese content reduced the grayish tint in the blue, and with proper firing it could produce a sapphire blue color. At the same time, due to the high iron content, black iron flecks often appeared in the blue, and these naturally occurring black iron flecks yielded an interesting contrast with the rich blue color. The three Yongle and Xuande blue-and-white pieces in this exhibition (cats. 142–44) are excellent examples of well-made blue-and-white works of this period.

Although blue-and-white dominated production, the Yongle and Xuande eras also saw the manufacture of a small number of extraordinary monochrome-glazed pieces, including red, brown, jade green, shadow blue, yellow, yellow-green, blue, Ge-type, Ru-type, and low-temperature green glazes.

From the late 1430s through the early 1460s, political turmoil in the Ming court caused porcelain production at the official (i.e., court-controlled) kilns in Jingdezhen to decline. Orders from the court revived with the start of the Chenghua era in 1465. Doucai porcelains of the Chenghua era, whose decoration combines blue painting under a clear glaze with polychrome enamels over the glaze, are works unmatched before or since. The Doucai vase with the floral pattern in this exhibition (cat. 146), though of the Yongzheng period, exemplifies the delicacy and soft, harmonious palette of Doucai designs.

Under Qing patronage Jingdezhen continued to thrive and its output to increase. The Ming repertoire continued in production, with the favored blue-and-white underglaze porcelains refined to a somewhat chilly perfection. Unflagging demand at home and abroad spurred technical innovation, producing a range of exquisitely subtle monochromes for the court and, to a very different taste, a huge variety of polychrome-enameled vessels (cat. 145) and figures of breathtaking virtuosity. The pieces in this show include choice items that embody five thousand years of Chinese history, and may leave viewers who are partial to Ming and Qing porcelains hungry for more. Perhaps this will provide the Guggenheim Museum with reason to organize a future exhibition of Ming and Qing treasures.

Translated, from the Chinese, by June Mei.

NOTES

1. Archaeology team of the Famen Temple, Shaanxi Province, "Brief Report on the Excavation of a Tang Dynasty Underground Palace at the Famen Temple Pagoda in Fufeng," *Wenwu*, 1988:10.

2. Wang Qingzheng, *Yue Ware Mise Porcelain* (Shanghai Classics Publishing House, 1996).

3. Li Linfu et al., comp., *Tang liudian*, vol. 23.

4. Shelagh Vainker, "Ge Ware Conference Report— Symposium on Ge Ware, Shanghai Museum, October 1992," *Oriental Art*, Summer 1993.

5. Zhao Qingyun, "Excavation of a Kiln Site at Diaotai, Yu County, Henan Province," *Wenwu*, 1975:6.

6. Wang Qingzheng, Fan Donqing, and Zhou Lili, *The Discovery of Ru Kilns* (The Woods Publishing Company, 1991).

7. Wang Qingzheng, "Some Issues in the Study of Song Dynasty Guan Ware," *Essays Celebrating the 30th Anniversary of the Minqiu Jingshe* (Liangmu Publishing House, 1995), p. 124.

Ceramics in China: Making Treasures from Earth

Regina Krahl

Independent Scholar,
Affiliated with the Royal Museums
of Art and History, Brussels

Earth is one of the most ubiquitous materials, and thus, in most cultures, one of the earliest from which vessels were made. Usually in plentiful supply, it tends to be versatile, easy to handle, and therefore very practical. It was used in most Neolithic cultures as it still is today.

Fig. 1. Bottle. Sui dynasty (581–618). High-fired white stoneware with translucent glaze; h. 21 cm. Hebei area. Meiyintang collection.

China is particularly rich in resources of earth, clay, and rock from which ceramics can be made. Chinese ceramics vary immensely in quality but basically divide into two types: low-fired earthenware (also called "pottery") and high-fired stoneware and porcelain. Simple, rough earthenware clay can be baked at low temperatures (up to about 1000° C) to a modest, fairly soft, porous brown or gray pottery. High-quality porcelain stone, when fired at high temperatures (to about 1200° C), turns into hard, dense, and usually gray stoneware; refined and upgraded and fired at even higher temperatures (to about 1350° C), it becomes a vitrified, translucent, hard, and dense glass-like white matter—which we call porcelain.

The fame of Chinese ceramics is built on these latter high-fired wares. Porcelain stone, or china stone, the raw material from which stoneware is made, is abundant in many areas of China, north and south. Very high quality porcelain stone can be used more or less as it is mined, without requiring any additions or much preparation. Stonewares have been made in China since the Shang dynasty (ca. 1600–ca. 1100 BCE), and predate their Western counterparts by over two and a half millennia.

The origin of porcelain is more difficult to specify, for it was not an invention but an evolution from stoneware, an advance along the continuum of high-fired wares. Where one ends and the other begins is a subjective decision. Distinguishing characteristics are body composition and firing temperature. Since these cannot easily be determined for ancient items, more superficial features have to be taken into account, such as the translucency and the whiteness of the body and the clarity of its sound when struck. The Chinese themselves do not distinguish at all between the two high-fired materials—stoneware and porcelain—and use the same name (*ci*) for both, as distinguished from low-fired earthenwares (*tao*).

The earliest pieces that could by any reckoning be called porcelain are some sixth-century white wares from the Northern Qi (550–77) or Sui (581–618) period (fig. 1). Between that period and the thirteenth century (Yuan dynasty; 1279–1368), a great variety of more or less "porcelaneous" stonewares was made throughout China, until in the second half of the Yuan dynasty the continuous production of nothing but porcelains began at the kilns of Jingdezhen and China's stoneware tradition came to an end.[1]

EARTHENWARE IN THE NEOLITHIC PERIOD
Only in prehistoric times was earthenware an important material in China. The most practical and versatile material available for vessels, earthenware served essential functions in many aspects of daily life. It was used throughout the vast area that we call China, which, between the sixth and the second millennium BCE, was inhabited by many independent and distinctive cultures. The ceramics produced during the Neolithic period (ca. 7000–ca. 2000 BCE) are as varied and complex as the cultures themselves, but they do not vary greatly in material and workmanship. The red or yellow pottery is often burnished and most frequently painted with abstract geometric designs in brownish black, tones of red, and white (cat. 113); more rarely it bears anthropomorphic,

zoomorphic, or other images, like the human heads and fish on a basin from Banpo near Xi'an, Shaanxi Province (cat. 114). Most of this pottery was probably made for practical use, although the more unusually painted pieces may have had a ritual function.

More remarkable than the Neolithic potters' efforts at painting are their ways of forming the clay. Vessels in sculpted three-dimensional forms are very rare, but occur in many different cultures. They include human, animal, and bird figures (cats. 115, 116), whose primary purpose does not seem to have been utilitarian.

Utility was certainly not a major concern of the Longshan potters in the region of Shandong Province who made some of the most beautiful Neolithic vessels. Their tall black goblets in daring shapes, turned on the potter's wheel, shaved to eggshell thinness, burnished, and pierced with lace-like openwork patterns (fig. 2), seem to have been designed to overcome the solid, weighty quality of the material. This imaginative and accomplished handling of earthenware clay was never achieved again in later periods. Yet even these most advanced Neolithic pots are technically nowhere near as remarkable as contemporaneous jades.

EARTHENWARE SINCE THE BRONZE AGE

From the middle of the second millennium BCE, earthenware was little used for quality crafts. It still had many other functions; all of them, however, were low in prestige. It was used at the building site, the foundry, and the tomb, for structural parts, models, molds, and replicas. Potters made earthenware roof tiles, wall tiles (cats. 103, 104), water pipes, bricks, and other structural parts; the wall tiles and bricks were mainly for underground structures, because Chinese buildings were held up by wooden pillars rather than supporting walls.

During the Shang (ca. 1600–ca. 1100 BCE) and Zhou (ca. 1100–256 BCE) dynasties, China's Bronze Age, earthenware had the important but naturally unglamorous function of supplying models and molds for bronze casting. Bronze Age potters thus left an imprint on the crafts of their time, but their actual works were not meant to be preserved and have survived in only a very fragmentary state.[2]

An exception is the white pottery jar from Anyang, in Henan Province (cat. 117)—a rare instance of a bronze vessel, presumably shaped after a pottery model, being in turn copied in clay.[3] Beautiful but impractical, it is made of white earthenware of finer quality and brighter color than that used for model making, yet is similarly soft, porous, and brittle. Not surprisingly, such pieces do not seem to have been made in any quantity, nor for long, and they do not

Fig. 2. Goblet with eggshell walls and openwork stem. Neolithic period, 3rd millennium BCE. Burnished black earthenware; h. 26.5 cm. Unearthed at Donghaiyu, Rizhao, Shandong Province. Shandong Provincial Museum.

represent an important step in the development of Chinese ceramics.

From the Warring States period (475–221 BCE) until the High Tang period (713–779) earthenware was in demand as an inexpensive, versatile, and attractive material for making replicas that played a vital role in funerary practices: figures of men and beasts (cats. 88–92, 96–97, 99–101, 105–7, 109), models of structures (cats. 100, 102), and copies of objects of daily life. These replicas were painted or glazed or both. The figures substituted for the living beings that previously had been sacrificed for important burials; the copies considerably reduced the costs of funerals by replacing more valuable goods.

The most remarkable aspect of this tomb pottery is the sculptural quality of some of the figures. Since burial goods were status symbols for both the deceased and the survivors, they became more and more ambitious over time. This trend reached its zenith in the High Tang period; grave figures of that time can be strikingly naturalistic and lively (cats. 105–7) or else highly imaginative and elaborate in their modeling (cats. 110–11).[4] They represent virtually the only type of secular sculpture ever made in China.

Funerary pottery inspired little innovation in ceramic technology. Glazes were used on Chinese earthenwares beginning only in the Han dynasty (206 BCE–220 CE), almost a thousand years after they had appeared on Chinese stonewares. The glazes have a wider range of bright colors than the early stonewares, beginning with a leaf green (cat. 100) and a reddish brown (cat. 101) in the Han dynasty, followed by a blackish brown in the Northern Wei (386–534), various tones of yellow and amber from the Northern Qi on, and eventually blue and turquoise in the Tang.[5]

Because funerary ceramics were generally made of soft and porous clays and either cold-painted with unstable pigments or covered with poisonous lead glazes, they were decorative but of very limited use to the living. This made them even more desirable for burials, as they held no attraction for tomb robbers.

STONEWARE FROM THE SHANG DYNASTY TO THE SIX DYNASTIES PERIOD

In the production of these various earthenwares since the Neolithic period, China was no more advanced than most other countries. The important and unique development of Chinese ceramics toward the production of porcelain took a separate route. Its origins can be traced back to the Bronze Age, when stonewares began to be produced simultaneously with earthenwares, but at different kiln centers and for different purposes.

The Shang dynasty gray-green jar in the exhibition (cat. 118) may have been considered less attractive than its white earthenware contemporary (cat. 117), but technically it is far more sophisticated. It has a stoneware body and a natural glaze derived from wood ash. Fired at a high temperature (over 1200° C), its body became hard and completely dense and wood ash on its surface turned liquid, forming a glaze over part of the vessel.

Since its properties are very similar to those of porcelain, even though it is neither white nor translucent, this type of ware is referred to as protoporcelain. It was by far the most advanced and practical ceramic ware of its period. Yet compared with contemporary bronzes, whose complex forms and intricate designs seem to have absorbed all artistic efforts of the time, it looks very modest indeed. Whether the porcelain stone that forms the body material was used in a pure state or enhanced by admixtures of kaolin (china clay) and other substances, it always remained gray and rather coarse. The glaze might have been accidental,

occurring when floating particles of ash in the wood-fired kiln landed on the vessel surface, or deliberate, achieved by dusting ash onto the vessel before firing. Whatever the process, the glaze was never smooth or even.

Vessels of glazed stoneware were made throughout the Bronze Age (ca. 2100 BCE–220 CE) without major changes. Whereas in the Eastern Zhou period bronze vessels became more and more flamboyant in shape and design, their surfaces often enhanced by dramatic inlay in silver, gold, malachite, and other materials, and lacquerware provided an elegant alternative in the form of far more delicate vessels with intricate polychrome painted designs, the finest ceramics were still rather dull.

After the Han dynasty fell, the empire fractured into a number of independent kingdoms. The kingdoms most important for the continuation of indigenous Chinese culture were all located in the southeast and all had their capitals in Nanjing. The manufacture of stonewares burgeoned in the south. Among the earliest ceramic centers to become famous by name are the Yue kilns of Zhejiang Province, not far from Nanjing. They were the earliest kilns to make stonewares with glazes that were applied in a liquid state and therefore evenly covered the whole vessel (cats. 119, 120). In color these liquid glazes, whose yellowish olive tone was derived from oxidized iron, are similar to ash glazes; but they tend to be brighter and more intense since the contents of a liquid glaze can more easily be manipulated than those of wood ash. Yue ware was made in much greater quantities than earlier stonewares, both for daily use and for burial.[6]

During this multistate period China was more receptive than ever before to foreign goods and ideas. Probably the most significant influence came from Western Asia with the introduction of Buddhism. The southern kingdom of Wu (220–80), in whose domain the Yue kilns were situated, was one of the first to embrace the new religion. Yue wares therefore show some of the earliest Chinese representations of the Buddha (cat. 120).[7]

As Buddhism spread throughout China it brought with it such foreign motifs as lotus flowers, palmettes, and applied decorations suggestive of encrusted jewels and strings of pearls. These motifs began to appear on the green-glazed stonewares from north of the Yangzi River (cat. 122). Although these ceramics with their exotic ornamentation and shapes seem to embody the taste of their time and to represent precious artifacts in which the period was otherwise poor, the most elaborate pieces were destined for burial; only the simpler ones were intended for use.[8]

STONEWARE DURING THE SUI AND TANG DYNASTIES

Although Buddhism remained enormously influential until the end of the High Tang period, ceramics did not reflect its influence for long. In the early Tang dynasty and during the two brief periods that led up to it artistically, the Northern Qi (550–577) and the Sui (581–618), Chinese potters again became more inward-looking. At the Yue kilns in the south, which continued to make green-glazed stonewares, and at the Xing and other kilns in Hebei and Henan provinces in the north, which began to make white stonewares, quality quickly improved. By the second half of the Tang, potters were creating ceramics with most desirable features: a clear and clean color, a glossy sheen, a smooth tactile surface, and an even, flawless appearance. The sheer beauty of such material made ornament superfluous.

Yue and Xing wares were more than merely practical; they were perhaps the first Chinese ceramics to be celebrated for their beauty. In the *Cha jing* ("Classic of Tea"), an eighth-century text, bowls of Yue (cats. 123–25) and of Xing ware (cats. 126, 127)[9] are recommended for tea drinking—then an activity of almost ritual intricacy—and are compared, respectively, to jade and silver, two of the most highly prized materials of the time.[10] Although the delicate green glaze of Yue ware can evoke the beauty and tactile quality of jade and the brilliant clear glaze over a white body of Xing ware can be reminiscent of silver, these ceramics were neither conceived nor regarded as substitutes for such elevated substances but rather as their equivalents. These early literary references signal the dawn of connoisseurship in Chinese ceramics.

In the early Tang dynasty, Buddhism had gripped not only the population at large but also the imperial household. Buddhist temples regularly received valuable offerings and thus became veritable treasure houses. One of the foremost temples of the time was the Famen Temple, not far from the Tang capital of Chang'an (present-day Xi'an); it held one of the most sacred relics, a finger bone of the Buddha. In the mid-Tang period this relic was repeatedly borne in procession with great ceremony from the temple to the palace, and then returned with lavish donations from the court. The last donations might have been added in 874, when the relic was sealed in a repository (see essay by Helmut Brinker in this volume).

When this repository was discovered in 1987 under the Famen Temple pagoda, the Buddha bone was found to be preserved among the most precious objects of gold and silver, the rarest pieces of rock crystal and glass, over seven thousand pieces of

silk—and fourteen green-glazed Yue ware vessels (cats. 124, 125). With their very pale bodies, highly glossy light-green glazes, and surfaces as tactile as a well-polished gem, they are exceptional indeed, unmatched in quality by any other pieces surviving from that time, even if closely related (cat. 123).[11] In the repository's inventory, they were listed as *mise* ("secret color") ware, a term well known from late Tang poetry, which tells us that *mise* ware was made at the Yue kilns.[12]

The fact that these green-glazed stonewares, produced far away in the south, should be included in one of the richest repositories, among the most exquisite and expensive gifts from the imperial court, clearly documents their elevated status. When the Tang empire began to break up into smaller kingdoms, not long after the Yue wares at the Famen Temple site were made, the kings of Wu-Yue, in whose domain the kilns were situated, reserved Yue ware for their own use.

White wares from the Ding or Xing kilns may have played a similar role at another court. Some of them are inscribed on the base with the character *guan* ("official") (cats. 126, 127) or with similar identifications. The significance of this inscription cannot yet be explained with any confidence, since such pieces have been discovered in Tang, Five Dynasties (907–960), Liao (916–1125), and Northern Song (960–1127) contexts.[13] One can therefore only speculate about what special status ceramics singled out in this way might have had. The only other Tang stonewares besides clear- and green-glazed ones were those with black glazes, often with light blue splashes, but for those no elevated status can be claimed.[14]

STONEWARE DURING THE SONG DYNASTY

Stylistically, these undecorated monochrome wares of the Tang are completely indigenous Chinese products. They initiated a taste in ceramics that found its fullest expression only during the Song dynasty (960–1279). Both aesthetically and technically, the Song dynasty represents a high point of Chinese culture and particularly of Chinese ceramics. It was a time when exquisite materials and sophisticated workmanship were combined with a calculated simplicity in form and design.

In contrast to the few workshops making fine ceramics in the Tang, dozens of kiln centers had mastered the basic principles by the early Song. Kilns that during the Tang had made only basic utensils which were not known by the kiln names, refined their body and glaze materials and improved potting and firing techniques to such a degree that by the tenth century they were able to produce beautiful and flawless wares. Technological mastery gave free rein to creativity and allowed the potters to concentrate on detail and subtle variation. The most important ceramic wares of the Song all developed from the three basic types of stoneware made in the Tang: those with green, clear, and black glazes.

Song shapes are almost invariably simple, functional, and well proportioned. Song vessels tend to be monochrome-glazed in subtle, rarely seen shades rather than bright primary colors. Often they are wholly undecorated, or have surfaces modestly enlivened by the faint tonal gradations created by incised or carved designs, or by the random patterns formed by a crackle, the decorative crazing of the glaze that can occur during the cooling process after firing.

The most admired features of Song ceramics look as if they had come about naturally, without all the effort and precision work that they in fact require. Only an intimate familiarity with the properties of all raw materials and a thorough understanding of their reactions during the firing cycle enabled potters to manipulate them as they wished.

The appeal of perfected simplicity achieved through exquisite craftsmanship is very subtle indeed. Ceramic masterpieces of the Song were not made for ostentatious display, but for handling by connoisseurs in an intimate, private setting. It was in the literati circles of the Song that ceramics were first appreciated as works of art, that they were deemed worth collecting, whether antique or new, and worth handing down from one generation to the next.

Although the preference for artifacts made of clay over precious metals or stones probably emanated from the literati circles of the Song, where understatement was a celebrated virtue, the imperial court manifested a similar taste. Of course, not all the vast and varied Song wares were officially appreciated, but some were made exclusively for the court. No comparable production of goods worked from gold or silver, or from jade or other stones exists for this period.

Through their absolute mastery of the technical process and their acute sense of aesthetic principles the potters, none of whom is known by name, were able to manipulate their medium so sensitively and intelligently that they turned one of the most basic raw materials—earth—into one of the most precious commodities.

By far the rarest and most desirable Chinese ceramics of all times were and are the green-glazed stonewares from the Ru kilns in Baofeng county, Henan Province (cat. 132), close to the capital at Kaifeng. They were made for the court for only some twenty years in the last two decades of the eleventh and first years of the twelfth century. Only some sixty examples have survived today, but collectors have lamented their rarity for centuries. Most Ru wares are accessories for the scholar's desk, such as brush washers (low bowls for cleaning the writing or painting brush). They are extremely simple, evenly and thinly potted, and almost invariably undecorated. Ru wares are fully glazed (including foot and base), having been placed in the kiln on supports that left only minute so-called sesame-seed marks on the glaze. The ware is celebrated above all for its tactile glaze in varying evocative shades of bluish and grayish green, usually with a crackle. The comparison with well-polished, well-colored, slightly veined jade is inevitable.

When the northern capital was captured by the Jin invaders and the Song fled south in 1127, they set up kilns at their new capital in present-day Hangzhou to make an "official" (*guan*) ware (cat. 133) modeled on Ru. Using the different raw materials of the south, the potters came up with a ware that appeals for the same reasons but looks different, having a thicker, clearer glaze and a more pronounced crackle. Guan and Ru wares represent the epitome of Chinese ceramics—the transformation of earth as a medium into a substance deemed more beautiful and more precious than the most valuable materials.

Since these two wares could not easily be obtained except by the imperial palace, their beauty was emulated by other kilns. "Celadon," as green-glazed stonewares are usually called in the West, was in fact in seemingly limitless supply.[15] The Yaozhou kilns in Shaanxi Province in the north were stylistically less immediately dependent on Ru; their wares bear swiftly incised, carved, or combed designs (cat. 130). But the Longquan kilns in Zhejiang Province in the south clearly aimed at imitating Guan (cat. 134). Some Longquan celadons do this so successfully that they were, and sometimes still are, mistaken for Guan ware.[16]

Among the white wares are two remarkable types of similar quality and style: both have a finely potted white body; clear, translucent glaze; and accomplished, swiftly carved designs. Ding ware (cat. 131 and its predecessors, cats. 128, 129), from Hebei Province in the north, has a characteristic ivory-tinged glaze and was used at the court. But the so-called *qingbai* ("bluish white") ware, which has a blue-tinged clear glaze (cat. 135) and came from Jingdezhen in Jiangxi Province in the south, was never highly appreciated. It was the Jingdezhen kilns, however, that were to establish a virtual monopoly on Chinese ceramics with their production of blue-and-white porcelain from the Yuan dynasty on.

During the Song dynasty the black-glazed, blue-splashed stonewares of the Tang developed in two directions: light blue-glazed wares, sometimes with purple suffusions, made by the Jun kilns of Henan Province (fig. 3),[17] which belong to the wares acclaimed at court, and black-glazed wares from kilns all over China,[18] which achieved no such eminence.

All these wares, which emanated from the traditions of Tang green-, white-, and black-glazed wares, embody the Song ideals of highly refined materials, exquisite workmanship, an unerring sense of proportion, and a judicious use of subtle decorative devices that contribute to the overall effect without compromising the general impression of simplicity.

The great exception to that aesthetic among Song dynasty ceramics are the wares from the Cizhou and related kilns of north China (cats. 136–38). They followed a different tradition, in which the potters were less concerned with the refinement of their materials than with producing striking decorations of calligraphic or painterly quality. Cizhou-type wares, which became particularly popular during the foreign-ruled Jin and Yuan periods, can be seen as foreshadowing a new direction in Chinese ceramics.

PORCELAINS SINCE THE YUAN DYNASTY

For some time the Jingdezhen kilns of Jiangxi Province had been able to create a clean, white, and translucent porcelain. Perhaps the most valuable aspect of this material is that it is totally neutral. A pristine ground such as this provides an ideal surface for painted decoration. The introduction of fine cobalt from the Middle East and experiments with copper in China suddenly introduced two striking pigments, a bright blue and a deep red, for painting with a brush on the dried but still unfired and unglazed porcelain body, very much like painting in ink on paper or silk. Sealed with glaze and fired at high temperatures, the colors are permanent. With this innovation, the stylistic concept of fine ceramics underwent a fundamental change.

The Yuan dynasty (1279–1368) therefore forms something like a watershed in the history of Chinese ceramics. The underglaze painting of cobalt and other pigments on porcelain represents the last great evolutionary step, after which no further dramatic innovations took place.[19] The development of Chinese ceramics during the last six hundred years could therefore be seen as a long sequence of variations on a single theme.

Fig. 3. Basin. Jin dynasty; 12th c. Blue-glazed stoneware with purple suffusions. Jun kilns, Henan Province, diam. 32.4 cm. Meiyintang collection.

In this respect, Chinese ceramics differ little from Chinese painting, and what James Cahill (q.v.) has stressed about later Chinese painting is equally true for later Chinese ceramics: the groundbreaking discoveries, both technical and conceptual, took place so remarkably early in China that all later craftsmen had to battle against a "near-overpowering weight of the past" to maintain their originality. Cahill's admiration for the "stratagems" the painters of the Ming and Qing period devised "for escaping repetition and stagnation" could equally be extended to the potters of the period, even though their ways of working were in no way comparable. In fact, the phases in which Chinese ceramics had the greatest impact on ceramics worldwide were yet to come.

From the early fourteenth century the most important aspect of a ceramic vessel was its decoration. A most spectacular early example of this emphasis is the covered jar (cat. 139) unearthed from a Yuan dynasty hoard at Baoding, Hebei Province: this jar combines painting in underglaze cobalt blue and underglaze copper red with applied openwork and pearl beading. A tour de force such as this vessel did not find immediate favor with Chinese connoisseurs, whose taste was much more restrained. Early blue-and-white and related porcelains were largely exported to the Middle East and Southeast Asia and were used, to a lesser

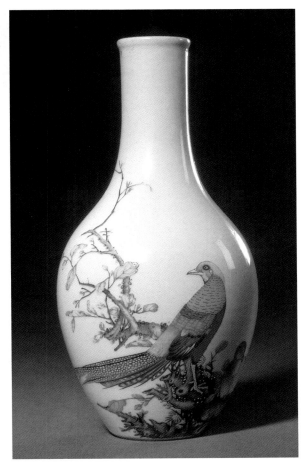

Fig. 4. "Chicken" cup. Ming dynasty, Chenghua mark and period (1465–1487). Porcelain with Doucai decoration, Jingdezhen kilns; diam. 8.2 cm.

degree, by the ruling Mongols. But since no other kiln could equal the striking visual appeal of these porcelains, Jingdezhen soon eclipsed all other kiln centers.

At first, however, the native Chinese Ming court, still influenced by Song aesthetics, preferred the more sober monochrome porcelains from Jingdezhen (cats. 140, 141). Blue-and-white found favor only gradually. The large and impressive blue-and-white porcelains made during the Yongle period (1403–1424) (cats. 142, 143) still went mainly abroad. Small, delicately potted and painted pieces such as the stem bowl from the Xuande reign (1426–1435) (cat. 144) may have been among the first blue-and-white porcelains to appeal at the Chinese court, about one hundred years after the ware was first made.

Once the court had "discovered" blue-and-white porcelain, it instantly monopolized the entire output of the Jingdezhen kilns. At the same time, virtually everything made for the imperial household was inscribed with a reign mark—that is, the auspiciously worded designation of the current emperor's reign period. To begin with, the reign mark truly indicated a ware made exclusively for court use; in later periods such marks were also inscribed on nonimperial porcelains and earlier reign marks were copied on later pieces. The palace required large numbers of identical objects. Stringent quality controls assured that shapes and patterns were precise and materials absolutely

Fig. 5. Vase with design of golden pheasants and calligraphy. Qing dynasty, Qianlong mark and period (1736–1795). Porcelain from Jingdezhen kilns, enamel painting by imperial workshops in Forbidden City, Beijing; h. 20.3 cm. Private collection.

flawless. Uniformity was more appreciated than individuality.

Although the porcelains of the Ming and Qing (1644–1911) are rarely unique, their painted decoration remained spirited. Painting in overglaze enamel colors, applied on the glazed, fired porcelain which is then refired, was perfected in the Chenghua period (1465–1487). Enamel colors such as red, green, yellow, aubergine, and turquoise were used first in the *doucai* ("matched" or "clashing" colors) technique, in which those overglaze colors were combined with underglaze blue outlines and sometimes washes. Later, enamels were used in varying *wucai* ("five-color") combinations, for which underglaze blue outlines were considered unnecessary. The *doucai* "chicken cups" of the Chenghua period, with their charmingly painted scenes of chickens and chicks (fig. 4), were and still are deemed the most desirable of all Ming porcelains. Both *doucai* and *wucai* continued to be popular throughout the Qing dynasty (cats. 145, 146).

Porcelain painting that approached the quality of traditional ink painting was an achievement of the Qing dynasty. It can be credited to a man named Tang Ying, who supervised the imperial porcelain production in the Yongzheng (1723–1735) and early Qianlong (1736–1795) periods, when it reached its greatest heights. It required not only more highly trained artists but also a much larger palette of suitable pigments to achieve a flexible range of colors and shades.

Imperial workshops had been set up within the palace precincts in the Forbidden City under the Kangxi emperor (1662–1722), for painting enamels on copper, porcelain, and glass. For this purpose the most accomplished porcelain painters were sent from Jingdezhen to Beijing together with ready-made plain white porcelains suitable for enameling. In addition, some of the Jesuits residing at the court, valued for their knowledge of Western science and technology, were assigned to these workshops from time to time, to their great chagrin. Among these artists it was Giuseppe Castiglione (1698–1766), known to the Chinese as Lang Shining, who greatly influenced the decorative arts through his naturalistic painting style, with its sharply defined contrasts between light and shade and emphasis on three-dimensionality and perspective.

At about the same time, the palette of enamel colors was enlarged by the introduction of two new pigments developed in Europe, whose use on porcelain was rapidly perfected in China: a rose pink and, more important, an opaque white enamel which, mixed with other colors, could create whole new ranges of opaque pastel shades.

The flower-and-bird or landscape scenes from the palace workshops are academic but exquisite little paintings. To emphasize their close connection with

painting, they are generally accompanied by a poetic colophon written in black in a calligraphic hand, followed by (painted) "seals" (fig. 5). The subtly nuanced color and the microscopic precision with which minute details are rendered make this the most sophisticated porcelain painting ever achieved.

SOURCES FOR FIGURES
Fig. 1. Copyright Azimuth Editions.

Fig. 2. After Zhongguo meishu Quanji, Vol. I, Arts and Crafts Edition (Shanghai: People's Arts Publishing Company, 1988).

Fig. 3. Copyright Sotheby's.

Fig. 4. Copyright Sotheby's.

Fig. 5. Copyright Sotheby's.

NOTES
1. For the purpose of this exhibition, the term "porcelain" has been used very conservatively—that is, only for wares from the Yuan dynasty or later, even though some earlier pieces may also seem to qualify for that designation.

2. Fragments of pottery molds have been discovered at many Shang and Zhou dynasty sites, particularly at the Eastern Zhou bronze foundry at Houma, Shanxi Province; see Institute of Archaeology of Shanxi Province, ed., *Art of the Houma Foundry* (Princeton: Princeton University Press, 1996); and Robert Bagley, "Debris from the Houma Foundry," *Orientations* (October 1996), pp. 50–58.

3. Compare a very similar Shang dynasty bronze jar (*you*), complete with cover and swing handle, excavated from a hoard in Zhengzhou, Henan Province, published in *Quanguo chutu wenwu zhenpin xuan* (*A Selection of the Treasure of Archaeological Finds of the Peoples' Republic of China*) (Beijing: Wenwu chubanshe, 1987), pl. 166.

4. For a good selection of fine tomb figures excavated in China, see *Zhongguo wenwu jinghua daquan: Taoci juan* ("Complete Series on the

Finest Cultural Relics of China: Ceramics Volume") (Taipei: Shangwu yinshuguan, 1993), pp. 76–163.

5. For an early example of a blackish brown glaze, see the figure of a horse from a Northern Wei tomb dated to 484, in *Zhongguo meishu quanji; Gongyi meishu bian 1: Taoci* ("Complete Series on Chinese Art; Crafts Section 1: Ceramics"), vol. 1 (Shanghai: Shanghai renmin meishu chubanshe, 1988), pl. 238; for a pale yellow and an amber glaze, see a covered bottle and a pilgrim flask from two Northern Qi tombs, the latter dated to 575, ibid., pls. 236, 237. One of the most impressive blue-glazed pieces is a large jar and cover from the Anthony de Rothschild collection at Ascott House, Buckinghamshire; see Margaret Medley, *T'ang Pottery and Porcelain* (London: Faber, 1981), cpl. B; and for a rare example of a Tang turquoise glaze, see the figure of an earth spirit in *The Tsui Museum of Art: Chinese Ceramics I, Neolithic to Liao* (Hong Kong: The Tsui Museum of Art, 1993), pl. 121.

6. In addition to functional containers, Yue wares of the Six Dynasties include unmistakable funerary wares such as plates with permanently affixed cups and spoons, and burial figures.

7. For Yue wares with Buddha figures predating the Western Jin bowl in the exhibition (cat. 120), see *Fojiao chuchuan nanfang zhi lu* ("The Southern Route of the Dissemination of the Buddhist Faith") (Beijing: Wenwu chubanshe, 1993), passim.

8. A series of the most lavishly embellished funerary vases of the Northern Qi dynasty is illustrated in Yutaka Mino and Katherine R. Tsiang, *Ice and Green Clouds: Traditions of Chinese Celadon* (Indianapolis: Indiana University Press, 1986), no. 38.

9. The white wares of the Xing and the Ding kilns, both in Hebei Province, are extremely difficult to distinguish. Generally speaking, the Xing kiln centers were more advanced during the Tang and Five Dynasties periods, but by the Northern Song period were outshone by the Ding

kilns and eventually eclipsed. Individual pieces are not always easy to attribute, however. White wares inscribed with the character *guan* ("official") are generally associated with the Ding kilns, but are not exclusive to them.

10. For a translation of Lu Yu's *Cha jing* ("Classic of Tea"), see Francis Ross Carpenter, *The Classic of Tea by Lu Yü* (Boston and Toronto: Little, Brown, 1974), where this discussion appears on pp. 90–93.

11. The two octagonal bottles (cats. 123, 125), which superficially look very similar, are in fact very different. The bottle from Famen Temple (cat. 125) shows a much whiter clay and glossier glaze and has more elegant proportions than the one in the Palace Museum, Beijing, whose history is not recorded (cat. 123). The Famen Temple Yue wares are of unmatched quality and at present seem to be the only ones to qualify for the distinction of being called *mise* ware. The Palace Museum bottle represents what used to be considered fine Yue ware of the period. Fragments of such bottles have been found at Shanglinhu, the main Yue kiln site, and one such piece comes from a burial datable to 871; see Ho Chuimei, ed., *New Light on Chinese Yue and Longquan Wares*, Centre of Asian Studies Occasional Papers and Monographs, no. 110 (Hong Kong: The University of Hong Kong, 1994), p. 341, pl. 1G. The two types therefore appear to be contemporary products of the same kilns; why they should be so different cannot yet be explained.

12. For discussions on *mise* (formerly called *bise*) ware, see S. W. Bushell, *Description of Chinese Pottery and Porcelain, Being a Translation of the T'ao Shuo* (Oxford, 1910), pp. 37, 131; and Sir Percival David, "Some Notes on Pi-sê Yao," *Eastern Art* 1 (January 1929), pp. 137–43.

13. White wares inscribed with the character *guan* have come to light in many tombs and pagoda foundations in

Zhejiang, Beijing, Liaoning, and Hebei, some of which are datable to the years 895–900, 958, 959, 977, and 1031, respectively: see *Wenwu*, no. 12 (1979), pp. 18–23; and *Wenwu*, no. 12 (1975), p. 41.

14. For a representative selection of Tang black wares from kilns in Henan Province, with and without light blue glaze splashes, see Regina Krahl, *Chinese Ceramics from the Meiyintang Collection*, vol. 1 (London: Azimuth Editions, 1994), pp. 126–35. The only other important Tang stoneware kilns not represented here are those of Changsha in Hunan Province, which made green wares, partly with designs painted under the glaze; see Timothy See-Yin Lam, *Tang Ceramics: Changsha Kilns* (Hong Kong: Lammett Arts, 1990).

15. "Celadon" is a Western collector's term that refers to green-glazed stonewares, usually those from the Song dynasty on. The origin of the term is not absolutely clear. It may derive either from Saladin, a twelfth-century sultan of Syria and Egypt, where the ware was popular, or from a seventeenth-century play by Honoré d'Urfé. The play, in which a young shepherd named Céladon appears dressed in pale green, was fashionable in nineteenth-century France, as was the ware.

16. Several of the most exquisite Longquan copies of Guan ware presented as tributes to the court during the first Qing reigns were included in the National Palace Museum exhibition *Song guanyao tezhan* (*Special Exhibition of Song Dynasty Kuan Ware*) (Taipei: National Palace Museum, 1989); three of them—cats. 33, 84, 110—were identified as such by Ts'ai Ho-pi in the catalogue, p. 31.

17. Two types of Jun ware can be distinguished whose dating and thus importance for the court is still much debated: a group of vessels of simple rounded forms characteristic of the Song and Jin dynasties, with even-toned blue glazes with or without distinct purple

splashes; and a group of flowerpots and vases in a range of sizes (marked from 1 to 10), made in complicated bronze shapes characteristic of the Yuan and Ming dynasties, with shaded blue and purple glazes. An attribution to the Northern Song is undisputed for the former; on the basis of controversial archaeological evidence some scholars also attribute the latter to that period. For examples of the two types, see Zhao Qingyun, *Henan taoci shi* ("History of Henan Ceramics") (Beijing: Zijincheng chubanshe, 1993), pl. 18 and cpl. 11, nos. 42, 43, 45 for the former, and pl. 19 and cpl. 11, no. 44 for the latter.

18. For a representative selection of Song black wares, see the exhibition catalogue by Robert D. Mowry, *Hare's Fur, Tortoiseshell, and Partridge Feathers: Chinese Brown- and Black-Glazed Ceramics, 400–1400* (Cambridge, Mass.: Harvard University Art Museums, 1996).

19. Isolated experiments with underglaze painting in cobalt blue on white stonewares that could be called porcelains had already been made in the Tang dynasty. The beginnings of blue-and-white porcelain are therefore by some scholars associated with the Tang. But these Tang wares appear to be totally unconnected with the continuous production of blue-and-white porcelain at Jingdezhen in Jiangxi Province, which can be traced back no earlier than the first quarter of the fourteenth century.

Origins and Trends in the Depiction of Human Figures in China of the Fifth and Sixth Centuries

Su Bai

Professor, Beijing University

In the sculpture and painting of central and northern China two successive changes occurred in the fifth and sixth centuries that were particularly evident in the depiction of human figures. These two changes were directly related to a deliberate attempt on the part of the non-Han ruling classes in central and northern China to adopt Han culture

Fig. 1. Buddha Amitābha. Dated to 420. Rock carving. Bingling Temple, Cave 169:6, Liujiaxia city, Gansu Province.

Fig. 2. Buddha Amitābha. Ca. 420. Cave painting. Bingling Temple, Cave 169:12, Liujiaxia city, Gansu Province.

and copy the native institutions of southern China. Hence, the origins of these changes must be traced back to the southern dynasties of Eastern Jin (317–420), Liu Song (420–479), and Liang (502–557).

I.

In April 1963 a work team from the Gansu Provincial Bureau of Relics discovered a grotto containing a sculpture of Buddha Amitābha (numbered 169:6 in the archaeologists' report) in Cave 169 of the Bingling Temple in Yongjing (present-day Liujiaxia city, about fifty miles southwest of Lanzhou) (fig. 1). This bore an inscription dated to the year 420, making it the earliest known cave sculpture in China with an explicit date. The grotto contains a configuration consisting of a Buddha sitting in meditation and attendant bodhisattvas; to the lower left of the grotto is a group of murals of similar date and subject matter (169:12; fig. 2). Both groups of Buddha images are characterized by broad shoulders, large torsos, and a sense of geometric solidity and weightiness. The same features recur in Tanyao's Caves 16–20 at Yungang in Datong, Shanxi Province. These were carved at the urging of Tanyao, overseer of monks under the Northern Wei dynasty, in 460. Among these images, the large seated Buddha in Cave 20 is the most typical (fig. 3). In 1949 a Buddha seated cross-legged in meditation was unearthed in Xingping county, Shaanxi Province, which dates from 471 (cat. 147).

Fig. 3. Seated Buddha. Dated to 460. Rock carving. Cave 20, Yungang, Shanxi Province.

Although it retains vestiges of the features mentioned above, it also shows changes in the direction of simpler and stronger lines. This transformation may have occurred during the period when the dowager empress Feng, widow of Emperor Wencheng, exerted great influence at court.

II.

According to the History of the Northern Dynasties, in 476 the dowager empress Feng "sat in Court and held all power." During her ascendancy the

Fig. 4. Buddha Śākyāmuni (below); Buddhas Śākyamuni and Prabhutaratna (above). Rock carvings. Cave 11, Yungang, Shanxi Province.

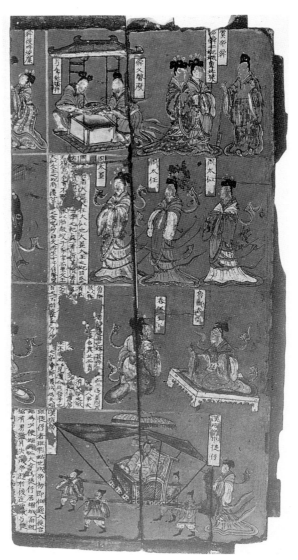

Fig. 5. Biographies of Virtuous Women. Dated to 484. Painted lacquer screen. Tomb of Sima Jinlong and his wife, Shijiazhai village, Datong, Shanxi Province.

Northern Wei policy of adopting Han culture intensified, and was reflected in Buddhist sculpture: the previously common garment that draped both shoulders or bared the right shoulder was no longer Śākyamuni's attire; rather, he was portrayed wearing the Confucian scholar's loose gown and wide sash. The face and torso also were transformed increasingly from square and powerful to thin and elongated. The earliest dated example of this new type of Buddha statue is found on the upper east side outside Cave 11 at Yungang (No. 11:14, which is numbered 11d by Mizuno Seiichi and Nagahiro Toshio in *The Yungang Caves*). An inscription dated to 489 is carved below the grotto. Thereafter, elaborate flowing drapery and elongated faces and figures became the vogue and spread throughout the Northern Wei domains (fig. 4). The Yungang cave sculptures from 489 to 524 are the most representative of this style. In 493 the capital was moved from Datong in Shanxi Province, near the Yungang caves, to Luoyang in Henan Province. The various sculptures from the Guyang Cave at Longmen near Luoyang similarly display the characteristics of this era. During the late Qing dynasty a carved stone panel donated by one Liu Gen, dated to 524, was unearthed in Dongyipu, Luoyang (cat. 152). Some of the figures in the middle of the tablet exquisitely exemplify the slender, linearly rendered figures of relatively late date. Buddhist icons were not the only images in this style: good examples of the same style are found among the figures of worshipers in the above-mentioned Yungang and Longmen caves, as well as among the earthen burial figures and the paintings and stone carvings in Northern Wei tombs of the Luoyang years. Among these secular figures, the earliest known examples from the north are the persons painted on a lacquer screen found in the tomb of Sima Jinlong and his wife. The screen, discovered in the village of Shijiazhai in Datong, dates from 474–484 (fig. 5).[1] There is some speculation that this screen may have been imported from southern China at about that time.

The scholar's loose robe and sash, elegant physiognomy, and purity of image characterize human figures of the Eastern Jin and Liu Song eras. In 847 Zhang Yanyuan of the Tang dynasty (618–907) compiled the *Lidai minghua ji* ("Record of Famous Painters of Successive Dynasties").[2] In it, the Jin and Liu Song dynasties are referred to as the Era of Middle Antiquity, and in volume 2 of this work the painters of the Era of Middle Antiquity are thus critiqued:

Those of Middle Antiquity who can compare with those of High Antiquity are Gu and Lu.

Gu Kaizhi (ca. 344–ca. 406) and Lu Tanwei (ca. 440–ca. 500) are cited as representative painters of Middle Antiquity. In volume 6 Zhang Yanyuan explicitly endorses the high assessment of Lu Tanwei by Zhang Huaiguan[3] during the Kaiyuan years of the Tang dynasty (713–741):

> Lu infuses his soul marvelously into his work. He combines motion with spirit, and his brush strokes are powerful as if chiseled with a knife. The elegant bones of his figures seem almost alive; they leave one in awe, as if in the presence of a god, yet though the image is wondrous it is conceived in nothing more than ink. In painting figures . . . Lu gets the bones right, while Gu [Kaizhi] gets the spirit. . . . Yanyuan considers this an appropriate assessment.

From this we know that representative painters of the Jin and Liu Song dynasties strove for an artistic style that stressed "spirit," or a sense of life, and "bones," or refined physiognomy. The human figures in the extant Song copies of Gu Kaizhi's *Admonitions to the Court Ladies* (fig. 6) and *Goddess of the Luo River*[4] do indeed emphasize "spirit and bone." Other figures with elegant physiognomy are the Pure Land (school of Buddhism) stone carvings of 425, which were found at the Wanfo Temple site in Chengdu, Sichuan Province, and the two extant gilded bronze seated Buddhas of 437 (fig. 7) and 451. These typical stylizations are similarly found in depictions of people from contemporary tombs of the Six Dynasties in the lower Yangzi River basin, such as images of the *Seven Sages of the Bamboo Grove and Rong Qiqi*, painted on bricks embedded in the walls of a tomb beneath the north face of Mt. Gong in Xishanqiao, Nanjing. These, as well as earthern figures of men and women from this tomb, probably date from the Liu Song dynasty, and their style is markedly refined and attenuated (fig. 8).[5] Such figures were particularly in vogue during the Liu Song and Southern Qi dynasties. Hence the contemporary writer Xie He of Wu, in his *Guhua pinlu* ("Classification of Ancient Painters"), ranks Lu Tanwei first among painters:

> He goes to the limits of understanding and nature, and there are no words to describe his achievements; he encompasses the past and bears the seeds of the future, yet stands out among both past and present; he cannot be praised by mere effusiveness, yet (his work) is of the greatest value. There is nothing to say except that he is the best of the best, but the most I can do is place him in the first rank.[6]

Slender images were even more popular in the

Fig. 6. Gu Kaizhi (ca. 344–ca. 406). Admonitions to the Court Ladies *(last section). Song dynasty copy. Handscroll, ink and color on silk. British Museum.*

Fig. 7. Seated Buddha. Dated to 437. Gilt bronze. Wanfo Temple site, Chengdu, Sichuan Province.

central Yangzi River basin during the period of the Liang dynasty. For instance, the images in the wall paintings and the earthen tomb figures from the brick tomb in Xuezhuang village of Deng county, Henan Province, which is on the west bank of the Tuan tributary of the Han River, are primarily of the slender type (fig. 9).[7] But some of the pottery tomb figures from a slightly later painted brick

Fig. 8. Seven Sages of the Bamboo Grove and Rong Qiqi. *Six Dynasties (222–589). Tomb mural of painted bricks. Mt. Gong, Xishanqiao, Nanjing, Jiangsu Province.*

tomb in Jiajiachong in Xiangfan, Hubei Province, are markedly fuller (fig. 10). The amplitude of the earthen figures from that tomb is especially noticeable.[8]

III.

Xiao Yan (r. 502–549), who founded the Liang dynasty, adapted many institutions of the Southern Qi dynasty,[9] and "for fifty years the south was uneventful."[10] A change in fashion at the southern courts was reflected in artistic styles, namely, the popularity of Zhang Sengyou's (act. ca. 500–ca. 550) school of painting. Zhang Yanyuan praised Zhang Sengyou's paintings of people as "marvelous" and "wonderful," and he noted that "the Zhangs, father and sons [Sengyou's sons Shanguo and Rutong] are

Fig. 9. Figures. Liang dynasty (502–557). Stamped brick with traces of pigment. Xuezhang village, Deng county, Henan Province.

Fig. 10. Figure of a civil official. Liang dynasty (502–557). Pottery. Painted brick tomb, Jiajiachong, Xiang fan, Hubei Province.

in the ultimate rank" (vol. 9, *Lidai minghua ji*). He also cites this comment from the *Duoyishu* ("Enumeration of the Myriad Arts") of Gao Zongshi (649–683)[11] and from Li Sizhen (d. 696), who compiled *Paintings:*[12]

> Gu and Lu are now gone, and in terms of being the best, only Sengyou can claim to be a worthy successor. Scholars of today look up to him as they would to the Duke of Zhou and Confucius. . . . Also, the attire of people drawn by Gu and Lu is incomparable, to the point where you notice little else. As for the marvelous sense of bones in Zhang, he has studied everything, so he is not only adept in the Six Methods, he is actually marvelous in every way. He has infinite variety, and an abundance of forms, which are seen by his eye and shaped in his palm; his hand responds to every thought in his mind, till you sense that here is a sage sent by heaven who can create as

Fig. 11. Buddha Amitābha and Buddha Maitreya. Dated to 483. Rock carvings. Mao county, Sichuan Province.

wondrously as a magician. So I suggest ranking him at the top with Gu and Lu (preface to vol. 7, *Lidai minghua ji*).

Li and Zhang are both certainly unstinting[13] in their praise of Sengyou, but for a specific description of Zhang's style we have only Li's remark about his marvelous sense of bones. What should we make of this phrase? After the previous passage, the *Lidai minghua ji* goes on to quote Zhang Huaiguan:

> In the subtleties of drawing people, Zhang gets the flesh right.

This is most crucial. Elsewhere, the *Lidai minghua ji* is even more explicit:

> In drawing the bones of people, Zhang falls behind Gu and Lu. Zhang gets the flesh right (vol. 6).

In contrast to the styles of the great masters who preceded Sengyou, the main point about Sengyou's "marvelous sense of bones" is his shift in emphasis from spirit and bones to "getting the flesh right," that is, the shift from slender to ample. Hence, the terms used in temple inscriptions of the time to describe the Buddha's image included "a relaxed moon face"[14] and "a face like a full moon."[15] These round faces are very different from the narrow faces so highly regarded before. Early signs of this change from the slender style, and of the gradual emergence of the fuller-bodied figures that "get the

flesh right," can be seen in the two stone carvings of Amitābha and Maitreya Buddha from Mao county, Sichuan Province, dating from 483 (fig. 11). Fuller and rounder figures can also be seen clearly in the stone carvings from the Wanfo Temple in Chengdu, which date from 523 (cat. 150), 529, 537, and 548, all bearing inscriptions from the Wuji period of the Liang dynasty. (The above are all in the collection of the Sichuan Provincial Museum.) These same traits are also evident in the carved images of female attendants from the painted brick tomb of the late Southern dynasties period in Qijia village of Changzhou, Jiangsu Province.[16] And as the bodies grew fleshier, the garments became simpler.

By about the second quarter of the sixth century the new Southern style represented by Zhang Sengyou had probably diffused all the way north to Luoyang, the new capital of the Northern Wei, which was again turning avidly to southern China for models in conduct and in art. According to the "Biography of the monk Fazhen":

> The monk Fazhen . . . was well versed in the *Chengshilun*, and had a profound grasp of its meaning. His lectures were brilliant and original, and he was peerless between the Yi and Luo rivers. His fame was as great as that of the monk Jian. At the time the virtues of the Wei were in decline, women were in the ascendant, predictions of doom were increasingly common, suspicions were rampant, envy was excessive—this is what the world was

Fig. 12. Fragments of sculptures. Dated to 519 (Northern Wei dynasty). Stone. Pagoda of the Yongning Temple, Luoyang, Henan Province.

Fig. 13. Figures of patrons. Mid-6th c. Rock carvings. Dalishan cave-temples, Gong county, Henan Province.

coming to. Zhen said to Jian, "The Liang is a nation which follows the rites, they have bodhisattvas and observe the rules and customs, and they preach the correct ways. Let us go there." . . . Jian said, "The moment is not to be lost. I have also had the same intention." So in the second year of the Putong period of the Liang (521) they headed south together. Zhen was overtaken by pursuing cavalry and killed. . . . [Jian then] travelled to the kingdom in the south and reached Jiangyin, where he lived in the Heyuan Temple.[17]

Given that the polities of southern China were perceived as authentically Chinese and admirable, it naturally became the fashion among artistic circles in central and northern China to emulate the new styles of the south. Thus, after the eighth month of 519 a group of sculptures was made and placed within the pagoda of the Yongning Temple, built by the Northern Wei royal family at Luoyang.[18] The surviving heads are about seven centimeters high, and greatly resemble those of the Liang dynasty (fig. 12).[19] The trend toward simpler draperies and fleshier bodies is increasingly evident in the slightly later figures of patrons from caves 1, 4, and 3 of the Dalishan caves in Gong county, Henan Province

(fig. 13). From the late Wei, this trend became pronounced. The "Biography of Du Bi" in volume 24 of the *Beiqi shu* ("History of the Northern Qi") records the following conversation that Gao Huanping had with Du Bi after he pacified the capital, Luoyang (532):

Bi noted that when Wenwu reigned, there was a level of clean government seldom seen, and he mentioned it to Emperor Gaozu. Gaozu said, "Come here, Bi, let me tell you something. It has long been the custom for the country to be corrupt and chaotic. Nowadays many of the generals' families live west of the pass where Heita [i.e., Yuwen Tai] is constantly beckoning to them, and it is unclear if their loyalties will be to stay or to go. In East China there is an old man named Xiao Yan living in Wu who specializes in the proper dress and rites. The gentry of the central plains regard him as the guardian of the correct ways.[20] I am eager to establish laws and rules, and would not mind borrowing, for I fear that if the generals go over to Heita and the gentry leave to follow Xiao Yan, then our talents will have all dispersed, and how then could I run the country?"

In light of this historical background, it was almost inevitable that the Eastern Wei and Northern Qi should copy the southern style. Hence, the following all reveal the fuller-figured style: the Gushan caves in Handan, Hebei Province (i.e., the North and South Xiangtangshan caves); the stone carvings in the Shuiyu cave-temple; and the figures on the steles unearthed in Xiangcheng and Luoning counties in Henan Province in 1963, which date from 559 (Northern Qi) and 565 (Northern Zhou) (cats. 157, 158); the carved stone grotto statues of the Northern Qi unearthed in 1954 at the Huata Temple in Taiyuan, Shanxi Province (cat. 156); and the earthen figures from Eastern Wei and Northern Qi tombs recently unearthed in Henan, Hebei, and Shanxi. In 1975 a group of figures within a square setting, made of white marble and believed to date from the Northern Zhou, was discovered in Caotan, a northern suburb of Xi'an in Shaanxi Province (cat. 159). These figures, most likely from a multistoried stone pagoda, are also of the Northern Qi style. Because many white marble figures came from Dingzhou, in Qi territory, there is speculation that these stone pagoda images may also have been made in Qi territory. In 1987 a tomb discovered at Wanzhang in Ci county, Hebei Province, proved to be the Wuning Mausoleum in which Gao Yang was buried, and its date is believed to be 560 (Northern Qi). In this tomb, as in the tomb of Lou Rui, Prince of Dong'an, discovered in 1979 at Wangguo village in Taiyuan, Shanxi Province, and dated to 570, there are large murals depicting a cavalry honor guard; in both murals the full-fleshed bodies are particularly obvious (fig. 14).[21] Both tomb murals are drawn with simple and forceful lines, and show a vitality in keeping with the high social standing of those buried there.[22] Quite a number of commentators believe that they may have been done by the Northern Qi court painter Yang Zihua.[23] Yang Zihua was the most highly regarded of the Qi painters, and the early Tang artist Yan Liben praised his works thus:

As for painting people, the subtlest lines, the utmost beauty in simplicity, having little enough so that not a single thing can be omitted, yet just enough that nothing should be added—only Zihua can do this![24]

Although it is not certain that Yang did the murals in the tombs of Gao Yang and Lou Rui, it is probably safe to say that they were in the style of

Fig. 14. Mounted honor guard. Dated to 570. Mural. Tomb of Lou Rui, Prince of Dong'an, Wangguo village, Taiyuan, Shanxi Province.

the Yang school, which was so popular during the Northern Qi. Zhang Yanyuan calls the period from the Qi and Liang through the Chen and Zhou the Period of Recent Antiquity, and he discusses the paintings of Recent Antiquity thus:

Those from Recent Antiquity who can compare with those of Middle Antiquity are Sengyou and Zihua.[25]

Just as Gu and Lu were contemporaries, practiced similar styles, were ranked as equals, and were considered comparable in excellence to the best painters of the preceding age, so Zhang and Yang were paired with each other and compared with their predecessors Gu and Lu. Volume 2 of the *Lidai minghua ji* lists Yang Zihua among those painters in central China during the Northern Qi period who had learned from Gu, Lu, and Zhang Sengyou:

Tian Sengliang, Yang Zihua, Yang Qidan, Zheng Fashi, Dong Boren, Zhan Ziqian, Sun Shangzi, Yan Lide, and Yan Liben learned from Gu, Lu, and Sengyou.[26]

Of these, Tian Sengliang, Yang Zihua, Zheng Fashi, Dong Boren, and Zhan Ziqian were famous during the Northern Qi and Zhou,[27] while Sun Shangzi and Yang Qidan were active during the Sui, and the Yan brothers during the early Tang. Sengyou, in the phrase "learned from Gu, Lu, and Sengyou," actually taught Tian, Yang, and the rest, whereas Gu and Lu were the originators of the style they studied. Hence, the *Lidai minghua ji* also cites earlier commentators on the subject of Zheng Fashi, Sun Shangzi, and the Yan brothers purportedly studying with Zhang Sengyou:

> [About] Zheng Fashi . . . the monk Zong[28] said: "He learned Zhang's methods, and could paint anything . . . . Li [Sizhen] said, "He studied the school of Zhang, and was considered his disciple" (vol. 8).

> Li said: "Sun [Shangzi] and Zheng [Fashi] both studied with Zhang. Zheng was incomparable at drawing people and buildings, whereas Sun was supernatural in the way his spirit infused his work" (vol. 8).

> Pei [Xiaoyuan] said: "Yan [Lide and Liben] studied with Mr. Zhang and surpassed their teacher. They mastered all the subtleties of drawing people, garments, horses, chariots, and buildings" (vol. 9).[29]

Moreover, according to Zhang Yanyuan, Li Ya, Fan Changshou, and He Changshou also had studied with Zhang:

> Li Ya [of the Sui] studied with Zhang Sengyou (vol. 2).

> [At the beginning of the dynasty] Fan Changshou studied with Zhang Sengyou. . . . He Changshou had the same teacher as Fan, but was slightly less skillful than Fan. Fan and He's *Drunken Daoist Priest* is extant. People say this was done by Sengyou, but that is untrue (vol. 9).

We can see what a profound influence Sengyou's quality of "getting the flesh right" had on the artists of the central plains from the Northern Qi and Zhou on. Many extant images continue to follow the tradition of fuller figures—for instance, the Zhou and Sui paintings and reliefs from the Maijishan caves of Tianshui in Gansu Province, the Mogao grottoes of Dunhuang, and Mt. Sumeru at Guyuan in Ningxia; stone carvings from various pre-High Tang tombs north of the Wei River in Shaanxi Province; funerary murals and incised carvings from the Qianling, the mausoleum of Tang Gaozong and Wu Zetian; and extant Song copies of early Tang *Portraits of Emperors through the Ages* (fig. 15).[30] The great artist Wu Daozi of the High Tang era drew people in relaxed poses that, according to the *Lidai minghua ji*, can also be traced back to Sengyou:

> Wu Daoxuan [Daozi] studied under Zhang Sengyou (vol. 2).

Fig. 15. Portrait of Sun Quan. Song dynasty (960–1279) copy from early Tang (618–907) Portraits of Emperors through the Ages *(Lidai dihuang tu). Handscroll, ink and light color on silk. Museum of Fine Arts, Boston.*

Zhang Huaiguan also remarked:

> Wu Daoxuan probed all the subtleties of painting, and he was probably a student of Zhang Sengyou ("Huaduan," cited in vol. 751 of *Taiping yulan*).[31]

He also notes:

> The brushwork in Wu's paintings has a soul. He is a reincarnation of Zhang Sengyou (*Lidai minghua ji*, introduction to vol. 9).

Thus, Sengyou's influence lasted through the reign of Emperor Xuanzong of the Tang.

IV.

Painting and sculpture have long been closely linked, and as Chinese sculptures were always colored, those engaged in sculpting had to have a solid foundation in painting. In his *Wudai minghua buyi* ("A Supplement to Famous Paintings of the Five Dynasties"), Liu Daochun of the Northern Song noted that among those who studied alongside Wu Daozi under Zhang Sengyou was Yang Huizhi, who was famous for his sculptures:

Yang Huizhi's hometown is unknown. During the middle of the Kaiyuan period of the Tang dynasty (713–741), he and Wu Daozi learned brushwork together from Zhang Sengyou, and they called each other "friends through art." They were both highly skilled, yet only Daozi had a great reputation. Huizhi then burned his brushes and inkstones, and threw himself into sculpting. He was able to capture the look of Sengyou's paintings, and thus could rival Daozi. It was said at the time, "Daozi's paintings and Huizhi's sculptures capture the spirit of Sengyou's brush." He was also praised for this.[32]

The *Lidai minghua ji* noted in vol. 9 that the great sculptors of the day all had a mastery of painting:

At the time, there was a Zhang Aier who was unsuccessful at learning [Wu Daozi's] painting, and so turned to sculpting. Emperor Xuanzong personally wrote and changed his name to Xianqiao. His paintings of insects were superb. Yang Huizhi of the same era was also adept at sculpting. Yuan Ming and Cheng Jin carved works in stone. Han Botong of the Sui dynasty was adept at sculpting. During the reign of the Empress, the local officials Dou Hongguo and Mao Poluo, Supervisor of the Eastern Garden Sun Rengui, and the general Quan Zhongyi at the Court of Emperor Dezong were all exceptionally skilled. This generation also [studied] painting. They were all excellent draftsmen, but their tone was not very high.

Since the earliest times it had been natural for great sculptors to also excel at painting. According to the *Lidai minghua ji*,

There was a man named Dai Kui [d. 395] [during the Eastern Jin dynasty]. He was styled Andao, and was a native of Zhi in Qiao Prefecture. He was very gifted even as a child, was intelligent and widely read. He played musical instruments well, and was a skillful calligrapher and painter . . . his paintings of scenery in the ancient style were wonderful. While in his teens, he was painting in the Waguan Temple. General Secretary Wang [Meng] saw him and said, "This child is not just good at painting. Sooner or later he will make a great name for himself." . . . He was also adept at casting images of Buddha and at sculpting. He had made a wooden statue of Amitābha Buddha 1.6 zhang tall, together with attendant bodhisattvas. Kui used the simple ancient style, and when the work was initially unable to move people's hearts, he sat silently behind a curtain, listening secretly to everyone's comments. He gave careful consideration to both praise and criticism, and collected his

Fig. 16. Mural and carved figure of Śākyamuni. 8th c. (High Tang period). Mogao Cave 328, Dunhuang, Gansu Province.

thoughts for three years, whereupon he completed the sculpture. . . . Also, in middle age, Dai Andao drew figures of great draftsmanship (vol. 5).[33]

Kui's son Yong was styled Zhongruo. His quickness of mind was comparable to Kui's. . . . He carried on his father's mastery of music, calligraphy, and painting. . . . The [Liu] Song crown prince was casting a 1.6 zhang golden image at the Waguan Temple. When it was completed, he was annoyed that the face seemed so thin, but the workmen could do nothing about it. He then invited Yong over and asked him about this. Yong said, "It is not that the face is thin, but that the shoulders are too big." He then pared down the shoulders, and the face's proportions then became right. Everyone was impressed by the sharpness of his thinking (vol. 5).[34]

Jiang Shaoyou [of the Later Wei] was a native of Bochang in Le'an. He had a keen and nimble mind, and was adept at calligraphy and painting. He was skilled at painting people and at sculpting (vol. 8).[35]

The Indian monk Tanmozhuoyi [of the Sui dynasty] was also skilled at painting. During the reign of Emperor Wen of the Sui, he came from his own country and visited all the pagodas of King Aśoka in China. When he came to the Dashi Temple at Luo county in Chengdu, he saw the forms of twelve spirits in the sky, whereupon he studied the looks of each one and then carved their images at the base of the temple's pagoda. They still survive today (vol. 8).[36]

These are all well-known examples. Extant sites such as the Mogao grottoes at Dunhuang indicate that even the earliest surviving caves show a consistency of layout and a uniformity in design and style among both paintings and sculptures that could only have been achieved by a single creator (fig. 16). That accounts for the roughly synchronous development of sculpture and painting in China prior to the late Tang. From the Northern Song, painters increasingly specialized in particular genres, and neither court painters nor literati painters deigned any longer to sculpt.[37] Popular art preserved the tradition of linking painting and sculpture, but in vulgarized styles that could no longer properly reflect the tastes of the times.

Translated, from the Chinese, by June Mei.

SOURCES FOR FIGURES

Fig. 1. See Zhongguo shiku: Yongjing Binglingsi *("Chinese Cave Sculptures: The Bingling Temple"), pl. 21.*

Fig. 2. See Zhongguo shiku: Yongjing Binglingsi 9*"Chinese Cave Sculptures: The Bingling Temple"), pl. 36.*

Fig. 3. See Yungang shiku *("The Yungang Caves"), pl. 92.*

Fig. 4. See Zhongguo shiku: Yungang shiku er *("Chinese Cave Sculptures: The Yungang Caves, Part 2"), pl. 124.*

Fig. 5. See Wenhua dageming qijian chutu wenwu *("Archaeological Relics Unearthed During the Cultural Revolution"), pl. 143.*

Fig. 7. See Zhongguo Jintongfo *("Gilded Bronze Buddhas in China"), fig. 5, p. 236.*

Fig. 8. See Liuchao yishu *("The Arts of the Six Dynasties"), fig. 163.*

Fig. 9. See Dengxian caise huaxiang zhuanmu *("A Color-Painted Brick Tomb at Deng County"), fig. 24.*

Fig. 11. See Zhongguo shikusi yanjiu *("Studies of Temples in Chinese Caves"), p. 108, fig. 4, and p. 109, fig. 5.*

Fig. 12. See Xinzhongguo de kaogu faxian yu yanjiu *("Archaeological Discoveries and Studies of New China"), pl. 148.*

Fig. 13. See Zhongguo shikusi: Gongxian shikusi *("Chinese Cave Sculptures: The Cave Temples of Gong County"), pl. 38.*

Fig. 14. See Wenwu, *1983:10, lower illustration on color page.*

Fig. 16. See Zhongguo shiku: Dunhuang Mogao san *("Chinese Cave Sculptures: The Mogao Grottoes, Part 3"), pl. 114.*

NOTES

1. *Wenhua dageming qijian chutu wenwu ("Archaeological Relics Unearthed During the Cultural Revolution")* (1990), vol. 1, pp. 143–44.

2. The edition of *Lidai minghua ji* ("Record of Famous Painters of All the Dynasties") cited in this paper is based on the original Xunyang edition of *Wangshi huayuan* ("Wang's Garden of Paintings"), which is now in the Beijing University Library collection and which dates back to the early Wanli period. Although this version contains more errors than the one in Mao's Jiuguge edition of *Jindi mishu* ("Secret Works of the Jindi"), it is nevertheless a reprint of the Shupeng half-page, 11-line edition published in Lin'an during the Southern Song, and is the earliest extant copy of the *Lidai minghua ji.*

3. Zhang Huaiguan compiled the three-volume *Shuduan* ("Opinions on Calligraphy"); see vol. 57, the "Arts and Letters, Part 1," of the *Xin Tangshu* ("New Tang History"). He also compiled *Huaduan* ("Opinions on Paintings"); see vol. 1 of *Tuhua jianwen zhi* ("Notes on Pictures and Paintings") by Guo Ruoxu of the Northern Song dynasty.

4. Xu Bangda, "Gu Kaizhi's 'The Goddess of the Luo River,'" in vol. 1 of *Gushuhua wei'e kaoshi* ("Studies of Errata in Ancient Calligraphy and Paintings"), 1984.

5. Yao Qian et al, *Liuchao yishu* ("Arts of the Six Dynasties") (1981), pp. 162–79.

6. In vol. 6 of the *Lidai minghua ji*, this excerpt is rendered thus: "He goes to the limits of understanding and nature, and there are no words to describe

his achievements; he encompasses the past and bears the seeds of the future, yet stands out among both past and present; he cannot be praised merely by effusiveness, and exhausts all description. He is the best of the best, there is nothing left to say . . . so the most I can do is place him in the first rank. He is the foremost person of the first rank."

7. Work team of the Henan Provincial Bureau of Relics, *Dengxian caise huaxiang zhuangwu* ("Color Paintings from a Brick Tomb in Deng County"), 1958.

8. Relics Administration Office of Xiangfan, "Xiangfan Jiajiachong huaxiang zhuanmu" ("A Painted Brick Tomb in Jiajiachong, Xiangfan"), *Jianghan Archaeology*, 1986:1.

9. According to the "Lidianxu" ("Preface to the Book of Rituals") in vol. 41 of the *Tongdian*, "By an edict in the second year of Yongming during the reign of Emperor Wu of the Qi, the Minister ordered the officials to establish the Five Rituals. Then Emperor Wu of the Liang ordered the scholars to refine and complete them. When Emperor Wu of the Chen succeeded to the throne, he mostly adhered to the Liang standards."

10. Geng Xin, "Lament for Jiangnan," in *Zhou shu* ("History of the Zhou"), vol. 41, "Biography of Geng Xin." Also "Biography of Baochang" in vol. 1 of *Xu Gaoseng zhuan* ("Sequel to Lives of Eminent Monks"): "For fifty-odd years, the south was uneventful."

11. Vol. 90, *Xin Tangshu* ("New History of the Tang"): "Biography of Li Sizhen."

12. Vol. 190 of the *Jiu Tangshu* ("Old History of the Tang"). "Diviners: Biography of Li Sizhen" notes that Sizhen compiled one volume each of "Books" and "Paintings." Chapters 1 and 3 respectively of the "Bibliography" section in vols. 57 and 59 of the *Xin Tangshu* list separately "Addendum to Calligraphy" and "Addendum to Paintings." Vol. 1 of *Notes on Drawings and Paintings* mentions the *Catalogue of Later Paintings* compiled by Li Sizhen. In vol. 3 of his *Junzhai's Reading Notes*, Chao Gongwu of the Southern Song writes *Sequel to Notes on Paintings* in one volume by Li Sizhen (Yuanzhou edition), the extant edition now known

as *Sequel to Catalogue of Paintings.*

13. Vol. 6 of the *Lidai minghua ji* cites Zhang Huaidan thus: "As for Lu, Gu, and Zhang Sengyou, commentators stress each of their strengths, and these are all appropriate." This can be taken to mean that the styles in vogue during the three periods following the Eastern Jin—Liu Song, Qi, and Liang—all differed, and hence different emphases were placed on them.

14. *Yiwen leiju*, vol. 76, quoting the stele of the Buddha Amitābha in the Jinxiang Temple of Yongzhou, carved by Liu Xiaoyi of the Liang dynasty.

15. *Yiwen leiju*, vol. 77, quoting the inscription for the Buddha Śākyamuni by Emperor Jianwen of the Liang.

16. See Lin Shuzhong, "Dating the Painted Brick Tomb of Changzhou and the Art of the Painted Bricks," *Wenwu*, 1979:3.

17. In vol. 6 of *Xu gaoseng zhuan* ("Further Lives of Eminent Monks"), by the monk Daoxuan of the Tang dynasty.

18. According to the "Biography of Cui Guang" in vol. 67 of the *Weishi* ("History of the Wei Dynasty"), "In the eighth month of the second year [of Shengui], Dowager Empress Ling visited the Yongning Temple and climbed up the nine-story pagoda. Guang submitted a memorial, saying ...'Although the image has not yet been constructed, this is already the home of the deity.' " From this, we know that the figures were built after the eighth month of the second year of Shengui.

19. Luoyang work team of the Institute of Archaeology, Chinese Academy of Social Sciences, "Brief Report on the Excavation around the Base of the Northern Wei Yongning Temple Pagoda," *Kaogu*, 1981:3.

20. The "Annals of Wenxiang" in vol. 3 of the *Beiqishu* ("History of the Northern Qi") notes that in the fourth year of Wuding (546), "[Marquis] Jing's general, Cai Zundao, returned from the north saying that Jing felt repentant. The Prince (Wenxiang) believed this, and thought he could lure him over, so he ignored Jing's letter. Jing had written, '. . . Nowadays in Liang, we were beckoned to with every courtesy, given tiger

skins for blankets and urged to stay with fine cups. . . . Leave the dangerous for the safe, and return now to the correct ways; change disaster into good fortune, we have escaped the net.'" This mention of the correct ways refers to the Liang dynasty kingdom in southern China.

21. See Xu Guangji, "Excavation and Studies of Large Tomb Murals of the Northern Dynasties at Wanzhang in Ci County, Hebei," *Wenwu*, 1996:9; also the Shanxi Provincial Institute of Archaeology et al., "Brief Report on the Excavation of the Tomb of Lou Rui of the Northern Qi in Taiyuan," *Wenwu*, 1983:10.

22. See *Beiqishu*, vol. 4, "Annals of Wenxuan"; vol. 48, "Relatives of the Empress: Biography of Lou Rui"; and *Beishi* ("History of the Northern Dynasties"), vol. 54, "Biography of Lou Zhao, with Appended Biography of His Nephew Rui."

23. See "Notes on the Northern Qi Tomb of Lou Rui in Taiyuan," *Wenwu*, 1983:10.

24. *Lidai minghua ji*, preface to vol. 8. Vol. 8 of the *Lidai minghua ji* further says about Yang Zihua: "Emperor Shizu [Gao Zhan, of the Northern Qi] held him in high esteem, and let him live in the palace. He was known throughout the land as the Divine Painter, and was forbidden to paint for outsiders, except by imperial edict. At the time there was a prince named Chong Shan whose chess-playing was godlike, and the two of them were known as the Two Ultimates."

25. *Lidai minghua ji*, vol. 2.

26. In *Zhenguan gongsi hualu* ("A Record of Paintings in Public and Private Collections in the Zhenguan Era [627-650]"), Pei Xiaoyuan notes that "after Yang Zihua, they are all northern painters." The six listed after Yang Zihua are Cao Zhongda, Dong Boren, Zheng Fashi, Yang Qidan, Zhan Ziqian, and Sun Shangzi.

27. About the five artists mentioned, vol. 8 of the *Lidai minghua ji* makes the following comments on all other than Yang Zihua: "Tian Zengliang reached the official position of *Sangong Zhonglangjiang* [during the Qi], and entering the Zhou period he became a *Changshi*,

and at the time had a higher reputation than Dong and Zhan"; "During the Zhou, Zheng Fashi was a *Dadou Duzuo Yuanwai Shilang*, a *Jianzhong* General, and was given the fief of Changshe county, and entering the Sui period he was made a *Zhongsan Daifu*; his *Images of the Northern Qi* . . . is still extant"; "Dong Boren was from Ru'nan, and a man of many talents . . . . [During the Sui] he reached the positions of *Guanglu Daifu* and *Dianzhong* General. . . . Initially both Dong and Zhan were summoned together to the Sui Court, one from Hebei, the other from southern China. Initially they were not taken seriously, but later they were rather well regarded. Dong's *Emperor Ming of the Zhou Hunting* is still extant"; "Zhan Ziqian lived through the Northern Qi, Zhou, and Sui dynasties, and became *Chaosan Daifu* and *Zhangnei Doudu*. His *The Later Ruler of the Northern Qi Visiting Jinyang* is still extant." From this, we know that they were all famous during the Qi and Zhou.

28. The monk Zong is the same person as the monk Yanzong, who compiled *Houhualu* ("Sequel to Catalogue of Paintings"). See *Tushu jianwenzhi*, vol. 1, and *Junzhai dushuzhi*, vol. 3, pt. 2.

29. According to part 3 of the *Yiwenzhi* ("Bibliography") section in vol. 59 of the *Xin Tangshu* ("New Tang History"): "Pei Xiaoyuan wrote *Huapin lu* ["Ranked Catalogue of Paintings"] in one volume. He was a *Zhongshu Sheren*, and recorded events of the Zhenguan and Xianqing periods." Vol. 1 of *Tuhua jianwen zhi* ("Notes on Drawings and Paintings") refers to the work as *Gongsihua lu* ("Catalogue of Public and Private Paintings"). The extant version is titled *Zhenguan gongsihua shi* ("History of Public and Private Paintings of the Zhenguan Period"). The text in the extant version is more detailed than the passage cited by Zhang, and reads, "The Yans originally studied with Mr. Zhang, and can be said to surpass their teacher. As for drawing people and garments, soldiers, horses and buildings, they have mastered the subtleties of both south and north."

30. See Jin Weinuo, "The Dates and Artists of Ancient Portraits of Emperors," in *Collected Essays on Chinese Art History*, 1981.

31. See n. 3.

32. Wu Daozi and Yang Huizhi were regarded equally highly at the time. Vol. 212 of the *Taiping guangji* cites Tang Kangping's *Jutanlu* thus: "There is a Xuanyuan Monastery on Mt. Beimang of the Eastern capital. To the south of the monastery stands a temple to Laozi. Its buildings are tall and imposing, and overlook Yiluo. All of its clay sculptures of the deities were done by Yang Huizhi during the Kaiyuan period. They are extraordinarily well done and meticulous, and everyone who sees them is filled with admiration. The walls have paintings by Wu Daozi of the Five Sages and of stories from Laozi. The paintings are exquisite, and have no peer either past or present."

33. At the end of his comments on Dai Kui, Zhang Yanyuan appends the following notes: "See the *Jinshu* ['History of the Jin'], *Songshu* ['History of the (Liu) Song'], and *Kuibiezhuan* ['Biography of Kui'], Xu Guang's *Jinji* ['Record of the Jin'], *Huigiji* ['Record of the Huiqi'], *Guozi*, Liu Yiqing's *Shishuo*, and the *Mingyanji* by Wang from Linchuan of the [Liu] Song dynasty."

34. At the end of his comments on Dai Kui, Zhang Yanyuan appends the following notes: "See the 'Biographies of Hermits' section in the *Songshu* ['History of the (Liu) Song'], and Wang Zhishen's *Songji* ['Record of the (Liu) Song']."

35. At the end of his comments on Jiang Shaoyou, Zhang Yanyuan appends the following note: "See the *Houweishu* ['History of the Later Wei']."

36. At the end of his comments on Tanmozhuoyi, Zhang Yanyuan appends the following notes: "See the *Insights into the Three Treasures*."

37. There were also exceptions, such as Zhai Ruwen, who was the *Anfushi* of both Zhiyue Prefecture and Andong in Zhejiang during the late Northern Song. The "Inscription for Sir Zhai" which is appended to the *Zhonghuizi* notes that Ruwen "was conversant with painting, and had himself painted some sixty-odd scrolls, including *Heights of the Three Locales*, *Various Sages of the Ten Ultimates*, *The Nine Heavens as One*, *The Four Holy Men Subduing the Demons*, etc. . . . He was also an expert sculptor,

and taught craftsmen to carve the images of the Three Holies, the Jade Emperor, and Zhenwu which are in the Zaocheng Monastery at Huiqi. These all display the greatest dignity and gentleness in their visages, and their expression is one of natural ease as if they were human, such that all who saw them were awestruck. People of that prefecture call them treasures of wood. . . . Zhai felt that the old work was not well done, and personally resculpted it. He captured the Rulai [Tathāgata] Buddha's compassion for the world and sympathy for the weak, and even if Dai Andao and Yang Huizhi were to be reborn, they would have a hard time surpassing him." For more on Zhai Ruwen's life, see his biography in vol. 131 of the *History of the Song* (*Song shu*).

Transfiguring Divinities: Buddhist Sculpture in China

Helmut Brinker

Professor, University of Zurich

The advent of Buddhism in China more than two thousand years ago heralded profound changes in almost every aspect of life and thought, state and society. Buddhism differed markedly from earlier Chinese religions and philosophies. It challenged and in part even flatly contradicted some of the most cherished concepts and ideals of the ancient

Chinese. Indian Buddhism arrived as a complex religious system based on a variety of doctrines, practices, and premises that the ancients would never have understood. The new faith assumed that life was transitory and illusory, essentially painful, and thus inevitably unsatisfactory. It offered, however, the consoling prospect of finding release from fatal destiny and breaking through the endless chain of causality in the illusory world of phenomena, in Sanskrit called *saṃsāra*.

Following the Noble Eightfold Path—that is, the Buddha's rules for right living—one could escape the perpetual cycle of rebirth by the virtues of sincere belief, compassion, meditative discipline, exemplary moral conduct, accumulation of religious merit, development of wisdom, and renunciation of worldly wealth and status in order to seek the truth. The doctrine of *karma* (literally, "work" or "action") was thought of as a system of moral causalities. Good or bad actions of an individual would be rewarded or punished either in this life or in the next. To attain supreme enlightenment was the ultimate goal for the practitioners of the faith. A person who had reached this awakened stage became a Buddha and qualified for entering into *nirvāna*. For the first time the Chinese had to come to grips with totally alien beliefs and highly sophisticated religious concepts. The success of Buddhism in China was due mainly to its tolerance for other philosophical paths and religious practices, its readiness to adopt and adapt to Daoism and Confucianism.

This exposure to foreign ideas and images, languages and metaphors inevitably caused a radical transformation of older traditions in Chinese culture and art. In India, the homeland of faith, mysticism, and magic, Buddhism was originally an aniconic religion. Since the Buddha stood ultimately for an abstract, metaphysical concept, initially he was not depicted as a human figure. Rather, his salvific presence and power were evoked by such representative symbols as his footprints, the wheel that stands for his preaching, or the *stūpa*, a tumulus-like monument erected over his holy bodily remains. During the time of the Kushan empire, established in the latter half of the first century CE, the worship of images at last triumphed, and soon thereafter iconographic schemes and forms of great intricacy and complexity rapidly evolved. Buddhism's historic founder, known as Śākyamuni, or Gautama Siddhārtha, is naturally the most widely worshiped figure of the Buddhist pantheon. He is said to have lived between 565 and 486 BCE—the dates are not precisely fixed—in what is now southern Nepal. Śākyamuni achieved enlightenment in his lifetime by discovering the middle path between severe ascetic self-mortification and self-indulgence. After spreading his new insights, performing miracles, and gathering disciples, he entered into nirvana at the age of eighty and receded far beyond the imagination and reach of mortal believers. His truly unfathomable reality could only be experienced and visualized through supreme insight, assisted by sacred images and rituals, by magic words, gestures, and symbols, by the mysteries of faith and worship.

BUDDHIST CULTURE IN CHINA— FORMATIVE STAGES, EXPANSION, CURTAILMENT

In Buddhism's formative stages in China, Buddhist imagery appears only sporadically, and mingled into indigenous Han contexts. Traditional Buddhist motifs of Indian origin were fused with Daoist beliefs, figures, and customs, and rendered in stylistic and technical patterns familiar from tomb decoration and furnishings. Buddhist imagery had to be translated into forms and modes that Chinese could understand, as was true for Buddhist scriptures. We must assume that the early missionaries from the West knew little if any Chinese and that their local collaborators probably had no comprehensive knowledge of Central Asian or Indian languages. Pertinent Daoist terms and metaphors as well as loanwords from the Confucian classics were appropriated in the attempt to render religious concepts such as impermanence and insubstantiality and to describe the transcendental notions of transmigration and reincarnation.

According to tradition, extensive translation activities began with the arrival of two Indian monks, Dharmaratna and Kāśyapa Mātaṅga. They allegedly joined a group of Chinese envoys that had been dispatched by Emperor Ming of the Eastern Han dynasty (r. 57–75 CE) in order to track down the import of a miraculous dream apparition. We are told that the two missionaries brought with them a copy of "The Scripture in Forty-Two Sections," which they translated into Chinese as *Sishi'er zhang jing*—traditionally the first Chinese rendition of an Indian Buddhist text. The true origin and date of this work, however, have been subjects of scholarly controversy. By medieval times, Dharmaratna and Kāśyapa Mātaṅga were regularly credited with the translation of this "short collection of aphorisms and pithy moralistic parables."[1] The emperor is said to have established the Temple of the White Horse (Baimasi), the first official Buddhist institution on Chinese soil, as their new residence in Luoyang.

Another pioneer missionary and translator was the Parthian prince known to the Chinese as An Shigao, who came to Luoyang in 148 CE. The impact of the Central Asian missionary translator Kumārajīva (344–409/413?) was even greater. A Kuchean aristocrat turned monk, he had been invited to China by the ruler of one of the Sixteen Kingdoms, but en route was captured by a rogue general and held for nearly two decades in the area of present-day Gansu Province. There the Kuchean monk learned Chinese. A new ruler, equally pro-Buddhist, finally destroyed the rogue general, at least partly in order to secure Kumārajīva's release. Kumārajīva arrived in Chang'an in 402 and became the *spiritus rector* of one of the greatest Buddhist translation projects of sacred scriptures.

At first, Buddhist congregations existed primarily in the foreign merchant quarters of larger cities; only gradually did the new religion gain a substantial following among native Chinese. From roughly the fourth century, however, religious life in China was largely dominated by Buddhism. In his preface to the *Luoyang qielan ji* ("Record of Buddhist Temples in Luoyang"), completed in 547, the military leader and chronicler Yang Xuanzhi noted:

> The people and wealthy families parted with their treasures as easily as with forgotten rubbish. As a result, Buddhist temples were built side by side, and stūpas [pagodas] rose up in row after row. People competed among themselves in making or copying the Buddha's portraits. Golden stūpas matched the imperial observatory in height, and Buddhist lecture halls were as magnificent as the [ostentatiously wasteful] Efang [palaces of the Qin dynasty (221–207 BCE)]. Indeed, [Buddhist activity was so intense] that it was not merely a matter of clothing wooden [figures] in silk or painting earthen [idols] in rich colors.[2]

Yang Xuanzhi reports that there were forty-two temples in Luoyang by the beginning of the fourth century CE and that this number increased rapidly; by the end of the Wei dynasty in the second half of the sixth century we have an estimate of no less than 1,367 Buddhist temples in and around the capital city. Medieval Chang'an was also early famed for its magnificent temples. Notwithstanding two serious persecutions—during 446–452 under Emperor Taiwu of the Northern Wei and again during 574–578 under Emperor Wu of the Northern Zhou—the Buddhist church continued to flourish during the Period of Disunity (220–589), the Sui (589–618), and most of the Tang (618–907) dynasty.

The third and most severe suppression, gathering head from about about 841 and culminating in 844–845, under the reign of the Tang emperor Wuzong, marked the beginning of a gradual decline in influence, power, and wealth of the Buddhist church as an established institution. A series of increasingly harsh imperial edicts was directed toward confiscation of monastic property and secularization of the clergy. The violent return to secular life of more than a quarter of a million nuns and priests was witnessed and recorded by the Japanese pilgrim Ennin (793–864), who kept a detailed diary of his sojourn in China. The vast properties and monetary wealth of the Buddhist church were confiscated by the government, and some of the splendid temple compounds in Chang'an were converted into imperial parks. Buddhist bronze bells and metal icons were ordered to be surrendered to the state authorities and were eventually melted down. In the entire empire no images of bronze, iron, gold, or silver were permitted for public or private worship. Only sculptures made of stone, wood, clay, or other nonmetallic materials are said to have been exempt from the tragic suppression and devastation. The actual extent of the loss of religious art and architecture and of Buddhist literature, icons, and sacred paraphernalia toward the end of the Tang dynasty can hardly be imagined. Arriving in Dengzhou after his own expulsion from Chang'an, the Japanese pilgrim Ennin noted in his diary:

> Although it [Dengzhou] is a remote place, it has been no different from the capital in the regulation of monks and nuns, the destruction of the monasteries, the banning of the

scriptures, the breaking of the images, and the confiscation of the property of the monasteries. Moreover they have peeled off the gold from the Buddhas and smashed the bronze and iron Buddhas and measured their weight. What a pity! What limit was there to the bronze, iron, and gold Buddhas of the land? And yet, in accordance with the Imperial edict, all have been destroyed and have been turned into trash.[3]

EVIDENCE OF EARLY BUDDHIST IMAGERY IN CHINA

Tradition holds that the first Buddha image was introduced into China sometime between 64 and 75 CE, as the result of a dream of Han Mingdi. The emperor saw a divine man whose body was

golden in color, wearing a solar halo about the crown of his head. He inquired of his courtiers, one of whom said: "In the West there is a deity known as the Buddha, whose form is like what Your Majesty dreamed of; may it not have been he?" Thereupon envoys were dispatched to India, who had copies made of a Sūtra [scripture] and [obtained] an image, which they displayed in China. There from the Son of Heaven on down through the princes and nobles, all paid them honor; for when they heard that a man's soul is not extinguished by death, there was none who was not fearful of being lost.[4]

This famous dream-and-envoy story was considerably embellished over time. It occurred initially in an early preface of the Sishi'er zhang jing ("The Scripture in Forty-Two Sections"), which may be dated to the Eastern Han (25–220 CE) or shortly thereafter. Such edifying anecdotes later acquired an aura of fact, and were often cited as literal truth by Chinese buddhologists.[5] By the fifth century the icon mentioned among the Buddhist paraphernalia in the luggage of Mingdi's returning delegation had been identified in Chinese records either as the original or as a faithful, equally sacred replica of the celebrated Śākyamuni portrait commissioned by the youthful king Udayana, Buddha's ardent admirer and pious patron. Although this account of the legendary Udayana icon is apocryphal, it tells us something about the significance of imagery in the transmission of Buddhism and the early Chinese concern and respect for the foreign religion and its art.

A century after the purported introduction of the first Buddhist scripture and image, a lavish religious ceremony in honor of Śākyamuni and of Laozi, the founding figure of Daoism, is mentioned by the astrologer and scholar Xiang Kai in his well-known memorial presented to the Han emperor Huan in 166. His text refers to the belief that Buddha was in reality none other than the deified Laozi. Images of the two Sacred Ones were installed under sumptuous floral canopies in a special palace building. Rituals and sacrifices were performed with pomp and ostentation, using precious vessels of gold and silver, consecrated beads, and embroidered textiles.[6]

Fairly reliable information has been preserved regarding the installation of yet another golden Buddha image in what is now Jiangsu Province. About the year 190, Zhai Rong, an active propagandist for Buddhism, reportedly built a structure of considerable size to house a gilded bronze statue and to accommodate a large congregation: "He erected a Buddha shrine, making a human figure of bronze whose body he coated with gold and clad in brocades. He hung up nine tiers of bronze plates [on the spire] over a multi-storied pavilion; his covered galleries could contain three thousand men or more."[7]

Buddhist icons must have been in ritual use in China well before this date; they probably arrived in the luggage of foreign merchants and missionaries who had come along the ancient overland trade routes of Central Asia or by sea around Southeast Asia. Most of these images were probably made of gilded bronze. Their shining surface was intended to reproduce the sunlike radiance of the Buddha's body. It is only toward the end of the Eastern Han dynasty, about the year 200, that the Chinese themselves may have started to experiment with casting such icons. We are informed by the noted Vinaya master, translator, and biographer Daoxuan (596–667) that a certain monk Huihu made a gilded Śākyamuni image at the Shaoling Temple in Wujun in the year 377. According to Daoxuan, the sixteen-foot-high statue was cast in a cave dug on the steep south side of the temple.[8]

In general, bronze casters and sculptors enjoyed little social eminence. Like their craftsmen ancestors, they remained anonymous. Very few won recognition comparable to that of contemporary painters. One of the earliest sculptors—perhaps the first—whose name entered historical records was Dai Kui (d. 395). He is said to have made monumental configurations for various temples and to have achieved an unprecedented technical versatility and inventiveness, beauty and expressiveness in casting bronze icons, carving wood sculptures, and making portable lacquer statues. In Daoxuan's view, Dai Kui's genius contributed decisively to the progressive disuse of exotic foreign styles in favor of Sinicized Buddhist imagery:

In [Dai] Kui's opinion the images made in Middle Antiquity had almost all been rude and oversimple, and in their function of inspiring worship lacked the power to stir men's hearts. Since he was both pure in faith and highly inventive, he was spurred to alter the carving of the August Visage, so as to attain the utmost in truthfulness. He pondered the problem for years on end and finally succeeded in producing a statue in which the excellence of Chinese figure sculpture exceeded anything previously known.[9]

Early sources record miraculous finds of golden or gilded statues deep underground at Buddhist temple sites. When the Yongning Temple ("Temple of Eternal Peace") was built in Luoyang by decree of the dowager empress in 516, thirty golden icons were unearthed during the construction process. The Yongning Temple, which was in the inner city, is said to have rivaled the magnificence of the imperial palace. Writing three decades later, Yang Xuanzhi tells us that the unexpected discovery of thirty sacred images "was interpreted as an auspicious reward for the dowager empress's conversion to Buddhism. As a result, she spent all the more lavishly on its construction." He describes the splendor of the temple in great and admiring detail:

North of the stūpa [pagoda] was a Buddhist hall, which was shaped like the Palace of the Great Ultimate (Tianjidian). In the hall was a golden statue of the Buddha eighteen feet high, along with ten medium-sized images—three of sewn pearls, five of woven golden threads, and two of jade. The superb artistry was matchless, unparalleled in its day. . . . Here were kept all the Sūtras and Buddhist images presented by foreign countries.[10]

ASPECTS OF BUDDHIST FAITH AND RITUAL

The most common Chinese terms for Buddhist icons are *foxiang* and *foxingxiang*, both meaning "Buddha images." Since ancient times the main object of veneration or prime statue worshiped in a particular ritual or enshrined in a building of a Buddhist temple has been called *benzun* ("Original Honored One"); as a rule, the chapel or hall is dedicated to and named after that particular deity. The word *benzun* can be traced back at least as far as the Northern Wei dynasty (386–534). Stronger emphasis on the intimate relationship between the devotee and the deity addressed in an icon is connoted by the word *zizun* ("Personal Honored One"), defined in early exegetic medieval texts as "the venerated deity to which one's Self is clinging." We may assume that icons of this category were preferably set up on the private altar of a practitioner. Another key term frequently encountered in Buddhist scriptures is *xingxiang* ("form image"), emphasizing the perceptible

appearance, the formal likeness, and iconographic appropriateness of the represented deity. *Yingxiang* ("shadow image") characterizes the icon as an ultimately illusory reflection without inherent reality, and is regularly used to designate the visualized image of a deity and its pictorial representation. In his instructions on the methods of performing such visualization, the extremely learned Tang monk Zhiyan (602–668), who is regarded as the second patriarch of the Huayan school, remarks:

How does one attain to dwelling in quiet meditation? During day and night one should visualize with energy the form image [*xingxiang*] of the Buddha, but without sticking to [the illusion of] its characteristics [as being real]. . . . Should this Buddha have been made by man, then the practitioner ought to reflect as follows: Is this Buddha made out of clay or wood, or is it made out of gold or bronze? After such a visualization he truly recognizes the Buddha whom he sees. If you, only relying on your own self, visualize the form image [*xingxiang*] of the Buddha in a pure abode, and remember it day and night, then this Buddha will appear constantly before your eyes.[11]

Icons were a means to the fundamental goal of every devoted Buddhist, a goal the Chinese called *jianfo* ("seeing the Buddha"). Material substance and form remain a totally worthless "shadow"— that is, a mere visual perception—as long as an icon has not received its proper spiritual enlivenment through consecration in an adequate ritual. Only then does a sculpture change from a piece of stone, wood, bronze, clay, or lacquer to a sacred image: it metamorphoses from form image (*xingxiang*) or shadow image (*yingxiang*) into the Original Honored One (*benzun*), imbued with the potency to assist and guide believers on their way to true enlightenment and salvation. The final step in creating an icon—depicting the pupils of the eyes—was an act of ritual as well as representation. The practice seems to have been known in ancient Indian Buddhism as well as in Brahmanism, and it was common cultic practice (along with the "mouth-opening" ritual) in Mesopotamia perhaps as early as the third millennium BCE. Called the "eye-opening" ritual (*kaiyan*), it is the most important process in consecrating a new icon: endowing the image with gaze endows it with a sense of life. The Tang emperor Taizong (r. 627–649) himself attended such an inaugural "eye-opening" ceremony for the main Buddha image in the Xingfu Temple (formerly Hongfu Temple) in Chang'an, which in 634 he had renamed and rededicated to the spiritual felicity of his mother. Unfortunately, the sources give no further details of this dedication service, but the monarch probably played an active part in the ritual of invoking the Buddha and endowing his image with beneficial and protective power.[12]

Since early times Buddhist theologians have speculated and commented on the relation of the outer form and the inner principle, the actual and spiritual presence of deities or saints in images made by human hands. They were deeply concerned with the degree of reality and potency dwelling in a pictorial representation. The efficacy of Buddhist icons, and therefore of the rituals addressed to them, was thought to depend to a great extent on their magic essence. To reinforce the potency ascribed to the images, all sorts of objects—precious relics, ritual implements, holy scriptures and pictures, printed or written magic spells, miniature figures of deities, even textile models of human organs—were sometimes deposited in special cavities or in the hollow interior of a sculpture before it received its finishing touches and initial consecration. Literary evidence and extant statues bear witness to the early existence of this magic-religious practice in China, which was not limited to any particular Buddhist school or category of religious imagery.

SACRED ICONS AND THE BUDDHIST CULT OF RELICS

One of the earliest references to a sacred deposit in a Buddhist figure appears in the biography of the distinguished evangelist and translator Dao'an (312–385), who once received a foreign gilded-bronze statue that was seven feet high:

Whenever there was a lecture or assembly, the holy images would be set out. Banners and canopies would be hung up; festoons of beads would swing; everywhere would be incense smoke and flowers; so that those who mounted the steps and crossed the threshold were awestruck and paid the utmost in devotion. The foreign bronze image was so archaic in form and workmanship that most people had no great respect for it. [Dao-] An said: "The shape and the body-marks are excellent; the only fault is that the form of the uṣṇīṣa [the protuberance on top of the head] is incongruous." So he ordered a disciple to fire and re-mould the uṣṇīṣa. At once a light flamed up with such brilliance that it filled the whole hall. On close inspection it was discovered that inside the uṣṇīṣa there was a relic. The brothers were filled with consternation; but [Dao-] An said: "The statue is already a wonder-working one, and will not be disturbed by recasting."[13]

The unexpected discovery of a sacred relic in the Buddha's head secured this rare foreign statue a special rank as miraculous icon, and therefore even

minor changes of iconographic features due to repair or finishing work essentially would not impair its efficacy.

In the orthodox Buddhist sense, the śarīra (C: sheli) refers to the pure crystallized grains found after the historical Buddha's cremation; to his ashes and other bodily remains, such as teeth, hair, finger bones and fingernails; or to the ashes, bones, and similar physical fragments of saints. According to ancient tradition, Śākyamuni's body was incinerated after he had attained his final nirvana. His ashes and physical remains were divided with diplomatic skill and interred in eight separate tumulus-like burial mounds, or stupas. In the third century BCE, India's first Buddhist ruler, Aśoka of the Mauryas, recovered and brought these relics together again, later dispersing them throughout his far-flung kingdom in 84,000 stupas that are said to have been erected in a single day.

The miraculous division and widespread veneration of the Buddha's remains established a powerful precedent. The process of dividing the śarīra again and again—not only those of Śākyamuni himself, but also those of his disciples and of later saints and patriarchs of the various Buddhist schools—created an almost inexhaustible supply of minute holy objects for the entire Buddhist world. The enormous number of 84,000 refers to the number of atoms in the Buddha's corpus as well as to the corpus of his sacred words. Thus, by erecting these stupas, the pious king Aśoka intended to recreate Śākyamuni's physical body symbolically and to reconstruct his myriad teachings. The śarīra of the historical Buddha and his doctrines were considered equivalent manifestations of the same reality and sacred presence. The possession of "authentic" relics ensured the possessor an elevated place in the ecclesiastical hierarchy as well as in society. At the same time, it was a powerful instrument of monastic and imperial legitimacy and, by stimulating donations from the faithful, guaranteed economic independence.

In recent years discoveries of Buddhist reliquary deposits have been reported from almost every part of China, from Liaoning in the northeast to Yunnan in the southwest. Sacred Buddhist relic assemblages were mostly found within or on the site of pagodas, which served as monumental architectural reliquaries and usually stood at a distinguished place on the temple grounds. Relics might be enshrined not only in a sealed crypt but in other parts of the structure as well—for example, at the base of the mast atop the pagoda. The finds date from the time of the initial impact of Buddhism and its arts on Chinese culture and increase concomitantly with the faith's subsequent powerful spread from the fourth century through the Ming dynasty

(1368–1644). The most spectacular *śarīra* discovery was made in 1987 at the Famen Temple ("Temple of the Gate to the Law"), in Fufeng county, west of Xi'an, Shaanxi Province (cats. 63–65). There the Chinese excavators claim to have found (among much else) four authentic finger bones (*fogu*) of Śākyamuni. The *śarīra* were well preserved and concealed in precious reliquaries in the Tang dynasty underground palace (*digong*) of the Famen Temple's sixteenth-century octagonal brick pagoda. The collapse of the pagoda in 1981 made possible the investigation of its crypt. Thus well-known literary evidence for the cult of relics, such as Han Yu's (768–824) forthright memorial to the Throne (819) condemning veneration of the Buddha's bones, was substantiated more than a millennium later by archaeological evidence.

Han Yu had serious grounds for protest. Śākyamuni's physical remains had several times been carried in lavish procession between Famen Temple and the Tang capital, a distance of more than 100 kilometers. Like many conservative literati of the day, Han Yu was appalled by the religious frenzy pervading all strata of society, and he proposed drastic measures to suppress the enormous influence of the Buddhist church. When, in 819, the Famen Temple finger-bone relics were received by an enthusiastic crowd in Chang'an and temporarily placed on view at the imperial palace, he wrote the *Lun fogu biao* ("Memorial Discussing the Buddha's Bones") and presented it to the Throne. Han Yu criticized His Majesty in harsh words: "You are . . . putting on for the citizens of the capital this extraordinary spectacle which is nothing more than a sort of theatrical amusement. . . . Now that the Buddha has long been dead, is it fitting that his decayed and rotten bones, his ill-omened and filthy remains, should be allowed to enter in the forbidden precincts of the palace? . . . Without reason you have taken up unclean things and examined them in person."[14]

DEITIES OF THE BUDDHIST PANTHEON AND THEIR ICONOGRAPHY

Three major doctrinal divisions, emerging successively, coexisted within the Buddhist faith. First in time is Hīnayāna, the "Small Vehicle," a conservative form of Buddhism based almost exclusively on the Pāli canon and asserting that enlightenment comes only through one's own efforts. The second is Mahāyāna, the "Great Vehicle," the doctrinal outlines of which seem to have been formulated in India as early as the first century BCE, advocating salvation for everyone through the assistance of a vast pantheon of compassionate divinities. The third is Esoteric Buddhism, also called tantric or Vajrayāna ("Diamond Vehicle") Buddhism, known in China as *mijiao*, "Secret Teachings." This form of

Buddhism, depending largely on "mysteries" taught and transmitted by Esoteric masters, developed from the fifth century CE as part of a most complex religio-philosophic movement.

Each Buddhist school—there were eight major schools by the Tang period—emphasized different aspects of faith and worship and thus favored particular figures from the vast pantheon. Sacred texts offered clear-cut descriptions of the special qualities and appearance of the Buddha and all the other figures of the Buddhist pantheon, providing a basic assurance of iconographic correctness and conformity.[15]

In artistic representations the Buddha's ideal figure appears very austere in stature, pose, and dress. Usually, his modest monk's robe and the near absence of specific attributes and individualizing features convincingly indicate his holy status of utmost unworldliness (cats. 147–49, 156, 162). Such utter simplicity gives his human figure a lofty majesty. Several unusual, seemingly aesthetic or miraculous features were assigned to the Buddha. They are manifestations of the Sacred, and basically statements of ontological quality, like the *mudrās*, the gestures (literally, "seal marks"; C: *yin[xiang]*) formed with the hands to convey such actions as preaching, meditating, wish granting, protecting, or releasing from fear. The Buddha's thirty-two major distinguishing physical marks are called *lakshana* (C: *xiang*). One of the most important is the protuberance on top of his head symbolizing the absolute perfect wisdom of the Enlightened One. It is usually referred to by the Sanskrit term *ushnīsha* (C: *rouji* or *dingxiang*); ancient Buddhist scriptures sometimes explain it as a "mark of the crown that is invisible" to ordinary people and list it as the sixty-sixth among the eighty minor distinctive marks of the Buddha. Another sign of supreme enlightenment is the *ūrnā* on his forehead; originally a white curl (C: *baihao*) between the Buddha's eyebrows, it was later simplified to a light-emanating spot that illuminated the world. Most of the exceptional marks and supernatural qualities were either derived from legends associated with the Buddha's life and virtues or devised as symbols of ultimate truth beyond human imagination, of unworldly beauty, holy distinction, and the sublime power of omnipresence.

In accordance with their salvific mandate, bodhisattvas appear less austere and inward than figures of the Buddha in sculpture and painting. Bodhisattvas are compassionate figures "whose essence is enlightenment." Renouncing their own salvation and immediate entrance into nirvana, they devote all their power and energy to saving suffering beings in this world. As intercessionary figures, majestic in power and sublime in compassion, bodhisattvas are usually represented in graceful postures, dressed in elegant garments with sophisticated drapery. They are adorned with crowns and precious jewelry, and often they are equipped with specific emblems and attributes (cats. 163, 165, 166, 172–76). Some bodhisattvas are depicted riding on a powerful animal (an elephant or lion, for example), indicating the irresistible nature of the Buddhist Law. Others appear with multiple heads or arms to signify their limitless compassion and their suprahuman potential as beneficent intercessors (cat. 164). Perhaps the single most popular focus of Buddhist art and devotion is Avalokiteśvara (C: Guan[shi]yin or Guanyin; "One Who Perceives [with compassion] the Sounds [of the suffering world]"). Religious imagination has endowed this widely adored bodhisattva with the greatest variety of attributes and manifestations. No less than thirty-three forms became canonized in the *Lotus Sūtra*. They are indications of his compassionate omnipotence to save sentient beings in different states of existence. As a benign emanation and agent of Amitābha, the Buddha of the Western Paradise (cat. 160), he has a small image of this Buddha in his crown. This image alone suffices to identify him as Guanyin (cat. 176).

Like the bodhisattvas, the *vidyārājas* ("Bright Kings [of Esoteric Wisdom]"; C: *mingwang*) are easily recognized. The *vidyārājas*, however, are wrathful deities, terrifying in appearance and often depicted in belligerent poses, with abnormal multiplication of limbs and heads, ferocious facial expressions, threatening weapons in their hands, and flame-edged halos (cat. 170). But their anger is beneficent. They embody the militant energy and retaliatory power of the Tathāgatas when confronted with such evils as heresy, ignorance, illusion, passion, and other spiritual obstacles. Tathāgatas are a class of fully enlightened Buddhas. The Chinese epithet, *rulai*, means something like "he who has thus come," that is, like other Buddhas before him. Although the Five Bright Kings, their names, and their function are of Indian origin, they were probably conceived as a distinct group of five in Chinese Esoteric Buddhism during the seventh to eighth centuries. The Five Bright Kings, or protectors of faith, correspond to the Five Tathāgatas, just as the five cosmic elements, the five cardinal points, the five transcendental wisdoms, the five senses, the five colors, the five vitality centers, and the five viscera of the human body do. These Tathāgatas of the Five Wisdoms (*wuzhi rulai*) were thought of as spiritual principles constituting the body of the universe; and the relationship among them was clarified by the use of schematic diagrams, known as mandalas. Such formal geometric diagrams, depicting Buddhist deities in a highly abstract theological schema, originated in India. In China mandalas of painted or sculptural images were employed in

liturgies and special rituals, such as ordination and baptism, and also as aids to private exercises such as the visualization of deities.

The cosmic All-Buddha Mahāvairocana ("Great Radiance of Illumination"; C: Dari) was established as the highest of these principles, penetrating with his light the darkness of ignorance. Each Tathāgata had a particular bodhisattva and *vidyārāja* as his pair of agents, representing his benign (*śānta*) and wrathful (*krodha*) aspects. Practitioners of the *mijiao*, or "Secret Teachings," believed that each person's body, mind, and speech were inherently divine and that his or her deeds, thoughts, and words were actually those of Mahāvairocana. Through such ritual practices as incantations, recitation of magic spells, mystical hand gestures, and trances the deities could be constrained to fulfill material goals—cure illness, defeat one's enemies, protect the state and government—and spiritual goals—hasten one's enlightenment or progress to a higher state of consciousness. Correct performance of such rituals was believed to offer access to the power of the expansive Buddhist pantheon. That pantheon was systematically defined and organized into a highly intricate and complex schema, more elaborate than any previously known in the Buddhist world. Picturing that pantheon presented a new challenge to the imagination and skill of Chinese artists of the Tang dynasty.

A large class of lesser deities, or *devas* (C: *tian*), rank just below *vidyārājas* in the order of sanctity (cats. 167, 169). Among them are the belligerent *dvārapālas*, who evolved out of Indian demonic creatures (*yakshas*) and Chinese warrior heroes and who protected the entrance of a sanctuary. In China they became known as *erwang* ("Two Kings"), a pair of guardian deities. Four *lokapālas*, or "Divine Kings" (C: *tianwang*) were responsible for protecting the Buddha and his Law, the sanctuary, and the Buddhist congregation from dangers and threats of evil forces arising from the four cardinal directions of the compass. Their images became standard furnishing on a Buddhist altar platform and at the four corners of a stupa or a mandala.

Symbolically, figures on the human level of existence, such as arhats (C: *luohan*; supranatural persons who, having attained enlightenment, will enter into nirvana after death) and the Buddha's major disciples, were more important as a group than as individuals. Arhats received a much simpler iconographical treatment than bodhisattvas, *vidyārājas*, and other suprahuman beings; on the other hand, they were represented with greater artistic and doctrinal freedom. The legendary, wonder-working arhats were often depicted as a group—groups of eight, sixteen, or five hundred being the most traditional. Arhats are frequently accompanied by animals and other companions (cat. 177). Originally worshiped as saints of the Hīnayāna pantheon, in China by the fifth century the sixteen arhats would become guardians of Mahāyāna Buddhism. Their names and abodes appear in a scripture translated into Chinese in 654 by the famous pilgrim-monk Xuanzang (600–664). According to this text, the Buddha advised the arhats to remain in this world to await the advent of the redeeming Buddha, Maitreya.

COMMISSIONING AND INSCRIBING BUDDHIST IMAGES

Despite the great variety of savior figures, the scope of artistic creativity and innovation in Buddhist imagery was limited on the whole by iconographic and iconometric constraints. Needless to say, statues were appreciated not primarily as art objects but as sacred icons. Nevertheless, such variables as the nature and intensity of piety in various parts of the vast country; locally available materials; patrons' preferences; the function, purpose, placement, and installation of a given icon; as well as adaptations of Indian and Central Asian aesthetics and stylistic traits to traditional Chinese taste and modes of representation brought about a surprising variety in Buddhist sculpture.

If we are able—despite the canonical uniformity—to perceive connections and variations in the process by which Buddhist art was slowly assimilated in China and in the complicated development of style and iconography, it is largely owing to the Chinese urge for accurate documentation. Dates, names, and facts were inscribed on Buddhist sculptures with such thoroughness that, with the aid of more or less accidentally surviving material, we can reconstruct almost uninterrupted chronological sequences of dated works. This, at any rate, is generally the case in northern China, where the new religion and its arts were strongly supported by the Tuoba, the foreign rulers of the Wei dynasties (386–557). In southern China many of the ancient Buddhist monuments have not survived. Besides the date of completion or consecration of an icon and the names of its donors and beneficiaries, inscriptions often indicate the dual motivation for commissioning a Buddhist statue. The devotee intended to provide a main object of worship and at the same time to incur the manifold blessings promised by the sacred texts to those who, solely or jointly, sponsored the making of an icon. In compliance with the doctrine of karma, the pious donor could even transfer or extend merits and virtues to others—to the imperial house, to ancestors, to living members of the family, to "all sentient beings."

"The Scripture on the Production of Buddha Images" (*Zuo fo xingxiang jing*) elaborates in great detail on the marvelous rewards that may be expected in a future life by those who make and commission sacred icons. This short text is among the most popular and earliest Buddhist scriptures to be translated into Chinese, perhaps in the first half of the third century. Virtually nothing is known of its provenance or translators. The scripture does not give any ritual, artistic, or technical instructions on the actual making of Buddhist icons. But it provides the background for the production of the first "authentic" Buddha image, the earliest known reference to the mysterious Udayana statue:

> The king addressed the Buddha further saying: "When people perform virtuous acts they gain good fortune, but where does this lead them? I dread no longer being able to look upon the Buddha after the Buddha is gone. I want to produce an image of the Buddha to venerate and bequeath to later generations. What sorts of good fortune will I obtain thereby? I ask the Buddha to take compassion upon me and explain this matter, as I earnestly desire to understand."[16]

What follows is a list of salvific aspects of rebirths to be gained through the production of sacred icons. One of these promulgations reads:

> One who produces an image of the Buddha will, in a later life, always honour the Buddha and revere his scriptures. He will continually make offerings to the relics of the Buddha of variegated silk, fine flowers, exquisite incense, lamps, and all the precious jewels and rare objects of the world. Afterward for innumerable aeons he will practice the path to nirvana. Those who aspire to present precious jewels to the Buddha are not common men; they have all practiced the Buddhist path in previous lives. Such is the fortune obtained by one who produces an image of the Buddha.[17]

On the pedestal of a gilded bronze altar of the Sui dynasty (581–618), representing the Buddha Amitābha and his retinue, we find a long engraved inscription (cat. 160). This masterwork of bronze casting, made up of twenty-three components, once served a pious person and his family members for their private worship. It was discovered in 1974 near the village of Bali on the outskirts of Xi'an, in Shaanxi Province. The beginning of the inscription is almost formulaic: "On the fifteenth day of the seventh month in the fourth year of the Kaihuang [era, i.e., 584] the general of Ningyuan and deputy district magistrate of Wujiang [in present-day Hebei Province, by the name of] Dong Qin had this Amitābha image made, so that His Majesty the emperor and his inner circle above and father and mother, brothers and sisters, wife and children below all may perceive the correct Law [of the Buddha]." There follows a panegyric in four verses on the prospects of salvation, the true marks of the Buddha's body becoming manifest, cause and effect, illusion and rebirth, and finally on salvation in Amitābha's paradise. A red sandstone stele more than sixty years older than the Sui altar was unearthed in 1954 at the ancient site of the Wanfo Temple ("Thousand Buddha Temple"), at Chengdu in Sichuan Province (cat. 150). Tradition holds that the Wanfo Temple was established shortly after the middle of the second century; under the Liang dynasty (502–557) it was known as Anpu Temple ("Temple of the Peaceful Riverbank"), and under the Tang (618–907) as Jingzhong Temple ("Temple of the Cleansed Multitude"). The first Buddhist sculptures were discovered at this site in 1882. Subsequent investigations in 1937, 1945, and 1953–54 brought to light a total of about two hundred figures and fragments (cats. 151, 163, 168, 176). The elaborate configuration of this stele depicts the standing Buddha Śākyamuni surrounded by pairs of bodhisattvas, deities, and disciples. A scenic composition in shallow relief on the rear of the stele shows Śākyamuni worshiped by ceremonially aligned men and women in a landscape setting as he sits in meditation under a tree. The inscription below may be translated:

> On the eighth day of the third month in the fourth year of the Putong [era] of the Liang [dynasty, i.e., 523] the [Buddha] disciple Kang Sheng, upon his awakening, reverently had one stone image of Śākyamuni made. We pray that his present relatives may always be at peace and quiet, and that by giving up the world [entering priesthood] his body will be blessed with receiving a state in which he forever will see the Buddha and hear his Law. May his fathers and mothers for the past seven generations, together with all sentient beings, share one and all in this prayer. May they quickly attain Buddhahood and altogether magnificent salvation.

ON THE PRODUCTION AND ICONOMETRY OF BUDDHIST IMAGES

A few Buddhist image makers may have been ecclesiastics or artists loosely associated with a religious institution; most were probably professional lay craftsmen who may have been organized in workshops through which they handed down their technical skills and experience to following generations. Ancient Chinese prejudice condemned even the most talented masters in the laborious art of sculpture to social inferiority and anonymity. Not until the end of the Tang dynasty is any individual sculptor known to have left his signature on an extant work. A few sculptors are known by name solely through literary sources.

Chinese sculptors rarely had the opportunity to see Western Buddhist monuments with their own eyes. Only now and then could they draw inspiration from major Western prototypes that had been imported or officially presented to the court or to a renowned temple in China. Instead, sculptors had to rely largely on oral descriptions by missionaries and returning pilgrims, perhaps on their sketches and drawings made en route, on manuals handed down, and on images made for private worship—small and therefore easily portable.

Canonical scriptures—some of Indian origin, some apocryphal—contain detailed accounts of the *imagining*, in the true meaning of the word, of Buddhist deities. These compilations of ritual prescriptions read like iconographic handbooks. They provide accurate descriptions of the figures with all their features and attributes. Although no early Chinese manuals on designing and making Buddhist images have survived, there must have been guides—plus strong oral traditions—with rules, instructions, perhaps even illustrations. The famous *Pratimāmāna lakshana* was translated from a Tibetan version as late as 1742 by the Manchu prince Gongbu Chabu and published under the title *Zaoxiang liangdu jing* ("Classic of Measurements for Making [Buddhist] Images").[18] As with the canon of classical Greek sculpture, Buddhist imagery followed elaborate rules: proportions and measurements of a figure were of fundamental significance and may be traced back to the old Indian iconometric system called *tālamāna*.[19] The Buddhist "doctrine of measuring icons" (S: *pratimāmāna*) is based on various modules. For example, the smallest unit is the width of a finger (S: *angula*; C: *zhiliang*). Next comes the span of a hand (S: *tāla* or *vitasti*; C: *shouliang*): this maximum distance between tips of thumb and middle finger corresponds to the length of the face from hairline to the tip of the chin. The length of the forearm from elbow to the tip of the thumb (C: *zhouliang*) constitutes another unit. Standard measurements of this sort provide the fabric and grid for the canon of proportions. Although derived from parts of the human body, the proportions were not used to represent observed reality or to depict the natural beauty and harmony of the human figure. Rather, this system of proportions embodies spiritual and metaphysical laws of the Sacred, symbolic norms of abstract character: it prescribes different mathematical relationships for the various categories of figures, according to their level of existence in the Buddhist pantheon. Multiples of the modules determine the size of a standing or a seated figure as well as the height and proportions of a Buddha, bodhisattva, deity, guardian, or an ordinary human being. In sculpture, configurations are dominated by this principle of hieratic scaling. Individual figures are also distinguished by their volume and placement. In relief representations, for example (cats. 150, 161), they range from the central figure of the Buddha, on his supreme level of transcendence, who stands out against the background and is carved almost completely in the round, to the worldly donors, who occupy subordinate positions at the bottom and the edges and are rendered in low relief or simple line engraving.

Artists in the service of Buddhism sought to represent their religious figures with stylized beauty and sumptuous splendor, using a complex system of idealization beyond human forms. It was their aim to visualize the sacred essence of the faith through majestic manifestation of the deities, through their serene nobility, and through their lavish adornment—an aesthetic quality called *alamkāra* in Sanskrit (C: *zhuangyan*). The fine linear engraving on a horizontal panel depicting the Buddha surrounded by bodhisattvas and disciples suggests a convincing vision of the reward awaiting pious believers in paradise (cat. 152). Highlighted by a large mandorla and seated beneath a precious canopy, the central figure can probably be identified as "Śākyamuni Preaching the Law." Subsidiary figures, "varied in pose and expression, are hierarchically grouped in front of luxuriant trees. This hierarchical symmetry and concern with three-dimensional form extends to the entire composition, inviting comparison with wall paintings of Buddhist paradise scenes in cave-temples. The fluent draftsmanship creates an exquisite pictorial effect that must have been considerably heightened by the now-vanished polychromy. On both sides the figures are flanked by a long dedicatory inscription dated in accordance with 524, making this Northern Wei panel from Jingming Temple in Luoyang one of the most valuable early monuments in China's history of religious figure painting. To suggest these visionary conceptions of paradises and the suprahuman character of their sacred figures, artists rendered their icons ageless, passionless, and flawless, wearing an introspective, compassionate expression (cats. 163, 164, 166, 174, 176). Only figures of lesser sanctity were represented with a degree of pictorial realism.

The materials Chinese artists used for Buddhist images varied greatly over region and time. Besides bronze, clay, and lacquer, various kinds of stone and wood were very popular. We find sculptures made of sandstone, limestone, schist, and marble as well as statues carved in sandalwood, camphor, and pine. As a rule, they received a polychrome finish over preparatory coatings (cats. 161, 170–73). The technique for casting bronze icons employed traditional molds as well as the lost-wax method (cats. 160, 169). Overall fire gilding was favored. Additional engraving may be seen occasionally; in ancient times this technique was mainly reserved for dedicatory inscriptions. Portable miniature altars and small icons for private worship stood more chance of preservation than did the monumental temple bronze statuary, almost all of which was destroyed in the course of infrequent but ferocious persecutions of Buddhism or in other disasters, such as revolts, wars, earthquakes, fires, or floods.

CATEGORIES OF CHINESE BUDDHIST SCULPTURE

The spread of Buddhism and its art can to some extent be traced through the chronological sequence of the establishment of cave-temples. The architecture of the earliest Chinese cave-temples follows Central Asian models and clearly reveals its Indian origins. Textual evidence suggests that the first was built in 366 at Dunhuang in the extreme northwest, a junction of the great trade routes and a gateway to Western influence. Soon afterward, extensive work was carried out in the southeast and east. The construction of the Bingling cave-temple at Mount Xiaojishi in northwestern Yongjing county, Gansu Province, seems to have begun early in the fifth century; in 1963 a votive inscription in ink bearing a Western Qin date corresponding to 420 was discovered in Cave 169. The cave-temple at Maijishan, east of the ancient Buddhist center of Liangzhou in Tianshui county, Gansu Province, may have been founded at about the same time. In his biographical account *Gaoseng zhuan* ("Lives of Eminent Monks"), Huijiao (497–554) records that the monk Tanhong from Chang'an, who was living as a hermit at Maijishan in the early 420s, was joined there by another monk, Xuangao.[20] At that time, a congregation of more than a hundred monks is said to have resided at Maijishan.

The first series of cave-chapels at Yungang, near Datong in Shanxi Province, was begun at the instigation of the monk Tanyao in 460 under the patronage of the Northern Wei sovereigns. Far into the sixth century caves with sculptural ensembles continued to be carved into the rock. In 493 the Tuoba ruler Xiaowen (r. 471–499) abandoned the flourishing and populous center of Datong and transferred the Wei court to Luoyang in Henan Province. This move into the heartland of Chinese civilization was a significant historical event and a profoundly political statement. Soon afterward, the laborious chiseling of cave-temples with extensive sculptural programs began afresh on a long cliff of dark gray limestone at Longmen, seven miles south of the new capital. At Gongxian, approximately forty miles downstream from Longmen, caves with superb sculptures were carved in a colossal cliffside overlooking the Luo River. A votive inscription dated in accordance with 531 has been discovered under niche 227 outside Cave 5.

The commission of the imperial caves at Xiangtangshan was also connected with the founding of an ancient capital: Ye, capital of Northern Qi (550–577), in southwestern Hebei Province. Literary evidence and inscriptions on steles permit us to assume that the emperor Wenxuan (r. 550–559) initiated this project. In Buddhist texts he is described as a "devoted and generous follower of the Church." The work on the large complex of Buddhist caves on the southwestern slope of Tianlongshan, southwest of present-day Taiyuan in Shanxi Province, is likely to have begun around 535 and seems to have continued until the middle of the eighth century, after more than a hundred years of suspended activity, under the patronage of influential people closely connected with the ruling Tang dynasty.

In addition to Buddhist images in cave-temples, images of stone, clay, bronze, and other materials were worshiped in wood-constructed buildings, temple courtyards, domestic shrines, and private homes. Although we have a general view of the development of Buddhist sculpture in China, it will require further investigation to more precisely identify regional schools and individual workshops and to determine their characteristics, patrons, and periods of flourishing. More research is also needed to discover when the first freestanding stone Buddhist images were created and where this process began. The oldest freestanding stone statues in the round are not likely to predate the first half of the sixth century. The use of micaceous white marble known as *Han baiyushi* ("white jade[-like] stone of Han") may have played an important role; it was an almost ideal material for the sculptors working in the Dingzhou and Baoding areas in Hebei Province. Besides smaller sculptures and steles, monumental statues in the round have been found in this area that exhibit a delicate smoothness. The flat drapery folds cling to the body and flow in subtle, graceful lines, contrasting with the rounded forms of the head. A large number of marble sculptures, several inscribed and dated to the 520s, were excavated from the ruins of the ancient Xiude Temple near Quyang in Hebei.

Most important for the study of Buddhist sculpture is the comparatively large corpus of votive steles (*huanyuan fobei*) richly decorated with engravings and reliefs of various depths and heights. They were usually installed in temple compounds, in monasteries and nunneries or their courtyards, and also in cave-chapels. Their prototypes may be seen in the memorial and other inscribed steles customary in China since Han times. Four-sided pier-steles resting on a pedestal usually have a simulated roof that serves as a top member and are adorned in several registers with Buddhist images, often set in niches on each of the four sides.

Another major type is a rectangular monolith set up vertically on a low base. On the front of the stele is a triad or a larger configuration centered on a seated Buddha and placed in a recess with imitated architectural elements, draped curtains, and canopy at the front (cats. 154, 155, 157, 158, 161). This arrangement is strongly reminiscent of the walls of cave-chapels. The reverse side of such steles may also be sculptured in relief, with groups of figures from the Buddhist pantheon, narrative scenes of sacred events and locations, or assemblages of donors. Often the rear is reserved for inscriptions, including long lists of donors' names. In some cases, pairs of intertwined dragons crown the work (cat. 157). Steles with images in relief on the front only, leaving the rear unworked, were originally most likely set into the walls of a temple structure. In 1975 seventeen marble steles of this sort were unearthed near the village of Caotan, at Xi'an, in Shaanxi Province (cat. 159). They were discovered standing in pairs, face to face, which accounts for their excellent state of preservation. Further archaeological evidence suggests that they were carefully buried at the site of an ancient Buddhist temple for safety reasons—probably to protect them from the iconoclasts of one of the devastating Buddhist persecutions in old Chang'an. Steles with a multitude of miniature Buddha niches surrounding the central image are customarily referred to as "Thousand Buddha" steles.

One of the earliest and most enduringly popular types of votive stele represents a seated or standing Buddha haloed by a leaf-shaped mandorla, or aureole (cats. 147–49). The Buddha thus represented is often Śākyamuni, the historical Buddha, or the redeeming Buddha of the Future, Maitreya, identified as a rule by his cross-ankled pose. The Buddha is presented in solemn frontality and high relief, almost in the round—a stately figure, imbued with majestic grandeur. A blissfully withdrawn smile on his face radiates tranquility and salvific certitude. The symbolic gestures of the hands, or *mudrās*, effectively convey powerful instructive messages to the devout beholder. On the front of the aureole, dense patterns and ornaments are often interspersed with miniature Buddha figures called "Transformation Buddhas" (*huafo*). Occasionally, the pointed mandorla curves gently forward at the top. This, along with other features such as the engraved wreath of flames, may have been inspired by gilded bronze images. On the reverse, carved in low relief or incised, we find groups of minor deities and donors, along with narrative scenes of the Buddha's life and depictions of holy or miraculous deeds, events, and encounters. Most of these features may be seen on a stele reportedly unearthed in Xingping county, Shaanxi Province (cat. 147). The inscription on the rear of its pedestal is partly damaged, but the date can be safely read: it corresponds to the year 471. The soft modeling and conspicuous parallel folds of the drapery suggest that the sculptor intended to transfer the qualities of a molded clay prototype into stone carving, which may reflect stylistic influences from Taxila in Gandhāra (in present-day Pakistan) or Bāmiyān in Afghanistan.

A great variety of freestanding Buddhist sculptures have been preserved from the Tang dynasty (618–907). One of the finest works is the white marble torso of a standing bodhisattva that was excavated in the old precincts of Daminggong, the Tang imperial "Palace of Great Brightness," in Xi'an (cat. 165). Only traces of gold and colors remain on the polished stone surface. The attractively rounded, swelling forms of the body and the pliant pose imbue this statue with the sensuous and tactile beauty that so emphatically marks Tang sculpture at its zenith, about the middle of the eighth century. The triple-bend posture, or *tribhaṅga*, suggesting a gentle sway at the hips, demonstrates the sculptor's interest in organic movement. At the same time this torso shows the influence of India's mature Gupta art. An elegant scarf across the naked chest and a dhoti covering the lower body are draped in graceful folds and pleats that closely follow the forms of the body. A precious necklace contributes to the effects of elegant courtly refinement, splendor, and grandeur.

A totally different stylistic approach is seen in a nearly contemporaneous sandstone torso of a powerful guardian figure (cat. 168). This statue was excavated in 1954 at the site of the Tang dynasty Jingzhong Temple (known as Wanfo Temple in late Han times) at Chengdu, in Sichuan Province. The threatening attitude of the robust guardian deity and his physical dynamism testify to his role as protector of the sanctuary. Forceful workmanship creates an almost overly emphatic, manneristic muscularity, reinforced by manneristic elements in the agitated treatment of the garment.

TANG MARBLE SCULPTURE FROM THE METROPOLITAN ANGUO TEMPLE
In the arts of Esoteric Buddhism flourishing under the Tang dynasty, wrathful figures such as *vidyārājas* and bodhisattvas in their awesome (S: *krodha*) incarnations played a prominent role. Of ten icons made of finely grained white marble with traces of gold and polychromy, excavated in 1959 in the old Changle ward of the Tang capital Chang'an, at least eight qualify as members of the Esoteric Buddhist pantheon (cats. 166, 170–72). Two depict the ferocious-looking Bright King Budong (S: Acala[nātha]; "Immovable One"), who was the unshakable, indomitable adherent and protector of the Buddhist Law. Two other terrifying deities on bizarre, layered rock pedestals most likely represent

Trailokyavijaya (C: Xiangsanshi; "Victor over the Three Worlds [of greed, hatred, and folly]") (cat. 170). One of his characteristic attributes is the ancient Indo-Aryan *vajra*, the magic thunderbolt or diamond scepter (C: *jingangchu*), which symbolizes the diamond-like, indestructible character of the ultimate truth. In one of his emanations, Trailokyavijaya has three, sometimes even four heads and eight arms. His furious, scowling visage, with bulging eyes, bestial fangs, and knotted eyebrows expresses his holy wrath (S: *krodha*; C: *fennu*), while his combative attitude and flamboyant hair point to his destructive energies and militant opposition to evil, both physical and spiritual. The Bodhisattva Hayagrīva, the "horse-headed" Matou Guanyin, also has three heads and eight arms. He is shown sitting on a lotus-and-rock pedestal in front of an aureole of swirling flames. Another prominent member of the Esoteric Buddhist pantheon is the mystic Buddha of the South, Ratnasambhava (C: Baosheng; "Producer of Treasures"). This figure, now headless, is seated with legs crossed in *vajrāsana* pose (legs folded in the "adamant," or unshakable, posture) on a lotus throne that rests on seven winged horses (cat. 171). Among the finest works in this group of marble sculptures is the image of Mañjuśrī (C: Wenshu), one of the agents of the Buddha Śākyamuni (cat. 172). In his left hand he holds the stem of a lotus. A palm-leaf book of Indian type placed on the blossom above his left shoulder allows us to identify him as the Bodhisattva of Great Wisdom. His cultic center was on Mount Wutai in Shanxi Province, which was thought to be his sacred abode. Richly adorned with heavy jewelry, Mañjuśrī is seated on an elaborate throne of overlapping lotus petals. Deeply sculptured, scrolling leaves create an almost baroque quality.

The sculptural refinement of all these marble statues and fragments is exceptional. Their subtle and elaborate surface treatment—including the original polychromy and gilding—attests to the artist's or the metropolitan atelier's remarkable technical skill and sensitivity in imparting a forceful expressiveness and an extraordinary lively grace to the works. In their original setting the icons may have constituted a complete mandala. It is likely that they were commissioned for the great Anguo Temple ("Temple for Pacifying the Country") in Chang'an, which historical records locate at the ancient Changle ward in the immediate neighborhood of the imperial palaces, just outside present-day Xi'an. Local government workers digging for a water conduit discovered the sculptures, several in badly damaged condition, in a small tunnel; they had been buried deep and were found at a depth of over ten meters.

The Anguo Temple was founded in 710. According to Duan Chengshi's (d. 863) *Sita ji* ("Notes on

Temples and Pagodas"), published in 853, the Anguo Temple's Buddha Hall was originally the bed-chamber hall of the emperor Xuanzong (r. 712–756).[21] The structure was purportedly dismantled and transferred to the temple grounds by imperial decree in 713. Its main image seems to have been a Maitreya statue that frequently emitted miraculous light. Unfortunately, there is no mention of any other icons. As a renowned study center for Esoteric Buddhism and a colossal monument to piety and the arts in the capital city of Chang'an, the Anguo Temple was a chief target in the violent persecution of 845. Anti-Buddhist iconoclasts may have buried the sculptures at such a great depth because they feared revenge and punishment through the magical powers of the terrifying deities embodied in the images. The turmoil accompanying general An Lushan's insurrection of 755–763 had far-reaching negative effects, not only on the subsequent political, economic, and social structure of Tang China, but also on the prestige and development of the Buddhist church and its arts. The Anguo Temple sculptures probably predate this dramatic decline, and thus may have been completed in the second quarter of the eighth century.

It was just at this time, during Xuanzong's reign, that Esoteric Buddhism first received official recognition and active encouragement from the court. In 716 the famous Indian Tantric theologian Subhakarasimha (637–735), known to the Chinese as Shanwuwei, arrived in Chang'an with a number of Sanskrit texts. Eight years later his Chinese disciple Yixing (638–727) assisted him in translating and commenting on one of the fundamental Esoteric Buddhist scriptures, the *Mahāvairocana Sūtra* (C: *Dari jing*; "Sūtra of the Great Radiance of Illumination"). This text describes most of the important Esoteric Buddhist deities in some detail: they were novel and infinitely more varied in their iconography than their traditional counterparts. The powerful presence of the Bright Kings, in particular, must have overshadowed the appeal of the bodhisattvas, whose prominence they were usurping.

STYLISTIC TRENDS IN BUDDHIST SCULPTURE

The number of securely dated Chinese Buddhist icons—mainly gilded bronzes—of the fourth century is very small, and their style is reminiscent of images from Gandhāra. Although attached canopies are also known in early Indian sculpture, the leaf-shaped mandorla with flaming border seems to be a Chinese innovation. The attempt to emulate the Indian naturalism soon fused with indigenous Chinese tendencies toward stylization and abstraction. Early Chinese Buddhist images tend to ignore rather than emphasize human anatomy. Thus, the robes do not drape easily; on the contrary, they are stiffly modeled and rigidly symmetrical, creating a rather austere, disincarnate image, but one of compelling majestic poise. By the end of the fifth century all the stylistic idioms of Buddhist sculpture that had reached China from Gandhāra, India, and Central Asia had been slowly assimilated into a consistent Chinese declaration of faith and zeal. Throughout the first half of the sixth century traditional styles and motifs persisted in the Chinese Buddhist sculptor's art, but from about the mid-sixth century a novel style was evolving in north China.

The sculpture of the Northern Qi and Sui periods is clearly distinct from earlier linear, geometric treatments of Buddhist images. In this new stage of the development we see a genuine attempt to indicate the human body beneath the garments, an attempt that was stimulated by Indian influences of the classic Gupta period. In their striving for volume and graceful movement in their figures, Tang sculptors of the seventh and eighth centuries went even a step further, combining solid, almost weighty reality with voluptuous fleshiness. Suave, rhythmic drapery patterns follow the form of the body so closely that one senses the texture, weight, and fall of the cloth. As the figures became substantial, often plump, there was an ever-increasing tendency toward rich detail, complexity of forms, and restless movement in the sweeping curves of the drapery folds. Their extraordinary technical skill allowed the sculptors to reproduce the finest details of hair, ribbons, and jewelry with utmost accuracy. In the end the monumental solidity of the mature Tang style was diminished through an overconscious striving for aristocratic elegance and sensuous beauty.

Over the past decades several of the large cave-temple sites have been thoroughly investigated; a number of individual temples and buildings have been restored; groups of religious icons as well as isolated images have been excavated; and several spectacular reliquary deposits have been recovered from China's great Buddhist heritage. All these substantive archaeological finds and results of recent restoration and research have greatly clarified and enriched our understanding of historical records and literary sources. They help to document changes in Buddhist piety, worship, and faith; developments in the structure and importance of various schools and temples; prominence of individual deities, saints, patriarchs, donors, and rulers over the centuries. They also allow us deeper insight into the nature and living tradition of Chinese Buddhist art, its liturgical foundations, iconography, style, materials, techniques, and last but not least, its perfect Sinicization.

NOTES

1. Robert H. Sharf, "The Scripture in Forty-Two Sections," in *Religions of China in Practice*, ed. Donald S. Lopez, Jr., Princeton Readings in Religions (Princeton: Princeton University Press, 1996), p. 360; for a concise introduction to and full translation of the text, ibid., pp. 360–71; and for the Chinese version see *Taishō shinshū daizōkyō*, ed. Takakusu Junjirō and Watanabe Kaigyoku (Tokyo, 1925; reprint, Tokyo: Taishō shinshū daizōkyō kankōkai, 1968), vol. 17, no. 784, pp. 722a–724a.

2. See *Taishō shinshū daizōkyō* (Tokyo, 1928; reprint, Tokyo: Taishō shinshū daizōkyō kankōkai, 1973), vol. 51, no. 2092, p. 999a. Translation, with minor changes, by Yi-t'ung Wang, *A Record of Buddhist Monasteries in Lo-yang by Yang Hsuan-chih* (Princeton: Princeton University Press, 1984), pp. 5f.

3. Edwin O. Reischauer, trans., *Ennin's Diary: The Record of a Pilgrimage to China in Search of the Law* (New York: Ronald Press, 1955), pp. 381f.

4. Translation by Alexander C. Soper, *Literary Evidence for Early Buddhist Art in China*, Artibus Asiae, Suppl. 19 (Ascona: Artibus Asiae, 1959), pp. 1f.

5. Another version of this apparition tale has been preserved in the *Mingxiang ji* ("Records of Miraculous Omens"), by Wang Yan (act. late 5th–early 6th c.). The 131 stories that can be attributed to the now lost *Mingxiang ji* make Wang Yan's compilation one of the most fascinating early Buddhist miracle-tale collections. In 664 Daoxuan included this anecdote as the first in a series of famous images in chapter 2 of his *Ji shenzhou san-*

bao gantong lu ("Catalogue of the Salvific Influence of the Three Jewels on China's Assembled [Temples and Pagodas]"), in *Taishō shinshū daizōkyō* (Tokyo, 1927; reprint, Tokyo: Taishō shinshū daizōkyō kankōkai, 1960), vol. 52, no. 2106, p. 413c.

6. Soper, *Literary Evidence*, p. 4.

7. Soper, *Literary Evidence*, p. 4.

8. See Daoxuan, *Ji shenzhou sanbao gantong lu*, chap. 2, pp. 416c–417a.

9. Daoxuan, *Ji shenzhou sanbao gantong lu*, p. 416c. Translation, with minor changes by Soper, in *Literary Evidence*, p. 21; for the Chinese text, see "Quotations and Technical Terms," in *Literary Evidence*, p. 296:G.

10. Yang Xuanzhi, *Luoyang qielan ji*, in *Taishō shinshū daizōkyō*, vol. 51, no. 2092, p. 1000a; translation by Wang, *Record of Buddhist Monasteries*, pp. 16f.

11. Translation, with minor changes, by Roger Goepper, "Some Thoughts on the Icon in Esoteric Buddhism in East Asia," in *Studia Sino-Mongolica: Festschrift für Herbert Franke,* herausgegeben von Wolfgang Bauer, Münchener Ostasiatische Studien, vol. 25 (Wiesbaden: Franz Steiner Verlag, 1980), p. 248.

12. See Arthur F. Wright, "Tang T'ai-tsung and Buddhism," in Arthur F. Wright and Denis Twitchett, eds., *Perspectives on the T'ang* (New Haven and London: Yale University Press, 1973), p. 256.

13. Soper, *Literary Evidence*, pp. 15f. Cf. also in Daoxuan's *Guang hongming ji* ("Expanded Collection on Propagating the Light"), the panegyric on the celebrated icon by Dao'an's distinguished disciple Huiyuan (334–416), in *Taishō shinshū daizōkyō*, vol. 52, no. 2103, p. 198b–c.

14. Translation, with minor changes, by James Hightower, in Edwin O. Reischauer, *Ennin's Travels in China* (New York: Reginald Press, 1955), pp. 223f.; and in Stanley

Weinstein, *Buddhism under the T'ang* (New York and Melbourne: Cambridge University Press, 1987), p. 104.

15. Mahāyāna doctrines hold that the Buddha exists simultaneously in three essentially identical "bodies": the *dharmakāya*, the *sambhogakāya*, and the *nirmānakāya*. The *dharmakāya*, or true "body of the Law" (C: *fashen*), transcends personality and the multitude of forms and colors in the phenomenal world. Thus, it can neither be depicted, nor expressed in words, nor contemplated by the unenlightened human mind. The *sambhogakāya*, or "body of requital" (C: *baoshen*), is the Buddha's level of existence upon entering Buddhahood as a result of vows, exercises, and religious merit. This aspect of the Buddha may be visualized by enlightened beings. The *nirmānakāya*, or "shadow body" (C: *yingshen*), is the Buddha's perceptible incarnation for the benefit of unenlightened sentient beings. In the aspect of this body, the devotee is able to perceive the Buddha as a human figure, in the person of Śākyamuni. The latter two bodies are also referred to as *rūpakāya*, "form bodies" or "color bodies" (C: *seshen*). Images for worship and devotion may be made only of these two bodies.

16. See *Taishō shinshū daizōkyō* (Tokyo, 1925; reprint, Tokyo: Taishō shinshū daizōkyō kankōkai, 1964), vol. 16, no. 692, p. 788a; Robert H. Scharf, trans., "The Scripture on the Production of Buddha Images," in *Religions of China*, p. 265.

17. Scharf, trans., "Production of Buddha Images," p. 266.

18. *Taishō shinshū daizōkyō* (Tokyo, 1928; reprint, Tokyo: Taishō shinshū daizōkyō kankōkai, 1968), vol. 21, no. 1419, pp. 936–56.

19. "The word *tāla*, of ancient origin and uncertain derivation, has from a very early time served as a basic term for the standard of measure (*pramāna*) in the visual and performing arts.... The basic meaning of *tāla* is 'span'—a span of space

(as measured from the tip of the outstretched thumb to the tip of the middle finger) [or] a span of time (as marked off and articulated by audible and silent gestures performed by the hand[s])." See Kapila Vatsyayan, ed., *Kalātattvakośa, A Lexicon of Fundamental Concepts of the Indian Arts,* vol. 2, *Concepts of Space and Time*, ed. Bettina Bäumer (New Delhi: Śri Jainendra Press, 1992), pp. 333, 335.

20. See *Taishō shinshū daizōkyō* (Tokyo, 1928; reprint, Tokyo: Taishō shinshū daizōkyō kankōkai, 1968), chap. 11, vol. 50, no. 2059, p. 397a.

21. See the translation by Alexander C. Soper, "A Vacation Glimpse of the T'ang Temples of Ch'ang-an: The *Ssu-t'a Chi* by Tuan Ch'eng-shih," *Artibus Asiae* 23, no. 1 (1960), pp. 23f. The *Taishō shinshū daizōkyō*, vol. 51, no. 2093, pp. 1022b–1024a, gives only an abridged version of the text.

Calligraphy

Peter Sturman

Associate Professor, Department of the
History of Art and Architecture,
University of California, Santa Barbara

Calligraphy is often called the most
Chinese of arts. This is a label of praise,
perhaps, but one that is also problematic,
for it exoticizes calligraphy by prompting
associations of the "mysterious East" and
by reinforcing the natural tendency
among those who do not read Chinese
to believe that this art of dynamic but
seemingly incomprehensible strokes

Fig. 1. *Cang Jie, legendary inventor of the Chinese characters. Computer-generated image.*

Fig. 2a. *Oracle bone, inscribed. Shang dynasty. Ox or deer scapula. Unearthed at Anyang, Henan Province, beginning of 20th century. Liaoning Provincial Museum, Shenyang.*

Fig. 2b. *Oracle bone, inscribed. Shang dynasty. Tortoise plastron. National Museum of Chinese History, Beijing.*

and dots is inaccessible to outsiders. It is true that the well-trained viewer of calligraphy must, at a minimum, be able to read Chinese characters, but it is largely unknown that Chinese calligraphy is, in fact, a remarkably open art, one that actively engages its viewer in a manner unlike that of any other art form of any culture. Little can be done about the language divide—hence, that sense of democratic engagement will remain largely beyond the reach of most of us. Nonetheless, a fairly informed appreciation is possible once some of the rules, techniques, aesthetic qualities, and history of Chinese calligraphy are introduced. Most important, one can understand why calligraphy is so engaging and thus why it is truly a unique art.

FROM ORACLE TO AUTOGRAPH

Early sources attribute the creation of the Chinese written language to Cang Jie, an official in the employment of the legendary Yellow Emperor and a man whose remarkable vision and ability to communicate with the spirit world was signified by his four eyes (fig. 1). Ancient texts recount that Cang Jie fashioned graphs in the form of pictorial images after being inspired by such natural phenomena as bird tracks, animal paw prints, and shadows cast by trees. "Millet rained from heaven and demons howled in the night,"[1] reads one, a clear indication of how momentous was Cang Jie's

accomplishment. There is no need to dwell on this ancient myth—Cang Jie joins such other celebrated culture heroes as Fuxi (inventor of the trigrams) and Shennong (the inventor of agriculture) as curious personifications, convenient though vague markers of the early progress of Chinese civilization. There is, however, an important point to be noted in Cang Jie's story: the characters, or graphs, in a sense are found, determined from patterns cast by images of the natural world. Cang Jie, or whomever Cang Jie represents, created not by forging something new, but by carefully examining what already existed. In other words, he did not write so much as he *read*.

Cang Jie's story resonates suggestively with the earliest fully developed and sustained system of writing in China: the oracle bones from the Anyang phase of the Shang dynasty (ca. 1300–ca. 1100 BCE) (fig. 2a). "Oracle bones" is the general term used for the ox and deer scapulae (fig. 2a) and tortoise carapaces and plastrons (fig. 2b) that were used to communicate with Heaven. To specific questions incised onto the bones ("Will it rain?" "Will the hunt be good?" and so on), Heaven responded in the form of cracks that appeared on the surface of the bone after the application of a heated point to drilled holes. These cracks were auguries, and professional scribes in charge of this vital communication interpreted their patterns and then recorded the interpretation on the bone surface. The scratchy appearance of the incised forms echoed the original fissures resulting from the applied heat. The writing was not an imposition but an evocation, the giving of form to what was understood to be embedded within.

The significance of Cang Jie's story is twofold: the presumption that writing in China is rooted in natural process and that writing carries inherent meanings. More than a millennium separates the oracle bones from our earliest evidence of calligraphy being recognized as an art of personal expression (in the Eastern Han period, 1st c. CE),[2] yet these two presumptions remained a consistent, if slightly modified, foundation of the art. The source of the writing changed—it was now a person rather than Heaven that communicated—but what issued forth was still considered the embodiment of inherent truths. "Writing is pictures of the heart," wrote Yang Xiong (55 BCE–18 CE) in the Han dynasty.[3] The beauty of Chinese calligraphy is that the tools of writing, as well as the rules, allow practice to concur with this promise of expression. Deceptively simple in appearance, the brush proves capable of conveying the slightest nuance of movement. It is a direct line from that point where the ink-charged brush meets the paper or silk through the fingers, hand, and wrist to the eye and brain; and as anyone who has tried to wield the calligrapher's tool would know, skill or ineptitude is readily apparent. Equally important, Chinese characters are essentially of fixed form, composed of an established number of brush strokes. There is a predetermined order to the writing of the individual strokes in a given character, and a predetermined direction for the writing of each stroke. These rules are integral to calligraphy's expressive dimension, for they allow a later viewer to retrace visually the process of writing, to re-experience the spatial and temporal unfolding of

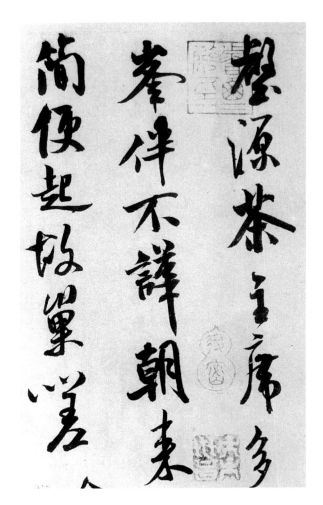

Fig. 3. Mi Fu (1052–1107/8). "Poems Playfully Written and Presented to My Friends, About to Embark for Tiao Stream." Dated to 1088. Detail of a handscroll, ink on paper. Palace Museum, Beijing.

the text. Stroke by stroke, character by character, column by column (from right to left), one "reviews" the original performance of writing. The more informed the viewer, the more familiar with using the brush to write, the more vividly that viewer will sense the brush's original movements and pacing. Some say that the visual retracing of a particularly dynamic piece of calligraphy evokes an unearthly sense of the calligrapher writing it for the first time. No other art can claim such immediacy. No other art captures the process of creativity so vividly.

The immediacy of Chinese calligraphy can create an aura of timelessness. An informed viewer attuned to the subtle art of reading calligraphy may feel as familiar with the author of a piece of writing done centuries earlier as with a contemporary. No one illustrates this effect better than the Northern Song calligrapher Mi Fu (1052–1107/8), a celebrated eccentric and dedicated student of his art. Throughout his life Mi Fu diligently collected ancient bits of writing, savoring them to the point of obsession. "I have no desire for wealth or noble rank," he wrote, "My only love is for those letters from the brushes of the men of antiquity. Every time I clean the inkstone and spread out a scroll, I am oblivious even to the roar of thunder by my side, and the taste of food is forgotten. . . . I suspect that after I die I will become a silverfish who enters into scrolls of prized calligraphy, with gold-lettered title inscriptions and jade rollers, roaming about but without causing harm."[4] "Letters" by "the men of antiquity" refers primarily to casual notes written by calligraphers of the Jin dynasty (265–420), especially those of Wang Xizhi (307?–365?) and his son Wang Xianzhi (344–388), who were long considered the most brilliant writers active during a golden age of calligraphy. By the eleventh century these were extremely rare works, prized not only for the quality of the writing but also for the untrammeled personalities of the writers themselves, who lived, it was imagined, at leisure in the beautiful landscape of the Yangzi River basin. Mi Fu and others knew of the quirks and follies of the men of Jin from collections of miscellaneous anecdotes, such as *Shishuo xinyu* ("A New Account of Tales of the World"), compiled under the aegis of Liu Yiqing (403–444), biographies in the official history, and various early writings on calligraphy.

In the autumn of 1088, at the height of Mi Fu's infatuation with Jin calligraphy, he was invited by a local magistrate to participate in an outing along Tiao Stream, a scenic stretch of landscape just south of Lake Tai in what is now Zhejiang Province. In anticipation of the excursion, Mi Fu wrote and sent to his host a number of poems on one scroll (fig. 3); afterward he recorded on another scroll the poems he had written during the trip.[5] Both sets of poems repeatedly refer to people of the Jin dynasty as if they were alive and present, sometimes conflating them with other members of the outing. In one poem, written for their gathering on the Double Ninth Festival, Mi Fu quotes a line directly from the most celebrated of all works of calligraphy, *Lanting xu* ("Preface for the Poems Written at the Orchid Pavilion"), written by Wang Xizhi in 353, thereby suggesting that their own gathering in 1088 had somehow merged with that famous meeting of seven hundred years earlier. The likely source for Mi Fu's flight of fancy was a superb Tang dynasty tracing copy of Wang's "Preface," which Mi Fu had acquired earlier in the year and no doubt was proudly showing off to his friends. Needless to say, Mi Fu's calligraphy in these two scrolls of poems closely follows the Jin dynasty style associated with Wang Xizhi and the Orchid Pavilion Preface. Although Jin calligraphy, even copies, became increasingly rare in later dynasties, the spirit of Wang Xizhi and the Orchid Pavilion gathering would still be invoked through such writing objects as inkstones carved with scenes from the life of Wang Xizhi.

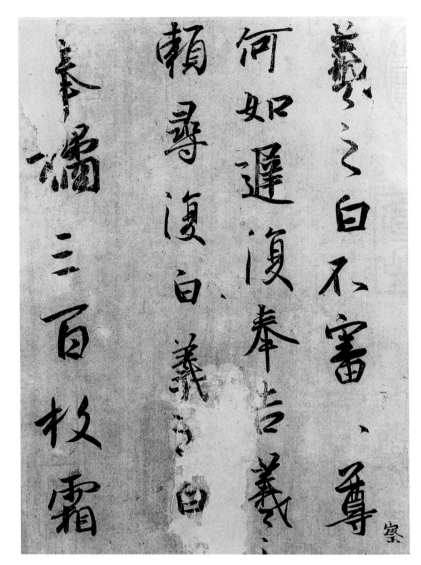

Fig. 4. Wang Xizhi (307?–365?). "Ping'an tie, Heju tie, Fengju tie." Tang dynasty (618–907) tracing copy. Detail of letters mounted as a handscroll, ink on paper. Palace Museum, Taipei.

As Mi Fu's story illustrates, in Chinese calligraphy the vertical expanse of history can seemingly be transformed into the horizontal space of the present. This combined sense of unity and continuity is an important characteristic of calligraphy. Moreover, it extends back to the so-called high tradition that began with Wang Xizhi and Jin calligraphy. With the preservation and continued, if limited, practice of such ancient scripts as seal (*zhuanshu*) and clerical (*lishu*) (see cat. 183 for an example of the latter), later calligraphers felt conversant with a spectrum of writing that literally spanned millennia. The catalyst for the interaction could be a masterful genuine work or a rare tracing copy of the type Mi Fu sought; it could be a faded rubbing from a compendium of collected writings engraved in stone or from some ancient stele accidentally discovered in a farmer's field. In each case, the right viewer under the right circumstances would become engaged, assimilate what had been learned, and thereby invigorate his or her own art. It is an ever-expanding circle.

Looking back on the long history of calligraphy that preceded him, the Ming dynasty theorist Dong Qichang (1555–1636) recognized three epochs fundamental to the formation of the canon and succinctly characterized each one: Jin dynasty calligraphy is governed by *yun* ("resonance"), Tang dynasty (618–907) calligraphy by *fa* ("methods"), and Song dynasty (960–1279) calligraphy by *yi* ("ideas").[6] Terse formulations such as this oversimplify the complexities of history. Nonetheless, it remains an insightful observation and a useful point of departure for a brief discussion of some of Chinese calligraphy's aesthetic qualities.

By Jin dynasty calligraphy, Dong Qichang was referring to the tradition exemplified by Wang Xizhi and Wang Xianzhi, or the Two Wangs, that developed during the fourth century. Wang Xizhi's calligraphy, in particular, was considered representative of the artistically graceful writing adopted for casual notes and letters by the aristocrats of his day. What can be gleaned from extant Tang dynasty tracing copies of calligraphy attributed to Wang Xizhi suggests a remarkably controlled hand that demanded nothing less than perfection of beauty from the brush (fig. 4). Each stroke is utterly smooth and tensile, ribbon-like in its twists and turns. At the same time, the calligraphy displays an extraordinary sense of ease. It appears absolutely unforced and natural, which was precisely the writer's aim. Early critiques of calligraphy almost invariably utilize metaphors of the natural world to describe the forms and forces of the writing. Suo Jing (239–303), for example, wrote the following in reference to the informal and abbreviated cursive script:

> Quivering like a startled phoenix,
> Not yet aloft, wings spread,
> Ready to rise,
> It returns to a state of rest.
> Insects and snakes coiled and poised:
> Some advancing, others retreating,
> Some fragile, soft and willowy,
> Others aggressive, charging forward.
> Wandering freely, this way and that,
> Suddenly upright, suddenly twisted.
> An outstanding steed bolts in anger,
> Struggling against the bridle.[7]

Suo Jing's emphasis is on the energy of the calligraphy, its sense of movement and liveliness. The general term used to describe such energy is *shi*, which can be roughly translated as "configural force," or "momentum." *Shi* is the manifestation of both potential and kinetic energy—process about to happen and already realized. It can be embodied

Fig. 5. Shuang ("frost"). Computer-generated image; (left) from Wang Xizhi (307?–365?), "Fengju tie"; (right) from Lu Jianzhi (7th c.), Rhapsody on Literature.

in a single brush stroke, but *shi* more commonly emerges through the interaction of two or more elements in the calligraphy—brush strokes interacting to create perceptions of continuity and discontinuity, balance and confrontation. *Shi* is an essential component of all good calligraphy from all periods, but its manner of presentation differs depending on both personal and period styles. In writings attributed to the Jin period that energy seems muted by refinement and decorum. Individual elements tend to achieve subtle balancing of forms and forces, with generous spaces created between the traces of ink. A quiet, self-contained energy seemingly resonates about the writing like an electrical field. This, I would suggest, is what Dong Qichang refers to as *yun* ("resonance").

A single character from one Wang Xizhi attribution will help to illustrate (fig. 5, left). The graph *shuang* ("frost") is composed of two basic elements: the upper portion, which by itself means "rain," and the lower portion, which is composed of left and right units. Note the length of the stroke at the upper left. This was the second stroke to be written (after the topmost horizontal stroke), and it is so pronounced that in writing the rest of the character the calligrapher had to consider ways to counter a threatened imbalance in the overall structure. Two solutions are apparent: a strong right-to-left curving stroke that connects the upper portion of the character to the lower left element, and the vertical stroke on the right side of the lower right element. The former parallels and balances that problematic second stroke while echoing and amplifying the curving stroke immediately above and to the right (which preceded it), thus creating a strong cascading movement that helps to anchor the top element. The vertical stroke at the lower right was the very last stroke of the character. It extends a bit lower than it otherwise might have—a last, minor correction to balance the entire composition. This character radiates harmony, balance, and classical beauty, but also, as we have seen, a strong inner tension. It is this perfect balance of energy and restraint that characterizes *yun*.

To illustrate *fa* ("methods"), which Dong Qichang associated with the Tang dynasty, we use the same character, *shuang*, this time written by Lu Jianzhi, a seventh-century follower of Wang Xizhi (fig. 5, right). At first glance, Lu Jianzhi's *shuang* appears almost identical to Wang Xizhi's; and this is as one may expect, considering that Lu's calligraphy style was founded on a slavish study of the earlier writer. There is, however, an important difference: Lu's character is a pasteurized version of Wang's. Achieving overall balance and harmony was now such a paramount concern that there were no self-generated challenges and hence no creative solutions. That second stroke is not as long now, and it is positioned in a way that makes the entire upper element much more stable. Each element of the character is carefully balanced and spaced. No slips have been made, but then no risks were taken. *Fa* suggests regimen and discipline imposed from above by a higher authority. The association of *fa* with the Tang dynasty calls to mind the Tang emphasis on structure, on rules and their codification, all in the interest of assuring stable continuity. Singling out Wang Xizhi's calligraphy as a canonical model to be emulated at the court was one such standardization. Lu Jianzhi's calligraphy, as well as that of many of the other early Tang writers, demonstrates the result: the spontaneity of Jin has been transformed into an image of wrought perfection.

Methods, of course, did not appear first in Tang calligraphy. Rules, propriety, and established standards of aesthetic quality are the foundation for the practice of calligraphy in any period. Similarly, *yun* is not necessarily absent from Tang calligraphy. It is true, however, that these two very significant periods in the development of Chinese calligraphy—the fourth and seventh centuries—are distinguished by different emphases on what was considered important. In the Jin dynasty it was spontaneity, naturalness, the images and energies of the natural world; in the Tang dynasty it was elegance tempered by propriety, stateliness, decorum, and orthodoxy. Both sets of aesthetic criteria are essential components of Chinese calligraphy. "Resonance" and "methods" are simply convenient terms to designate these two different aspects of the calligrapher's art.

But what of "ideas," which Dong Qichang associated with the Song dynasty? *Yi* ("ideas") means "intent, will, reason." It refers to the cognitive processes that distinguish an individual, along with his or her idiosyncrasies. In calligraphy it suggests

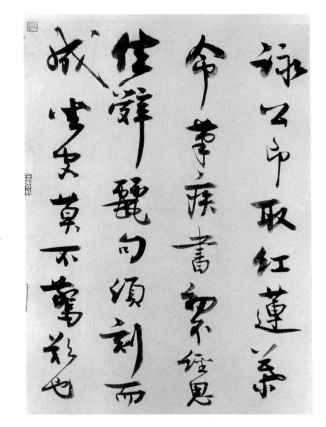

Fig. 6. Wang Shen (ca. 1048–after 1104). "Poem Written on the Lake at Yingchang and Song to the Tune of Dielan hua." Dated to 1086. Detail of a handscroll, ink on paper. Palace Museum, Beijing.

an imposition of the self, qualities of singularity that draw attention to the distinguishing characteristics of a particular person. Qualities of individuality are not absent in the earlier calligraphy, but never are "ideas" more strongly sensed and the individual more directly celebrated than in the writing of the Song calligraphers active in the second half of the eleventh century. When Dong Qichang wrote of "Song ideas," he most likely had in mind the triumvirate of great Song calligraphers—Su Shi (1037–1101), Huang Tingjian (1045–1105), and Mi Fu—but what he points to, in fact, was a widespread phenomenon apparent in the work of a number of calligraphers. Wang Shen (ca. 1048–after 1104), a close friend of the above three, wrote in a particularly distinctive style (fig. 6), which Huang Tingjian made fun of by likening it to the images of strange demonic creatures he once saw in a piece of embroidery from a foreign land—some without hands and feet, some with too many. "This kind of strangeness is not what is normally studied in calligraphy," Huang wrote, "but Wang Shen certainly has developed his own style."[8] There is a tone of grudging approval in Huang Tingjian's comment, admiration for Wang Shen's ability to distinguish his writing from that of others, even if it means unorthodox results.

Historically, the "ideas" of Song calligraphy proved the most problematic for later Chinese

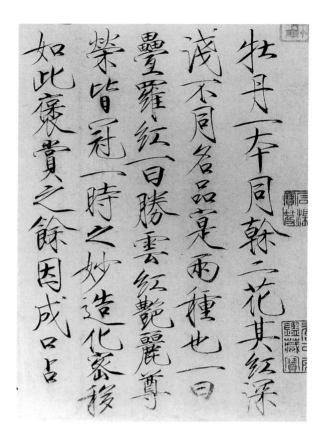

Fig. 7. Song Huizong (Zhao Ji; 1082–1135, r. 1100–1126). "Poem on Peonies." Ca. 1100–26. Detail of an album leaf, ink on paper. Palace Museum, Taipei.

Fig. 8. "Geyang ling Cao Quan bei." Dated to 185 CE.

calligraphers. Just as Huang Tingjian felt compelled to poke fun at his friend Wang Shen, many later critics felt a compulsion to dismiss the unconventional aspects of Song calligraphy as indulgent and heterodox. Certainly, "ideas" tend to manifest themselves at the expense of the classical norms of beauty evident in both Jin and Tang calligraphy. The educated class of scholar-officials, who were the primary practitioners of calligraphy, took it as their incumbent duty to represent the state, tradition, and orthodoxy. Excessive expression of one's individuality was at best irrelevant to this responsibility, at worst contradictory. By unhappy coincidence, the Song dynasty came perilously close to total collapse just one generation after the great individualist calligraphers of the Northern Song. For those who truly believed in the expressiveness of calligraphy—its ability to reflect inherent truths—the idiosyncrasies of Song "ideas" were symptomatic of the graver ills that ultimately led to the loss of the northern half of China in 1127.

Despite such reservations, most, if not all, calligraphers wished to develop singular styles of calligraphy that would distinguish them as individuals and serve as the evidence from which others would read their characters (or "understand their sounds," as an old saying goes, in reference to expressive music). Certainly one of the most enjoyable aspects of viewing calligraphy is the intangible pleasure that stems from the sense of the writer's presence or personality, and this happens most readily with calligraphy that is particularly distinctive. To give an extreme example, one twentieth-century author goes so far as to read physical as well as behavioral traits from the calligraphy of Northern Song writers: Mi Fu was "tubby"; Shu Shi, "fatter, shorter and careless in nature"; Huang Tingjian, "tall, lean and obstinate"; Emperor Huizong (r. 1100–1126), "handsome, slim, meticulous, and somewhat effeminate" (fig. 7). "We can even affirm that he [Huizong] was slow and measured of speech," the author goes on to write![9] If it does nothing else, this imaginative critique presents one positive aspect of Song ideas: the opportunity to establish so personal an imprint on the tradition that later viewers would be inspired to imagine what one was like.

PARAMETERS OF INNOVATION IN THE LATER TRADITION

"Resonance," "methods," and "ideas" are vague labels, but they are useful for designating three different aspects of Chinese calligraphy: naturalness associated with spontaneity, skill and practice associated with tradition, and personal expression. By choosing these terms to epitomize the three great epochs of writing that preceded the seventeenth century, Dong Qichang suggests both the aesthetic and historical parameters within which later calligraphers worked at their art. After Dong Qichang's time another epochal movement would take place in Chinese calligraphy, known as *jinshixue* ("metal-and-stone study"), referring to the careful examination of earlier calligraphy incised on old steles (many of them newly excavated) (fig. 8) as well as cast on ancient ritual bronzes. Perhaps if Dong Qichang had lived in the twentieth century he would have coined a fourth category for Qing dynasty (1644–1911) calligraphy: *gu*, or "antique." Again, this was not a quality lacking in the earlier periods—in fact, the pursuit of antiquity was almost always a concern of Chinese calligraphers, and the systematic study of steles and bronzes began as early as the Northern Song—but the dominant trend in Qing calligraphy sought inspiration in antiquity to an unprecedented degree. Written in the clerical script (*lishu*), "Couplet in seven-character lines" (cat. 183) by Deng Shiru (1743–1805) provides an excellent example.

Each of the works in the exhibition reveals the calligrapher's attempt to create something new within the parameters of the tradition. This was no simple matter, considering the longevity and weight of that tradition by the sixteenth century, when the earliest of the included works was written. Moreover, the parameters differed, depending on the specific circumstances of the calligrapher and which particular aspect of the tradition was being tapped. Consider, for example, Zhang Zhao's (1691–1745) transcription of "Seventh Month" from the *Odes of Bin* (cat. 182). Zhang Zhao was an important minister and cultural figure at the Qing dynasty court, rising to such high positions as president of the Censorate and of the Board of Punishments under the Yongzheng (r. 1723–1735) and Qianlong (r. 1736–1795) emperors. Zhang's skill as a calligrapher was much admired by Qianlong in particular, who employed him as a ghostwriter early in his reign.[10] In keeping with Zhang Zhao's high profile at the court and the pressures of conservatism that accompanied such prominence, both the content and style of Zhang's transcription of "Seventh Month" are unfailingly orthodox, even predictable. The poem is from the ancient compilation *Shi jing* ("Classic of Poetry"), long a favorite source for lessons of good government, and the calligraphy is written in a precise standard script that instantly recalls the *fa* ("methods") of such early Tang dynasty exemplars of standard script as Yu Shi'nan (558–638), Ouyang Xun (557–641), and Chu Suiliang (596–658).[11] The writing is a definitive statement of orthodoxy and, as such, allows only the most tightly controlled expression of individual creativity. We admire Zhang Zhao's ability to carry off such a lengthy, if constrained, performance, and politely applaud his handsome

character compositions; but innovation here is revealed only by the most subtle of indications and only to those who recognize hints of the brush modes and compositions of past masters under this highly polished formal veneer.

Zhang Zhao wrote under the most restrictive of circumstances. In contrast, both Deng Shiru (cat. 183) and Zhang Ruitu (cat. 180) worked within considerably broader spaces of the tradition. Writing at a time when the rediscovery of ancient steles acted to liberate calligraphers from the torpid repetition of learned habits, Deng Shiru found plenty to play with in archaic styles of writing that appeared fresh and unusual to a largely jaded audience of scholars and merchants eager for something different and sophisticated. Here the solemnity of the clerical script is subtly tweaked with whimsical touches in composition and brushwork so that the end result is a buoyancy within the weighty forms. The earlier Zhang Ruitu (1570–1641), on the other hand, sought an innovative image by deliberately tapping into that portion of the tradition which was already inextricably associated with individualism. In the late 1620s, Zhang Ruitu retired from important positions at the Ming court and pursued personal interests in Chan (Zen) Buddhism. Chan had its own tradition of calligraphy, one that had been strongly influenced by the Song dynasty emphasis on "ideas" and personality. In the context of the late Ming and such influential thinkers as Li Zhi (1527–1602) and Yuan Hongdao (1568–1610), Chan-inflected calligraphy discarded rules, methods, and standards in favor of recapturing the "child's heart," or original nature, of the writer. Zhang Ruitu's cursive script in his transcription of Wang Wei's "Song of the Aged General" (cat. 180) is highly spirited, yet by emphasizing an even tempo down his columns he manages to suggest an overall uniformity, almost a placidity, that is most fitting for the Chan devotee in search of personal enlightenment.

These general observations about the calligraphy of Zhang Zhao, Deng Shiru, and Zhang Ruitu suggest how later writers established their art in the context of their immediate surroundings largely by positioning it in a working relationship to some aspect of the past tradition. The same can be said of two major works by Zhu Yunming (1461–1527) and Wang Duo (1592–1652), to which we turn now in order to explore this act of positioning in finer detail (cats. 179, 181). The goal is not to clarify Zhu Yunming's and Wang Duo's contributions to the history of Chinese calligraphy—a task that would demand much more time and space than is granted here—but rather to elucidate the practice of the calligrapher's art by considering specific concerns reflected in the writers' choices of script, style, and technique.

Zhu Yunming, often considered the greatest calligrapher of the Ming dynasty, wrote in a wide array of styles and scripts. Such versatility reflects broad training, which, we learn from Zhu Yunming's own words, was strictly directed by paternal guidance to well-established models of the Jin and Tang dynasties.[12] Although the work in the exhibition, a scroll of poems composed by Zhu Yunming himself (cat. 179), appears absolutely free, it in fact belongs to a long and curious tradition of writing that is generally referred to as *kuangcao* ("wild cursive"). Two basic historical transformations are recognized in the cursive-script tradition. The first occurred about the fourth century and within the milieu of Wang Xizhi, with the development of what was then called "modern cursive" (*jincao*). Four hundred years later another epochal change took place with the appearance of wild cursive. It was associated almost exclusively with Zhang Xu (ca. 700–ca. 750), one of the "Eight Immortals of Wine" and a spirited fellow given to wild tantrums while in his cups. According to a number of sources, Zhang Xu would temper his drunken fits by channeling his energy through an ink-charged brush. Some claim that on occasion he would even dip his unbound hair into the ink and use that to write.[13] This was writing aimed at revealing the fundamental nature of the calligrapher and based on the assumption that wine was an essential element in dissolving all inhibitions and intentions. After this mode of writing became established in the eighth century, a number of wild-cursive specialists emerged in quick succession. *Poems by Yu Xin and Xie Lingyun*, a celebrated piece that for many years was erroneously attributed to Zhang Xu, provides an excellent example of eleventh-century *kuangcao* (fig. 9).[14]

Kuangcao presents interesting problems in all three of the aesthetic domains previously described. *Yun* resonance is an important desideratum for all forms of cursive script, but wild-cursive script promotes an outward display of raw energy. Containment, that subtle sense of resonating energies rippling across characters or columns, is often lost in the calligrapher's eagerness to open the emotional floodgates. Similarly, methods (*fa*), reflective of diligence and restraint, at first seem totally irrelevant. As for ideas (*yi*), their presence would be antithetical to the absolute naturalness demanded of the calligrapher. But herein precisely lies the problem. Later critics recognized that *kuangcao*, in fact, often was written with intention—the intention to be as wild as possible. Wildness was not to be equated with genuineness, especially when there was a ready audience and market for this new, exciting form of performance calligraphy. Eleventh-century critics like Su Shi and Huang Tingjian were careful to emphasize that Zhang Xu's wild-cursive writing was built on a solid foundation of

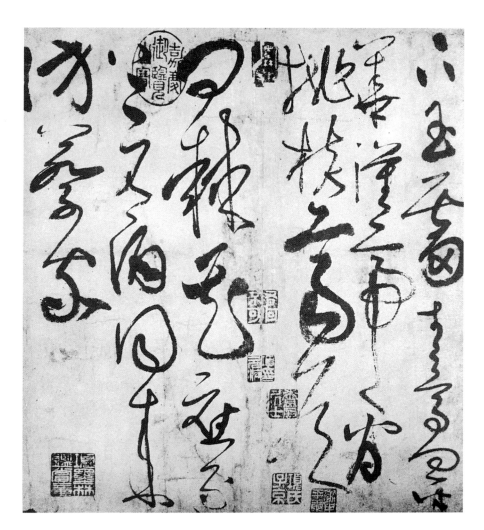

Fig. 9. Anonymous (11th c.). Poems by Yu Xin and Xie Lingyun. Northern Song dynasty (960–1127). Detail of a handscroll, ink on "five-colored paper." Liaoning Provincial Museum, Shenyang.

orthodox study, without which his wilder experiments would have been unacceptable. The proof lay in a stele exhibiting Zhang Xu's standard script, which was a considered a model of Tang discipline and suggested to Song dynasty viewers some relationship with the earlier Jin tradition because of its relatively open, sparse structures— aesthetic qualities generally associated with Jin writing.[15] The existence of this standard-script writing was extremely important, for it validated Zhang Xu's unconventional cursive by proving that Zhang was steeped in rules and methods. Huang Tingjian prided himself on the ability to spot Zhang Xu fakes—wild writing by pretenders and followers—precisely because rules and methods were lacking.[16] Both Su Shi and Huang Tingjian strongly emphasized the propriety—the solid foundation rooted in orthodoxy—governing the dots and dashes of Zhang's drunken brush. It was what separated Zhang Xu from his followers, who, by merely imitating the wildness of his writing, were guilty of using conscious intent to write that which should have emerged spontaneously.

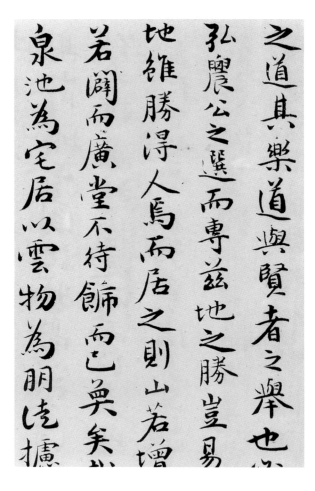

Fig. 10. *Zhu Yunming (1461–1527). Examples of prose by four masters of the Tang and Song. Ming dynasty (1368–1644). Palace Museum, Beijing.*

Fig. 11. *Yan Zhenqing (709–785). "Record of the Yan Family Ancestral Shrine." Dated to 780. Detail of a rubbing.*

Zhu Yunming was probably well aware of the controversy that surrounded the wild-cursive script. In fact, his own writing was also mired in it. Although supporters were willing to see Zhu's *kuangcao* as a natural outlet for his personality, described by one friend as "bold and direct, with no patience for strictness and reserve," critics disparaged it as "undisciplined," "careless," "self-indulgent," and "bordering on the heretical." Interestingly, Zhu Yunming's wild-cursive writing, like Zhang Xu's, was apparently much forged. As the contemporary scholar Fu Shen has documented, one later calligrapher went so far as to claim that all of Zhu Yunming's wild-cursive works in circulation were outright fakes.[17]

The approach taken in the present scroll (cat. 179), a late work dated to 1523, suggests Zhu Yunming's solution to the problems posed by the *kuangcao* tradition. Unlike the eleventh-century "Poems" (fig. 9), which emphasizes a kind of zigzagging columnar speed, Zhu's wild cursive explores a broad horizontal dimension. He purposely leaves many of the structures loose and open so that dots and lines almost seem to disperse instead of connecting to form distinct characters. In fact, the untutored eye may have a difficult time distinguishing Zhu Yunming's individual columns of

writing. There is evidence here of the influence of Huang Tingjian's cursive calligraphy, and this is significant, for Huang Tingjian repeatedly emphasized the importance of *yun* ("resonance") in cursive calligraphy. Viewers cognizant of Zhu Yunming's standard-script calligraphy will also be tempted to recognize in the writing compositional principles that Zhu had mastered from his study of the very early calligrapher Zhong You (151–230) (fig. 10). Samples of writing attributed to Zhong You epitomize that association of loose compositional structures with early writing. If Zhu Yunming did apply the methods of standard-script writing to his wild cursive, it would have been reassuring to the viewer that the underlying quality of propriety so important to Song dynasty critics was indeed present. Zhu Yunming refrained from interconnecting many of the characters, opting instead for measured compositional interplay. The writing is dynamic and inspired, but the overall feeling is of a deep pool of complex, interweaving energies, like swirling eddies, rather than a cascading release. Zhu Yunming successfully realized a delicate balance between containment and vigor. He explains at the end of the scroll that he wrote after drinking and that though he was fatigued, the brush moved spiritedly, without urging. No ideas; in other words, no intentions—just Zhu Yunming.

Wang Duo's large, standard-script (kaishu) transcription of poems by the Tang dynasty poet Wang Wei (699–759) taps into a rather different tradition (cat. 181). This is unusual writing by Wang Duo, who is better known for the highly individualistic style of semicursive and cursive calligraphy exhibited in the inscription at the left of the scroll, following his transcriptions. The poems themselves are written in the unmistakable manner of the great Tang calligrapher Yan Zhenqing (709–785), whose bold, assertive standard-script writing has served as one of the canonical models for calligraphers throughout the ages (fig. 11). Wang Duo, like Zhu Yunming, was a devoted student of the art, and he avidly devoted himself to copying classical models. It is not surprising to find him writing a rather diligent rendition of Yan Zhenqing's style. But Wang Duo was first and foremost an individualist who commonly used the ancient models as a point of departure for his own expressive means. A more careful comparison is merited, beginning with Yan Zhenqing.

Yan's style is one of the most easily recognized of all Chinese calligraphers. The brush strokes are muscular, the character compositions expansive. Not everyone appreciated this style of writing. For example, Li Yu (r. 961–975), ruler of the Southern Tang kingdom, found Yan's calligraphy offensively direct—"like an uncouth farmer facing forward with arms folded and legs spread apart."[18] Almost all, however, considered this confrontational style an appropriate correlative to the larger-than-life image Yan Zhenqing cast as a high minister of unquestioned loyalty and courage. Yan Zhenqing was well known as a stalwart defender of the court and as a martyr who died at the hands of a would-be usurper. This identification between the moral qualities of Yan Zhenqing and his forceful style of writing was well ensconced by the eleventh century, when Ouyang Xiu (1007–1072) announced that Yan's calligraphy resembled a loyal minister: correct, severe, and serious.[19] And so it has been perceived through the later dynasties. Beginning students of calligraphy are often given Yan Zhenqing's writing as a model, no doubt in hopes that some of the Tang minister's virtuous character would be passed along with his particular brush habits. Yan Zhenqing's style is so widely known that one's immediate perception of any later rendition of the Yan style is colored by associations of propriety, moral fortitude, and orthodoxy.

That is precisely what makes Wang Duo's scroll so interesting. In the 1620s and 1630s, Wang had served in high offices, culminating in his promotion to Minister of Rites in 1640. He retired after only two months because of his father's death and remained in mourning until spring of 1644, when he was recalled to the same office. Unfortunately, before Wang could resume his duties the Ming dynasty collapsed. Wang Duo wrote this transcription of Wang Wei's poems in the late autumn of 1643, while staying with friends. Those were chaotic times, and one is tempted to read into Wang Duo's adoption of Yan Zhenqing's style a statement of dynastic loyalty and political resolve. Yet the two poems Wang chose to transcribe are largely celebrations of a reclusive lifestyle, and Wang's own inscription at the end speaks not of the nation's ills but of the camaraderie of friends, the sweetness of their wine, the clear sounds of a bubbling brook by his window, and tomorrow's planned outing to scenic spots. Viewed retrospectively, the writing is even more curious, because Wang Duo would later earn the unenviable historical reputation of a turncoat: he was one of a number of high officials who joined in ignominious surrender to the Manchus, founders of the Qing dynasty (1644–1911), and he immediately began to serve under the new regime, resuming his position of Minister of Rites in the spring of 1646 (Wang's official biography is listed in the section Er chen juan ["Officials who Served Two Houses"].)[20]

In the light of such infelicities, Wang Duo's copying of the Yan style begins to appear somewhat questionable. A closer look at Wang Duo's inscription confirms that he was not exclusively concerned with the state of the nation. He writes, "Few are those who attempt to write standard-script calligraphy on satin. One does not even find such a combination among the works of Xuanzai of Huating. . . . In the future, upon opening this scroll, those who have made some progress in the art of calligraphy will certainly reject this [i.e., my writing], even wish to spit upon it. But what's to be done???" Xuanzai is Dong Qichang, Wang Duo's older contemporary and the dominant figure in the world of calligraphy circa 1640. Whatever Wang Duo's initial inspiration for this essay in the Yan Zhenqing style, it quickly became a personal challenge, an opportunity to do what few, if any, had attempted before—in other words, a forum for the expression of Wang's individualism. The decidedly unpolished quality of Wang Duo's writing here helps to explain his last modest remarks. At the same time, such self-deprecation should not be taken seriously. One can imagine the calligrapher being somewhat pleased with the results, knobby strokes, bleeding ink, and all. This calligraphy may not exactly be a work of beauty, but it certainly makes an impression; and that, ultimately, was Wang Duo's goal.

The point here is not to question Wang Duo's integrity or moral fiber, nor is it to accuse him of debasing the hallowed heritage of Yan Zhenqing. It is, rather, to reveal some of the complexities attending the practice of calligraphy in the later dynasties. The weight of the tradition had become so massive that the creative artist found himself constantly negotiating with the landscape of the past in an attempt to explore new territories of the present. Wang Duo's appropriation and handling of the Yan style so that this most familiar of images became recast into something peculiarly appropriate to the circumstances of a late Ming high official who cultivated a distinctive voice is, I believe, the mark of an exceptional artist. Similarly, Zhu Yunming's delicate balancing act between propriety and wildness in his *kuangcao*, a balance achieved through the creative utilization of earlier styles, demonstrates how a great calligrapher could rise to the challenge posed by an ancient debate and achieve a creative resolution.

Innovation in calligraphy is defined by creative engagement with tradition. Mastery of rules and methods is prerequisite, but must be conjoined with the confidence and ability to express one's own vision. Ultimately, what allows Zhu Yunming's and Wang Duo's calligraphy to succeed is not a reprising of what others had done before, but the palpable sense of two artists molding the past to suit the needs of the present. In their works, calligraphy's immediacy is once more confirmed.

SOURCES FOR FIGURES

Fig. 1. After Sancai tuhui (Taipei, 1970).

Fig. 3. After Gugong bowuyuan cang lidai fashu xuanji, *vol. 3* (Beijing, 1982).

Fig. 6. After Gugong bowuyuan cang lidai fashu xuanji, *vol. 3* (Beijing, 1982).

Fig. 8. After Shodō zenshū, *vol. 2, pl. 118 (Tokyo, 1954–1961).*

Fig. 9. After Tang Zhang Xu caoshu gushi sitie *(Beijing, 1962).*

Fig. 10. After Gugong bowuyuan cang lidai fashu xuanji, *vol. 1 (Beijing, 1982).*

Fig. 11. After Yan Zhenqing, *vol. 5, pl. 241 (Beijing, 1985).*

NOTES

1. *Huainanzi zhuyi* (reprint, Taibei: Hualian chubanshe, 1968), p. 116.

2. Stories of individuals active in the Eastern Han whose writing was preserved by those who read qualities of personality into the calligraphy are recounted by Lothar Ledderose, *Mi Fu and the Classical Tradition of Chinese Calligraphy* (Princeton: Princeton University Press, 1979), pp. 30–31.

3. "For presenting the desires of the inner heart and communicating that which others do not comprehend, nothing can compare with words (*yan*). For spreading and explicating the affairs of the world, recording them for longevity and illuminating them far, making manifest that which cannot be seen of antiquity and transmitting for a thousand miles that which is not understood, nothing can compare with writing (*shu*). Thus, words are the sounds of the heart. Writing is pictures of the heart. By the forms of the sounds and pictures, superior and lesser people are distinguished. Sounds and pictures—by these, superior and lesser people move one's feelings." Yang Xiong, *Fa yan*, *juan* 4, pp. 2b–3a, in *Han Wei congshu*, vol. 24 (Taipei: Yiwen yinshuguan, 1967). It would appear that by "writing," Yang Xiong is referring primarily to the content of the written word. In later times, however, Yang Xiong's comment was clearly associated with the art of calligraphy.

4. Mi Fu, "Ba mige fatie," in Huang Bosi, *Dongguan yulun* (reprint, Taipei: Guoli zhongyang tushuguan, 1974), *juan* 1, p. 46a–b.

5. The two scrolls are "Poems Playfully Written and Presented to My Friends, About to Embark for Tiao Stream," in the collection of the Palace Museum, Beijing, and "Poems on Sichuan Silk," in the collection of the National Palace Museum, Taipei. See Peter Sturman, *Mi Fu: Style and the Art of Calligraphy in Northern Song China* (New Haven: Yale University Press, 1997), chap. 2.

6. Dong Qichang, *Rongtai ji* (reprint, Taipei: Zhongyang tushuguan, 1968), *juan* 4, p. 23b.

7. Suo Jing, "Caoshu zhuang,"

in *Peiwenzhai shuhuapu*, *juan* 1, pp. 11b–12a, *Siku quanshu* ed. (reprint, Shanghai: Shanghai guji chubanshe, 1987).

8. Huang Tingjian, "Ba Wang Jinqing shu," in *Shangu ji*, *Siku quanshu* ed., *juan* 29, p. 19a–b.

9. Chiang Yee, *Chinese Calligraphy* (reprint, Cambridge: Harvard University Press, 1973), pp. 11–12.

10. When Zhang Zhao was found delinquent in his task of helping to pacify the Miao tribe of the southwest in 1735 and consequently ordered to be executed, he was pardoned by Qianlong, owing, it is said, to their mutual interest in calligraphy. Zhang Zhao was also an eminent painter at the Qing court and a prominent figure in the compilation of *Shiqu baoji*, the Qing imperial catalogue of paintings and calligraphy. Arthur Hummel, ed., *Eminent Chinese of the Ch'ing Period* (Washington, D.C.: Library of Congress, 1943), pp. 24–25.

11. Zhang Zhao's models for standard script were Dong Qichang (1555–1636) and Yan Zhenqing (709–785). I am referring here to the meticulous manner in which Zhang Zhao writes, which recalls that of the early Tang writers.

12. Shen C. Y. Fu, *Traces of the Brush* (New Haven: Yale University Art Gallery, 1977), p. 211, citing a colophon by Zhu Yunming in which he discusses copying a range of Jin, Tang, Song, and Yuan calligraphers.

13. Zhang Xu was celebrated as one of the Eight Immortals of Wine in Du Fu's poem "Yinzhong baxian ge," in *Du shi xiangzhu* (Beijing: Zhonghua shuju, 1979), *juan* 2, pp. 80–85. Other early sources on Zhang Xu include Zhu Changwen, *Xu shu duan*, *juan* 1, in *Chūgoku shoron taikei* (Tokyo: Nigensha shuppansha, 1977–92), vol. 4, pp. 403–4, and *Xuanhe shupu*, *juan* 18, in *Chūgoku shoron taikei*, vol. 6, p. 47.

14. This scroll of four transcribed poems, two by Yu Xin (513–581) and two by Xie Lingyun (385–433), is

erroneously recorded under Xie Lingyun's name in Huizong's *Xuanhe shupu* (*juan* 16) of circa 1120. In recent years both Xu Bangda and Qi Gong have both pointed out that a changed character in one of the verses may reflect the avoidance of a character that was taboo in the early Northern Song period. By this reasoning, the calligraphy would date from after 1012 (but somewhat before Huizong's reign). See Xu Bangda, *Gu shuhua weie kaobian* (Nanjing: Jiangsu guji chubanshe, 1984), pp. 94–98; and Qi Gong, "Jiu ti Zhang Xu caoshu gushi tie bian," in *Qi Gong conggao* (Beijing: Zhonghua shuju, 1981), pp. 90–100.

15. The stele is titled "Record of the Langguan Stone." See Su Shi, "Shu Tang shi liujia shu hou," in *Su Shi wenji* (reprint, Beijing: Zhonghua shuju, 1986), *juan* 69, p. 2206.

16. Huang Tingjian, "Ti Jiangben fatie," in *Shanggu ji*, *juan* 28, pp. 10b–11a.

17. Fu, *Traces of the Brush*, pp. 214–15.

18. Dong Shi, *Shu lu*, *Siku quanshu* ed., *juan* 2, p. 6b.

19. "Tang Yan Lugong shu Cao bei," in Ouyang Xiu, *Ouyang Xiu quanji* (reprint, Hong Kong: Guanzhi shuju, n.d.), *juan* 6, p. 31. See also Ronald Egan, "Ou-yang Hsiu and Su Shih on Calligraphy," *Harvard Journal of Asiatic Studies* 49, no. 2 (December 1989), p. 372.

20. See Mingshui Hung's entry on Wang Duo in L. Carrington Goodrich, ed., *Dictionary of Ming Biography* (New York and London: Columbia University Press, 1976), vol. 2, pp. 1434–36.

Calligraphy and Painting—The Essence of a Civilization

Liu Jiu'an

Researcher, Palace Museum, Beijing

The five-thousand-year history of Chinese civilization has shaped the culture and art of the Chinese people. The arts of painting and calligraphy are rooted in this ancient civilization. They are fruits borne by it, and through their unique artistic expressiveness and profound artistic inner content, they also epitomize one aspect of it. Just as Chinese civilization is generally regarded as one of the classic civilizations of world history, so too are Chinese painting and calligraphy classic types among the world's art forms.

This exhibition features the works of thirty-seven painters and calligraphers, ranging from the middle of the Northern Song dynasty in the mid-eleventh century through the middle of the late Qing dynasty in the eighteenth century. These outstanding works, selected from museums throughout mainland China, compose in microcosm a history of the development of painting and calligraphy during this period. For instance, Wang Shen's *Misty River and Layered Hills* (cat. 184), the Southern Song *Snowy Landscape* (cat. 186), and Zhao Kui's *In the Spirit of Poems by Du Fu* (cat. 185), taken together, succinctly epitomize the rapid developments in landscape painting during the Northern and Southern Song dynasties.

Misty River and Layered Hills invokes a vast panorama in the depiction of a single scene. *Snowy Landscape* uses instead the classic allusive technique of the renowned Southern Song landscape artist Ma Yuan (act. late 12th–early 13th c.), suggesting the immensity of the mountains by showing only their peaks and not their bases. The buildings have been drawn not as architectural renderings but freehand, without benefit of straightedge, and the dominant mood is one of quiet and solitude in a setting of great beauty. Very few of Ma Yuan's paintings have survived to the present, but this anonymous scroll conveys some sense of them. The Qianlong emperor of the Qing dynasty sought to express the essence of Zhao Kui's small painting of a bamboo grove (cat. 185) in the following couplet:

> The tranquil lotus and verdant creek reject the summer's heat,
> And in the depths of the bamboo grove fans are unfurled in the little pavilion.

This emperor's couplet alludes consciously to a verse by the renowned Tang dynasty poet Du Fu:

> The depths of the bamboo grove urge the visitor to stay
> And enjoy the coolness of the tranquil lotus.

Hence the title of the painting. To paraphrase the great Song poet Su Dongpo: In the words of the poem we find the painting; in the lines of the painting we find the poem. This masterpiece of Chinese "poetic painting" is also the only known work by Zhao Kui.

During the Yuan dynasty paintings as pictures of things and paintings as cosmic metaphors began to be displaced by literati paintings—executed by members of the educated elite using a deliberately plain, even awkward manner intended to signify their status as noble-minded amateurs. They claimed to paint only for self-expression, "as a lodging for [their] feelings" (Ni Zan), never at the behest of a patron or for the marketplace. Wang Meng's *Dwelling in the Qingbian Mountains* (cat. 189) reveals only to the closest inspection the dwelling of a recluse, to which the craggy, bristling mountain seems to deny all access—an emblem of the literati ideal of literally forsaking and spiritually transcending the mundane world. Ni Zan's *Six Gentlemen* (cat. 188) uses six trees, upright and unbending, to allude to the austere integrity of the literati. Though the first painting teems with writhing forms and the second is almost minimalist, both of them slight pictorial description and emphasize instead the quality of the brush stroke, which was held to express the character of the painter.

From the mid-Ming period prosperous southeastern cities such as Suzhou and Songjiang in Jiangsu tended to attract literati painters. These urban literati transferred their love of nature and the bucolic life to their gardens and studios, which became favorite artistic subjects. Wen Zhengming's *Studio of True Appreciation* (cat. 197) depicted the study of Hua Xia (b. ca. 1498), the most famous collector of his day. Shen Zhou, in *Eastern Villa* (cat. 196), abjured his usual broad brush strokes in favor of a meticulously detailed picture of the garden residence of his literatus friend Wu Kuan (1435–1504). Likewise, Qiu Ying's *Playing the Flute by Pine and Stream* (cat. 195) expresses the literati pastoral ideal. From the mid-Ming onward, the literati ideal dominated Chinese culture and society, and the less rigorously austere examples of literati painting found acceptance at court and among the mercantile class as well as among the scholar-official elite.

From the outset Qing painting displayed a rich diversity. Wang Shimin (1592–1680), Wang Jian (1598–1677), Wang Hui (1632–1717), and Wang Yuanqi (1642–1715), collectively known as the "Four Wangs" of Chinese art history, primarily carried on the literati landscape traditions of the early Song and Yuan dynasties. Artistic archaism—paintings alluding to the styles of earlier masters—became fashionable at court and among the upper classes generally. The literati style, revolutionary during the Ming, became the new orthodoxy of Qing painting, exemplified by the "Four Wangs" (especially the first three) and their epigones. Contemporaneously, Bada Shanren, Shitao, Hongren, and Kuncan, collectively known as the "Four Monks" of art history, expressed their inner turmoil at the fall of the Ming and triumph of the non-Han Qing dynasty in powerfully individualistic works. Take, for instance, *Ducks and Lotuses* (cat. 210) by Bada Shanren (Zhu Da), who was a descendant of the Ming imperial family. He used the splashed-ink method to draw the lotus blossoms, and hooked brush strokes to depict the rocks in the pond, with just the slightest use of pale ink to limn the rocks. The Qing painter Zheng Xie (1693–1765) inscribed on this painting, "Few ink drops, many teardrops," alluding both to the drawing and to the artist's grief and anger over the loss of his country and family.

Distinct regional schools in abundance arose during the Qing. Gong Xian (cat. 209), Zou Zhe (cat. 212), Gao Cen (cat. 214), and others who were active around the Nanjing area were known as the Jinling school, while Gao Xiang (cat. 215), Yuan Jiang (cat. 213), and others were active in the Yangzhou area. Even artists working in the same region and grouped into the same school show distinctive characteristics. The style and method of painting of Yuan Jiang's *Garden for Gazing* clearly differ from Gao Xiang's *Finger-snap Pavilion*. This wealth of expressiveness, the artistic hallmark of the period, reflected the variety of artistic traditions available to painters during the Qing dynasty.

Elevating the writing of words into an art form was an inspired development. The five pieces of calligraphy exhibited here exemplify four principal calligraphic scripts, namely, clerical, standard, cursive, and wild cursive. Perhaps no other art form is as condensed and abbreviated as calligraphy, or as expressive of the artist. For instance, the Ming calligrapher Zhu Yunming, known as a free spirit and unbridled personality, was a master of all scripts but with a particular affinity for the wild cursive script. In *The Terrace of Ode to the Wind* (cat. 179) his brush moves with abandon—a display of the writer's naturally uninhibited character—yet the writing shows a firm and steady hand. Zhang Zhao's scroll of the poem "Seventh Month" from the *Odes of Bin* (cat. 182) uses a dignified and poised standard script that shows the influence of the calligrapher Yan Zhenqing (709–785) of the Tang, while also reflecting, in its poise and elegance, Zhang's long tenure at court. In contrast, Deng Shiru, who never held any official post, took as his models the inscriptions on stone tablets of the Han and Wei dynasties, and these helped shape the dense, archaic style seen in his *Couplet in seven-character lines, written in clerical script* (cat. 183).

Taken together, the works in this exhibition disclose the distinctive characteristics—the leitmotifs—of Chinese painting and calligraphy. First is the central role of people as subjects. Even unpeopled landscapes embody the adage attributed to Confucius, "The virtuous delight in mountains, and the wise delight in waters," an association deeply rooted in the ancient philosophic concept that "Heaven and man are one." Second is the allusiveness made possible by that concept, the freedom from the need to depict literally and completely. In *Snowy Landscape*, for example, only the mountaintops are shown, while the bases are left to our imaginations, lending the landscape far greater monumentality than if the mountains had been shown in their entirety. The Chinese use of monochrome ink alone is a prime example of the penchant for allusion. Third is the creative leeway given to subjectivity and expressiveness without ever abandoning description in favor of abstraction; this fusion of expression and objective description is summed up in Bada Shanren's *Ducks and Lotuses*. Even calligraphy, which is wholly abstract, involves a complex process of "encompassing a million particularities and abstracting them into a single image." The theory that calligraphy and painting had a common divine origin, and that the two arts have "different names but a common form," dates at least from the ninth century and has never been questioned since. That same theory has given rise to "the three perfections"—works in which poetry, calligraphy, and painting are integrated into one totality, in which each form alludes to and completes the others. Fourth is the insistence on inner refinement—"freedom from vulgarity"—of the artists and of their works, for the simple reason that only a person of great understanding and cultivation could comprehend the preceding three characteristics. Last is the honor paid to the creation and even the collecting of paintings and calligraphy, activities generally considered to denote persons of understanding, delicacy of perception, and moral fastidiousness.

These ancient works of Chinese painting and calligraphy are material embodiments of the Chinese civilization. They touch our hearts, stimulate our minds, and nurture our continuing growth.

Translated, from the Chinese, by June Mei.

Chinese Painting: Innovation After "Progress" Ends

James Cahill

Professor Emeritus, History of Art,
University of California, Berkeley

The time is long past when Western specialists in the history of Chinese painting have had to be defensive about the status of their subject within world art. A succession of major exhibitions, the building of impressive museum and private collections, and an outpouring of substantial publications both scholarly and popular over the past half-century or so have instilled it firmly in the consciousness of both academics and the larger community of art-lovers as ranking among the supreme artistic achievements of any culture. And yet a curious belief about Chinese painting persists—that in its later phases it is essentially a performance art, within which the artist is reduced to making individual interpretations of long-established formulae.

Two examples can represent quite a few more. E. H. Gombrich, in his influential *Art and Illusion,* reproduces from a seventeenth-century Chinese manual for beginning painters a page of instructions for painting orchids in ink, stroke by stroke. This he takes to exemplify China's "complete reliance on acquired vocabularies," commenting that "there is nothing in Western art which compares with this conception of painting," which he characterizes as a "combination of traditionalism and respect for the uniqueness of every *performance*."[1] More recently, Arthur Danto, in "Ming and Qing Paintings," misunderstands Sherman Lee's opening statement in a catalogue essay that by the beginning of the Ming dynasty "the materials, formats, and techniques of painting had developed in flexibility and complexity to a point where further subtlety was both unimaginable and superfluous."[2] Danto takes Lee's statement to mean that, in Danto's words, "all the truths of Chinese painting were in place before that protracted [Ming–Qing] period began." And Danto, too, contrasts this reading of the Chinese situation with what happened during the same period in Western art: "Imagine, then, an exhibition which begins with Giotto and ends with Gauguin." One scarcely could say of Western painting during that time, as Danto believes we can say of Ming and Qing painting, that "everything was already in place at the beginning, further development of which [sic] was 'unimaginable and superfluous.'"[3] In support of his view, Danto cites observations by Roger Fry about the "strange atrophy of the creative spirit" that afflicted later Chinese art and about its "excessive reverence for the tradition."[4]

One might see these simply as misreadings: there is a large gap between the woodblock-printed painting manual cited by Gombrich and the practice of serious later Chinese artists that he wrongly took it to represent; and there is an even larger gap between Sherman Lee's unobjectionable statement that further *subtlety* was unimaginable in the later centuries in China (one could persuasively argue that Gauguin does not represent any advance in subtlety over Giotto) and Danto's construing this to mean that no further *development* took place. But it is less a misreading, I think, than a proclivity among Western scholars (even good ones) unfamiliar with Chinese painting: to believe a version of its history in which innovation ended about the fourteenth century and to take what they see and read as evidence for that version.

What lies behind this inclination to see the later centuries of Chinese painting as essentially repeating the earlier ones? In part, it is a carry-over from the ill-informed belief of pioneer Western writers on Chinese painting that its great creative period ended with the Song dynasty in the late thirteenth century, and that all beyond was repetition and decline. No one seriously engaged with Chinese painting believes that now, but this attitude no doubt continues to resonate in the minds of people who have read the old books or taken courses with the old teachers. Another important reason is the inability of even sensitive observers to recognize stylistic distinctions, including large and crucial ones, within an unfamiliar art, whether it be painting or music or poetry. I noted this often-encountered phenomenon at the beginning of my book *The Compelling Image*, recalling the experience of taking a distinguished and recently arrived Chinese connoisseur around the National Gallery in Washington (yes, from Giotto to Gauguin and beyond) and being told: "Very nice, but they all look alike."[5] Danto's admission that the works in the Ming–Qing exhibition, spanning some six centuries, seemed to him "oddly contemporaneous" is another case of the same; both responses betray limitations not in the art but in the observer, who infers sameness from his own failure to perceive, or at least to properly evaluate, difference. Of course Chinese painting appears to have had no development if the later ones appear no different from the early ones.

Also accounting in some part for this phenomenon is the insistence of many of the Chinese painters themselves, in inscriptions on their works, that they are "imitating" some old master: taken literally, such inscriptions would indeed attest to derivativeness. But to accept such statements at face value would be equivalent to charging T. S. Eliot with being derivative because he claims in a certain passage to be "imitating" Chaucer. When one looks beyond the inscriptions to compare the paintings themselves with their putative models, it is immediately obvious that the old style is usually no more than a frame of reference, a jumping-off point for formal explorations that can be as original as any in painting. All art, in some sense, imitates other art; the Chinese have simply recognized and institutionalized such derivation and made it more self-conscious, more a matter of deliberate and sophisticated allusion than Western artists generally have, at least until very recent times.

Even after we have recognized all these reasons for the derogation of later Chinese painting, however, we must admit and come to terms with certain elements of truth that underlie the perceptions of repetitiveness. It is generally true (with exceptions, as always) that later Chinese artists were more open in their reliance on established convention and insisted less on direct observation of the world than Western artists of the same period usually did. One must quickly add, however, that the best of them accomplished such creative and even radical manipulations of the conventions that, again, the outcomes can scarcely be seen as any real loss of originality. It can also be argued that after the end of the Song dynasty in the late thirteenth century no clear, unilinear development can be observed in Chinese painting, in the sense of successive advances in representational techniques, or in pervasive stylistic shifts like those defined by the old art historians for European painting—from Medieval to early to high to late Renaissance, Baroque to Rococo to Romantic to Modern.

But granting this need not carry any implication that Chinese painting ceased to be innovative. It might, alternatively, be argued that the great global shifts took place earlier in China—that their equivalent of the Giotto-to-Gauguin phase happened between the Tang and Yuan dynasties (i.e., between the eighth and fourteenth centuries)—and ended sooner, so that the Chinese

arrived in their painting, long before we did, at "the end of the history of art." This is not the place to make that argument at length, nor am I the person to make it; an unpublished book by James Elkins, entitled "Chinese Landscape Painting as Object Lesson" (1995) presents an interesting case for this large and highly controversial proposal, in terms with which I am generally in agreement. In any case, leaving aside particulars of argument, this is the direction in which any real understanding of later Chinese painting's "failure to develop" must be charted out. Instead of, in effect, writing off later Chinese painting as attractive but more or less irrelevant to our own artistic concerns, we might better look to it for ways out of what may seem perilously like an end-game situation (Elkins's term, adopted from chess and Duchamp). A tradition that folds so insistently back on itself, that comes to be caught up in such a potentially paralyzing engagement with its own past, obliges its artists to devise stratagems for escaping repetition and stagnation. An account of Ming and Qing painting—a non-history, it might be called—could be constructed around the successive stratagems that were devised to this end, both by individual masters and within particular movements and schools. Such an account would acknowledge some of these stratagems to have been relatively conservative—the disciplined, somewhat intellectualized uses of old styles by such Ming masters as Shen Zhou and Wen Zhengming, for instance; it would recognize others, such as the brilliant transformations of older pictorial materials carried out by the Individualist masters of the seventeenth century, as radical, even revolutionary.

Most of all, such an account would recognize that critical theorizing, in writings that are sophisticated and often contentious, affected the later practice of Chinese painting much as such theorizing has affected the recent practice of painting in the West. Many of the Ming and Qing artists, along with their scholar-critic contemporaries, argued vehemently and interestingly for this or that position on what the artist should paint and how, drawing their arguments from a diversity of grounds—aesthetic, philosophical, moral, political, economic. In both traditions, the artists themselves might talk themselves into corners. But proponents of established ideologies could also make moralizing judgments—Confucian or Marxist or other—proclaiming certain kinds of painting to be low-class or inauthentic or otherwise unacceptable, thus effectively shutting off broad ranges of options that artists might otherwise have found viable and fruitful. Or, if they did not manage to shut them off completely, at least they made them difficult and unrewarding to pursue, so that those who pursued them risked, and usually incurred, critical condemnation. No artistic dilemma could resonate more painfully with the predicament of artists today. It is not that the Chinese artists, freed of such pressures, would have made their choices purely on aesthetic grounds, unconcerned with the broader issues of their time; but they surely had their own agendas, as their writings sometimes indicate, which did not necessarily correspond with the established systems that sought to control them and usually did. Counterforces to the coercion of the literati critics were few and mostly weak.

Two opposing forces, one aimed at narrowing options for artists and so inducing them to paint in the "right" way, the other at broadening again the spectrum of acceptable styles or breaking the boundaries altogether, are represented by the two major writers on painting in the late Ming and early Qing: Dong Qichang (1555–1636) and Shitao (1642–1707). The two can be seen also as arguing in opposite directions about what was for both of them the central dilemma: how to stand up, as creative and highly original artists, against the nearly overpowering weight of the past. They establish themselves as the most powerful proponents of two different ways out.

Dong's way was to reduce and absorb the past by making a rigorous selection of suitable models from it, simplifying the history of painting into two "schools," or lineages, only one of which he judged to be appropriate for the practice of a cultivated literatus-amateur like himself. He then "imitated" the models in this established canon so freely that the old styles virtually vanished under his hand, transmuted into new structures within which the old are scarcely recognizable. Shitao's way out, based on a desperate recognition of the advanced state of conventionalization into which much of the art had descended, was to reject the past entirely and start over, as if situated at the first dawn of painting. That, at least, would be his claim and the ideal toward which he would strive in some of his late and more extreme works. It was a magnificent but ultimately unrealizable attempt—painters can no more return to a state of pristine simplicity than anyone else—and incapable of pointing a clear direction out of their common predicament for artists who followed. Dong Qichang's direction, carried on in ever more exclusionary ways by the Orthodox landscape masters who claimed to be his legitimate successors, was to prove more influential, but its authority was sapped by the quick debilitation of that landscape tradition.

The capsulized account of Chinese painting that follows, while it certainly will not substantiate the proposal outlined above, will accommodate it, as conventional histories that attempt broad characterizations of the "period styles" of the successive periods cannot.

EARLY PAINTING: REPRESENTATIONAL CONQUESTS

Early Chinese writings about painting praise its capacity to arouse the feelings and responses that the depicted thing would arouse if seen in reality. Portraits, for example, captured salient qualities of the sitter and presented them to the viewer, thus taking on the Confucian function of preserving for contemplation models of moral worth or depravity. The painting could fool the viewer into confusing it with the real thing: a picture of a beautiful woman would be mistaken for the person, a painting of fish hung on the riverbank would attract otters to leap at it. For this criterion of excellence, a high degree of verisimilitude and even "magic realism" are obviously appropriate. But these naive views (as we would see them) were supplanted relatively early by recognition of the evocative powers of paintings that transcended simple representation and required of the artist more than descriptive techniques. Brief essays by Zong Bing (375–443) and Wang Wei (415–443) already credit landscape painting with the power to present expansive and absorbing vistas to the entranced viewer, who can enjoy vicariously, through the artist's subtle understanding and technical skill, journeys among mountains and rivers that refresh the spirit.

Pictures with the capacity to affect their viewers that way, however, were preceded by centuries of simpler landscape representation, a formative stage that can be traced in designs on bronze vessels and other objects, including several in this exhibition. An Eastern Han (25–220 CE) gilt-bronze vessel with hills and animals (cat. 51) represents hilltops and clouds in the simplest schematic forms. By contrast, on an inlaid bronze chariot fitting (cat. 49) the hills on which the animals scamper are drawn in intricate linear arabesques derived from earlier dragon forms, a metamorphic process common in early Chinese art. Simple, overlapping triangular peaks make up a schematic landscape (a "magic mountain") to which trees and animals and figures are added in the splendid gilded bronze incense burner from the tomb of Prince Liu Sheng (cat. 50). The landscape scenes on a late Han relief tile from Sichuan Province (cat. 103) achieve remarkable (for that time) integrations of the pictorial materials in space, and some transcending of schematic forms, but the achievement was not followed up, at least on extant objects. Three centuries later, for instance, the landscape settings for Buddhist narratives on a Liang dynasty (502–557) stele (cat. 151) still display an archaic system in which rocks and trees and hilltops compartmentalize the composition into "space cells" within which the figures and other narrative elements are placed.

Surviving early landscape paintings, or believable copies of them, seem designed to fulfill the aims set forth in the texts. They typically offer densely filled scenes of mountains and rivers within which travelers, mounted or on foot, move among trees; cross bridges; pass by rustic residences and temples. The compositions may recede to high horizons, demonstrating the painter's ability to carry the viewer's gaze into depth. The individual entities that make up these pictures, especially those of the Tang dynasty (618–906), are typically drawn in fine outline and colored with mineral pigments. This analytical outline-and-color mode, characteristic of early Chinese painting, encourages the viewer to read the picture part by part while moving over its richly detailed surface.

By the tenth and eleventh centuries, the Five Dynasties (907–960) and Northern Song (960–1127) periods that followed the collapse of the Tang, this archaic mode was seen as charming but unsuited to new directions in landscape painting, which in these centuries was rising to displace figural subjects as the central concern of leading artists and critics. Landscapes in the new manner are dominated by earth masses rendered in broader, scumbled brush strokes of monochrome ink, strongly varied in tone, which shape the forms with light and shadow while also rendering the tactile qualities of their pitted surfaces. Indications of human presence—buildings, figures, bridges—are diminished in size and visually integrated into the landscape setting, so that they no longer command the viewer's attention. Beside the attractive artificialities of the archaic landscape mode, this new manner can be seen (admittedly, in terms unacceptable to "new art history" practitioners) as a great leap forward in naturalism—in its power to engage the beholder's vision with forms that read as truer to one's experience of the physical world and as all but palpable. It was exactly the development of this new manner, combining refinements of monochrome ink tonality for effects of light and shade with systems of overlaid brushwork to differentiate textures, that opened the way to the towering achievements of monumental landscape in the Five Dynasties and Northern Song periods.

The supplanting of figural themes, including narrative, historical, and religious, by landscape at such an early period distinguishes the Chinese tradition of painting from all others, prompting us to ask what conditions and objectives underlay this crucial change. It is another question too large to address here, except to say that in the hands of a succession of great masters, Chinese landscape painting not only developed to a sublime point its function of "making the viewer feel as though he were in the very place," thus allowing it to serve as spiritual refreshment for people who could not physically retire into the mountains, but also acquired the capacity to embody metaphysical concepts in forms and so convey them to its viewers. The rise of monumental landscape paralleled, not coincidentally, the great age of Neo-Confucian philosophy, which similarly attributes a coherence and order to natural phenomena. It corresponded also to the ascendancy of expressive theories of painting: Mi Fu (1052–1107/8) wrote that landscape "is a creation of the mind and is intrinsically a superior art"—superior, that is, to pictures of animals or human figures, which could, in his view, be done by simply copying their appearances. These are, to be sure, Chinese formulations; our own account of the rise of landscape painting in China would follow other lines.

Underlying the "great leap forward in naturalism" was the development by tenth- and eleventh-century artists of representational techniques that opened the way to all these achievements. Specialists in portraying birds and animals were creating systems of patiently repeated brush strokes for natural-looking renditions of plumage and fur, while painters of interior scenes with figures were working out spatial schemes as intricately readable as any that Chinese artists would ever attempt. Early Song landscapists would refine the device of atmospheric perspective so as to create breathtaking effects of height and deep space, within which strongly volumetric forms were shaped and geologically differentiated with new texture-stroke systems. We are, that is to say, at that apogee, or roll-off point, arrived at by the Chinese relatively early in the collective mastery of representational techniques that allowed them to create, when they wished, paintings that could be read as close and convincing likenesses of the persons, things, or scenes portrayed.

No painting could better exemplify this observation than the astonishing *Bamboo, Old Tree, and Stones in Winter* (fig. 1), attributed to a tenth-century master named Xu Xi but in truth an anonymous work of the late tenth or early eleventh century. The subject carries a metaphorical meaning of survival and integrity under harsh conditions, but we know this only from external literary evidence: nothing in the picture itself suggests that it is other than a meticulously detailed, objective portrayal of a passage of nature. The unknown artist, who has not signed his name but has inscribed "This bamboo is worth more than a hundred pieces of gold" in tiny archaic characters (upside down! on a bamboo stalk) has concealed his hand throughout, using virtually no outlining or other conspicuous brush strokes, creating the image as if entirely out of light and dark, making the picture seem more a work of nature than a product of human artifice. In truth,

Fig. 1. Anonymous (attrib. Xu Xi, 10th c.).
Bamboo, Old Tree, and Stones in Winter.
Late 10th or early 11th c. Shanghai Museum.

put into proper context the "non-development" of later Chinese painting, along with the complaints of seventeenth-century Jesuits and other early Western writers that the failure of Chinese artists to employ linear perspective and chiaroscuro made their pictures flat and dead. A recognition of the true attainment of early Chinese painting can only be humbling.

LATER SONG PAINTING: THE PURSUIT OF POETIC MOOD

If, as argued here, the Chinese reached their highpoint in the development of representational techniques as early as the tenth–eleventh century, all the later history of Chinese painting can be constructed as a series of moves away from that point, "retreats from likeness" that take many different directions. One of these is the literati, or scholar-amateur, movement in painting, which began in the late Northern Song period but is represented in this exhibition only from the Yuan dynasty on, and so will be discussed below. Spokesmen for this new movement were inclined to adopt antirepresentational positions. Mi Fu, quoted above, saw landscape painting as a creation of the artist's mind; Su Shi (1037–1101), the central figure in the movement, wrote in a poem that "If someone talks of painting as formal likeness/ His way of looking is like a child's."

the technical achievement it displays is nothing short of amazing. Some technique of reserve was probably used for the light-against-dark passages; but how the subtle shifts from these to dark-against-light were accomplished is not easy to reconstruct. Like other moves toward realism in Chinese painting, this one is abortive and produced no following; it was suppressed, presumably, by a critical dogma that condemned the pursuit of verisimilitude, or "form-likeness," as an unworthy objective for painting. The work has come down to modern times unrecorded and unnoticed by critics, with none of the collectors' seals and adulatory inscriptions that embellish old paintings of more prestigious kinds.

As an exercise in comparative chronology, we might ask, "In what other artistic culture, at this time, could such a feat of descriptive naturalism— avoidance of artificed patterning, near-photographic depiction—have been accomplished?" And if the answer must be, "No other," the next question is, "How many centuries must one wait for anything comparable in the West?" In descriptive painting techniques as in technology, the Chinese far outstripped the West in early centuries, then *by choice* largely turned away from that mode to pursue other directions, while Western artists took up (more or less) the descriptive vein the Chinese had abandoned. This understanding of the matter will

About the same time that these scholar-amateurs, some of whom held official posts in the government, were working out their new styles and genres so as to separate themselves clearly from the professional tradition, another group of semi-amateur artists were taking a somewhat different course, aimed at endowing their paintings both with poetic content and with a cultivated kind of archaism through allusions to early styles. This group might be called aristocrat-amateurs, since they were associated with the court and imperial family; their socially and economically privileged positions gave them access to old masterworks, and their "quoting" of these in their own paintings credited their viewers with a correspondingly sophisticated understanding of historical styles. This was an art by and for the elite.

Misty River and Layered Hills by Wang Shen (ca. 1048–after 1104) is a fine example of this courtly poetic-archaizing mode (cat. 184). Wang Shen, descendant of a military hero, son-in-law of an emperor, friend of Su Shi, and himself a distinguished connoisseur and collector, began painting landscape during a period of political banishment from the capital—his works have been read (by Richard Barnhart, who has written most interestingly about him) as landscapes of exile.[6] As a style-conscious amateur, he could choose among styles with a freedom normally denied the full-time, vocational masters, adopting the manner of his great court-academy contemporary Guo Xi for one painting, reviving the old outline-and-color mode from the Tang for another. *Misty River* belongs to the latter style, using green mineral pigment within decoratively repeated outlines. Unrolling the scroll from right to left, one traverses a long stretch of empty silk that stands for water and that renders the farther shore of cloud-veiled hills, when it eventually appears, even more remote. The picture echoes, presumably by intent, paradise or isles-of-immortals imagery in which the green and blue colors represent jade and chalcedony. The flattening and decorative richness that can be seen as genuinely archaic in early works (or close copies after them) are here elements in an archaistic mode consciously adopted for the cultural values it carried.

Other members of the Song imperial family (surnamed Zhao) who painted include Zhao Lingrang (also called Zhao Danian; act. ca. 1070–ca. 1100), who did bucolic scenes of thatched houses on the riverside which evoked the ideal of escaping the sordor of the city for a simple life in the (morally and physically) purer air of the countryside (as none of these artists could do in reality); and Zhao Ji, the emperor Huizong (r. 1100–1126), who painted bird-and-flower subjects and was especially taken with the ideal of making paintings that embodied poetic concepts, enforcing it on the artists who served in his academy. The late Song painter Zhao Kui (1185–1266) did not belong to the imperial family but held a high ministerial post. The handscroll titled *In the Spirit of Poems by Du Fu* (cat. 185) originally bore his signature, according to a colophon by a slightly later writer, but the signature has been lost, probably in remounting. The painting echoes a couplet from a poem by the great poet Du Fu (712–770): "The depths of the bamboo grove urge the visitor to stay/ And enjoy the cool of the tranquil lotus." Unrolling the scroll, we are taken through groves of bamboo by a stream and glimpse the top of a thatched kiosk hidden among them, then two servants bringing donkeys along a path, and finally, toward the end, a man who sits in a waterside pavilion and is fanned by a servant as he gazes out over water lilies. The scroll recreates the quiet experience of escaping from the city and the heat into cool seclusion; it may represent scenery around Yangzhou, where Zhao Kui lived for some years.

The ideal of poetic painting advocated by Emperor Huizong continued to pervade the output of the imperial painting academy in the Southern Song, or late Song, where masters of transcending technique and sensitivity created works that are among the glories of Chinese painting. One of the greatest of them is Ma Yuan (act. late 12th–early 13th century). An unsigned *Snowy Landscape* (cat. 186) is not attributed to him but is closely in his style and may well be from his hand. Whatever its authorship, it belongs to a mode of poetic terseness that became popular in the late Song. The scenery is simple: a traveler with his servant carrying the luggage approaches a Buddhist temple in a ravine. Dark mists capture the wintry mood; earth banks and hilltops recede in clear stages, the nearer ones given volume, the farthest in simple silhouette. With all technical problems of creating effects of space and atmosphere long solved, insofar as China was ever to address them, the artist could work in a broad, sparse manner, reducing the pictorial materials as a poet might evoke an extensive scene in a couplet. Art-historical hindsight allows us to see this as an end-of-an-era work, attenuated in both its composition and its poetic content.

Another work that reveals the late Song passion for poetic imagery is the woodblock-printed book *Meihua xishen pu* ("Album of Plum Blossom Portraits") by Song Boren. First printed in 1238, it survives in a single copy of a 1261 reprint and has been called the world's first known printed art book (cat. 187). In text and pictures it presents one hundred aspects, or "moods," of blossoming plum branches, each comprising a poetic title, a simple pictorial image, and a quatrain (four five-character lines) arranged on a single page with an elegance that is astonishing: the book appears to be the earliest attempt at anything of the kind, in China or elsewhere. A craze for blossoming plum had swept China in the Southern Song, producing thousands of poems and paintings that celebrate its pure and fragile beauty. A range of meanings, including the erotic and the political, had come to be attached to the theme (as explored in Maggie Bickford's recent book *Ink Plum*).[7] Song Boren's poems are full of allusions to the plight of his country—the Mongols had already conquered the north, and the Song was soon to fall—and admonishments to strength and loyalty, themes that the various stages of the blossoming plum are made, somewhat forcedly, to symbolize.

YUAN PAINTING: LANDSCAPE AS SELF-EXPRESSION

The Song dynasty ended with the conquest of south China by the Mongols under Khubilai Khan, grandson of Chinggis Khan and first emperor of the Mongol dynasty in China, which they named the Yuan. Although Mongol rule was to last less than a century (1279–1368), it was a traumatic time for the Chinese: never before had their entire territory been under the control of one of the northern nomadic peoples whom the Han Chinese had traditionally regarded as "barbarians." In the early Yuan period the civil-service examinations

Fig. 2. Zhao Mengfu (1254–1322). Villa by the Water. *Dated to 1302, Yuan dynasty (1279–1368). Handscroll, ink on paper; 24.9 x 120.5 cm. Palace Museum, Beijing.*

were abolished, and although Khubilai Khan sought to surround himself with traditionally educated Chinese advisers, many such scholars who would normally have attempted government careers withdrew instead from public life, supporting themselves through various activities for which their scholarly backgrounds fitted them, among which were calligraphy and painting. The literati, or scholar-amateur, movement in painting, inaugurated in the eleventh century but eclipsed during the later Song by the brilliant achievements of the professional and Academy masters, came to the fore during the Yuan and maintained its primacy during most of the later centuries.

The Song-Yuan transition is accordingly seen as a great turning point in the history of Chinese painting, when (to oversimplify) a primarily representational tradition gave way to one primarily aimed at individual expression. A Yuan-period critic, reflecting a view that had already become orthodox among the literati, put "form-likeness" last on a list of criteria for judging paintings; what was to be esteemed, he wrote, was "plays with brush and ink in which lofty-minded men and superior scholars have lodged their exhilaration [intense feeling] and sketched their ideas." The move from painting as pictorial description of appearances to painting as an expressive art concerned with its own conventions and its own past, the very shift that in the West (according to one common view) marks the beginnings of modernism, thus happened at least half a millennium earlier in China.

A central figure in the creation of new literati styles in landscape painting during the early Yuan was Zhao Mengfu (1254–1322). Although a descendant of the Song imperial house, he did not adopt the stance of a Song loyalist, but accepted high posts in the Mongol administration under Khubilai Khan and had a distinguished official career. As a painter he rejected, like most others in his time, what he saw as the polish and overt appeal of Song painting, choosing instead to revive styles from the more distant past, especially the Tang and Five Dynasties periods. His *Villa by the Water* of 1302 (fig. 2), painted for a friend whose retreat bore that name, is for Chinese connoisseurs "in the style of" the tenth-century landscapist Dong Yuan, whose deliberately plain scenery and lulling repetitions

of brush strokes were admired as the antithesis to the now-unacceptable drama and diversity of later Song painting. Zhao's picture is even flatter and simpler than any of Dong Yuan's, with minimal detail absorbed into the fabric of brushwork to the point of being barely discernible. It is executed in brush strokes that reject everything gestural and overtly expressive; the ink is rubbed on dry to catch the slight nap of the paper, for an effect not unlike charcoal drawing. Here for the first time landscape takes on the capacity to express in its forms and execution both the reclusiveness of the recipient and a tranquil state of mind— considered an essential attribute of high character— in the artist.

This expressive capacity of landscape painting is fully expanded in the late Yuan, especially in the works of two artists who are often paired in a relationship more of contrast than of similarity: Ni Zan (1306[?]–1374) and Wang Meng (ca. 1308–1385). Ni Zan spent his early years as a rich, cultivated youth who collected antiques, entertained a rigorously selected group of friends (he was neurotically cleanly, washing his hands frequently and shunning anyone he considered "vulgar"), and practiced poetry, calligraphy, and painting. When he was in his thirties, however, the burden of taxes and the depredations of local uprisings drove him to disperse the family property and take up a wandering life. He traveled about by small boat, staying with friends and patrons, repaying their hospitality with his paintings, which were increasingly in demand—by the time of his death, we read, the ownership of a Ni Zan was a mark of elevated cultural status for families in the region. In his hands the sparse, dry-brush manner, with its effect of visual disengagement, became a metaphor for emotional alienation from what he saw as a contaminated world. His *Six Gentlemen* of 1345 (cat. 188), done for one of his hosts, presents his typical river scene with widely separated banks—a compositional device itself expressive of distance and loneliness—with six exiguous trees in the foreground "representing" the six men present at the gathering. This way of endowing the barest of materials with multilayered meaning would become another option and ideal for artists of later periods.

Ni Zan's younger contemporary Wang Meng was the grandson of Zhao Mengfu and grew up with a familiarity with old painting that informs his own works. Rejecting the reclusiveness of Ni Zan and others, he followed the family tradition of official service, holding a minor post in the 1340s and another after the founding of the Ming dynasty, eventually becoming implicated in a supposed treasonous plot and dying in prison. His landscapes, densely packed and tactilely rich, can be read as emblematic of engagement and thus as representing a stance opposed to that of Ni Zan. The highly activated forms that make up Wang Meng's best pictures create powerful tensions, even turbulence, which undermine the original implications of stability and coherence carried by the Song monumental landscapes on which they are distantly based. Such a calculated, expressionist distortion of an established type, intended to subvert its normal associations, seems, again, a very modern stratagem.

Finest among Wang Meng's surviving paintings is his 1366 *Dwelling in the Qingbian Mountains* (cat. 189), which, according to research by Richard Vinograd, was probably painted for the artist's cousin Zhao Lin and represents the Zhao family retreat at that place.[8] Depictions of secluded villas were a specialty of Yuan literati artists, who ordinarily portrayed them as securely sequestered from the outside world. Wang subverts this type too, by confounding the viewer's attempt to read his picture as made up of coherent geological forms and spaces, and by instilling a powerful restlessness through nervous, constantly shifting brushwork and an unnaturalistic play of light and shadow. The insecurity was real: the two principal contenders for the succession to Mongol rule were battling nearby at just this time; one of them, Zhu Yuanzhang, would become, two years later, the first emperor of the Ming dynasty.

EARLY AND MIDDLE MING PAINTING:
DIVERGENT DIRECTIONS

In the early Ming dynasty painters were called to court and assigned projects, as they had been in the Song. By the Xuande reign (1426–1435) of the emperor Xuanzong, a conscious attempt was underway to revive the Southern Song Painting Academy, employing court artists who basically continued the Song styles. Literati, or scholar-amateur, artists of the early Ming continued late Yuan literati styles in a similarly conservative way; the first century or so of the Ming might thus seem to support the idea of a stagnation in later Chinese painting. But the lull was not to last beyond the middle and later fifteenth century, when both currents were powerfully redirected by great original masters.

Imperial Academy artists made paintings, mostly under orders or on commission, for a diversity of uses—auspicious, decorative, seasonal—besides doing pictures that carried political meanings for presentation and hanging on special occasions such as the appointment and retirement of court officials. A competence in portraiture was normally required of these versatile artists, even when their primary specialty was flowers-and-birds or some other subject. Shang Xi, best known for what in the West are called history pictures, is credited with a huge painting (over 2 x 3.5 m.), which may have been mounted originally on a screen, representing Emperor Xuanzong and members of his court setting off on a hunt (cat. 190). The emperor, seen at the top, is the largest figure, as longstanding convention dictated; the principal figures among the mounted party in the foreground are given portrait-like faces and must represent particular people. We can assume that their inclusion in the picture, and their positions within it, reflected their ranks in the court. The creatures crowded into the upper right—deer, rabbits, ducks and other birds—stand for the intended quarry, but play only subsidiary roles in this grand display piece.

Another group portrait by a court master, this one in handscroll form and more modest in size, is *The Literary Gathering in the Apricot Garden*, an event that took place in 1437 and was depicted by Xie Huan (act. 1426–1452) (cat. 191). Xie had a long and successful career in the Academy, attaining great favor with the emperor, with whom he is said to have played chess every day. His status, and the place in society that a painter might attain by his time, is indicated by his including himself in the picture—at the beginning of the scroll, to be sure, farthest out from the garden that is its climactic scene, but still there. The central figures are the Three Yangs, members of the Grand Secretariat and the emperor's most trusted advisers. They have invited high-ranking friends for a day of banqueting and drinking, appreciating antiquities, doing calligraphy, and composing poems. Here, too, the sizes, poses, and positioning of the figures establish a clear hierarchy among them. Another, shorter version of the picture is in the Metropolitan Museum of Art; it may be that the composition was loosely replicated by lesser Academy masters for presentation to participants in the event.

Both these paintings were executed in the Song-derived, traditional manner of the early Ming Academy; neither artist allowed his personal style, or "handwriting," to intrude. The first significant break with that practice was accomplished by Dai Jin (1388–1462), who served in the Academy, if at all, only briefly, but whose stylistic innovations heavily influenced its later masters. His typical works, large landscape hanging scrolls on silk, are still relatively traditional in subject and composition, but are made up of massive, strongly contoured earth forms. The brush drawing is less constrained than before by its bounding and texturing function, more expressive of nervous energy in the artist's hand. This stylistic move is not only another assertion of the rising status of painters, including professionals, but also an incursion into the territory of the scholar-amateurs—who would, however, have been quick to point out that Dai Jin's brushwork-oriented paintings were still very different from theirs, less subtle, as befitting the work of a professional.

An untypical, very fine work by Dai Jin is the small picture on paper now titled, somewhat misleadingly, *Landscape in the Manner of Yan Wengui* (cat. 192). The association with this tenth- to eleventh-century landscapist comes from the inscription written on it by Dong Qichang (1555–1636), leading spokesman for the literati position, who was, we can imagine, shown the work and invited to inscribe it by some collector. Dong, to whom Dai Jin's typical work must have seemed heavy-handed and overcharged, could scarcely praise a painting without identifying in it the kind of style-conscious allusions to old masters that he and other literati artists practiced themselves; he felt obliged to find such allusions, however forcedly, in Dai's work. The words of heavily qualified, even evasive praise that Dong wrote on it reveal the uneasy relationship between artists occupying different socioeconomic positions in Ming China: "Among the professional painters of our dynasty, Dai Jin is considered a great master. This picture follows Yan Wengui's style, and is pure and empty, not at all like [Dai's] everyday work in character—it is highly unusual." Although the shape of the highest peak and a few other features may relate distantly to Yan Wengui, Dai's painting is not style-conscious at all, but is a sensitive, painterly evocation of a misty scene centered on the thatched retirement house of the man for whom it was done, identified in Dai's own inscription as "Old Teacher Yongyan."

The "school" or movement that Dai Jin is credited with founding was later named, after his birthplace in Zhejiang Province, the Zhe school. Among the artists who succeeded him in what is now called the Zhe school and who served in the Imperial Academy was Wu Wei (1459–1508). His career marks a further stage in the social elevation of the artist. He was much in demand as a drinking companion for men of high position and was a familiar of the emperor himself, who excused his aberrant behavior because of his artistic brilliance.

Wu Wei exemplifies a new type of artist, the urban eccentric, to whose personality the quick and spontaneous manner of execution seen in his paintings was taken to be a stylistic counterpart. His subjects and compositions are in themselves relatively conservative: *Fishermen on a Snowy River* (cat. 193), for instance, with a landmass on one side and a receding river on the other, follows a very old pattern. In the eyes of the audiences for whom Wu Wei worked, fishermen represented an ideal of escape from the pressures and spiritual contamination of city and court.

By the end of the fifteenth century the great city of Suzhou, which had been a gathering place for artists and poets in the late Yuan period but had declined under persecution by the first Ming emperor, was recovering its cultural preeminence, which it would retain for about a century. Besides being the principal locus for the revival of literati painting, it offered the most attractive patronage to professional artists, who could benefit also from the great collections of old paintings to be seen there. Among these professionals, three stand out: Zhou Chen (ca. 1455–after 1536) and two who learned from him—Qiu Ying (ca. 1495–1552) and Tang Yin (1470–1523). Zhou and Qiu are represented in this exhibition by excellent paintings that display the conservative side of their output; judged by these, they might seem to substantiate, once more, the idea that little had changed since the Song dynasty.

The subject of Zhou Chen's *Peach Blossom Spring* (cat. 194), which he painted in 1533, was a favorite among Suzhou and other big-city audiences, since it was another image of escape from the "dusty world." In the famous account by Tao Qian (365–427), a fisherman discovers a hidden elysium (the origin of the Shangri-la story) where refugees from an oppressive ruler had lived for centuries without aging. The fisherman returns to his town, and a search party is sent to find this blessed place; needless to say, they never do. The compartmentalized composition of Zhou's painting follows this narrative in its structure: passage from the foreground, the outside world, to the elysium is through a cave; beyond, in the sequestered space, the fisherman is seen being greeted by the village elders. The picture is executed in brushwork that conceals the hand of the artist, answering the continuing fondness of the Suzhou patrons for Song-style painting—preference for the styles of the Yuan literati masters had yet to become the dominant critical taste.

Qiu Ying's *Playing the Flute by Pine and Stream* (cat. 195) is another successful evocation of Song style and another image of reclusion. The man playing a flute in a boat is not a working fisherman, as portrayed, for instance, in Wu Wei's painting

(cat. 193), but, as his attributes (Daoist wine-gourd, loose robe, flute) indicate, a scholar-gentleman enjoying solitude, having come out, presumably, from the thatched house seen behind. The melancholy sound of the flute merging with the splash of water and wind in the pine is evoked as a familiar metaphor for harmony with nature. The spaces opening back successively beyond the flute player serve as sounding chambers for these imagined sounds and are accomplished with Song-like gradations of tonal values. Other works by Zhou Chen and Qiu Ying would bring out better their individual styles and innovations; these reveal them as heirs to a great tradition, who could still practice it on a high level.

The literati, or scholar-amateur, movement in painting, which had been concentrated in the Suzhou region in the late Yuan, had received a serious setback with the persecution of that city and its cultural elite by the first Ming emperor. Its real comeback, leaving aside a few secondary masters active during the first century of the Ming who bridged the hiatus without ending it, was accomplished by Shen Zhou (1427–1509). Born into a gentry family with land holdings, he was able to live comfortably without attempting an official career, and devoted much of his leisure to literary and artistic pursuits. His status also relieved him of the need to master high-level representational techniques as a painter; he developed instead an amiable and ingenuous personal style in which forms, simply textured and bounded by thick brush line, are made up into inventive compositions that read basically as strong, flat designs. In contrast to the escape-and-reclusion themes of so much of the output of the Zhe school and other professional masters, paintings by Shen Zhou and the Suzhou amateur artists who follow him typically take as their subjects the local scenery, occasions such as outings and gatherings and farewells, the villas and gardens of friends—idealized versions, that is, of the here-and-now of their real lives. The *Eastern Villa* album (cat. 196) depicts scenes on the estate of

Shen Zhou's friend Wu Kuan (1435–1504). Three of the original twenty-four leaves have been lost, one of them reportedly bearing Shen's own inscription, so that the attribution (first made in a colophon dated to 1611 by Dong Qichang) is not absolutely secure; this might be an exceptionally fine work in Shen's style by a follower. In any case, it exemplifies the flattening and abstracting direction that literati painting was taking in this period, notably in Shen Zhou's own hands.

That direction can be seen also in the works of Shen Zhou's principal follower Wen Zhengming (1470–1559), who came from a Suzhou gentry family, had a brief period of official service in the capital, and in principle painted as an amateur artist and "retired scholar" without thought of profit. In reality, he, Shen Zhou, and the others engaged in an intricate pattern of exchanges of goods, services, and favors through which they derived substantial "incomes" from their painting. Works such as Wen Zhengming's *Studio of True Appreciation*, painted in 1549 (cat. 197), were usually done at the request of the owner of a house or villa and portrayed him in it, receiving visitors, surrounded by the trappings of high culture and taste, including in this case the huge, fantastically eroded Taihu rocks brought from a nearby lake shore to be set up like natural sculptures in gardens. To have one's dwelling depicted by an artist of Wen's status and renown, in his cool, disciplined, irreproachably upper-class style, invested it with an aura of literati elegance.

The art of Shen Zhou and Wen Zhengming is highly style-conscious and self-reflective, deeply occupied with its past. Both artists sometimes painted landscapes in the manners of the Yuan masters Ni Zan and Wang Meng, among others. The cautious moves into abstraction in their works were in part expressions of disdain for the "form-likeness," or verisimilitude, toward which less cultivated artists were assumed to aspire; they must have impressed art-lovers of their time as strikingly original and "modern." To later Chinese

connoisseurs, and to us, they seem to foreshadow the truly revolutionary moves of the later Ming without quite realizing them—occupying art-historical positions, that is, somewhat like Courbet and Manet. If so, Dong Qichang (cat. 200) was to be the Chinese Cézanne. Such comparisons are perhaps idle and easily discredited; they are meant only as loose indicators of how large patterns of change in artistic styles, first slower and then more radical, might be seen as repeating themselves.

LATE MING PAINTING: RADICAL MOVES
The self-expressive concept of painting, by which the qualities of the work reflect the artist's personality and cultivation, was well established in Chinese literati painting theory of the Song period and was taken to be ideally exemplified, as we saw, in the work of such late Yuan masters as Ni Zan and Wang Meng. A corollary of this idea, popular in China as in the West (the "van Gogh's ear" notion), was that eccentricity or even aberration in the painter produced corresponding oddities in the picture. Audiences for artists identified as "mad," then, expected some evidence of "madness" in the paintings, and the artists responded. Those such as Wu Wei (cat. 193), who cultivated eccentricities of behavior and matched them with wild brushwork in their paintings, should be distinguished from those who suffered real, disabling bouts of mental disorder. Two of the latter are represented in this exhibition: Xu Wei and Bada Shanren.

Xu Wei (1521–1593) is another artist, like Ni Zan, whose paintings can scarcely be discussed apart from his life. After failing in successive attempts at an official career, he made his living as a playwright, calligrapher, and painter, exhibiting brilliance in all three pursuits. His emotional disorder sometimes took violent forms: he mutilated himself while in prison, and in a drunken fit beat his second wife to death, narrowly escaping execution for this. Xu Wei's favorite subjects as a painter have no implications of violence, however; he painted plants, including fruits and flowers,

Fig. 3. Xu Wei (1521–1593). Flowers and Other Plants (grapevines). *Ming dynasty (1368–1644). Handscroll, ink on paper; 30 x 1,053.5 cm. Nanjing Museum.*

which he depicts in assertive strokes of ink monochrome. An extreme example of his semicontrolled, gestural manner can be seen in a section representing grapevines in his great handscroll in the Nanjing Museum (fig. 3). Another kind of nonconformist brushwork, in which the ink is applied so wet that individual strokes cannot be distinguished within puddled areas and the image is blurred as if by atmosphere, is displayed in his large hanging scroll *Peonies, Banana Plant, and Rock* (cat. 198). By accepting a role outside normal social demands, Xu Wei freed himself to violate established literati disciplines of brushwork and form. At the same time, however, he creates here a moving evocation of what one might see in the corner of one's garden on a foggy morning. In all their moves to the very edge of abstraction, Chinese artists never renounced representation completely, presumably because doing so deprives the artist of the power to create visually arresting effects through tensions between image and abstraction.

The centuries after the Song dynasty had produced few distinguished figure painters, but that long-neglected subject category rose again to prominence in the late Ming, especially in the work of Chen Hongshou (1598–1652). Like Xu Wei, he lived in the region of Shaoxing in Zhejiang, and also like Xu he was an educated man and frustrated would-be official who failed the examinations repeatedly, settling finally and reluctantly into the role of professional painter. Both his level of cultivation and his bitterness can be read in his paintings. The nonconformity of his works, however, is not manifested in bold, gestural brush strokes; Chen paints mostly in the old manner of fastidious fine-line drawing with washes of color.

His nonconformity appears, instead, in highly cultivated archaisms of style that can turn quirky or even bizarre. His figures are often drawn in a pre-Tang mode, with elongated faces and flattened drapery drawing that implies no articulated body beneath it.

In Chen Hongshou's handscroll *The Pleasures of He Tianzhang* (cat. 199), done in collaboration with his studio assistant Yan Zhan and a portrait specialist named Li Wansheng (who painted the man's face, using the new illusionism derived from contacts with European pictures), three levels of "reality" and artifice are clearly distinguished. He Tianzhang, seated at a stone table surrounded by the trappings of high culture, is a "real person" looking complacently out at us; the diminutive flute player at the end (left) of the scroll is a conventional image from the past, without substance. He Tianzhang's wife or concubine, sitting between them on a banana leaf and holding an upright fan, occupies a mediating position also in mode of representation; she is given some weight and prominence but reduced to a type of beauty, presented more as a lovely attribute of his than as an individual person. Such refinements of style and plays on representation bespeak both a highly sophisticated audience and an art that can scarcely present its imagery any longer in a straightforward way.

Chen Hongshou is the author of an essay castigating both the professional masters, for not looking far enough into the past in their search for models, and the literati-amateurs, for using their social position to claim lofty achievements in art beyond their real merits.[9] It is true enough that by the late Ming period, a great many amateur artists of small technical prowess were engaging in a repetitive production of conventional river landscapes and the like. One great master, however, rescued the whole scholar-amateur tradition from its doldrums: Dong Qichang.

Dong Qichang (1555–1636) could be seen as a foil to Chen Hongshou in almost all respects. He took high honors in the official examinations and held several positions at court, including that of tutor to the heir apparent. During his long periods out of service he lived as a rich landholder in Songjiang, in Jiangsu Province. His paintings, writings, and expertise as a connoisseur were constantly in demand—and were always, we can assume, suitably recompensed. He was the most respected and influential painting theorist of his time, devising a grand formulation in which the history of painting was divided into two "schools," the "southern" and "northern"—the former corresponding loosely with the literati tradition, the latter with the professional and academy masters. As a painter, Dong limited himself almost exclusively to "pure" landscape, in which figures virtually never appear, much less the narrative or human-interest themes of other artists' works. Stylistically, he moved, moreover, in a profoundly antinaturalistic direction. "For splendid scenery," he wrote, "painting cannot equal the real landscape; but for marvels of brush and ink, real landscape is not at all the equal of painting." He advocated a kind of free "imitation" of old styles (*fang*), in which the canonical old masters are evoked in ways that reveal the artist's familiarity with them, at no real compromise to his originality; good analogies might be to Stravinsky in music or Ezra Pound in poetry. All three assume a knowing viewer-listener-reader whose experience of the work will include recognition of the learned allusions embedded in it.

Dong Qichang's *Poetic Feeling at Qixia Monastery*, painted in 1626 (cat. 200), can be read on a number of levels: as a quasi-topographical picture (it "represents" a mountain near Nanjing, with its famous Buddhist monastery); as a demonstration of the brushwork and compositional principles that Dong advocated in his theoretical writings; as a stark, diagrammatic exposition of Dong's understanding of old paintings (it invokes, among others, the monumental landscape type from the tenth and eleventh centuries); and as a near-abstract construction within which dynamic forms interact for powerfully unsettling effect. And this last reading, if one chooses, can be further linked to the political situation of the late Ming by seeing the picture as a consciously subversive distortion of an old type, a deliberate misreading of the monumental landscape in which established implications of stability and order are denied, as Wang Meng (cf. cat. 189) had denied them three centuries earlier.

When the achievements of Xu Wei, Chen Hongshou, and Dong Qichang, along with other late Ming masters not represented here (notably, Wu Bin), are set against Gombrich's "performance" art, Danto's "further development unimaginable," and Fry's "atrophy of the creative spirit," these Western assessments of later Chinese painting fall, I think, into true perspective. And the great early Qing Individualist masters are still to come.

The late Ming was also the peak period of pictorial woodblock printing, seeing notable advances in the quality of block-cutting, refinements of design, and the introduction of new techniques for color printing. Major artists, including Chen Hongshou, produced designs for printed illustrations. In a few of the pictures in the 1606 *Cheng shi mo yuan* ("Cheng Family Garden of Ink"), the linear designs were printed in color through the simple device, called *yitao* ("single block"), of putting pigments on different areas of the single woodblock in place of ink. This method was soon superseded by another, the *douban* ("pieced-together blocks") method of using a number of blocks, one for each color. The Chinese way of printing, with the block face-up, ink or color applied to it, and the paper laid over it and rubbed with a burin, permitted subtle effects of shading by applying the pigments unevenly or by wiping the block after applying them. No two impressions, then, are quite identical.

This process was superbly utilized in two works published in Nanjing by Hu Zhengyan. The *Shizhuzhai shuhuapu* ("Ten Bamboo Studio Manual of Calligraphy and Painting") (cat. 201), completed in 1627 and issued in eight volumes between then and 1633, reproduces paintings of flowers-and-birds, bamboo and blossoming plum, garden stones, and other subjects by a number of artists. It can be admired both as the finest reproductions of paintings made anywhere up to that time, and simply as color printing of a technical and aesthetic refinement similarly unmatched elsewhere. The *Shizhuzhai qianpu* ("Ten Bamboo Studio Letter Papers"), issued in four volumes by the same publisher in 1644 (cat. 202), added a further technical innovation: in addition to the designs in ink and colors, "blind blocks" were used to impress low-relief patterns into the paper, a process called *gauffrage*. It is hard to believe that these papers can really have been intended for use, with letters or poems written (in elegant calligraphy, to be sure) over their exquisite designs. Happily, examples that have survived have no such writing.

Color printing continued in China, but for economic and other reasons still to be explored, the achievements of the late Ming in this medium were never surpassed and seldom approached there afterward. The Japanese learned the techniques of color woodblock printing from China and used them brilliantly through the eighteenth and nineteenth centuries for the well-known Ukiyo-e prints, as well as for the less-known printed books called *gafu*, and these have understandably overshadowed later Chinese color printing in foreign writings. A late nineteenth–early twentieth-century Chinese publication titled *Baihua tupu* ("Album of a Hundred Flowers") (cat. 203), based on paintings by Zhang Chaoxiang, a flower-and-bird specialist active in Tianjin, illustrates this observation; the quality of the color printing is still high, but represents no real advance over the *Ten Bamboo Studio* publications. The finest pictorial printing of the late period is not in color but in the ink-line tradition: in stylistic and technical refinements, the books designed by Ren Xiong (1823–1857) nearly match those by his model, Chen Hongshou of the late Ming period.

EARLY QING PAINTING: ORTHODOXY AND INDIVIDUALISM

Dong Qichang was unquestionably the most influential painter of his age, but his following took two more or less opposed directions. In one, his creative manipulations of old compositions inspired the Individualist masters of the early Qing period to attempt similarly radical feats of transforming selected materials from their heritage while seeming to embrace them. In the other, Dong's authoritative pronouncements on the "right" way to paint, and the possibility of deriving a consistent set of compositional techniques, brushwork conventions, and type-forms from his more routine works, encouraged the emergence of an orthodoxy. Such an orthodoxy took shape, in fact, in the paintings and writings of the so-called Four Wangs of the Ming-Qing transition—Wang Shimin (1592–1680), Wang Jian (1598–1677), Wang Hui (1632–1717), and Wang Yuanqi (1642–1715)—along with Wu Li (1632–1718) and Yun Shouping (1633–1690), who have collectively come to be called the Six Orthodox Masters. Their following, in turn, has continued down to the present, although significant contributions to the style declined precipitously after their time. An appreciation of Orthodox school landscape, and the ability to discriminate between the different hands engaged in it, has remained the very hallmark of traditional connoisseurship in Chinese painting. Whole exhibitions, symposia, and book-length studies have been devoted to the Orthodox school, and deservedly. It will receive less attention here, in keeping with the argument of this essay and the direction of this exhibition, in which only one of the Four Wangs—Wang Yuanqi—is represented.

Wang Shimin is credited with establishing the school. As a well-to-do young collector he had studied painting with Dong Qichang, and it was he who reduced Dong's prodigious artistic achievements to a learnable system, in keeping with his own more limited talents and conservative taste. The "right" or "true" lineage of painting that Wang Shimin and his followers defined was set in opposition to other currents of painting in their time: what we would regard as a healthy, exuberant diversification of styles and subjects in late Ming–early Qing painting they saw as fragmentation and decline. Variety in subject matter was far from their purpose: an overall title such as *River Landscape with Houses and Trees* would cover most of their output. Spokesmen today for this kind of painting exhort us to "Look at the brushwork, not the scenery!" but one can wish nonetheless for a bit more variety in the scenery. Wang Shimin's fellow townsman and friend Wang Jian, through an abundant and consistently high-level output, helped to consolidate the style and establish its preeminence in the eyes of critics of their persuasion. The third of the Wangs, Wang Hui, was taken on while still young as a protégé by the older two and trained in the Orthodox manner. He had more natural talent and technique than his mentors and could imitate the old masters so successfully that he was much in demand as a forger. He went on to a highly successful career, including a period in the imperial court.

The youngest of the Four Wangs was Wang Yuanqi, who was the grandson of Wang Shimin and so belonged in the direct succession of the "true lineage." He held high positions in the Manchu court and edited an imperial anthology of writings on painting and calligraphy. Given his wealth and position, he could have achieved a successful career in painting merely by carrying on the family style. Instead, he became the most innovative and interesting of the four, the equal of the Individualist masters in his sophisticated manipulations of semiabstract form. Even more strikingly, he accomplished this within the boundaries of the Orthodox style. No artist who followed that lineage after him was to be so successful in revitalizing it. Wang Yuanqi's *Complete in Soul, Sufficient in Spirit* (cat. 204), painted in 1708, is a good example of how, while seeming to replicate the over-familiar river landscape type of his school, he could build a formal, near-abstract structure charged with complex tensions. In his inscription he argued that although paintings in the Dong Yuan–Juran manner (i.e., the "southern school" style) had to be sufficient in "spirit and soul," these qualities could not be attained apart from technical mastery. "But this," he flatteringly assured the dedicatee, "is not a matter one can discuss with shallow-minded people."

Wu Li has been of special interest to Western scholars because he was converted to Christianity, becoming a Catholic priest in 1688 and serving in his late years as a missionary in Shanghai. Only a few of his paintings, however, betray any contact with European art; most are pure landscapes in his version of the Orthodox manner, in which the earth masses seem to have been constructed in an almost modular way out of simple forms and are given an unnaturally consistent, sometimes furry texture that eliminates surface differentiation. Wu Li's *Reading "The Book of Changes" in a Streamside Pavilion* (cat. 205), painted in 1678, displays this manner, which could be seen, like Wang Yuanqi's painting, as doing for the traditional river landscape something comparable to, but far less radical than, what the Cubists would later do for still lifes.

Contemporaneous with the Orthodox landscapists, spanning the tumultuous Ming-Qing transition and affected by it in different ways, were the artists who have come to be loosely grouped as the Individualists. Five are represented here: Kuncan, Hongren, Gong Xian, Bada Shanren, and Shitao. They were mostly associated with local schools of painting in Nanjing and Yangzhou (Jiangsu Province), and in Anhui Province, places where patronage and other conditions were favorable. Only Bada Shanren was isolated from these great centers, working in Nanchang, in Jiangxi Province, where there was no notable tradition of painting. All except Gong Xian were Buddhist monks, having joined the order, as a great many did in the early Qing, either out of religious convictions (Kuncan) or as a way to escape involvement in politically dangerous secular affairs; Hongren had already been linked with an anti-Manchu movement, while Bada and Shitao were both descendants of the Ming imperial house and therefore under suspicion. Although more or less marginalized in their time by the "mainstream" Orthodox masters and their adherents, the Individualist artists had their own circles of admirers, and some following in the eighteenth century. Interest in them was reawakened in the second quarter of our century, when major artists took up their strikingly "modern-looking" styles as the basis for a revival of landscape painting.

The paintings of Kuncan (1612–ca. 1674) are a good beginning, since an understanding of how they differ fundamentally from those of the Four Wangs, to which they may at first appear similar, will illuminate the Orthodox-Individualist distinction. His *Clear Sky Over Verdant Hills*, painted in 1660 (cat. 206), is an outstanding example. Seen in the original or in a good reproduction, it reveals itself immediately as *not* made up, as Orthodox-school landscapes are, of repeated, conventional forms rendered in a neat system of brush strokes, nor are the forms so clearly demarcated. On the contrary, the heavily vegetated hillsides, depicted in loose, disorderly brushwork that imparts to them an earthy naturalism, read as richly variegated continuums of space and matter, imagery and texture; the visual experience of moving over the surface of one of Kuncan's pictures is, accordingly, more than usually akin to that of moving through natural terrain and absorbing transitory sensory stimuli. The effect is personal to the artist, a deeply troubled man who found no comfortable place in the tortured world of human affairs and took solace in immersion in nature. His paintings typically lay out an ideal narrative, the kind of excursion reported in his long inscriptions: from a secure base, a thatched house shown in the foreground, one moves upward along paths and through ravines, perhaps passing a Buddhist temple, sometimes (as here) going at last through a gate leading still farther outward. Implied always is the safe return to the security of one's hermitage.

Kuncan spent his later years in monasteries in the area of Nanjing, but also traveled to Anhui and knew the scenery of Huangshan, the spectacular range of granite peaks that has inspired poets and painters from the late Ming, when it was first made accessible to pilgrimages both religious and literary, down to the present day. In the early Qing a school of painters grew up in southern Anhui that took Huangshan as their principal subject; the central figure was Hongren (1610–1664). Responding in part to the bare, geometricized patterns of Huangshan rock formations, the Anhui landscapists most often worked in a dry-brush linear manner, taking Ni Zan and some works by Dong Qichang (cf. cats. 188, 200) as their principal models, relinquishing washes and texture-stroke systems for effects that are often stark and semiabstract. Their pictures thus occupy an opposite pole from Kuncan's dense textures and variegated forms. Hongren's *Peaks and Ravines at Jiuqi* (cat. 207) is less severe and geometricized than some others of his works (notably, the great *Sound of Autumn* in the Honolulu Academy of Arts), but exemplifies his ability to create, within his self-imposed limitations, effects of substantiality and even monumentality in his landscapes. Sparse pines and other trees grow from rocky crevices; in the lower right, a path leads up from a bridge to a simple pavilion. This, no less than Kuncan's, is a landscape inviting imaginary engagement with a somehow believable world.

Engaging the viewer in visionary worlds that cannot simply be dismissed as convention and artifice, as most of the landscapes of the Orthodox masters can, is the large project underlying the best painting of the Individualists. They too plunder the past, but less for style-conscious allusiveness, more to retrieve pictorial devices that enhance the power and presence of their images. For a few of them, including Gong Xian (1618–1689), the leading master of the Nanjing school in the early Qing, the search extended even outside the boundaries of their own painting tradition, to the European pictorial art that had by this time become known to Chinese artists through paintings and prints (principally, engravings in books) brought from Europe for proselytizing uses by Jesuit missionaries. The question of what seventeenth-century Chinese painters adopted from European pictorial art is complex and controversial, and it is enough for the present purpose to point out that the rendering of light and shade, air and space, seen in such Gong Xian paintings as his *Summer Mountains after Rain* (cat. 209) cannot be accounted for without looking beyond Chinese precedents to European pictures. The indistinct and overlapping brush strokes on the slopes, for instance, are not so much the texture strokes of Chinese practice as a brush equivalent of Western style stippling. The inky depths of the groves of leafy trees, set against strange, ambiguous

areas of light in which empty houses appear, seem similarly foreign to Chinese landscape. In Gong Xian's hands, the European illusionistic devices are used, not as one might expect for the portrayal of comfortingly real-world scenery, but for otherworldly visions; and the whole effect is somber and unsettling. Gong is another painter who was somehow involved in the throes of dynastic change—the short-lived court of the last Ming pretender was located in Nanjing—so that political readings of his dark landscapes seem warranted.

Bada Shanren, or Zhu Da (1626–1705), is the other famously "mad" artist (along with Xu Wei) in Chinese painting. In the late 1670s, after spending some years in Buddhist monasteries near Nanchang, he experienced bouts of crazy behavior; opinion is still divided over whether they were feigned to escape suspicion of political subversion or, as seems more likely, real. He burned his monk's robes and returned to secular life, but according to contemporary reports never spoke again, communicating instead by laughing and crying and gesturing. His paintings, which he produced prolifically in later years, came to be in great demand and probably were his chief means of support. He was not, like the other Individualist masters, primarily a landscapist; his best-known works are enigmatic portrayals of birds and fish, along with plants and rocks, in which the creatures strike unnaturally expressive poses, often seeming to project negative human feelings—suspicion, disgruntlement, anger—along with a dark humor. The models for these came chiefly from the mysterious pictures of such subjects by Muqi and other Chan (Zen) Buddhist monk-artists of the late Song and Yuan, which are known now only through examples in Japan, since Chinese collectors for the most part did not consider them worth preserving. Bada must have seen examples, and perhaps a contemporary practice by monk-amateurs, in the local monasteries. His *Ducks and Lotus* (cat. 210), painted in 1696, is a striking example. The off-balance poses and cryptic, mismatched interrelating of the two birds, the way the lower-right rock hovers without a solid base, and the way the contours of rock and lotus stalks repeat and intersect as they twist upward, confusing mass and space, are among the devices that give the picture, like others of Bada's, powerful instabilities which viewers both then and now are inclined to ascribe to his bottled-up "madness."

The youngest of the Individualist masters was Yuanji, or Shitao (1642–1707), who like Bada Shanren was descended from one of the Ming rulers. Since Shitao was only a child when the Ming dynasty fell, the rupture was for him less traumatic. Late in his life he renounced his Ming loyalist stance altogether, met the Kangxi emperor on one of his southern tours, and traveled to the capital in Beijing, probably as the guest of a Manchu official. During his active years he lived for periods of time in each of the major centers of painting—Anhui Province, Nanjing, and Yangzhou—and absorbed and utilized, always on his own terms, the local styles. In the end, he became independent of all of them, and an artist of unparalleled versatility. It was Shitao who, as noted earlier in a contrast with Dong Qichang, conceived the extraordinary project of relinquishing all established styles and making a fresh start, as if he could return to a state prior to the formulation of conventions. "Before the old masters established methods," he wrote, "I wonder what methods they followed." To raise the question was to challenge directly the Orthodox masters' insistence on "right method"; what Shitao advocated was a "method that is no method." The rhetoric of the claim, needless to say, could not be matched in his actual artistic practice. The attempt, however, while it ultimately led (along with ravages of age and illness, commercialization, and overproduction) to a marked decline in much of the work of his last years, produced some strange and wonderful pictures. It also, together with the drastic failure of creative energy within the Orthodox school of landscape around the same time, left a curious and not entirely healthy legacy for the artists who followed in the eighteenth century, confronting them with still another "end of the history of art." The most interesting of them turned away from landscape altogether to pursue other subjects, and landscape would not recover its central importance until the twentieth century.

Two of Shitao's finest landscapes are in the exhibition. Neither is dated. *Pure Sounds of Hills and Streams* (cat. 208) is probably from his years in Nanjing, 1680–1687, when he was affected by the styles of the local artists—notably Gong Xian (cf. cat. 209). The heavy application of dotting over the surface, which seems to vibrate apart from the solid masses and to convey a psychological rather than a physical state, is a feature also of Gong's late period, the 1680s. At the right of Shitao's picture, a path ascends a ravine to disappear in fog; at the left, in a similarly constricted space, a waterfall seen at the top emerges below to flow under a roofed bridge in which two men relax, listening to the sounds and enjoying the cool. *Clear Autumn in Huaiyang* (cat. 211), judging from its style, must be much later; Jonathan Hay dates it to 1705 and associates it with a flooding that Yangzhou suffered then.[10] In brushwork it stops well short of the more extreme essays toward "stylelessness" seen in other works of Shitao's last years; in its handling of the flat recession along the river, it would appear to betray some acquaintance with Western pictorial

techniques, which were easily accessible by this time to any artist who chose to draw on them—and many were doing so, in diverse ways. Huaiyang is an old name for the city of Yangzhou, where Shitao lived as a professional artist in his late years.

Gong Xian and seven other artists active in Nanjing in the early Qing period are designated in Chinese writings as the "Eight Masters of Jinling" (an old name for the city). Two of the others are Zou Zhe (1636–ca. 1708) and Gao Cen (active ca. 1645–1689.) A distinct school style runs through the output of the Nanjing masters and is well exemplified by Zou Zhe's twelve-leaf *Album of Landscapes* (cat. 212). The style includes a preference for angular divisions of the picture area—strong diagonals, V-shaped compositions—and a fondness for rich textures in both earth surfaces and vegetation. This textural richness responds to, among other factors, the richly forested terrain around Nanjing, just as the linear, geometricized style of the Anhui masters responds to the fractured rock masses of Huangshan. Dark, mysterious groves of trees often dominate Nanjing-school landscapes, and can even, as in two of Zou Zhe's album leaves, serve as the sole subject of the picture. By contrast, Gao Cen's large hanging scroll *The Temple on Jinshan* (cat. 214) avoids the local manner—or any established manner, in fact—to give a close visual report of a famous sight, using all the techniques for convincing representation that an artist of his time and place could muster, including some adopted from Western pictures. Jinshan ("Gold Mountain") is an island in the Yangzi River near the neighboring city of Zhenjiang; topped by a Buddhist temple and pagoda that were visible from afar, the island was a familiar landmark for travelers.

EIGHTEENTH-CENTURY PAINTING: THE YANGZHOU "ECCENTRICS"
By the early decades of the eighteenth century the older centers of painting had been replaced in importance by the city of Yangzhou. Artists and litterateurs were attracted by the generous patronage of salt merchants and other wealthy men who settled there. Painters with different styles and specialties, polished professionals and self-styled amateurs (who mostly depended, nonetheless, on their painting for income), responded to a diversity of tastes and demands.

Two depictions of real places by Yangzhou masters exemplify this diversity. One, in handscroll form (cat. 213), depicts the Zhan Yuan ("Garden for Gazing"), probably the garden of that name on the Qin-Huai Canal in Nanjing, which still can be seen today, although much altered and restored. The artist is Yuan Jiang, who was active from the 1690s until about 1746. Such a work was ordinarily commissioned by the owner of the garden, who would then invite noted literary people to add inscriptions to it. The choice of Yuan Jiang as painter indicates a desire for a detailed and descriptive picture in the conservative tradition stretching back to the Song dynasty. Yuan accomplished this on a high technical level, laying out his panorama of the garden so that the viewer can explore its spaces and appreciate its elegance.

The aim of Gao Xiang (1688–1753) in *Finger-Snap Pavilion* (cat. 215), by contrast, is certainly not close description, but rather to apply his loose, amiable style to conveying the rustic charm of the place, the residence of a noted monk at the Tianning Temple in Yangzhou. A Buddhist altar is visible in the upper story of the open building, and the monk himself and a visitor appear outside, under shaggy trees. Yuan Jiang's patron, given such a picture by his chosen artist, would have returned it indignantly, complaining of sloppiness; the recipient of Gao's would have reacted the same way to one in Yuan's style, calling it fussy and stiff. Both artists worked in response to well-understood expectations, instilling their paintings with visual pleasures of very different kinds. The ingenuous, technically less demanding mode seen in Gao Xiang's work would be favored and developed in interesting directions throughout the eighteenth century by the artists known collectively as the Eight Strange Masters of Yangzhou.

Some time in the second decade of the century, around the end of the Kangxi era, with the deaths within a few years of the major early Qing landscapists Wang Hui, Wang Yuanqi, and Shitao, Chinese painting seems to undergo a great change. Whatever economic and other factors we introduce in accounting for it and however we assess its effect—it might be seen as the onset of decline, but many specialists in Chinese painting would argue vehemently against such a reading—we must recognize that painting of the eighteenth and nineteenth centuries was on the whole milder, flatter in all senses than that of the late Ming and early Qing, less concerned with creating spacious and otherwise plausible worlds or stirring effects and less engaged in the large, complex formal and expressive problems of its predecessors. Interest in landscape declined among the best artists and their audiences, who turned their attention to figures (including portraits) and flower and plant subjects, along with some fresh imagery, unknown in earlier painting, that expanded the artists' thematic repertories. The fondness of some eighteenth-century artists, especially those active in Yangzhou, for sketchy, quirky, and otherwise unorthodox brush manners, and for compositions that are sometimes equally odd, has earned them reputations as nonconformists within Qing painting. Prominent among them are the Eight Strange Masters, or Eight Eccentrics of Yangzhou.

One of the eight, Gao Xiang, has already been introduced (cat. 215). A more serious and prolific artist numbered in the group is Hua Yan (1682–1756). Born in the southeast coastal province of Fujian, he was active in his later years in Hangzhou and Yangzhou, supporting himself by producing a large and heterogeneous body of painting that encompasses nearly all subjects and an astonishing range of styles, drawing on predecessors as diverse as the Song Academy masters and Shitao. He is unmatched in his time for group figure compositions, of which *The Golden Valley Garden* (cat. 219), painted in 1732, is an outstanding example. This was the garden of Shi Chong, a fabulously rich man of the third century. Hua Yan portrays him with his concubine Lü Zhu ("Green Pearl"), who was an accomplished flutist. Rocks, trees, flowers, and servants surround the two in an arrangement that harks back to the "space cells" of early painting.

Another who was attracted from his native place in Fujian by the richer patronage and livelier atmosphere of Yangzhou was Huang Shen (1687–after 1768). The local style he learned in Fujian was too finished and detailed for Yangzhou taste, to which he accommodated by moving into a looser brush manner that had the added benefit of permitting faster and more copious production. Best known for figures, he also painted landscapes and quickly rendered scenes from nature, such as *Willows and Egrets* (cat. 216). Here the gestural flourishing of a heavily loaded brush for the broad, suffusing strokes at the base of the trees and for the trees themselves creates a sense of the momentary, which is caught also in the stalking movements of the birds through shallow water. The picture demonstrates, among other things, how an artist with Huang Shen's solid training can make seemingly free, calligraphic brush strokes serve descriptive and evocative ends.

Li Shan (1686–after 1760) was born near Yangzhou into a scholar-official family. He himself attempted a government career and spent some time at the court in Beijing during the reign of the Kangxi emperor (1662–1722), whose special favor he enjoyed as a poet and painter. Later, after he had lost imperial support and become frustrated with officialdom, he settled in Yangzhou as a professional artist. In a stylistic shift like Huang Shen's, he gave up the more traditional and careful manner he had learned at court to do vigorously executed pictures of trees, flowers, and other plants, along with vegetables and other mundane subjects. In addition to their decorative value, all these carried auspicious and symbolic meanings that fitted them for hanging on particular occasions. Prominent in Li Shan's oeuvre, accordingly, are large hanging scrolls such as his 1755 *Pine, Wisteria, and Peonies* (cat. 217). Here the quirkiness appears in the attenuated, twisting shapes of the rock and trees, and the odd, quasi-postural way they answer each other, like partners in an ungainly dance. In some of his smaller works, notably album leaves, Li Shan used opaque pigments and run-together brush strokes in ways that opened new stylistic options for nineteenth- and twentieth-century painters.

The real amateur of the group was Jin Nong (1687–1764). Although his claim that he did not begin painting until he was fifty is exaggerated, it is true that most of his dated works are from his late years. Earlier he made his living as an itinerant antique dealer and calligrapher. It was, of course, not new for an amateur to paint and sell his works; what was audacious and attractive about Jin Nong was how he made no effort to conceal his amateurism, even flaunting it. Not limiting his paintings to the technically undemanding types favored by the scholar-amateurs (unpeopled river landscapes, ink monochrome bamboo and other plants), he took on subjects that usually required professional skills—figures, including religious images and portraits; horses; illustrations to old poems; figure-in-landscape compositions. All these and others he did with an ingenuous air, relying on his cultivated taste, familiarity with old painting, and a sure and sensitive hand developed through practicing antiquarian calligraphy. His inscriptions to paintings often claim illustrious models; on the leaf representing two men strolling and conversing in a forest from his 1759 *Album of Landscapes and Figures* (cat. 218), for instance, he wrote that it was based on a work by the twelfth-century Academy master Ma Hezhi. In an age and setting in which fine technique had become a bit boring, the demand for Jin Nong's paintings was more than he could keep up with, and he used "ghost-painters" to do works in his style for him to sign.

Most of these complex stratagems for instilling freshness into a very late stage in a very old tradition will seem familiar to us. We can conclude by recognizing also that Chinese painting from the fourteenth through the seventeenth centuries (the Yuan to early Qing periods) presents the single *other* case in world art of what can follow the deliberate relinquishing—even, on the theoretical level, the discrediting—of representation as the underlying project for a highly evolved tradition of painting. Later Chinese painting also demonstrates that after artistic "progress"—in the sense of a coherent series of pictorial modes that seems to exhibit a cumulative mastery of representational techniques—had come to an end, stagnation could still be staved off by successive manipulations of the past, some of them brilliantly conceived, all (at least until the late Shitao) preserving basic strengths from the tradition while transforming it. If Western

painting, at that future moment when three centuries will have elapsed since it passed through the corresponding turning point, can look back over those centuries and claim comparable successes, it will be cause for rejoicing.

SOURCES FOR FIGURES
Fig. 2. After James F. Cahill, The Compelling Image *(Cambridge, Mass.: Harvard University Press, 1982), pl. 2.15.*

Fig. 3. After James F. Cahill, Parting at the Shore *(New York and Tokyo: Weatherhill, 1978), pls. 78–80.*

NOTES
1. E. H. Gombrich, *Art and Illusion: A Study in the Psychology of Pictorial Representation*, The A.W. Mellon Lectures in the Fine Arts 1956, 2d ed. (New York: Pantheon, 1965), pp. 148–50 (italics added).

2. Sherman Lee, cited in Arthur C. Danto, "Ming and Qing Paintings," in *Embodied Meanings: Critical Essays & Aesthetic Meditations* (Farrar, Straus and Giroux, 1994), p. 35. For the catalog essay, see Sherman E. Lee, "Ming and Qing Painting," in Howard Rogers and Sherman E. Lee, *Masterworks of Ming and Qing Painting from the Forbidden City* (Lansdale, Pa.: International Arts Council, 1988), pp. 17–31; this quotation is on p. 17.

3. Danto, "Ming and Qing Paintings," pp. 34–35.

4. Roger Fry, cited in Danto, "Ming and Qing Paintings," p. 35.

5. James Cahill, *The Compelling Image: Nature and Style in Seventeeth-Century Painting*, The Charles Eliot Norton Lectures (Cambridge: Harvard University Press, 1982), p. 5.

6. Richard Barnhart, "Wang Shen and Late Northern Sung Painting," in *International Symposium on Art Historical Studies*, no. 2, "Ajiya ni okeru sanzui no hyogen" ("Landscape Expression in Asia") (Kyoto: Taniguchi Foundation, 1983), pp. 62–70.

7. Maggie Bickford, *Ink Plum: The Making of a Chinese Scholar-Painting Genre* (New York and Cambridge: Cambridge University Press, 1996).

8. Richard Vinograd, "Family Properties: Personal Context and Cultural Pattern in Wang Meng's *Pien Mountains* of 1366," *Ars Orientalis* 8 (1982), pp. 1–29.

9. A translation of Chen Hongshou is in James Cahill, *The Distant Mountains: Chinese Painting of the Late Ming Dynasty* (Tokyo and New York: Weatherhill, 1982), pp. 264–65.

10. Jonathan Hay, "Shitao's Late Work (1697–1707): A Thematic Map" (Ph.D. diss., Yale University), vol. 1, p. 45; and vol. 2, pp. 60–61, n. 55.

Catalogue

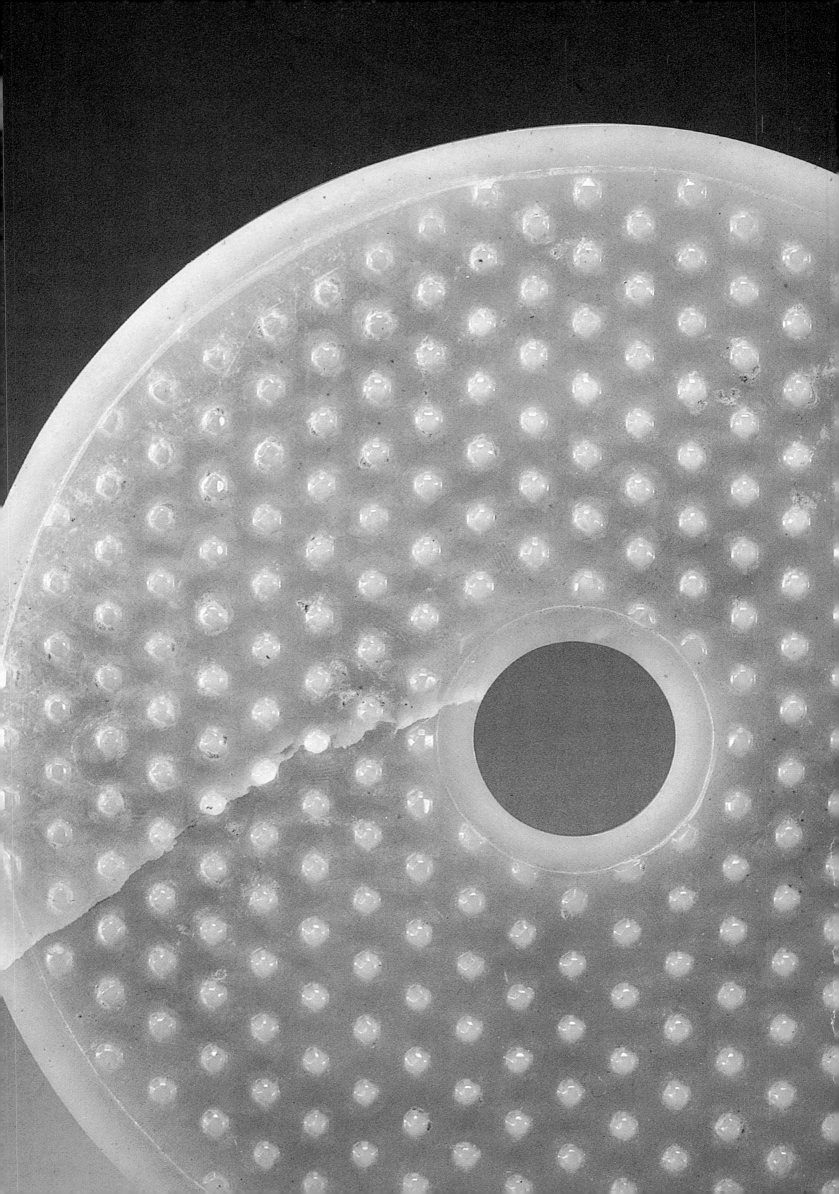

Jade

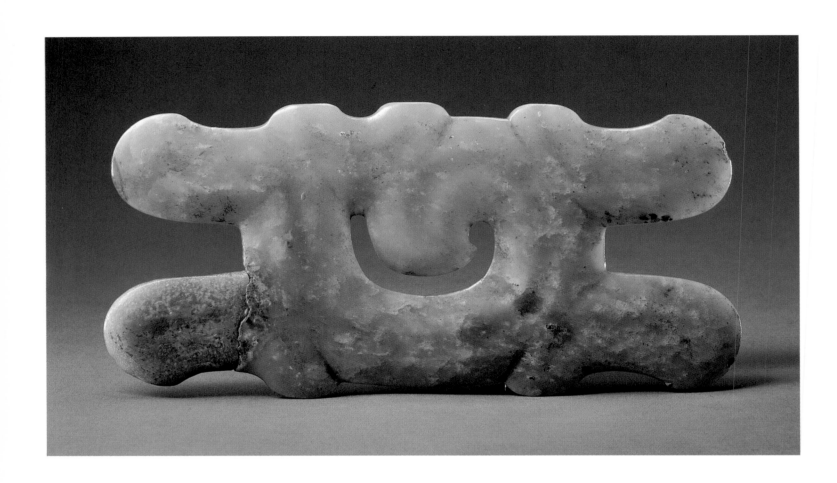

1.

Ornament in the shape of hooked clouds
with central bird motif
Neolithic period, Hongshan culture
(ca. 3600–ca. 2000 BCE)
Nephrite jade; l. 22.4 x w. 11.5 x d. 0.5 cm
Unearthed in 1979 at Sanguandianzi, Lingyuan city,
Liaoning Province
Liaoning Provincial Museum, Shenyang

2.

Ornament in the shape of a pig-dragon (*zhulong*)

NEOLITHIC PERIOD, HONGSHAN CULTURE

(ca. 3600–ca. 2000 BCE)

Nephrite jade; h. 15.7 x w. 10.4 x d. 4.3 cm

Found in Jianping county, Liaoning Province

Liaoning Provincial Museum, Shenyang

3.

Prismatic tube (*cong*)

Neolithic period, Liangzhu culture
(ca. 3600–ca. 2000 BCE)
Nephrite jade; h. 8.8 x max. width 17.6 cm
Unearthed in 1986 from Fanshan tomb No. 12, Yuhang,
Zhejiang Province
Zhejiang Provincial Institute of Cultural Relics and
Archaeology, Hangzhou

4.

Prismatic tube (*cong*)

NEOLITHIC PERIOD, LIANGZHU CULTURE

(ca. 3600–ca. 2000 BCE)

Nephrite jade; h. 5 x max. width 7.4 cm

Unearthed in 1982 from Fuquanshan tomb No. 9,

Qingpu county, Shanghai

Shanghai Museum

5.
Prismatic tube (*cong*)
Neolithic period, Liangzhu culture
(ca. 3600–ca. 2000 BCE)
Nephrite jade; h. 29.7 x max. width 6.1 cm
Unearthed in 1982 in Wujin county, Jiangsu Province
Nanjing Museum

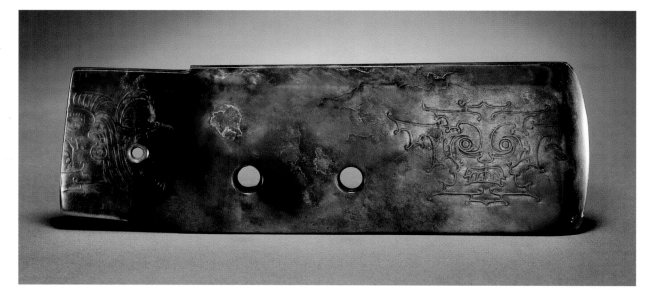

6.

Knife (*dao*) with semihuman mask motifs

Neolithic period, Longshan culture
(ca. 3000–ca. 1700 bce)
Nephrite jade; l. 23.7 x w. 7.7 cm
Shanghai Museum

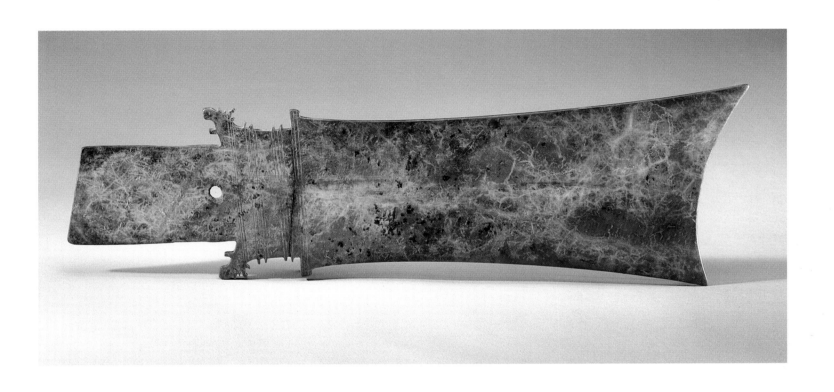

7.

Blade (*zhang*)

Xia or Shang period (ca. 2200–ca. 1100 BCE)

Nephrite jade; l. 37 x w. 11.2 x d. 0.6 cm

Palace Museum, Beijing

8.

Blade (*zhang*)

Shang period (ca. 1600–ca. 1100 BCE)

Nephrite jade; l. 68 x w. 10.8 cm

Unearthed in 1986 from Sanxingdui pit No. 2,
Guanghan, Sichuan Province

Sichuan Provincial Institute of Archaeology and Cultural
Relics, Chengdu

9.
Chime with design of crouching tiger
SHANG PERIOD (ca. 1600–ca. 1100 BCE)
Stone; l. 84 x w. 42 x d. 2.5 cm
Unearthed in 1950 at Wuguan village, Anyang,
Henan Province
National Museum of Chinese History, Beijing

10.

Four figures: (1) bird with ram's horns (2) kneeling human (3) bird (4) bird-headed human

Shang period (ca. 1600–ca. 1100 BCE)

Nephrite jade; (1) h. 4.9 cm (2) h. 5.6 cm (3) h. 10 cm
(4) h. 9.8 cm

Unearthed in 1976 from Fu Hao tomb No. 5, Anyang,
Henan Province

Henan Provincial Museum, Zhengzhou

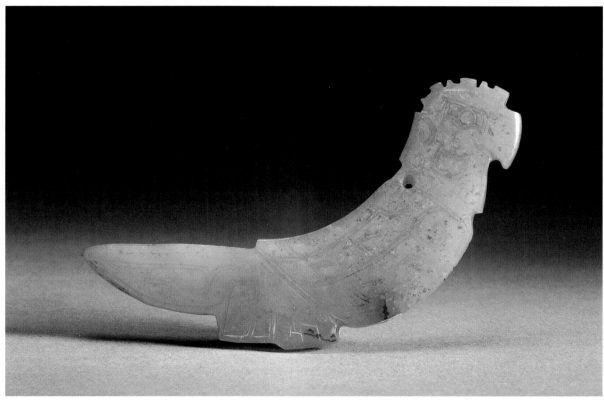

11.

Dagger-ax (*ge*) with grooved blade
WESTERN ZHOU PERIOD (ca. 1100–771 BCE)
Nephrite jade; l. 25.4 x w. 6.1 cm
Unearthed in 1983 at East Sidaoxiang, Xi'an,
Shaanxi Province
Shaanxi History Museum, Xi'an

12.

Fourteen-piece burial mask
WESTERN ZHOU PERIOD (ca. 1100–771 BCE)
Nephrite jade; max. width 10.7 cm
Unearthed in 1990 from Guo State tomb No. 2001,
Sanmenxia, Henan Province
Henan Provincial Institute of Archaeology and Cultural
Relics, Zhengzhou

13.

Ornamental plaque with interlacery and animal mask designs

EASTERN ZHOU, SPRING AND AUTUMN PERIOD (770–476 BCE)
Nephrite jade; h. 7.1 cm
Unearthed at Xiasi, Xichuan county, Henan Province
Henan Provincial Institute of Archaeology and Cultural
Relics, Zhengzhou

14.

A pair of dragon-shaped pendants

EASTERN ZHOU, WARRING STATES PERIOD (475–221 BCE)

Nephrite jade; l. 11.4 cm

Unearthed at Pingliangtai, Huaiyang county,

Henan Province

Henan Provincial Institute of Archaeology and Cultural

Relics, Zhengzhou

15.

Ring (*huan*) with abstract designs

Eastern Zhou, Warring States period (475–221 BCE)

Nephrite jade; diam. 10.6 cm

Unearthed in 1991 at Xujialing, Xichuan county,

Henan Province

Henan Provincial Institute of Archaeology and Cultural

Relics, Zhengzhou

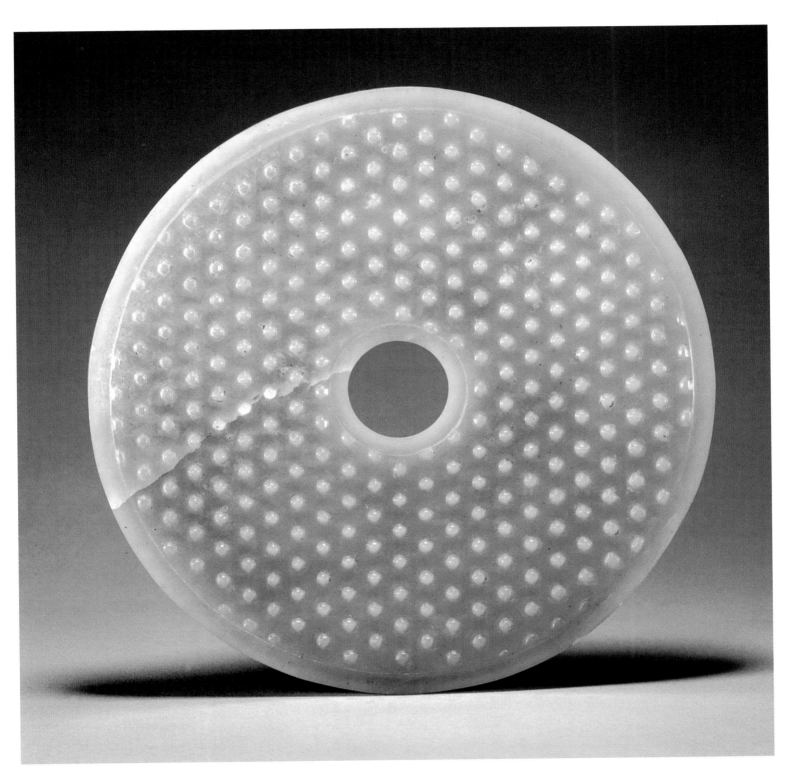

16.

Disk (*bi*) with grain pattern

WESTERN HAN DYNASTY (206 BCE–8 CE)

Nephrite jade; diam. 18.9 cm, depth 0.9 cm

Unearthed in Zhouzhi county, Shaanxi Province

Shaanxi History Museum, Xi'an

17.

Winged horse

HAN DYNASTY (206 BCE–220 CE)

Nephrite jade; h. 4.2 x l. 7.8 x w. 2.6 cm

Palace Museum, Beijing

18.
Chimera (*bixie*)
Han dynasty (206 bce–220 ce)
Nephrite jade; l. 13.5 x w. 8.5 cm
Palace Museum, Beijing

19.

Vessel (*lian* or *zun*) with design of deities, animals, and masks

(Detail on facing page)

WESTERN JIN DYNASTY (265–316)

Nephrite jade; h. 10.5 cm

Unearthed in 1991 from the tomb of Liu Hong,

Huangshantou, Anxiang county, Hunan Province

Administrative Office for Cultural Relics, Anxiang County,

Hunan Province

20.

Sixteen-piece belt

Tang dynasty (618–907)

Nephrite jade; l. of pieces 3.5–5 cm

Unearthed in 1970 at Hejia village, Xi'an, Shaanxi Province

Shaanxi History Museum, Xi'an

Bronze

21.

Vessel (*jue*)

XIA PERIOD (ca. 2100–ca. 1600 BCE)

Bronze; h. 11.7 x w. 14.1 cm

Shanghai Museum

22.

Square cauldron (*fang ding*) with thread-relief frieze of
animal masks, and nipple pattern

SHANG PERIOD (ca. 1600–ca. 1100 BCE)

Bronze; h. 82 x w. 50 cm

Unearthed in 1990 at Qian village, Pinglu county,

Shanxi Province

Shanxi Provincial Institute of Archaeology, Taiyuan

23.

Square vessel (*fang zun*) with four rams

(Detail on facing page)

Sᴴᴀɴɢ ᴘᴇʀɪᴏᴅ (ca. 1600–ca. 1100 ʙᴄᴇ)

Bronze; h. 58.3 cm, w. of mouth 52.4 cm

Found in 1938 at Yueshanpu, Ningxiang, Hunan Province

National Museum of Chinese History, Beijing

24.

Vessel (*zun*) in the shape of a bird, inscribed "Fu Hao"

SHANG PERIOD (ca. 1600–ca. 1100 BCE)

Bronze; h. 45.9 cm

Unearthed in 1976 from Fu Hao tomb No. 5, Anyang,
Henan Province

National Museum of Chinese History, Beijing

25.

Vessel (*zun*) in the shape of an elephant

Shang period (ca. 1600–ca. 1100 BCE)

Bronze; h. 26.5 x l. 22.8 cm

Found in 1975 at Shixingshan, Liling, Hunan Province

Hunan Provincial Museum, Changsha

26.

Vessel (*you*), inscribed

(Details on facing page)

SHANG PERIOD (ca. 1600–ca. 1100 BCE)

Bronze; h. 37.7 cm

Found in 1970 at Huangcai village, Ningxiang county,
Hunan Province

Hunan Provincial Museum, Changsha

27.

Vessel (*zun*) in the shape of a boar

SHANG PERIOD (ca. 1600–ca. 1100 BCE)

Bronze; h. 40 x l. 72 cm

Unearthed in 1981 at Chuanxingshan, Xiangtan county,

Hunan Province

Hunan Provincial Museum, Changsha

28.
Vessel (*gong*) in zoomorphic shape
SHANG PERIOD (ca. 1600–ca. 1100 BCE)
Bronze; h. 19 x l. 43 x w. 13.4 cm
Unearthed in 1959 at Taohua village, Shilou county,
Shanxi Province
Shanxi Provincial Museum, Taiyuan

29.

Basin (*pan*) with coiling dragon design

(Detail on facing page)

Sʜᴀɴɢ ᴘᴇʀɪᴏᴅ (ca. 1600–ca. 1100 ʙᴄᴇ)

Bronze; h. 26 cm, diam. of mouth 61.6 cm

Unearthed in 1984 at Chenshan village, Wenling,

Zhejiang Province

Administrative Office for Cultural Relics, Wenling

30.

Mask with protruding eyes

Shang period (ca. 1600–ca. 1100 BCE)

Bronze; h. 65 x w. 138 cm

Unearthed in 1986 from Sanxingdui pit No. 2,

Guanghan, Sichuan Province

Sichuan Provincial Institute of Archaeology and Cultural

Relics, Chengdu

31.
**Vessel (*lei*) with elephant trunk handles and
buffalo horns**
WESTERN ZHOU PERIOD (ca. 1100–771 BCE)
Bronze; h. 70.2 cm, diam. of mouth 22.8 cm
Unearthed in 1980 at Zhuwajie, Peng county,
Sichuan Province
Sichuan Provincial Museum, Chengdu

32.
Vessel (*zun*), inscribed
WESTERN ZHOU PERIOD (ca. 1100–771 BCE)
Bronze; h. 38.8 cm, diam. of mouth 28.6 cm
Unearthed in 1963 at Jia village, Baoji county,
Shaanxi Province
Baoji Municipal Museum

33.
Bell (*bo*) with four tigers
WESTERN ZHOU PERIOD (ca. 1100–771 BCE)
Bronze; h. 44.3 x w. 39.6 cm
Palace Museum, Beijing

34.
Drum (*gu*) with abstract zoomorphic designs
SHANG PERIOD (ca. 1600–ca. 1100 BCE)
Bronze; h. 75.5 cm, diam. of drum 39.5 cm
Found in 1977 in Chongyang county, Hubei Province
Hubei Provincial Museum, Wuhan

35.
Two-handled vessel (*gui*) with ox-head motifs,
inscribed

(Detail on facing page)

WESTERN ZHOU PERIOD (ca. 1100–771 BCE)

Bronze; h. 31 cm, diam. of mouth 25 cm

Unearthed in 1981 from tomb No. 1, Zhifangtou village,

Baoji county, Shaanxi Province

Baoji Municipal Museum

36.

Vessel (*gong*), inscribed

WESTERN ZHOU PERIOD (ca. 1100–771 BCE)

Bronze; h. 28.7 x l. 38 cm

Unearthed in 1976 at Zhuangbai village, Fufeng county,

Shaanxi Province

Zhouyuan Museum, Xi'an

37.

Vessel (*zun*) in the shape of an elephant

WESTERN ZHOU PERIOD (ca. 1100–771 BCE)

Bronze; h. 21 x l. 38 cm

Unearthed in 1975 at Rujia village, Baoji county,

Shaanxi Province

Baoji Municipal Museum

38.

Covered spouted vessel (*he*) in the shape of a
four-legged duck, inscribed

(Detail on facing page)

WESTERN ZHOU PERIOD (ca. 1100–771 BCE)

Bronze; h. 26 cm

Unearthed in 1980 from the Ying State tomb at

Pingdingshan, Henan Province

Henan Provincial Institute of Archaeology and Cultural

Relics, Zhengzhou

39.

Two-handled vessel (*gui*), inscribed

WESTERN ZHOU PERIOD (ca. 1100–771 BCE)

Bronze; h. 26.5 cm

Unearthed in 1986 from the Ying State tomb at
Pingdingshan, Henan Province

Henan Provincial Institute of Archaeology and Cultural
Relics, Zhengzhou

40.

Vessel (*hu*), inscribed

WESTERN ZHOU PERIOD (ca. 1100–771 BCE)

Bronze; h. 65.4 cm, diam. of mouth 19.7 cm

Unearthed in 1976 at Zhuangbai village, Fufeng county,

Shaanxi Province

Zhouyuan Museum, Xi'an

41.

Rectangular vessel (*fang yi*), inscribed

WESTERN ZHOU PERIOD (ca. 1100–771 BCE)

Bronze; h. 38.5 x l. of mouth 20 x w. of mouth 17 cm

Unearthed in 1963 at Qijia village, Fufeng county,

Shaanxi Province

Shaanxi History Museum, Xi'an

42.

Miniature carriage with human guardians including
one-legged watchman, birds, and crouching tigers

WESTERN ZHOU PERIOD (ca. 1100–771 BCE)

Bronze; h. 9.1 x l. 13.7 x w. 11.3 cm

Unearthed in 1989 at Shangguo village, Wenxi county,

Shanxi Province

Shanxi Provincial Institute of Archaeology, Taiyuan

43.
**Four-sided vessel (*fang hu*) with square base and
lotus-petal crown**
EASTERN ZHOU, SPRING AND AUTUMN PERIOD (770–476 BCE)
Bronze; h. 66 x max. width 34 cm
Unearthed in 1988 from tomb No. 251, Jinsheng village,
Taiyuan, Shanxi Province
Shanxi Provincial Institute of Archaeology, Taiyuan

44.
Vessel (*hu*) with bird-shaped lid
EASTERN ZHOU, SPRING AND AUTUMN PERIOD (770–476 BCE)
Bronze; h. 41 x w. 23.5 cm
Unearthed in 1988 from tomb No. 251, Jinsheng village,
Taiyuan, Shanxi Province
Shanxi Provincial Institute of Archaeology, Taiyuan

45.

Square-based vessel (*fang hu*) with lotus-petal crown and crane

EASTERN ZHOU, SPRING AND AUTUMN PERIOD (770–476 BCE)
Bronze; h. 126 x l. of mouth 30.5 x w. of mouth 24.9 cm
Unearthed in 1923 at Lijialou, Xinzheng county,
Henan Province
Henan Provincial Museum, Zhengzhou

46.

Mythical beast

Eastern Zhou, Spring and Autumn period (770–476 bce)

Bronze inlaid with malachite; h. 48 cm

Unearthed in 1990 from Xujialing tomb No. 9,

Xichuan county, Henan Province

Henan Provincial Institute of Archaeology and Cultural

Relics, Zhengzhou

47.

Tapir bearing figure holding interlace tray

Eastern Zhou, Warring States period (475–221 BCE)

Bronze; h. 15 cm, diam. of tray 11 cm

Unearthed in 1965 at Fenshuiling, Changzhi,

Shanxi Province

Shanxi Provincial Museum, Taiyuan

48.

**Rectangular basin (*pan*) with turtle, fish, and
interlacing dragon designs**

(Detail on facing page)

EASTERN ZHOU, WARRING STATES PERIOD (475–221 BCE)

Bronze; h. 22.5 x l. 73.2 x w. 45.2 cm

Palace Museum, Beijing

49.

Chariot fitting with mythical hunting scenes

(Detail on facing page)

WESTERN HAN DYNASTY (206 BCE–8 CE)

Bronze inlaid with gold, silver, and turquoise; h. 26.4 cm, diam. 3.5 cm

Unearthed in 1965 from Sanpanshan tomb No. 122, Ding county, Hebei Province

Hebei Provincial Institute of Cultural Relics, Shijiazhuang

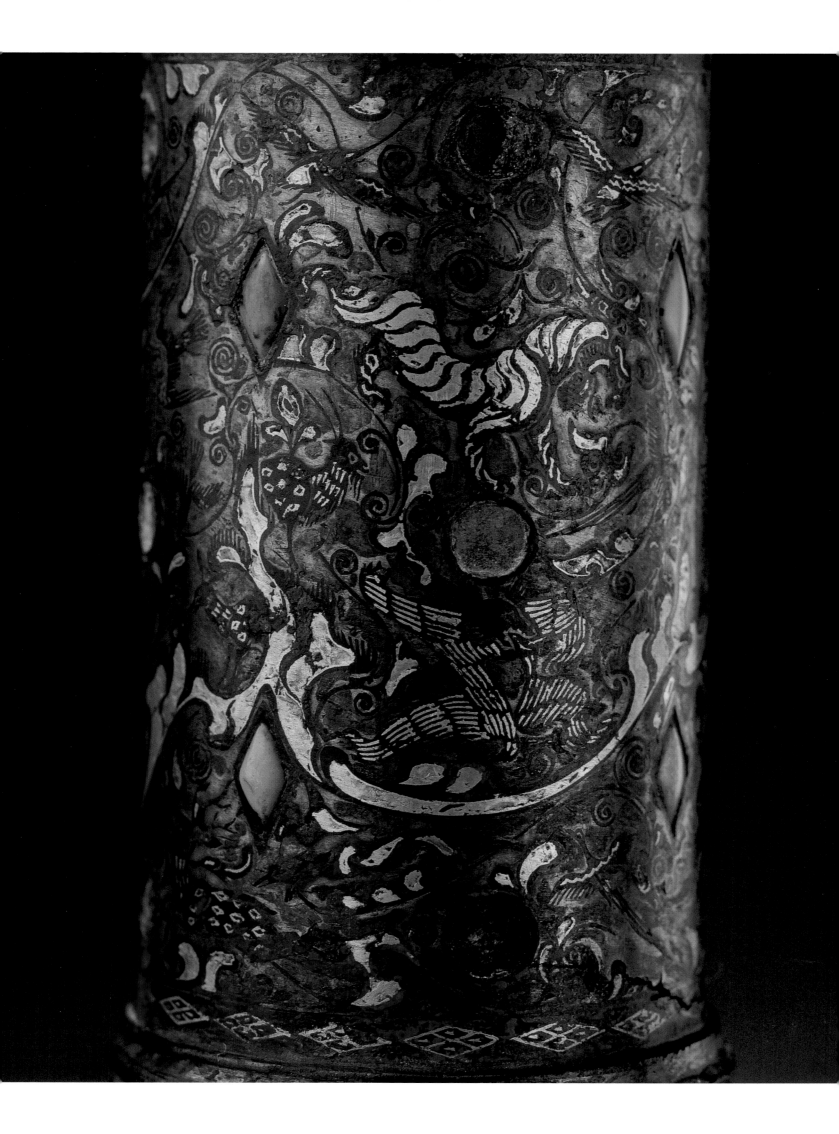

50.

**Incense burner in the shape of a magical mountain isle
of the immortals**

WESTERN HAN DYNASTY (206 BCE–8 CE)

Bronze inlaid with silver, gold, and turquoise; h. 26 cm,
max. diam. 12.3 cm, diam. of foot 9.7 cm

Unearthed in 1968 from the tomb of Prince Liu Sheng,
Mancheng county, Hebei Province

Hebei Provincial Museum, Shijiazhuang

51.

**Covered vessel (*lian* or *zun*) with mythical hunting
scenes, inscribed and dated (26 CE?)**

Eastern Han dynasty (25–220)

Gilt bronze; h. 24.5 cm, diam. of mouth 23.4 cm

Unearthed in 1962 at Dachuan village, Youyu county,
Shanxi Province

Shanxi Provincial Museum, Taiyuan

52.

**Screen support in the shape of a kneeling figure biting
and holding snakes**

WESTERN HAN DYNASTY (206 BCE–8 CE)

Gilt bronze; h. 31.5 x l. 15.8 cm

Unearthed in 1983 from the tomb of the king of Nanyue,
Guangzhou, Guangdong Province

Museum of the Tomb of the Nanyue King of the Western
Han Dynasty, Guangzhou

53.
Lamp in the shape of a goose holding a fish
WESTERN HAN DYNASTY (206 BCE–8 CE)
Bronze with paint; h. 53.8 x l. 31.3 cm
Unearthed in 1985 at Zhaoshiba village, Pingshuo,
Shanxi Province
Shanxi Provincial Museum, Taiyuan

54.

**Lamp with fifteen oil saucers in the form of a
mythical tree**

(Detail on facing page)

Eastern Zhou, Warring States period (475–221 BCE)

Bronze; h. 82.6 cm

Unearthed in 1977 from the tomb of the king of
Zhongshan, Pingshan county, Hebei Province

Hebei Provincial Institute of Cultural Relics, Shijiazhuang

55.
Spear head with hanging men
WESTERN HAN DYNASTY (206 BCE–8 CE)
Bronze; h. 41.5 cm
Unearthed in 1956 at Shizhaishan, Jinning county,
Yunnan Province
Yunnan Provincial Museum, Kunming

56.

Buckle ornament with dancers holding cymbals

Western Han dynasty (206 bce–8 ce)

Gilt bronze; h. 12 x l. 18.5 cm

Unearthed in 1956 at Shizhaishan, Jinning county,

Yunnan Province

Yunnan Provincial Museum, Kunming

57.

Low offering stand with two bulls and pouncing tiger

EASTERN ZHOU, WARRING STATES PERIOD (475–221 BCE)

Bronze; h. 43 x l. 76 cm

Unearthed in 1972 from Lijiashan tomb No. 24,

Jiangchuan county, Yunnan Province

Yunnan Provincial Museum, Kunming

58.

Man holding parasol

WESTERN HAN DYNASTY (206 BCE–8 CE)

Bronze; h. of man 55.5 cm, h. of parasol 110.5 cm

Unearthed in 1956 at Shizhaishan, Jinning county,

Yunnan Province

Yunnan Provincial Museum, Kunming

59.

Rearing dragon

Tang dynasty (618–907)

Gilt bronze and iron; h. 34 x l. 28 cm

Unearthed in 1975 at Caochangpo in the southern suburb

of Xi'an, Shaanxi Province

Shaanxi History Museum, Xi'an

60.

Six-lobed plate with design of mythical beast

Tang dynasty (618–907)

Silver with gilding; h. 1.2 cm, diam. 15.3 cm

Unearthed in 1970 at Hejia village, Xi'an, Shaanxi Province

Shaanxi History Museum, Xi'an

61.

Six-lobed plate with design of bear

TANG DYNASTY (618–907)

Silver with gilding; h. 1 cm, diam. 13.4 cm

Unearthed in 1970 at Hejia village, Xi'an, Shaanxi Province

Shaanxi History Museum, Xi'an

62.

Plate in the shape of two peach halves with design of two foxes

Tang dynasty (618–907)

Silver with gilding; h. 1.5 x max. width 22.5 cm

Unearthed in 1970 at Hejia village, Xi'an, Shaanxi Province

Shaanxi History Museum, Xi'an

63.

Censer found with figure of Ganesha

(Detail on facing page)

TANG DYNASTY (618–907)

Silver with gilding; h. 41.8 cm, diam. of mouth 24.5 cm

Discovered in 1987 in underground chamber of the Famen

Temple Pagoda, Fufeng county, Shaanxi Province

Famen Temple Museum, Shaanxi Province

64.

**Storage container with bird designs for holding
brick tea**

TANG DYNASTY (618–907)

Silver with gilding; h. 17.8 cm, diam. 16.1 cm

Discovered in 1987 in underground chamber of the Famen
Temple Pagoda, Fufeng county, Shaanxi Province

Famen Temple Museum, Shaanxi Province

65.

Jar with design of figures in a landscape

TANG DYNASTY (618–907)

Silver with gilding; h. 24.7 cm, diam. of jar 12.3 cm,
diam. of foot 12.6 cm

Discovered in 1987 in underground chamber of the Famen
Temple Pagoda, Fufeng county, Shaanxi Province

Famen Temple Museum, Shaanxi Province

Lacquer

66.

Vessel based on bronze *hu* vessel

WESTERN HAN DYNASTY (206 BCE–8 CE)

Wood-core lacquer; h. 57 cm, diam. of mouth 18.1 cm,
diam. of foot 20 cm

Unearthed in 1972 from Mawangdui tomb No. 1,
Changsha, Hunan Province

Hunan Provincial Museum, Changsha

67.
Set of eight cups
Western Han dynasty (206 BCE–8 CE)
Wood-core lacquer; h. 12.2 cm, w. 16–19 cm
Unearthed in 1972 from Mawangdui tomb No. 1,
Changsha, Hunan Province
Hunan Provincial Museum, Changsha

68.

Rectangular box with cloud designs

WESTERN HAN DYNASTY (206 BCE–8 CE)

Wood-core lacquer; h. 21 x l. 48.5 x w. 25.5 cm

Unearthed in 1972 from Mawangdui tomb No. 3,

Changsha, Hunan Province

Hunan Provincial Museum, Changsha

69.

Round tray with scroll designs

Western Han dynasty (206 bce–8 ce)

Wood-core lacquer; h. 4.5 cm, diam. 53.7 cm

Unearthed in 1972 from Mawangdui tomb No. 1,

Changsha, Hunan Province

Hunan Provincial Museum, Changsha

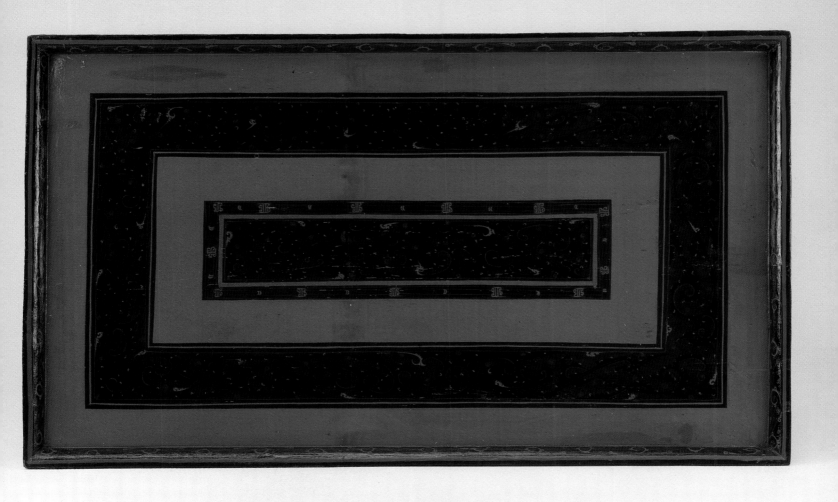

70.

Rectangular tray with scroll designs

WESTERN HAN DYNASTY (206 BCE–8 CE)

Wood-core lacquer; l. 75.6 cm

Unearthed in 1972 from Mawangdui tomb No. 1,

Changsha, Hunan Province

Hunan Provincial Museum, Changsha

71.

Round box with painted and incised designs

(Detail on facing page)

WESTERN HAN DYNASTY (206 BCE–8 CE)

Wood-core lacquer; h. 18 cm, diam. 32 cm

Unearthed in 1972 from Mawangdui tomb No. 3,

Changsha, Hunan Province

Hunan Provincial Museum, Changsha

72.

Reliquary with Buddhist figures

NORTHERN SONG DYNASTY (960–1127)

Wood-core lacquer with seed pearls; h. 41.2 x w. 24.5 cm

Unearthed in 1966 at the Huiguang Pagoda site, Rui'an,

Zhejiang Province

Zhejiang Provincial Museum, Hangzhou

73.

Sutra boxes with Buddhist figures

NORTHERN SONG DYNASTY (960–1127)

Wood-core lacquer with seed pearls; (outside box) h. 16 x
l. 40 x w. 18 cm, (inside box) h. 11.5 x l. 33.8 x w. 11 cm

Unearthed in 1966 at the Huiguang Pagoda site, Rui'an,
Zhejiang Province

Zhejiang Provincial Museum, Hangzhou

74.

Round covered box with aged scholar and servant

Dated to 1351

Yuan dynasty (1279–1368)

Carved lacquer on a fabric-covered wood core;

diam. 12.1 cm

Unearthed in 1953 from the tomb of the Ren family,

Qingpu county, Shanghai

Shanghai Museum

75.

**Round covered box with figures viewing a waterfall,
inscribed**

Ming dynasty, Yongle mark and period (1403–1424)

Carved lacquer on a fabric-covered wood core; h. 7.7 cm,
diam. of mouth 22 cm

Palace Museum, Beijing

Textiles

76.
Potpourri bag
WESTERN HAN DYNASTY (206 BCE–8 CE)
Chain-stitch embroidery on patterned silk; l. 48 cm
Unearthed in 1972 from Mawangdui tomb No. 1,
Changsha, Hunan Province
Hunan Provincial Museum, Changsha

77.
**Gauze with patterns of pine-bark lozenges, signifying
longevity**
WESTERN HAN DYNASTY (206 BCE–8 CE)
Silk gauze; l. 75 x w. 48 cm
Unearthed in 1972 from Mawangdui tomb No. 1,
Changsha, Hunan Province
Hunan Provincial Museum, Changsha

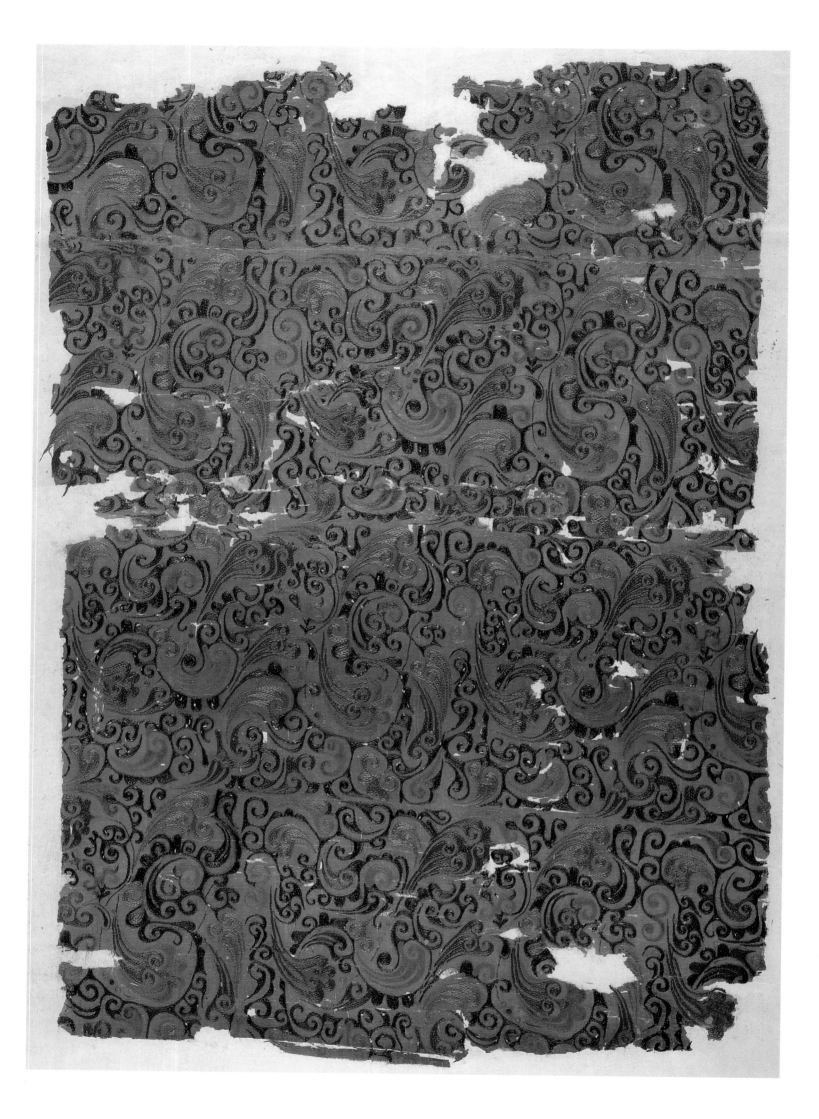

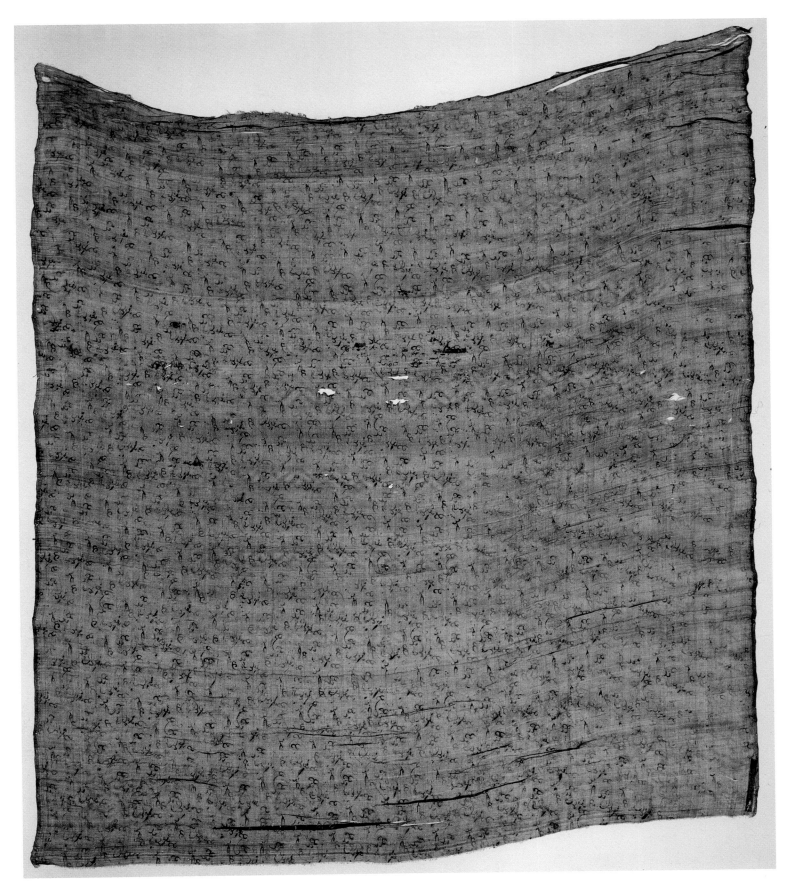

78.

Embroidered silk with designs signifying longevity

Western Han dynasty (206 bce–8 ce)

Chain-stitch embroidery on silk tabby; l. 23 x w. 16 cm

Unearthed in 1972 from Mawangdui tomb No. 1,

Changsha, Hunan Province

Hunan Provincial Museum, Changsha

79.

Printed silk with small scroll motifs

Western Han dynasty (206 bce–8 ce)

Silk tabby with printed and drawn designs; l. 48 x w. 53 cm

Unearthed in 1972 from Mawangdui tomb No. 1,

Changsha, Hunan Province

Hunan Provincial Museum, Changsha

80.

Embroidered textile with cloud design

WESTERN HAN DYNASTY (206 BCE–8 CE)

Chain-stitch embroidery on silk tabby; l. 17 x w. 14.5 cm

Unearthed in 1972 from Mawangdui tomb No. 1,

Changsha, Hunan Province

Hunan Provincial Museum, Changsha

81.

Coverlet with dragon design

LIAO DYNASTY (916–1125)

Silk tapestry (*kesi*) with gold threads; h. 90 x w. 56.5 cm

Unearthed in 1974 at Yemaotai, Faku county,

Liaoning Province

Liaoning Provincial Museum, Shenyang

82.

Zhu Kerou

Camellias

SOUTHERN SONG DYNASTY (1127–1279)

Silk tapestry (*kesi*), mounted as album leaf; 25. 6 x 25.3 cm

Liaoning Provincial Museum, Shenyang

83.

Garden rocks with chrysanthemum, high mallow, and begonia, after a painting by Cui Bai (act. ca. 1060–1085)

SOUTHERN SONG DYNASTY (1127–1279)

Silk tapestry (*kesi*); 102.5 x 43.6 cm

Liaoning Provincial Museum, Shenyang

84.

Heavenly King of the West

(Detail on facing page)

YUAN DYNASTY (1279–1368)

Silk embroidery; 250.8 x 247.7 cm

Donated in 1949 by Mr. Fei Zhenshan

National Museum of Chinese History, Beijing

85.

King of Bright Wisdom Budong

YUAN DYNASTY (1279–1368)

Silk tapestry (*kesi*); 90 x 56 cm

Administrative Office of Norbu Linka, Lhasa,

Autonomous Region of Tibet

86.

Śākyamuni Buddha

QING DYNASTY (1644–1911)

Silk tapestry (*kesi*); 182.7 x 77.6 cm

Liaoning Provincial Museum, Shenyang

87.

Li Bai's "Evening in the Peach and Plum Garden"

(Full image on facing page; detail above)

QING DYNASTY (1644–1911)

Silk tapestry (*kesi*); 135.5 x 70.2 cm

Liaoning Provincial Museum, Shenyang

Grave Goods

88.

General

Qin dynasty (221–207 bce)

Terra-cotta; h. 196 cm

Unearthed in 1977 from the Qin Shihuangdi tomb,
pit No. 1, Lintong county, Shaanxi Province

Museum of Terra-cotta Warriors and Horses of Qin
Shihuangdi, Xi'an

89.
Military officer
QIN DYNASTY (221–207 BCE)
Terra-cotta; h. 198 cm
Unearthed in 1977 from the Qin Shihuangdi tomb,
pit No. 1, Lintong county, Shaanxi Province
Museum of Terra-cotta Warriors and Horses of Qin
Shihuangdi, Xi'an

90.

Military officer

QIN DYNASTY (221–207 BCE)

Terra-cotta; h. 192 cm

Unearthed in 1977 from the Qin Shihuangdi tomb,

pit No. 1, Lintong county, Shaanxi Province

Museum of Terra-cotta Warriors and Horses of Qin

Shihuangdi, Xi'an

91.

Soldier

QIN DYNASTY (221–207 BCE)

Terra-cotta; h. 185 cm

Unearthed in 1977 from the Qin Shihuangdi tomb,
pit No. 1, Lintong county, Shaanxi Province
Museum of Terra-cotta Warriors and Horses of Qin
Shihuangdi, Xi'an

92.

Chariot horse

QIN DYNASTY (221–207 BCE)

Terra-cotta; h. 163 x l. 200 cm

Unearthed in 1977 from the Qin Shihuangdi tomb,
pit No. 1, Lintong county, Shaanxi Province

Museum of Terra-cotta Warriors and Horses of Qin
Shihuangdi, Xi'an

93.
Chimera (*bixie*)
EASTERN HAN DYNASTY (25–220)
Stone; h. 114 x l. 175 x w. 45 cm
Unearthed in Yichuan county, Henan Province
Guanlin Museum of Stone Sculpture, Luoyang

94.

Five kneeling musicians

WESTERN HAN DYNASTY (206 BCE–8 CE)

Painted wood; h. 32.5–38 cm

Unearthed in 1972 from Mawangdui tomb No. 1,

Changsha, Hunan Province

Hunan Provincial Museum, Changsha

95.

Standing figure

WESTERN HAN DYNASTY (206 BCE–8 CE)

Painted wood; h. 47 cm

Unearthed in 1972 from Mawangdui tomb No. 1,

Changsha, Hunan Province

Hunan Provincial Museum, Changsha

96.

Standing performer with a drum

Eastern Han dynasty (25–220)

Earthenware with pigment; h. 66.5 cm

Unearthed in 1963 in Pi county, Sichuan Province

Sichuan Provincial Museum, Chengdu

97.

Squatting performer with a drum

EASTERN HAN DYNASTY (25–220)

Earthenware with pigment; h. 48 cm

Unearthed in 1982 from Majiashan tomb No. 23,
Sanhexiang, Xindu county, Sichuan Province

Administrative Office for Cultural Relics, Xindu county,
Sichuan Province

98.

Tomb guardian holding an ax and a snake

EASTERN HAN DYNASTY (25–220)

Earthenware; h. 87.2 cm

Unearthed in 1957 from the Huangshui Xiang'ai tomb,

Shuangliu county, Sichuan Province

Sichuan Provincial Museum, Chengdu

99.

Kneeling woman holding a mirror

EASTERN HAN DYNASTY (25–220)

Earthenware with red pigments; h. 61.4 cm

Unearthed in 1963 in Pi county, Sichuan Province

Sichuan Provincial Museum, Chengdu

100.

Model of tower and pond with animals

EASTERN HAN DYNASTY (25–220)

Glazed earthenware; h. 45 cm, diam. of basin 55 cm

Unearthed in 1964 in Xichuan county, Henan Province

Henan Provincial Museum, Zhengzhou

101.

Recumbent dog

EASTERN HAN DYNASTY (25–220)

Glazed earthenware; h. 47 x l. 44 x w. 20 cm

Unearthed at Nanyang, Henan Province

Nanyang Municipal Museum

102.

Tower

Han dynasty (206 bce–220 ce)

Earthenware; h. 147 cm

Unearthed in 1952 at Jiunüzhong, Huaiyang county,
Henan Province

Henan Provincial Museum, Zhengzhou

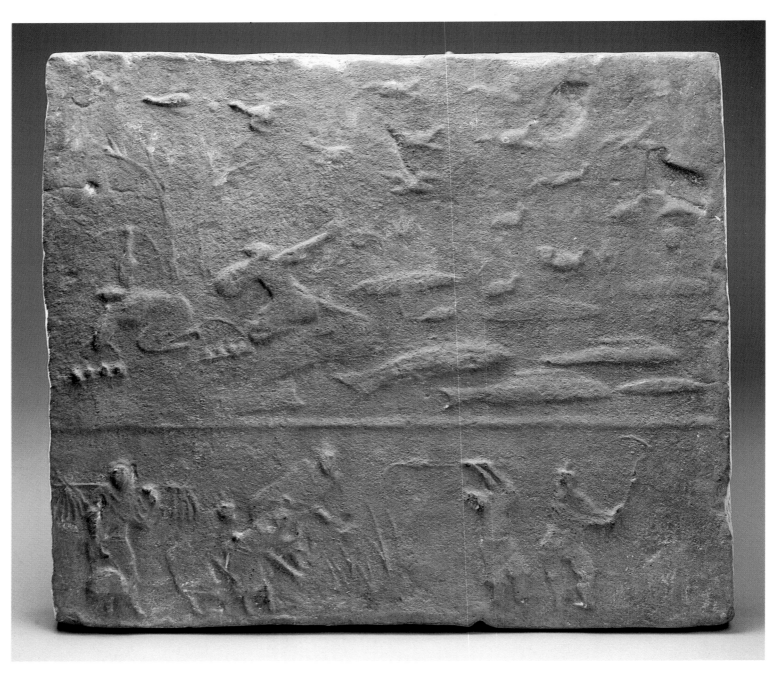

103.

Tomb tile with scenes of hunting and harvesting

(Rubbing at right)

Eastern Han dynasty (25–220)

Earthenware; l. 44.5 x w. 39.6 x d. 6.5 cm

Unearthed in 1972 at Anren village, Dayi county,

Sichuan Province

Sichuan Provincial Museum, Chengdu

104.

Tomb tile with carriage and horses

(Rubbing at right)

Eastern Han dynasty (25–220)

Earthenware; l. 45 x w. 39.5 x d. 6.5 cm

Unearthed in 1955 from Qingbaixiang tomb No. 1,

Xinfan county, Sichuan Province

Sichuan Provincial Museum, Chengdu

105.

Three aristocratic women

Tang dynasty (618–907)

Earthenware with pigment; h. 73–83 cm

Unearthed in 1985 at Hansenzhai, Xi'an, Shaanxi Province

Institute for the Protection of Cultural Relics, Xi'an

106.

Horse

Tang dynasty (618–907)

Earthenware with pigment; h. 87 x l. 93 cm

Unearthed in Luoyang, Henan Province

Henan Provincial Museum, Zhengzhou

107.

Camel

Tang dynasty (618–907)

Earthenware with *sancai* ("three-color") glaze;

h. 81 x l. 68 cm

Unearthed in 1973 at Guanlin, Luoyang, Henan Province

Luoyang Cultural Relics Work Team, Henan Province

108.

Set of twelve calendrical animals

(Detail on facing page)

Tang dynasty (618–907)

Earthenware with pigment; h. 38.5–41.5 cm

Unearthed in 1955 in the suburbs of Xi'an,

Shaanxi Province

Shaanxi History Museum, Xi'an

109.
Civil official
TANG DYNASTY (618–907)
Earthenware with *sancai* ("three-color") glaze; h. 107 cm
Unearthed at Guanlin, Luoyang, Henan Province
Luoyang Municipal Museum

110.

Tomb guardian

TANG DYNASTY (618–907)

Earthenware with *sancai* ("three-color") glaze; h. 103.5 cm

Unearthed in 1981 from the tomb of An Pu at Longmen, Luoyang, Henan Province

Luoyang Cultural Relics Work Team, Henan Province

III.
Heavenly king
TANG DYNASTY (618–907)
Earthenware with *sancai* ("three-color") glaze; h. 113 cm
Unearthed at Guanlin, Luoyang, Henan Province
Luoyang Municipal Museum

112.

Four brick reliefs with figures

YUAN DYNASTY (1279–1368)

Earthenware; (1) h. 35 x l. 35.8 x w. 21 cm (2) h. 34 x
l. 29 x w. 22.5 cm (3) h. 34 x l. 31 x w. 19.5 cm (4) h. 35 x
l. 19.5 x w. 10 cm

Unearthed in 1973 at Xifengfeng village, Jiaozuo,
Henan Province

Henan Provincial Museum, Zhengzhou

Ceramics

113.

Bowl with stylized floral or leaf designs

Neolithic period, Yangshao culture, Miaodigou type
(4th millennium BCE)
Red earthenware with black pigment;
h. 23 cm, max. diam. 36 cm
Unearthed in 1979 in Fangshan county, Shanxi Province
Shanxi Provincial Institute of Archaeology, Taiyuan

114.

Basin with human head and fish designs

Neolithic period, Yangshao culture, Banpo type
(late 6th–5th millennium BCE)
Red earthenware with black pigment; h. 15.5 cm,
diam. of mouth 39.5 cm
Unearthed in 1955 at Banpo village, near Xi'an,
Shaanxi Province
National Museum of Chinese History, Beijing

115.

Vessel in the shape of an owl

Neolithic period, Yangshao culture, Miaodigou type
(4th millennium BCE)

Black earthenware; h. 35.8 cm

Unearthed in 1959 at Taiping village, Hua county,
Shaanxi Province

National Museum of Chinese History, Beijing

116.

Bottle in the shape of a bird or dolphin

NEOLITHIC PERIOD, LIANGZHU CULTURE

(ca. 3600–ca. 2000 BCE)

Gray earthenware; l. 32.4 x w. 11.7 cm

Unearthed in 1960 at Meiyan, Wujiang county,

Jiangsu Province

Nanjing Museum

117.

Jar with incised animal mask designs

SHANG PERIOD (ca. 1600–ca. 1100 BCE)

White earthenware; h. 22.1 cm, diam. of mouth 9.1 cm,

diam. of foot 8.9 cm

Unearthed at Anyang, Henan Province

Palace Museum, Beijing

118.

Jar (*zun*) with mat impressions

SHANG PERIOD (ca. 1600–ca. 1100 BCE)

Ash-glazed stoneware (protoporcelain); h. 27 cm,
diam. of mouth 27 cm

Unearthed in 1965 at Zhengzhou, Henan Province

Zhengzhou Municipal Museum

119.
**Candleholder in the shape of a man riding
a mythical beast**
WESTERN JIN DYNASTY (265–316)
Green-glazed stoneware (Celadon), Yue kilns; h. 27.7 cm
Palace Museum, Beijing

120.
Basin with applied Buddha figure
WESTERN JIN DYNASTY (265–316)
Green-glazed stoneware (Celadon), Yue kilns; h. 7.5 cm,
diam. of mouth 19.4 cm, diam. of foot 10 cm
National Museum of Chinese History, Beijing

121.

Jar with six lugs and incised bird and tree motifs
NORTHERN QI DYNASTY (550–577)
Green-glazed stoneware (Celadon); h. 28.5 cm,
max. diam. of mouth 18.5 cm
Unearthed in 1958 from the tomb of Li Yun,
Puyang county, Henan Province
Henan Provincial Museum, Zhengzhou

122.

Chicken-headed ewer with dragon handle
NORTHERN QI DYNASTY (550–577)
Green-glazed stoneware (Celadon); h. 48.2 cm,
max. diam. 32.5 cm
Unearthed in 1978 from the tomb of Lou Rui, Taiyuan,
Shanxi Province
Shanxi Provincial Institute of Archaeology, Taiyuan

123.
Octagonal bottle
TANG DYNASTY (618–907)
Green-glazed stoneware (Celadon), Yue kilns; h. 21.7 cm,
diam. of mouth 2.3, diam. of foot 7.8 cm
Palace Museum, Beijing

124.
Bowl
TANG DYNASTY (618–907)
Green-glazed stoneware (Celadon), Yue kilns; h. 6.8 cm,
diam. of mouth 22.4 cm
Discovered in 1987 in underground chamber of the Famen
Temple Pagoda, Fufeng county, Shaanxi Province
Shaanxi History Museum, Xi'an

125.

Octagonal bottle

TANG DYNASTY (618–907)

Green-glazed stoneware (Celadon), Yue kilns; h. 21.5 cm,
diam. of mouth 2.2 cm, diam. of foot 8 cm

Discovered in 1987 in underground chamber of the Famen
Temple Pagoda, Fufeng county, Shaanxi Province

Famen Temple Museum, Shaanxi Province

126.

Dish in the shape of a five-petaled blossom, base inscribed with character *guan* ("official")

TANG DYNASTY (618–907)

White stoneware with transparent glaze, Xing or
Ding kilns; h. 3.5 cm, diam. of mouth 13.8 cm,
diam. of foot 6.45 cm
Unearthed in 1985 at Huoshaobi, Xi'an, Shaanxi Province
Institute for the Protection of Cultural Relics, Xi'an

127.

Dish in the shape of a three-petaled blossom, base inscribed with character *guan* ("official")

TANG DYNASTY (618–907)

White stoneware with transparent glaze, Xing or
Ding kilns; h. 2.3 x w. 11.7 cm, diam. of foot 5.9 cm
Unearthed in 1985 at Huoshaobi, Xi'an, Shaanxi Province
Institute for the Protection of Cultural Relics, Xi'an

128.

Covered jar with four lugs

FIVE DYNASTIES (907–960)

White stoneware with transparent glaze, Xing or
Ding kilns; h. 26.2 cm, diam. of mouth 10.4 cm,
diam. of foot 9.1 cm

Donated by Mr. Zhou Rui

Shanghai Museum

129.

Bowl inscribed with characters *yang ding*
("glorious Ding")

Five Dynasties (907–960)

White stoneware with transparent glaze, Ding kilns;

h. 6.3 cm, diam. of mouth 19.9 cm, diam. of foot 7.5 cm

Donated by Mr. Huang Zhaoxi

Shanghai Museum

130.

Bottle with carved and combed peony designs

NORTHERN SONG DYNASTY (960–1127)

Green-glazed stoneware, Yaozhou kilns; h. 19.9 cm,
diam. of mouth 6.9 cm, diam. of foot 7.8 cm

Palace Museum, Beijing

131.

Bowl with incised ducks and water weeds

NORTHERN SONG DYNASTY (960–1127)

White stoneware with transparent glaze and bronze
rim band, Ding kilns; h. 6.4 cm, diam. of mouth 23.5 cm,
diam. of foot 7.3 cm

Shanghai Museum

132.

**Tripod vessel in the shape of an archaic
bronze *lian* or *zun* vessel**

NORTHERN SONG DYNASTY (960–1127)
Pale blue-green–glazed stoneware, Ru kilns;
h. 12.9 cm, diam. of mouth 18 cm
Palace Museum, Beijing

133.
Mallow-shaped bowl
(View from below at right)
SOUTHERN SONG DYNASTY (1127–1279)
Crackled pale blue-green–glazed stoneware, Hangzhou
Guan ("official") kilns; h. 4.2 cm, diam. of mouth 17.3 cm,
diam. of foot 9.9 cm
Palace Museum, Beijing

134.
Vase with dish-shaped mouth and raised ribs
SOUTHERN SONG DYNASTY (1127–1279)
Crackled pale blue-green–glazed stoneware,
Longquan kilns; h. 31 cm, diam. of mouth 10.4 cm,
diam. of foot 11. 3 cm
Palace Museum, Beijing

135.
Jar with incised floral designs
NORTHERN SONG DYNASTY (960–1127)
Bluish–glazed white stoneware (*qingbai*), Jingdezhen kilns;
h. 26.6 cm, diam. of mouth 5 cm, diam. of foot 8.5 cm
Palace Museum, Beijing

136.

Vase with carved peony designs

NORTHERN SONG DYNASTY (960–1127)

Cizhou-type stoneware with white slip and transparent
glaze; h. 34 cm, diam. of mouth 6 cm

Unearthed in 1959 in Tangyin county, Henan Province

Henan Provincial Museum, Zhengzhou

137.
**Pillow with painted design of a hawk chasing
a rabbit among reeds**
JIN DYNASTY (1115–1234)
Cizhou-type stoneware with white slip, black pigment,
and transparent glaze; h. 9.7 x l. 24.7 x w. 17 cm
Henan Provincial Museum, Zhengzhou

138.

**Vase with two leopards incised on a
ring-matted ground**
Northern Song dynasty (960–1127)
Stoneware with white slip and transparent glaze,
Dengfeng kilns; h. 32.1 cm, diam. of mouth 7.1 cm,
diam. of foot 9.9 cm
Palace Museum, Beijing

139.

Covered jar with floral designs in painted applied openwork

(View of lid above; full view on facing page)

YUAN DYNASTY (1279–1368)

Porcelain with underglaze cobalt blue and copper red
painted and applied decoration, Jingdezhen kilns;
h. 42.3 cm, diam. of mouth 15.2 cm, diam. of foot 18.5 cm
Unearthed in 1964 from a Yuan dynasty hoard at Baoding,
Hebei Province
Palace Museum, Beijing

140.

Covered jar with three lugs

MING DYNASTY, YONGLE PERIOD (1403–1424)

Pale green-glazed porcelain, Jingdezhen kilns;

h. 10.4 cm, diam. of mouth 9.9 cm, diam. of foot 14.1 cm

Palace Museum, Beijing

141.

Flower-shaped brush washer

MING DYNASTY, XUANDE MARK AND PERIOD (1426–1435)

Copper red-glazed porcelain, Jingdezhen kilns;

h. 3.8 cm, width of mouth 15.9 cm, diam. of foot 13 cm

Palace Museum, Beijing

142.
Moon flask with dragons among lotus scrolls
MING DYNASTY, YONGLE PERIOD (1403–1424)
Porcelain with underglaze cobalt blue decoration,
Jingdezhen kilns; h. 44 cm, diam. of mouth 8 cm,
diam. of foot 14.5 cm
Palace Museum, Beijing

143.
Jar with flowering plum, bamboo, and pine
MING DYNASTY, YONGLE PERIOD (1403–1424)
Porcelain with underglaze cobalt blue decoration,
Jingdezhen kilns; h. 36 cm, diam. of mouth 6.7 cm,
diam. of foot 13.9 cm
Palace Museum, Beijing

144.
Stem bowl with scenes of ladies in a garden
MING DYNASTY, XUANDE MARK AND PERIOD (1426–1435)
Porcelain with underglaze cobalt blue decoration,
Jingdezhen kilns; h. 10.2 cm, diam. of mouth 15.5 cm,
diam. of foot 4.5 cm
Palace Museum, Beijing

145.
Vase with flower and bird designs
Qing dynasty, Kangxi period (1662–1722)
Porcelain with *wucai* ("five–color") decoration,
Jingdezhen kilns; h. 46.4 cm, diam. of mouth 11.2 cm,
diam. of foot 14.7 cm
Palace Museum, Beijing

146.
Vase with flower designs
Qing dynasty, Yongzheng mark and period (1723–1735)
Porcelain with *doucai* ("clashing" or "matched color")
decoration, Jingdezhen kilns; h. 26 cm, diam. of mouth
5.2 cm, diam. of foot 11.8 cm
Palace Museum, Beijing

Sculpture

147.
Stele with Maitreya
Dated to 471
NORTHERN WEI DYNASTY (386–534)
Sandstone; h. 86.9 x w. 55 cm
Unearthed in Xingping county, Shaanxi Province
Forest of Steles Museum, Xi'an

148.
Śākyamuni on lion throne
Dated to 502
NORTHERN WEI DYNASTY (386–534)
Sandstone; h. 48.5 x w. 27.7 cm
Found in 1952
Forest of Steles Museum, Xi'an

149.
Stele with Śākyamuni and bodhisattvas
NORTHERN WEI DYNASTY (386–534)
Stone; h. 96 x w. 43.5 cm
Unearthed in 1974 in Qi county, Henan Province
Henan Provincial Museum, Zhengzhou

150.

Stele with Śākyamuni and attendants

(Reverse on facing page)

Dated to 523

LIANG DYNASTY (502–557)

Sandstone; h. 35.8 x w. 30.3 x d. 20 cm

Unearthed in 1954 at the Wanfo Temple site, Chengdu,

Sichuan Province

Sichuan Provincial Museum, Chengdu

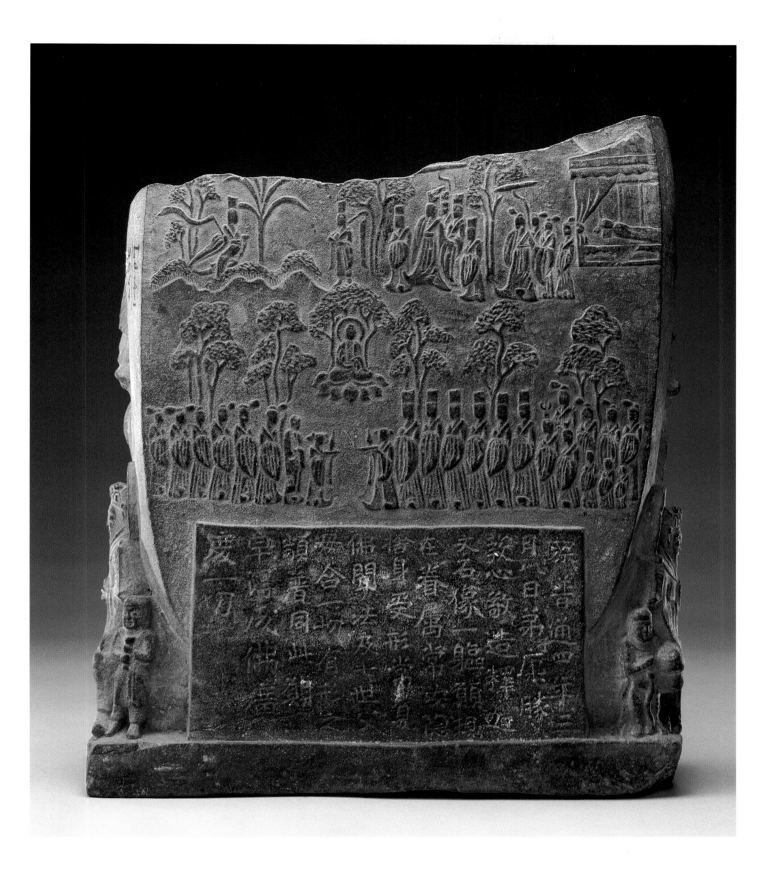

151.

Stele: (obverse) bodhisattvas; (reverse) lower tier, figures, animals, and buildings in mountainous landscape; middle panel, lotus pond; upper tier, Buddha preaching to monks in garden setting

(Detail of reverse on facing page)

LIANG DYNASTY (502–557)

Sandstone; h. 121 x w. 60 x d. 24.5 cm

Unearthed in 1954 at the Wanfo Temple site, Chengdu, Sichuan Province

Sichuan Provincial Museum, Chengdu

152.

Engraved panel with Buddha beneath canopy

Dated to 524

NORTHERN WEI DYNASTY (386–534)

Stone; h. 39.5 x l. 144 x w. 14 cm

Unearthed in the late 19th century in Luoyang,

Henan Province

Henan Provincial Museum, Zhengzhou

153.
Pillar base with mountains, dragons, and figures
NORTHERN WEI DYNASTY (386–534)
Stone; h. 16.5 x w. 32 cm
Unearthed in 1966 from the Sima Jinlong tomb, Shijiazhai,
Datong city, Shanxi Province
Shanxi Provincial Museum, Taiyuan

154.
Stele with Śākyamuni and Maitreya
Dated to 532
NORTHERN WEI DYNASTY (386–534)
Sandstone; h. 90 x w. 46 x d. 14 cm
Institute for the Protection of Cultural Relics, Xi'an

155.
Stele: (obverse) Śākyamuni and attendants;
(reverse) Maitreya
WESTERN WEI DYNASTY (535–557)
Sandstone; h. 48.2 x w. 21.5 x d. 12.1 cm
Institute for the Protection of Cultural Relics, Xi'an

156.
Śākyamuni
Dated to 540
EASTERN WEI DYNASTY (534–550)
Sandstone; h. 35 cm
Unearthed in 1954 at the Huata Temple site, Taiyuan,
Shanxi Province
Shanxi Provincial Museum, Taiyuan

157.
**Stele with enthroned Buddhas and attendant
bodhisattvas and monks**
Dated to 559
NORTHERN QI DYNASTY (550–577)
Limestone; h. 110 x w. 58.5 x d. 10 cm
Unearthed in 1963 in Xiangcheng county, Henan Province
Henan Provincial Museum, Zhengzhou

158.

Stele: (obverse) Śākyamuni and attendants;
(reverse) myriad Buddhas

(Detail on facing page)

Dated to 565

NORTHERN ZHOU DYNASTY (557–581)

Stone; h. 259 x w. 73.4 x d. 19.5 cm

Unearthed in 1963 in Luoning county, Henan Province

Henan Provincial Museum, Zhengzhou

159.

Stele with Buddhist trinity

NORTHERN ZHOU DYNASTY (557–581)

Marble; h. 40 x w. 28 x d. 8.5 cm

Unearthed in 1975 at Caotan in the northern suburb of
Xi'an, Shaanxi Province

Institute for the Protection of Cultural Relics, Xi'an

160.

Amitābha altar

Dated to 584

SUI DYNASTY (581–618)

Gilt bronze; h. 41 cm, l. of altar stand 24.3 cm, w. of altar
stand 24 cm

Unearthed in 1974 at Bali village, Xi'an, Shaanxi Province

Institute for the Protection of Cultural Relics, Xi'an

161.

Stele with Śākyamuni and attendants

NORTHERN QI DYNASTY (550–577)

Sandstone with polychrome; h. 46 x w. 27 cm

Unearthed in 1954 at the Huata Temple site, Taiyuan,

Shanxi Province

Shanxi Provincial Museum

162.

Seated Buddha

SUI DYNASTY (581–618)

Marble with pigments; h. 100.7 x w. 74.7 cm

Palace Museum, Beijing

163.

Head of a bodhisattva

TANG DYNASTY (618–907)

Sandstone; h. 36 cm

Unearthed in 1954 at the Wanfo Temple site, Chengdu,

Sichuan Province

Sichuan Provincial Museum, Chengdu

164.

Head of Eleven-Headed Avalokiteśvara

Tang dynasty (618–907)

Marble; h. 25.5 cm

Unearthed in 1983 in the western suburb of Xi'an,

Shaanxi Province

Forest of Steles Museum, Xi'an

165.

Torso of a bodhisattva

TANG DYNASTY (618–907)

Marble; h. 110 x w. 35 cm

Unearthed in 1959 in the precincts of the Daminggong, a

Tang dynasty imperial palace in Xi'an, Shaanxi Province

Forest of Steles Museum, Xi'an

166.

Head of a bodhisattva

TANG DYNASTY (618–907)

Marble with gold; h. 15.7 cm

Unearthed in 1959 at the Anguo Temple site, Xi'an,

Shaanxi Province

Forest of Steles Museum, Xi'an

167.

Torso of a guardian king

TANG DYNASTY (618–907)

Marble; h. 100 cm

Forest of Steles Museum, Xi'an

168.

Torso of a vajrasattva

TANG DYNASTY (618–907)

Sandstone; h. 86 cm

Unearthed in 1954 at the Wanfo Temple site, Chengdu,
Sichuan Province

Sichuan Provincial Museum, Chengdu

169.
Heavenly King
TANG DYNASTY (618–907)
Gilt bronze; h. 65 cm
Unearthed in Baoji, Shaanxi Province
Baoji Municipal Museum

170.
Trailokyavijaya
TANG DYNASTY (618–907)
Marble; h. 71 x w. 42 cm
Unearthed in 1959 at the Anguo Temple site, Xi'an,
Shaanxi Province
Forest of Steles Museum, Xi'an

171.

Ratnasaṃbhava

Tang dynasty (618–907)

Marble with traces of gold; h. 67.5 cm

Unearthed in 1959 at the Anguo Temple site, Xi'an,

Shaanxi Province

Forest of Steles Museum, Xi'an

172.

Mañjuśrī

Tang dynasty (618–907)

Marble; h. 75 cm

Unearthed in 1959 at the Anguo Temple site, Xi'an,

Shaanxi Province

Forest of Steles Museum, Xi'an

173.
Head of a bodhisattva
TANG DYNASTY (618–907)
Sandstone; h. 30 x w. 19 cm
Unearthed in 1957 at Nannieshui village, Qin county,
Shanxi Province
Shanxi Provincial Museum, Taiyuan

174.
Standing bodhisattva
TANG DYNASTY (618–907)
Sandstone with gold; h. 60 cm
Unearthed in 1954 at the Huata Temple site, Taiyuan,
Shanxi Province
Shanxi Provincial Museum, Taiyuan

175.
Torso of a bodhisattva
TANG DYNASTY (618–907)
Sandstone; h. 112 cm
Unearthed at the Guanghua Temple site, Baicheng village,
Taigu county, Shanxi Province
Shanxi Provincial Museum, Taiyuan

176.
Head of Avalokiteśvara
TANG DYNASTY (618–907)
Sandstone; h. 41 cm
Unearthed in 1954 at the Wanfo Temple site, Chengdu,
Sichuan Province
Sichuan Provincial Museum, Chengdu

177.

Two arhats, one with dragon, the other with tiger

NORTHERN SONG DYNASTY (960–1127)

Stone; (1) h. 38 cm (2) h. 38 cm

Discovered in 1980 at the Boshan Temple site, Fu county,

Shaanxi Province

Shaanxi History Museum, Xi'an

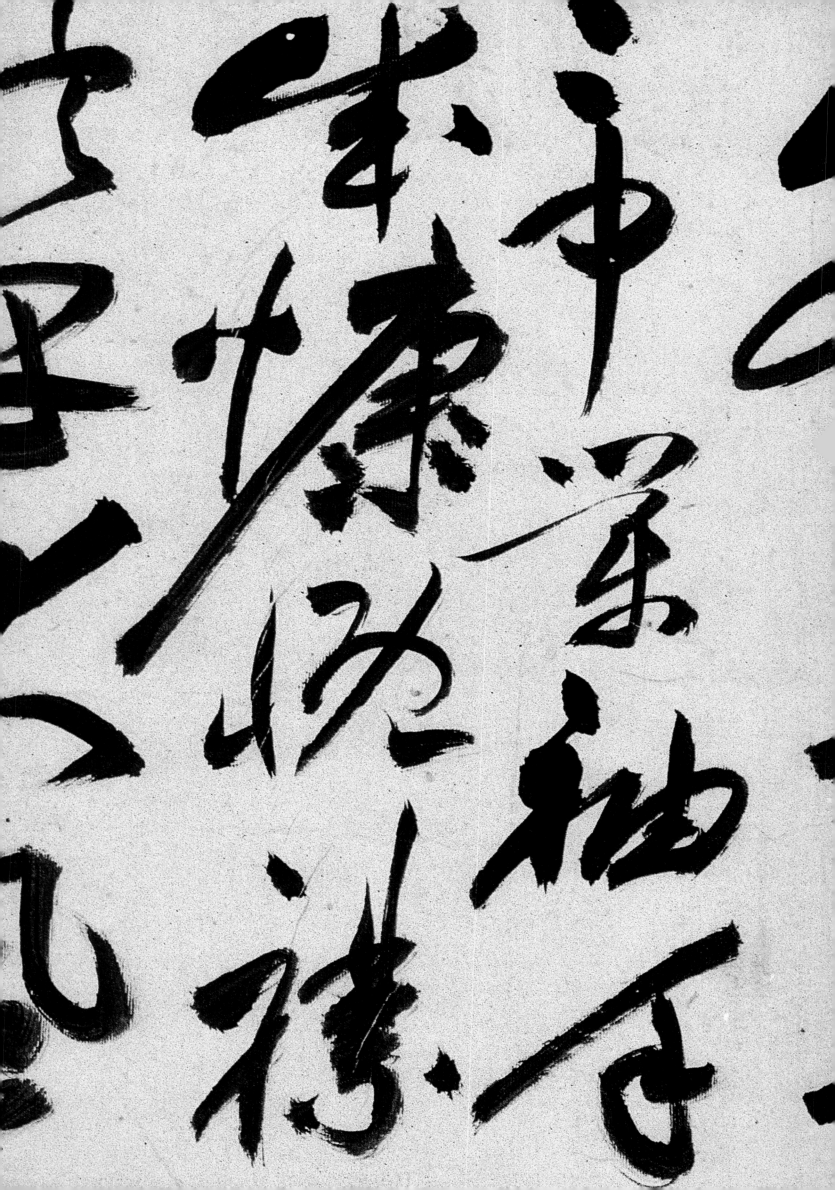

178.
Ink stone
NORTHERN WEI DYNASTY (386–534)
Stone; h. 8.5 x l. 21.2 x w. 21 cm
Unearthed in 1970 near Datong, Shanxi Province
Shanxi Provincial Museum, Taiyuan

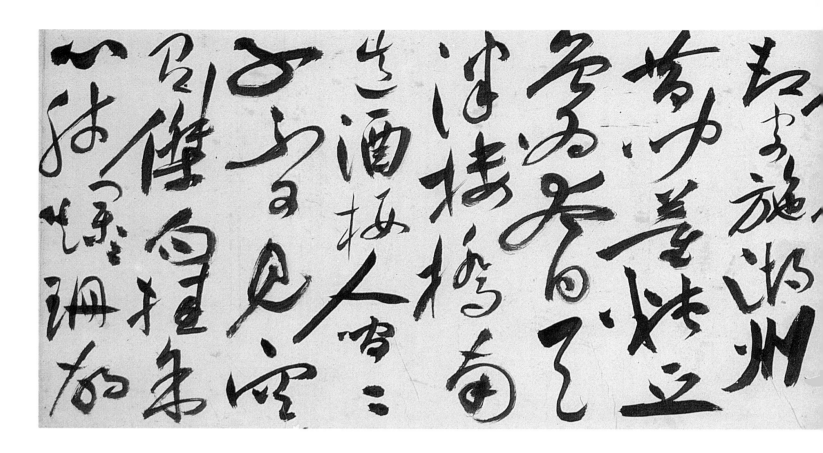

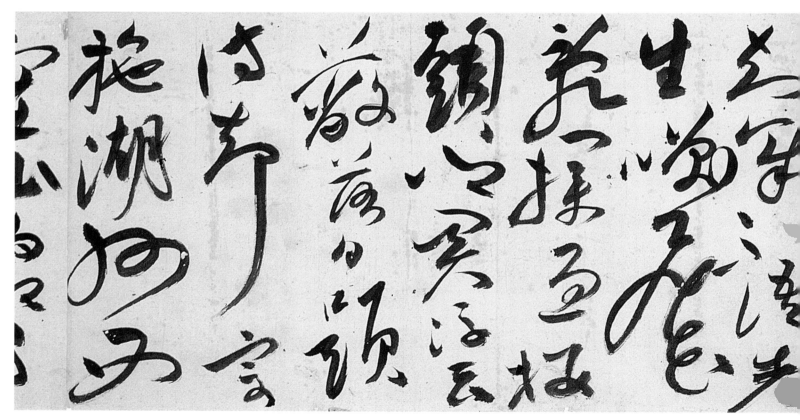

179.

Zhu Yunming (1461–1527)

"The Terrace of Ode to the Wind" and other poems
composed by Zhu Yunming, written in wild cursive
script (**kuangcao**)

Dated to 1523

MING DYNASTY (1368–1644)

Handscroll, ink on paper; 24.6 x 655.6 cm

Palace Museum, Beijing

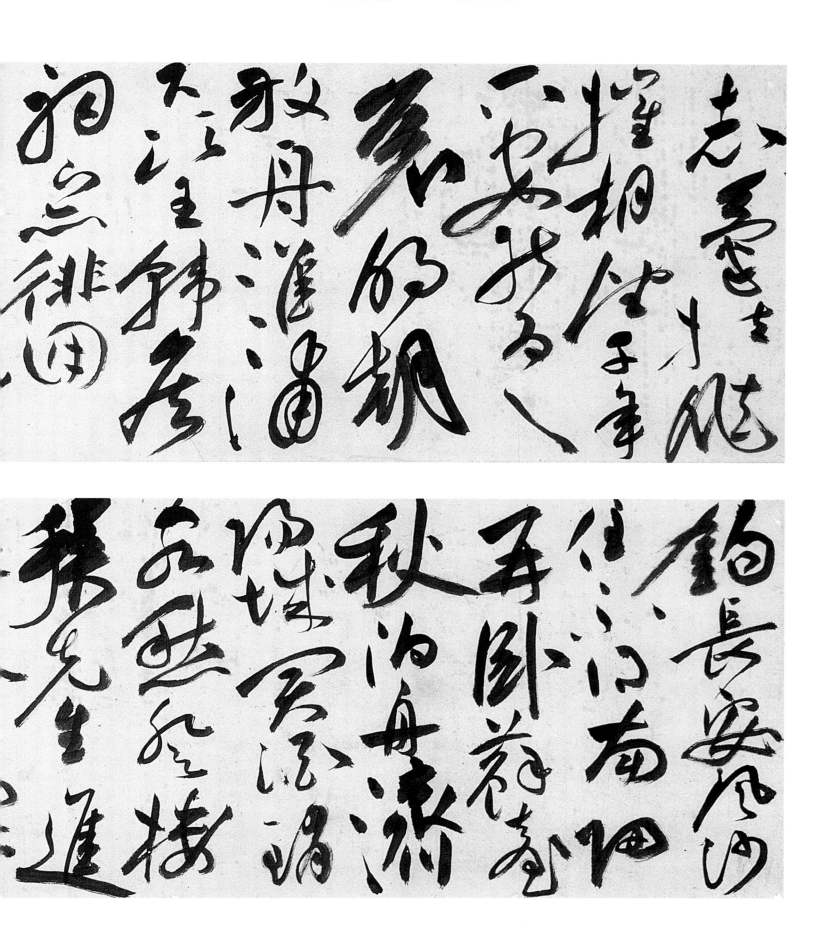

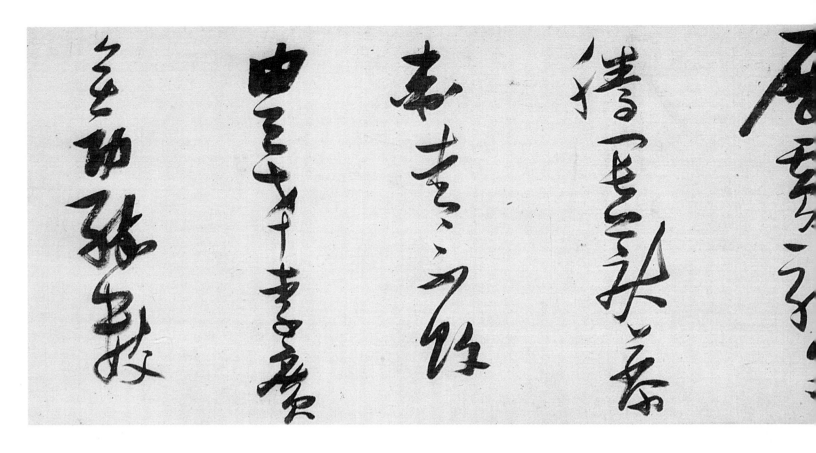

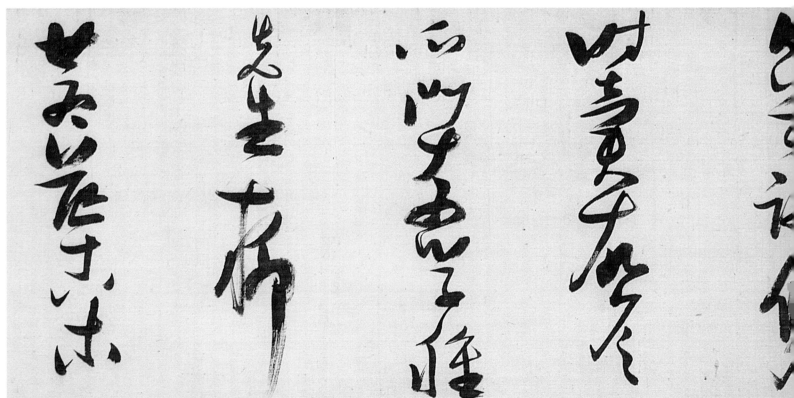

180.

Zhang Ruitu (1570–1641)

Transcription of Wang Wei's "Song of the Aged General," written in cursive script (*caoshu*)

Ming dynasty (1368–1644)

Handscroll, ink on silk; 29.5 x 629.5 cm

Palace Museum, Beijing

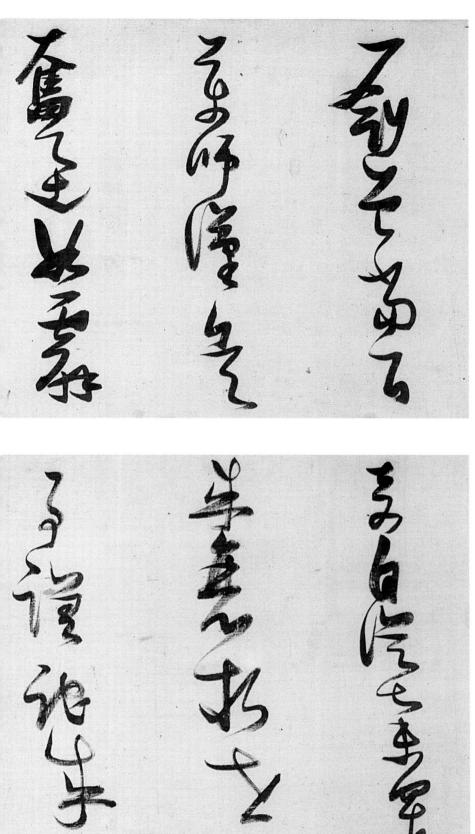

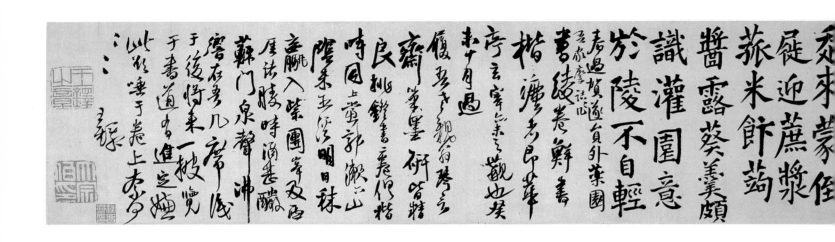

181.
Wang Duo (1592–1652)
Transcription of Wang Wei's "Enjoying a Repast at the
Home of Elder Zhao in Qizhou" and "Passing by the
Herbal Garden of Master Hesui in Spring," written in
standard script (*kaishu*)
Dated to 1643
Ming dynasty (1368–1644)
Handscroll, ink on satin; 21.2 x 165.5 cm
Palace Museum, Beijing

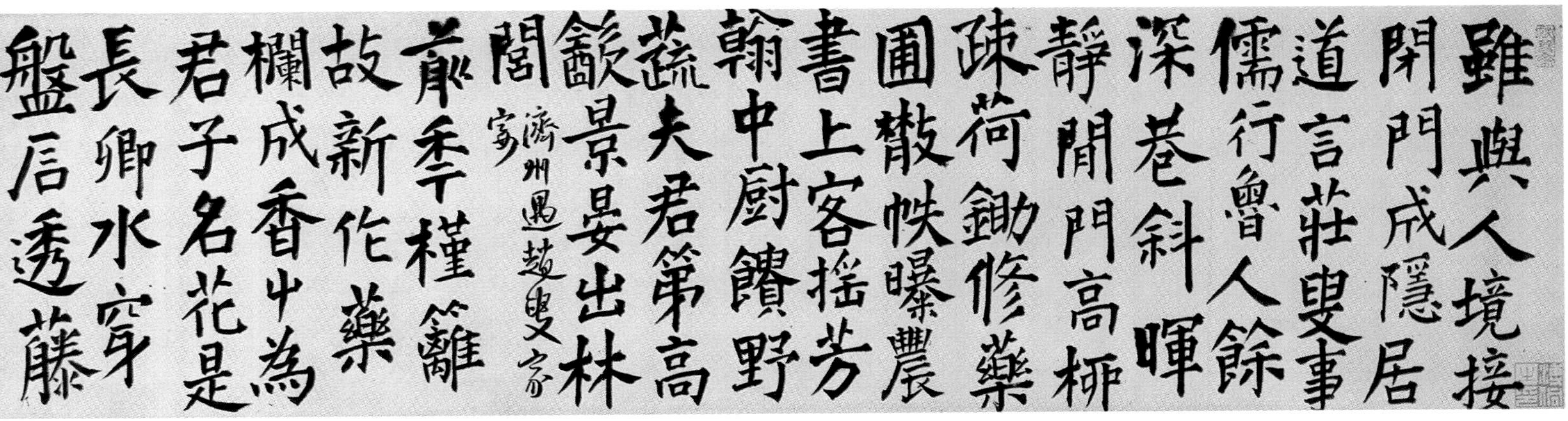

雖與人境接
閉門成隱居
道言莊叟事
儒行魯人餘
深巷斜暉
靜閉門高柳
疎荷鋤修藥
圃散帙曝農
書上客搖芳
翰中尉饋野
蔬夫君第高
飲景晏出林
閣家 濟州遇趙叟又為
蔖季槿籬
故新作藥
欄成香中為
君子名花是
長卿水穿
盤后透藤

七月流火九月授衣一之日觱發二之日栗烈無衣無褐何以卒歲三之日于耜四之日舉趾同我婦子饁彼南畝田畯至喜七月流火九月授衣春日載陽有鳴倉庚女執懿筐遵彼微行爰求柔桑春日遲遲采蘩祁祁女心傷悲殆及公子同歸七月流火八月萑葦蠶月條桑取彼斧斨以伐遠揚猗彼女桑七月鳴鵙八月載績載玄載黃我朱孔陽為公子裳四月秀葽五月鳴蜩八月其穫十月隕蘀一之日于貉取彼狐狸為公子裘二之日其同載纘武功言私其豵獻豜于公五月斯螽動股六月莎雞振羽七月在野八月在宇九月在戶十月蟋蟀入我床下穹窒熏鼠塞向墐戶嗟我婦子曰為改歲入此室處六月食鬱及薁七月亨葵及菽八月剝棗十月穫稻為此春酒以介眉壽七月食瓜八月斷壺九月叔苴采荼薪樗食我農夫九月築場圃十月納禾稼黍稷重穋禾麻菽麥嗟我農夫我稼既同上入執宮功晝爾于茅宵爾索綯亟其乘屋其始播百穀二之日鑿冰沖沖三之日納于凌陰四之日其蚤獻羔祭韭九月肅霜十月滌場朋酒斯饗曰殺羔羊躋彼公堂稱彼兕觥萬壽無疆

臣張照敬書

182.
Zhang Zhao (1691–1745)
Transcription of "Seventh Month" from the *Odes of Bin*, written in standard script (*kaishu*)
QING DYNASTY (1644–1911)
Hanging scroll, ink on paper; 176 × 92 cm
Palace Museum, Beijing

183.
Deng Shiru (1743–1805)
Couplet in seven-character lines, written in clerical script (*lishu*)
QING DYNASTY (1644–1911)
Hanging scrolls, ink on gold-flecked paper; 130.1 × 27.6 cm
Palace Museum, Beijing

Painting

184.
Wang Shen (ca. 1048–after 1104)
Misty River and Layered Hills
NORTHERN SONG DYNASTY (960–1127)
Handscroll, ink and color on silk; 45.2 x 166 cm
Shanghai Museum

185.

Zhao Kui (1185–1266)

In the Spirit of Poems by Du Fu

(Detail on facing page)

SOUTHERN SONG DYNASTY (1127–1279)

Handscroll, ink on silk; 24.7 x 212.2 cm

Shanghai Museum

宋趙葵畫杜甫詩意圖

186.

Anonymous

Snowy Landscape

SOUTHERN SONG DYNASTY (1127–1279)

Handscroll, ink and light color on paper; 24 x 48.2 cm

Shanghai Museum

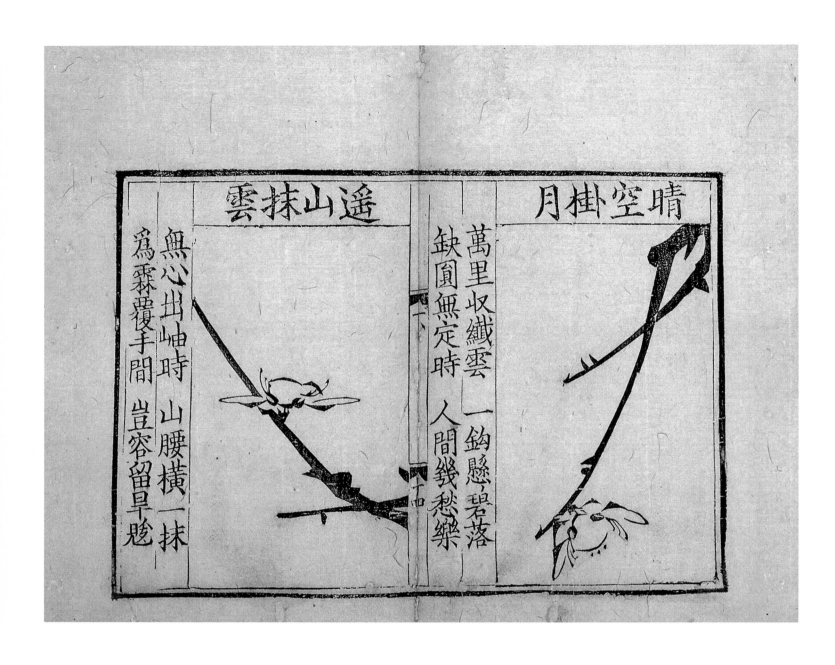

187.

Song Boren (act. mid-13th c.)
Album of Plum Blossom Portraits
(Above and following three pages)
1238; reprint, 1261
SOUTHERN SONG DYNASTY (1127–1279)
Woodblock print book; each leaf 23.1 x 28.6 cm
Shanghai Museum

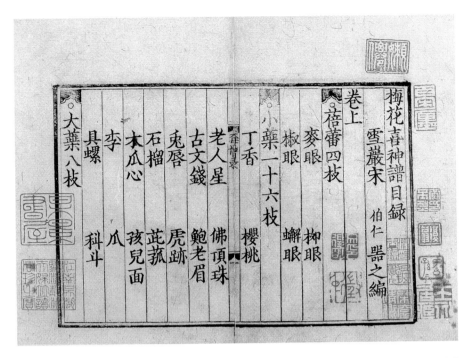

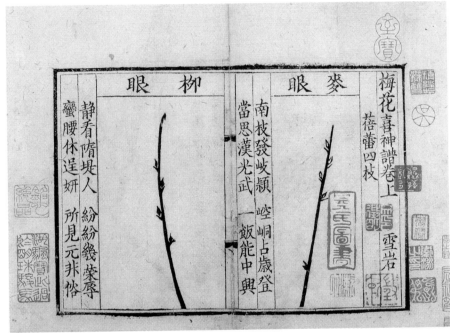

梅花喜神譜卷上　蓓蕾四枝　雪巖

麥眼

南枝發岐穎　嶙峋占歲登　當思漢光武　一飯能中興

柳眼

靜看隋堤人　紛紛幾榮辱　蠶腰体逞妍　所見元非俗

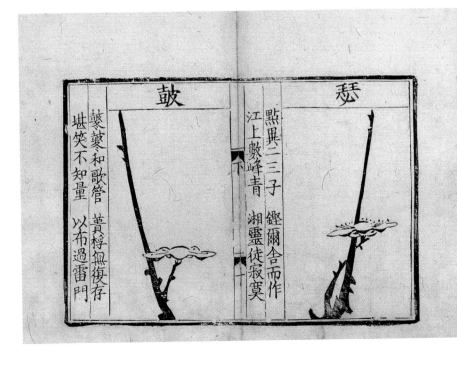

瑟

點異一二三子　鏗爾舍而作　江上數峰青　湘靈徒寂寞

敧

簇簇和歌管　黃桴無復存　堪笑不知量　以布過雷門

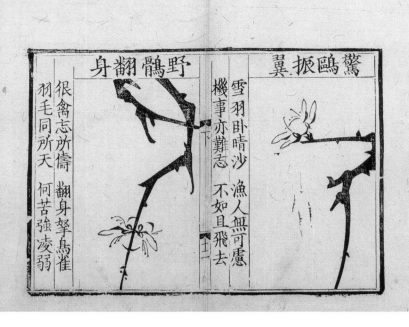

驚鷗振翼

雪羽卧晴沙　漁人無可慮　機事亦難忘　不如且飛去

下
十一

野鶻翻身

很禽志所償　翻身挐鳥雀　羽毛同所天　何苦強凌弱

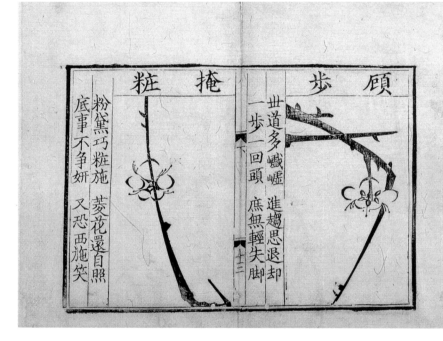

顧步

世道多巇嶮　進趨思退却　一步一回頭　庶無輕失脚

下
十三

掩粧

粉黛巧粧施　菱花還自照　底事不爭妍　又恐西施笑

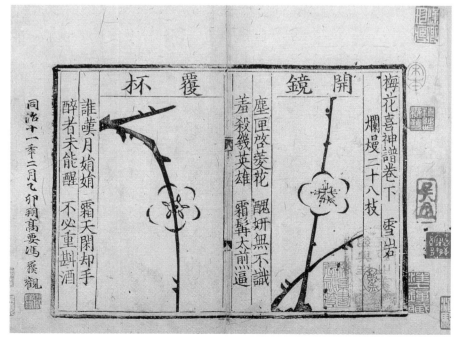

梅花喜神譜卷下　雪岩

爛熳二十八枝

開鏡

塵匣啓菱花　醜妍無不識　羞殺幾英雄　霜鬢太前逼

下
十

覆杯

誰嘆月娟娟　霜天閑却手　醉者未能醒　不必重斟酒

同治十一季二月乙卯翔高要馮溪觀

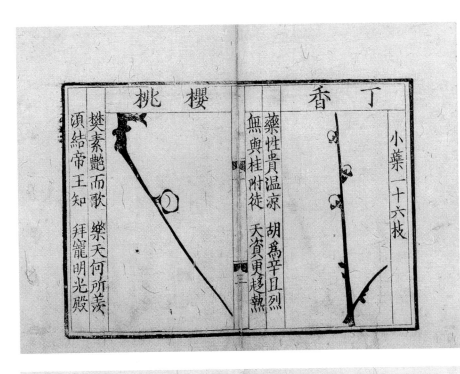

丁香
小葉一十六枚
藥性貴溫涼　胡爲辛且烈
無與桂附徒　天資更趨熱

櫻桃
樊素艷而歌　樂天何所羨
須結帝王知　拜寵明光殿

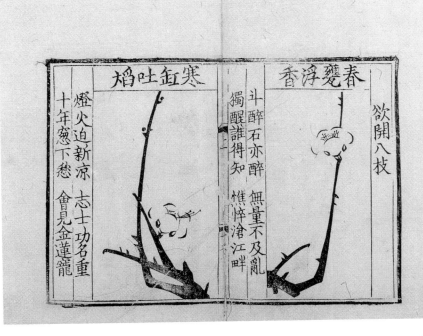

春甕浮香
欲開八枝
斗醉石亦醉　無量不及亂
獨醒誰得知　憔悴滄江畔

寒缸吐焰
燈火迫新涼　志士功名重
十年窻下愁　曾見金蓮寵

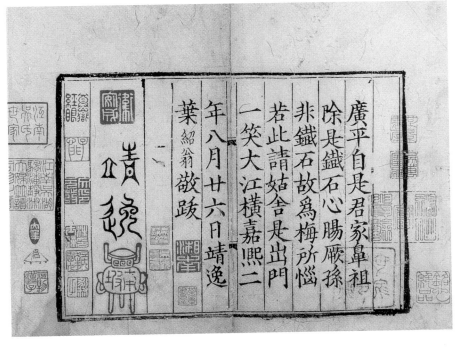

廣平自是君家鼻祖
除是鐵石心腸厭孫
非鐵石故爲梅所惱
若此請姑舍是出門
一笑大江橫嘉熙二
年八月廿六日靖逸
葉紹翁敬跋

188.

Ni Zan (1306[?]–1374)

Six Gentlemen

Dated to 1345

Yuan dynasty (1279–1368)

Hanging scroll, ink on paper; 61.9 x 33.3 cm

Shanghai Museum

189.

Wang Meng (ca. 1308–1385)

Dwelling in the Qingbian Mountains

Dated to 1366

YUAN DYNASTY (1279–1368)

Hanging scroll, ink on paper; 140.6 x 42.2 cm

Shanghai Museum

190.

Shang Xi (act. ca. 2nd quarter of 15th c.)

The Xuande Emperor on an Outing

MING DYNASTY (1368–1644)

Hanging scroll, ink and color on paper; 211 x 353 cm

Palace Museum, Beijing

191.

Xie Huan (act. 1426–1452)

The Literary Gathering in the Apricot Garden

Ca. 1437

MING DYNASTY (1368–1644)

Handscroll, ink and color on silk; h. 37 cm

Zhenjiang Municipal Museum

國朝畫史以戴文進為
大家此學燕文貴淡蕩
清空不作平日本色又
為奇絕 荣國昌欵

錢唐戴進寫奉
用言老師清供

192.

Dai Jin (1388–1462)

Landscape in the Manner of Yan Wengui

MING DYNASTY (1368–1644)

Hanging scroll, ink on paper; 98.2 x 45.8 cm

Shanghai Museum

193.

Wu Wei (1459–1508)

Fishermen on a Snowy River

MING DYNASTY (1368–1644)

Hanging scroll, ink on silk; 245 x 156 cm

Hubei Provincial Museum, Wuhan

194.
Zhou Chen (ca. 1455–after 1536)
Peach Blossom Spring
Dated to 1533
MING DYNASTY (1368–1644)
Hanging scroll, ink and color on silk; 161.5 x 102.5 cm
Suzhou Municipal Museum

195.
Qiu Ying (ca. 1495–1552)
Playing the Flute by Pine and Stream
MING DYNASTY (1368–1644)
Hanging scroll, ink and color on silk; 116.4 x 65.8 cm
Nanjing Museum

196.
Shen Zhou (1427–1509)
Eastern Villa
(Above and following three pages)
MING DYNASTY (1368–1644)
Album, ink and color on paper; each leaf 28.6 x 33 cm
Nanjing Museum

南濠

稻畦

鶴洞

知樂亭

197.

Wen Zhengming (1470–1559)

Studio of True Appreciation

Dated to 1549

MING DYNASTY (1368–1644)

Handscroll, ink and color on paper; 36 x 107.8 cm

Shanghai Museum

198.
Xu Wei (1521–1593)
Peonies, Banana Plant, and Rock
MING DYNASTY (1368–1644)
Hanging scroll, ink on paper; 120.6 x 58.4 cm
Shanghai Museum

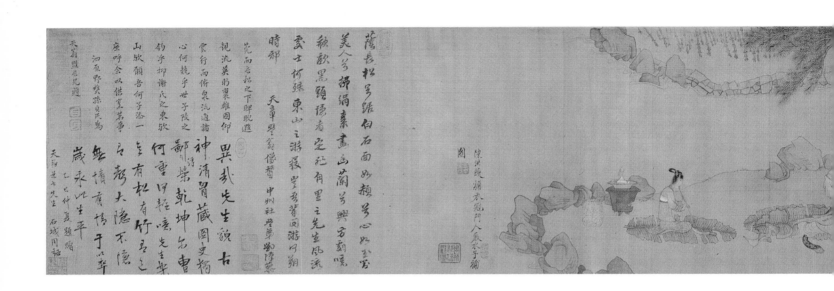

199.

Chen Hongshou (1598–1652)

The Pleasures of He Tianzhang

(Detail on facing page)

MING DYNASTY (1368–1644)

Handscroll, ink and color on silk; 25.3 x 163.2 cm

Suzhou Municipal Museum

200.
Dong Qichang (1555–1636)
Poetic Feeling at Qixia Monastery
Dated to 1626
MING DYNASTY (1368–1644)
Hanging scroll, ink on paper; 133.1 x 52.5 cm
Shanghai Museum

201.

**Ten Bamboo Studio Manual of Calligraphy
and Painting**

(Above and following three pages)

Published 1627–1633 by Hu Zhengyan (1584–1674)

MING DYNASTY (1368–1644)

Woodblock print book; each leaf 25.8 x 31 cm

Palace Museum, Beijing

芳倫步傳

何意羅浮色龍然後屋廖開
可因霜染出凝雲被遂吹来
个逐金颷轉長係玉樹瑝
孤山吟新咏子里際高臺

顧起元題

曉看粉動
趙芝

香靄晴酣
凌雲翰寫

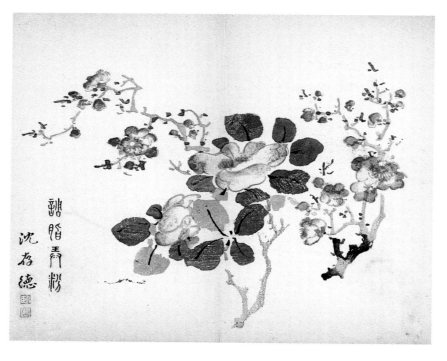

臙脂膏粉
沈存德

202.

Ten Bamboo Studio Letter Papers

(Above and facing page)

Published 1644 by Hu Zhengyan (1584–1674)

Ming dynasty (1368–1644)

Woodblock print book; each leaf 21 x 13.6 cm

Palace Museum, Beijing

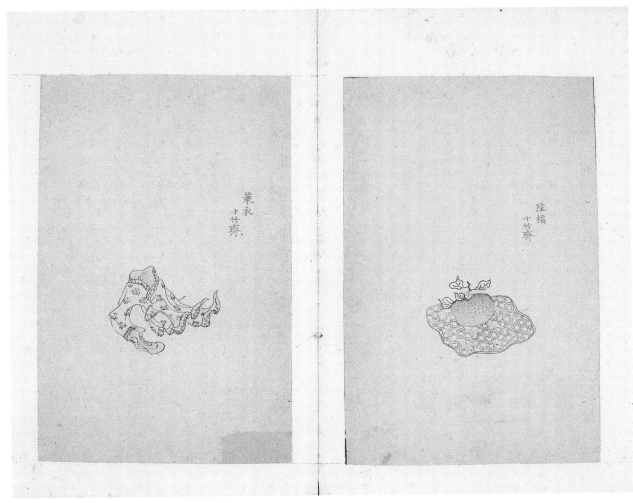

203.

Album of a Hundred Flowers, after paintings by

Zhang Chaoxiang (act. 19th c.)

(Above and facing page)

Qɪɴɢ ᴅʏɴᴀꜱᴛʏ, Tᴏɴɢᴢʜɪ ᴘᴇʀɪᴏᴅ (1862–1874)

Woodblock print book; each leaf 24.2 x 16.8 cm

Palace Museum, Beijing

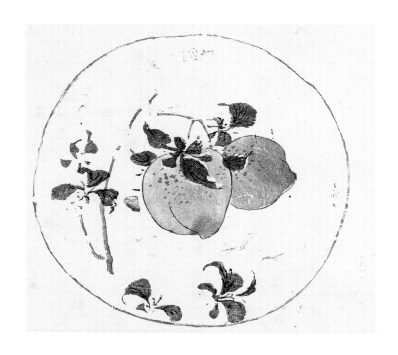
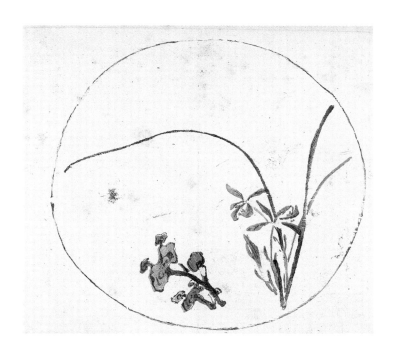
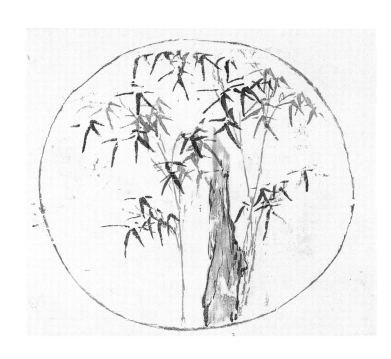

204.

Wang Yuanqi (1642–1715)

Complete in Soul, Sufficient in Spirit

Dated to 1708

QING DYNASTY (1644–1911)

Hanging scroll, ink on paper; 137.2 x 71.5 cm

Palace Museum, Beijing

205.

Wu Li (1632–1718)

Reading "The Book of Changes" in a Streamside Pavilion

Dated to 1678

QING DYNASTY (1644–1911)

Hanging scroll, ink on paper; 211.7 x 78.7 cm

Shanghai Museum

206.
Kuncan (1612–ca. 1674)
Clear Sky over Verdant Hills
Dated to 1660
QING DYNASTY (1644–1911)
Hanging scroll, ink and color on silk; 85 x 40.5 cm
Nanjing Museum

207.
Hongren (1610–1664)
Peaks and Ravines at Jiuqi
QING DYNASTY (1644–1911)
Hanging scroll, ink on paper; 110.6 x 58.9 cm
Shanghai Museum

208.

Yuanji (Shitao; 1642–1707)
Pure Sounds of Hills and Streams
QING DYNASTY (1644–1911)
Hanging scroll, ink on paper; 102.5 x 42.4 cm
Shanghai Museum

209.
Gong Xian (1618–1689)
Summer Mountains after Rain
QING DYNASTY (1644–1911)
Hanging scroll, ink on silk; 141.7 x 57.8 cm
Nanjing Museum

210.
Bada Shanren (1626–1705)
Ducks and Lotuses
Dated to 1696
QING DYNASTY (1644–1911)
Hanging scroll, ink on paper; 166 x 76.3 cm
Shanghai Museum

211.
Yuanji (Shitao; 1642–1707)
Clear Autumn in Huaiyang
QING DYNASTY (1644–1911)
Hanging scroll, ink and color on paper; 89 x 57.1 cm
Nanjing Museum

212.

Zou Zhe (1636–ca. 1708)

Album of Landscapes

(Above and facing page)

QING DYNASTY (1644–1911)

Album, ink and color on paper; three leaves each

12.6 x 28.6 cm, remaining leaves each 12.6 x 14 cm

Nanjing Museum

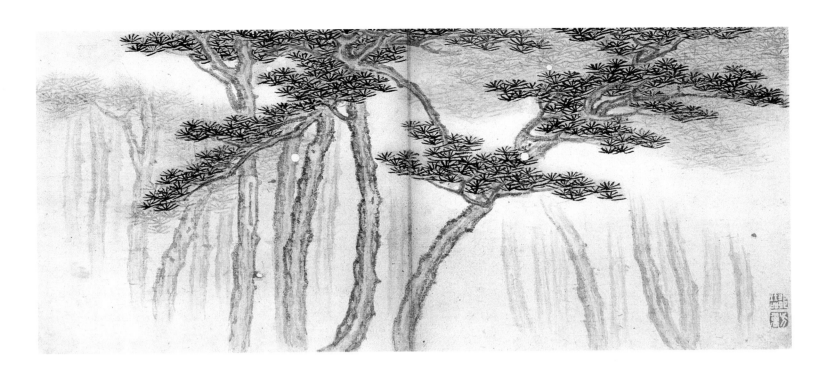

213.

Yuan Jiang (act. ca. 1690–ca. 1746)

Garden for Gazing

QING DYNASTY (1644–1911)

Handscroll, ink and light color on silk; 51.5 x 254.5 cm

Tianjin Municipal History Museum

214.
Gao Cen (act. ca. 1645–1689)
The Temple on Jinshan
QING DYNASTY (1644–1911)
Hanging scroll, ink and color on silk; 180.8 x 95.1 cm
Nanjing Museum

215.
Gao Xiang (1688–1754)
Finger-Snap Pavilion
QING DYNASTY (1644–1911)
Hanging scroll, ink on paper; 69 x 38 cm
Yangzhou Municipal Museum

216.

Huang Shen (1687–after 1768)

Willows and Egrets

QING DYNASTY (1644–1911)

Hanging scroll, ink and color on paper; 113.7 x 57.7 cm

Shanghai Museum

217.

Li Shan (1686–after 1760)

Pine, Wisteria, and Peonies

Dated to 1755

QING DYNASTY (1644–1911)

Hanging scroll, ink and color on paper; 238 x 118.2 cm

Shanghai Museum

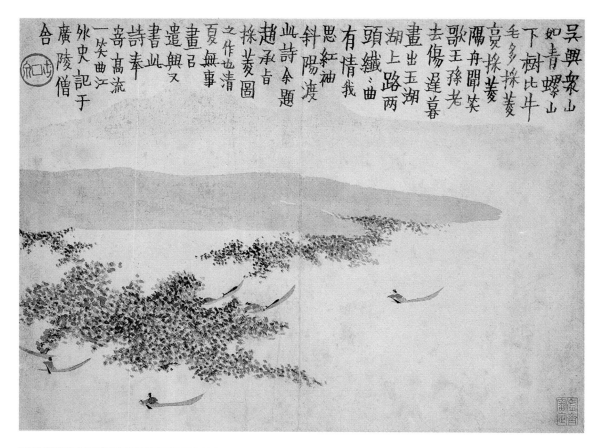

吳興衆山
如青螺山
下樹比牛
毛多採菱
亮採菱
陽舟間笑
歌王孫老
去傷遲暮
畫出玉湖
頭纖、曲
湖上路兩
有情我
思紅袖
斜陽渡
趙吳詩今題
採菱圖
之作也清
夏日無事
畫與又
書兼山
詩奉高流
寄曲江
一笑記于
外史記于
廣陵僧
含 [印]

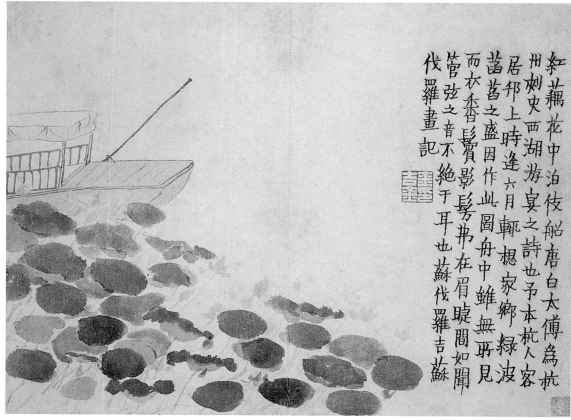

紅藕花中泊伎船唐白太傅為杭
州刺史西湖游宴之詩也予本杭人客
居邗上時逢六月輒想家鄉綠波
蒿苢之盛因作此圖舟中雖無所見
而衣香影鬢弗在眉睫間如聞
管弦之音不絶于耳也蘇伐羅吉蘇
伐羅畫記
[印]

218.

Jin Nong (1687–1764)

Album of Landscapes and Figures

(Above and following three pages)

Dated to 1759

Qing dynasty (1644–1911)

Album, ink and color on paper; each leaf 26.1 x 34.9 cm

Shanghai Museum

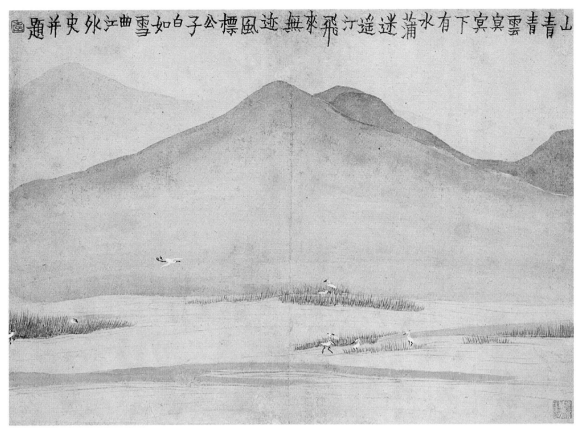

山青青雲冥冥下有水迷蒲蒲逍遙飛來無迹風標如公子白雪曲江外史題

八九峯如畫三二人倚闌偶猶雷雨山民寫于無夏扶

迴汀曲渚渚暖
生煙風柳風
蒲綠漲天我
是釣師人識
否白鷗前導
在春船予導
此予二十年前
凡蕭家湖之
作今追想昔
游風景漫畫
小幅并錄前
詩乃江外史
記

馬和之秋林共話圖用筆疎簡
作淺絳邑有楊妹子題詩其
上同鄉周微君少穆曾藏一幅
余贈以古青甕出軸葊之微君下
世為梁少師薊林所得進之內
府矣今追想其意畫于紙冊是
耶非耶吾不自知楷雷山民記

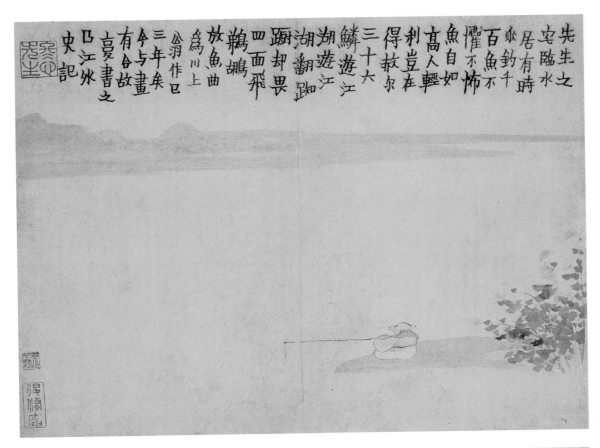

先生之宅臨水
宅臨水
居有時
濯不怖
百魚不
从釣千
魚自如
高人輕
利豈在
得枚爾
三十六
鱗遊江
湖遊江
湖翺翔
蹄却畏
四面飛
鶺鴒
放魚曲
烏川上
公翁作已
三年矣
今與畫
有台故
高夏書之
烏江外
史記

野竹無次頗多清風何方朝士
屏蔽從之來裵回竹下歌詠不
去得非王子猷之流輩乎此間
忽有斯人可想可想

乾隆二十四年立秋日
七十三翁杭郡金農

219.
Hua Yan (1682–1756)
The Golden Valley Garden
Dated to 1732
QING DYNASTY (1644–1911)
Hanging scroll, ink and color on paper; 178.9 x 94.1 cm
Shanghai Museum

List of colorplates

Objects are listed in catalogue order.

JADE

1. **Ornament in the shape of hooked clouds with central bird motif**
NEOLITHIC PERIOD, HONGSHAN CULTURE
(ca. 3600–ca. 2000 BCE)
Nephrite jade; l. 22.4 x w. 11.5 x d. 0.5 cm
Unearthed in 1979 at Sanguandianzi, Lingyuan city, Liaoning Province
Liaoning Provincial Museum, Shenyang

2. **Ornament in the shape of a pig-dragon (*zhulong*)**
NEOLITHIC PERIOD, HONGSHAN CULTURE
(ca. 3600–ca. 2000 BCE)
Nephrite jade; h. 15.7 x w. 10.4 x d. 4.3 cm
Found in Jianping county, Liaoning Province
Liaoning Provincial Museum, Shenyang

3. **Prismatic tube (*cong*)**
NEOLITHIC PERIOD, LIANGZHU CULTURE
(ca. 3600–ca. 2000 BCE)
Nephrite jade; h. 8.8 x max. width 17.6 cm
Unearthed in 1986 from Fanshan tomb No. 12, Yuhang, Zhejiang Province
Zhejiang Provincial Institute of Cultural Relics and Archaeology, Hangzhou

4. **Prismatic tube (*cong*)**
NEOLITHIC PERIOD, LIANGZHU CULTURE
(ca. 3600–ca. 2000 BCE)
Nephrite jade; h. 5 x max. width 7.4 cm
Unearthed in 1982 from Fuquanshan tomb No. 9, Qingpu county, Shanghai
Shanghai Museum

5. **Prismatic tube (*cong*)**
NEOLITHIC PERIOD, LIANGZHU CULTURE
(ca. 3600–ca. 2000 BCE)
Nephrite jade; h. 29.7 x max. width 6.1 cm
Unearthed in 1982 in Wujin county, Jiangsu Province
Nanjing Museum

6. **Knife (*dao*) with semihuman mask motifs**
NEOLITHIC PERIOD, LONGSHAN CULTURE
(ca. 3000–ca. 1700 BCE)
Nephrite jade; l. 23.7 x w. 7.7 cm
Shanghai Museum

7. **Blade (*zhang*)**
XIA OR SHANG PERIOD
(ca. 2200–ca. 1100 BCE)
Nephrite jade; l. 37 x w. 11.2 x d. 0.6 cm
Palace Museum, Beijing

8. **Blade (*zhang*)**
SHANG PERIOD (ca. 1600–ca. 1100 BCE)
Nephrite jade; l. 68 x w. 10.8 cm
Unearthed in 1986 from Sanxingdui pit No. 2, Guanghan, Sichuan Province
Sichuan Provincial Institute of Archaeology and Cultural Relics, Chengdu

9. **Chime with design of crouching tiger**
SHANG PERIOD (ca. 1600–ca. 1100 BCE)
Stone; l. 84 x w. 42 x d. 2.5 cm
Unearthed in 1950 at Wuguan village, Anyang, Henan Province
National Museum of Chinese History, Beijing

10. **Four figures: (1) bird with ram's horns (2) kneeling human (3) bird (4) bird-headed human**
SHANG PERIOD
(ca. 1600–ca. 1100 BCE)
Nephrite jade; (1) h. 4.9 cm
(2) h. 5.6 cm (3) h. 10 cm
(4) h. 9.8 cm
Unearthed in 1976 from Fu Hao tomb No. 5, Anyang, Henan Province
Henan Provincial Museum, Zhengzhou

11. **Dagger-ax (*ge*) with grooved blade**
WESTERN ZHOU PERIOD
(ca. 1100–771 BCE)
Nephrite jade; l. 25.4 x w. 6.1 cm
Unearthed in 1983 at East Sidaoxiang, Xi'an, Shaanxi Province
Shaanxi History Museum, Xi'an

12. **Fourteen-piece burial mask**
WESTERN ZHOU PERIOD
(ca. 1100–771 BCE)
Nephrite jade; max. width 10.7 cm
Unearthed in 1990 from Guo State tomb No. 2001, Sanmenxia, Henan Province
Henan Provincial Institute of Archaeology and Cultural Relics, Zhengzhou

13. **Ornamental plaque with interlacery and animal mask designs**
EASTERN ZHOU, SPRING AND AUTUMN PERIOD (770–476 BCE)
Nephrite jade; h. 7.1 cm
Unearthed in 1987 at Xiasi, Xichuan county, Henan Province
Henan Provincial Institute of Archaeology and Cultural Relics, Zhengzhou

14. **A pair of dragon-shaped pendants**
EASTERN ZHOU, WARRING STATES PERIOD (475–221 BCE)
Nephrite jade; l. 11.4 cm
Unearthed at Pingliangtai, Huaiyang county, Henan Province
Henan Provincial Institute of Archaeology and Cultural Relics, Zhengzhou

15. **Ring (*huan*) with abstract designs**
EASTERN ZHOU, WARRING STATES PERIOD (475–221 BCE)
Nephrite jade; diam. 10.6 cm
Unearthed in 1991 at Xujialing, Xichuan county, Henan Province
Henan Provincial Institute of Archaeology and Cultural Relics, Zhengzhou

16. **Disk (*bi*) with grain pattern**
WESTERN HAN DYNASTY
(206 BCE–8 CE)
Nephrite jade; diam. 18.9 cm, depth 0.9 cm
Unearthed in Zhouzhi county, Shaanxi Province
Shaanxi History Museum, Xi'an

17. **Winged horse**
HAN DYNASTY
(206 BCE–220 CE)
Nephrite jade; h. 4.2 x l. 7.8 x w. 2.6 cm
Palace Museum, Beijing

18. **Chimera (*bixie*)**
HAN DYNASTY
(206 BCE–220 CE)
Nephrite jade; l. 13.5 x w. 8.5 cm
Palace Museum, Beijing

19. **Vessel (*lian* or *zun*) with design of deities, animals, and masks**
WESTERN JIN DYNASTY
(265–316)
Nephrite jade; h. 10.5 cm
Unearthed in 1991 from the tomb of Liu Hong, Huangshantou, Anxiang county, Hunan Province
Administrative Office for Cultural Relics, Anxiang County, Hunan Province

20. **Sixteen-piece belt**
TANG DYNASTY (618–907)
Nephrite jade; l. of pieces 3.5–5 cm
Unearthed in 1970 at Hejia village, Xi'an, Shaanxi Province
Shaanxi History Museum, Xi'an

BRONZE

21. **Vessel (*jue*)**
XIA PERIOD (ca. 2100–ca. 1600 BCE)
Bronze; h. 11.7 x w. 14.1 cm
Shanghai Museum

22. **Square cauldron (*fang ding*) with thread-relief frieze of animal masks, and nipple pattern**
SHANG PERIOD (ca. 1600–ca. 1100 BCE)
Bronze; h. 82 x w. 50 cm
Unearthed in 1990 at Qian village, Pinglu county, Shanxi Province
Shanxi Provincial Institute of Archaeology, Taiyuan

23. **Square vessel (*fang zun*) with four rams**
SHANG PERIOD (ca. 1600–ca. 1100 BCE)
Bronze; h. 58.3 cm, w. of mouth 52.4 cm
Found in 1938 at Yueshanpu, Ningxiang, Hunan Province
National Museum of Chinese History, Beijing

24. **Vessel (*zun*) in the shape of a bird, inscribed "Fu Hao" (one of an identical pair)**
SHANG PERIOD (ca. 1600–ca. 1100 BCE)
Bronze; h. 45.9 cm
Unearthed in 1976 from Fu Hao tomb No. 5, Anyang, Henan Province
National Museum of Chinese History, Beijing

25. **Vessel (*zun*) in the shape of an elephant (one of an identical pair)**
SHANG PERIOD (ca. 1600–ca. 1100 BCE)
Bronze; h. 26.5 x l. 22.8 cm
Found in 1975 at Shixingshan, Liling, Hunan Province
Hunan Provincial Museum, Changsha

26. **Vessel (*you*), inscribed**
SHANG PERIOD (ca. 1600–ca. 1100 BCE)
Bronze; h. 37.7 cm
Found in 1970 at Huangcai village, Ningxiang county, Hunan Province
Hunan Provincial Museum, Changsha

27. **Vessel (*zun*) in the shape of a boar**
SHANG PERIOD (ca. 1600–ca. 1100 BCE)
Bronze; h. 40 x l. 72 cm
Unearthed in 1981 at Chuanxingshan, Xiangtan county, Hunan Province
Hunan Provincial Museum, Changsha

28. **Vessel (*gong*) in zoomorphic shape**
SHANG PERIOD (ca. 1600–ca. 1100 BCE)
Bronze; h. 19 x l. 43 x w. 13.4 cm
Unearthed in 1959 at Taohua village, Shilou county, Shanxi Province
Shanxi Provincial Museum, Taiyuan

29. **Basin (*pan*) with coiling dragon design**
SHANG PERIOD (ca. 1600–ca. 1100 BCE)
Bronze; h. 26 cm, diam. of mouth 61.6 cm
Unearthed in 1984 at Chenshan village, Wenling, Zhejiang Province
Administrative Office for Cultural Relics, Wenling

30. **Mask with protruding eyes**
SHANG PERIOD (ca. 1600–ca. 1100 BCE)
Bronze; h. 65 x w. 138 cm
Unearthed in 1986 from Sanxingdui pit No. 2, Guanghan, Sichuan Province
Sichuan Provincial Institute of Archaeology and Cultural Relics, Chengdu

31. **Vessel (*lei*) with elephant trunk handles and buffalo horns**
WESTERN ZHOU PERIOD (ca. 1100–771 BCE)
Bronze; h. 70.2 cm, diam. of mouth 22.8 cm
Unearthed in 1980 at Zhuwajie, Peng county, Sichuan Province
Sichuan Provincial Museum, Chengdu

32. **Vessel (*zun*), inscribed**
WESTERN ZHOU PERIOD (ca. 1100–771 BCE)
Bronze; h. 38.8 cm, diam. of mouth 28.6 cm
Unearthed in 1963 at Jia village, Baoji county, Shaanxi Province
Baoji Municipal Museum

33. **Bell (*bo*) with four tigers**
WESTERN ZHOU PERIOD (ca. 1100–771 BCE)
Bronze; h. 44.3 x w. 39.6 cm
Palace Museum, Beijing

34. **Drum (*gu*) with abstract zoomorphic designs**
SHANG PERIOD (ca. 1600–ca. 1100 BCE)
Bronze; h. 75.5 cm, diam. of drum 39.5 cm
Found in 1977 in Chongyang county, Hubei Province
Hubei Provincial Museum, Wuhan

35. **Two-handled vessel (*gui*) with ox-head motifs, inscribed**
WESTERN ZHOU PERIOD (ca. 1100–771 BCE)
Bronze; h. 31 cm, diam. of mouth 25 cm
Unearthed in 1981 from tomb No. 1, Zhifangtou village, Baoji county, Shaanxi Province
Baoji Municipal Museum

36. **Vessel (*gong*), inscribed**
WESTERN ZHOU PERIOD (ca. 1100–771 BCE)
Bronze; h. 28.7 x l. 38 cm
Unearthed in 1976 at Zhuangbai village, Fufeng county, Shaanxi Province
Zhouyuan Museum, Xi'an

37. **Vessel (*zun*) in the shape of an elephant**
WESTERN ZHOU PERIOD (ca. 1100–771 BCE)
Bronze; h. 21 x l. 38 cm
Unearthed in 1975 at Rujia village, Baoji county, Shaanxi Province
Baoji Municipal Museum

38. **Covered spouted vessel (*he*) in the shape of a four-legged duck, inscribed**
WESTERN ZHOU PERIOD (ca. 1100–771 BCE)
Bronze; h. 26 cm
Unearthed in 1980 from the Ying State tomb at Pingdingshan, Henan Province
Henan Provincial Institute of Archaeology and Cultural Relics, Zhengzhou

39. **Two-handled vessel (*gui*), inscribed**
WESTERN ZHOU PERIOD (ca. 1100–771 BCE)
Bronze; h. 26.5 cm
Unearthed in 1986 from the Ying State tomb at Pingdingshan, Henan Province
Henan Provincial Institute of Archaeology and Cultural Relics, Zhengzhou

40. **Vessel (*hu*), inscribed**
WESTERN ZHOU PERIOD (ca. 1100–771 BCE)
Bronze; h. 65.4 cm, diam. of mouth 19.7 cm
Unearthed in 1976 at Zhuangbai village, Fufeng county, Shaanxi Province
Zhouyuan Museum, Xi'an

41. **Rectangular vessel (*fang yi*), inscribed**
WESTERN ZHOU PERIOD (ca. 1100–771 BCE)
Bronze; h. 38.5 x l. of mouth 20 x w. of mouth 17 cm
Unearthed in 1963 at Qijia village, Fufeng county, Shaanxi Province
Shaanxi History Museum, Xi'an

42. **Miniature carriage with human guardians including one-legged watchman, birds, and crouching tigers**
WESTERN ZHOU PERIOD (ca. 1100–771 BCE)
Bronze; h. 9.1 x l. 13.7 x w. 11.3 cm
Unearthed in 1989 at Shangguo village, Wenxi county, Shanxi Province
Shanxi Provincial Institute of Archaeology, Taiyuan

43. **Four-sided vessel (*fang hu*) with square base and lotus-petal crown**
EASTERN ZHOU PERIOD (770–256 BCE)
Bronze; h. 66 x max. width 34 cm
Unearthed in 1988 from tomb No. 251, Jinsheng village, Taiyuan, Shanxi Province
Shanxi Provincial Institute of Archaeology, Taiyuan

44. **Vessel (*hu*) with bird-shaped lid**
EASTERN ZHOU, SPRING AND AUTUMN period (770–476 BCE)
Bronze; h. 41 x w. 23.5 cm
Unearthed in 1988 from tomb No. 251, Jinsheng village, Taiyuan, Shanxi Province
Shanxi Provincial Institute of Archaeology, Taiyuan

45. **Square-based vessel (*fang hu*) with lotus-petal crown and crane**
EASTERN ZHOU, SPRING AND AUTUMN period (770–476 BCE)
Bronze; h. 126 x l. of mouth 30.5 x w. of mouth 24.9 cm
Unearthed in 1923 at Lijialou, Xinzheng county, Henan Province
Henan Provincial Museum, Zhengzhou

46. **Mythical beast**
EASTERN ZHOU, SPRING AND AUTUMN period (770–476 BCE)
Bronze inlaid with malachite; h. 48 cm
Unearthed in 1990 from Xujialing tomb No. 9, Xichuan county, Henan Province
Henan Provincial Institute of Archaeology and Cultural Relics, Zhengzhou

47. **Tapir bearing figure holding interlace tray**
EASTERN ZHOU, WARRING STATES period (475–221 BCE)
Bronze; h. 15 cm, diam. of tray 11 cm
Unearthed in 1965 at Fenshuiling, Changzhi, Shanxi Province
Shanxi Provincial Museum, Taiyuan

48. **Rectangular basin (*pan*) with turtle, fish, and interlacing dragon designs**
EASTERN ZHOU, WARRING STATES period (475–221 BCE)
Bronze; h. 22.5 x l. 73.2 x w. 45.2 cm
Palace Museum, Beijing

49. **Chariot fitting with mythical hunting scenes**
WESTERN HAN DYNASTY (206 BCE–8 CE)
Bronze inlaid with gold, silver, and turquoise; h. 26.4 cm, diam. 3.5 cm
Unearthed in 1965 from Sanpanshan tomb No. 122, Ding county, Hebei Province
Hebei Provincial Institute of Cultural Relics, Shijiazhuang

50. **Incense burner in the shape of a magical mountain isle of the immortals**
WESTERN HAN DYNASTY (206 BCE–8 CE)
Bronze inlaid with silver, gold, and turquoise; h. 26 cm, max. diam. 12.3 cm, diam. of foot 9.7 cm
Unearthed in 1968 from the tomb of Prince Liu Sheng, Mancheng county, Hebei Province
Hebei Provincial Museum, Shijiazhuang

51. **Covered vessel (*lian* or *zun*) with mythical hunting scenes, inscribed and dated (26 CE?)**
EASTERN HAN DYNASTY (25–220)
Gilt bronze; h. 24.5 cm, diam. of mouth 23.4 cm
Unearthed in 1962 at Dachuan village, Youyu county, Shanxi Province
Shanxi Provincial Museum, Taiyuan

52. **Screen support in the shape of a kneeling figure biting and holding snakes**
WESTERN HAN DYNASTY (206 BCE–8 CE)
Gilt bronze; h. 31.5 x l. 15.8 cm
Unearthed in 1983 from the tomb of the king of Nanyue, Guangzhou, Guangdong Province
Museum of the Tomb of the Nanyue King of the Western Han Dynasty, Guangzhou

53. **Lamp in the shape of a goose holding a fish**
WESTERN HAN DYNASTY (206 BCE–8 CE)
Bronze with paint; h. 53.8 x l. 31.3 cm
Unearthed in 1985 at Zhaoshiba village, Pingshuo, Shanxi Province
Shanxi Provincial Museum, Taiyuan

54. **Lamp with fifteen oil saucers in the form of a mythical tree**
EASTERN ZHOU, WARRING STATES period (475–221 BCE)
Bronze; h. 82.6 cm
Unearthed in 1977 from the tomb of the king of Zhongshan, Pingshan county, Hebei Province
Hebei Provincial Institute of Cultural Relics, Shijiazhuang

55. **Spear head with hanging men**
WESTERN HAN DYNASTY (206 BCE–8 CE)
Bronze; h. 41.5 cm
Unearthed in 1956 at Shizhaishan, Jinning county, Yunnan Province
Yunnan Provincial Museum, Kunming

56. **Buckle ornament with dancers holding cymbals**
WESTERN HAN DYNASTY (206 BCE–8 CE)
Gilt bronze; h. 12 x l. 18.5 cm
Unearthed in 1956 at Shizhaishan, Jinning county, Yunnan Province
Yunnan Provincial Museum, Kunming

57. **Low offering stand with two bulls and pouncing tiger**
EASTERN ZHOU, WARRING STATES period (475–221 BCE)
Bronze; h. 43 x l. 76 cm
Unearthed in 1972 from Lijiashan tomb No. 24, Jiangchuan county, Yunnan Province
Yunnan Provincial Museum, Kunming

58. **Man holding parasol**
WESTERN HAN DYNASTY (206 BCE–8 CE)
Bronze; h. of man 55.5 cm, h. of parasol 110.5 cm
Unearthed in 1956 at Shizhaishan, Jinning county, Yunnan Province
Yunnan Provincial Museum, Kunming

LACQUER

59. **Rearing dragon**
TANG DYNASTY (618–907)
Gilt bronze and iron; h. 34 x
l. 28 cm
Unearthed in 1975 at
Caochangpo in the southern
suburb of Xi'an, Shaanxi
Province
Shaanxi History Museum, Xi'an

60. **Six-lobed plate with
design of mythical beast**
TANG DYNASTY (618–907)
Silver with gilding; h. 1.2 cm,
diam. 15.3 cm
Unearthed in 1970 at Hejia
village, Xi'an, Shaanxi Province
Shaanxi History Museum, Xi'an

61. **Six-lobed plate with
design of bear**
TANG DYNASTY (618–907)
Silver with gilding; h. 1 cm,
diam. 13.4 cm
Unearthed in 1970 at Hejia
village, Xi'an, Shaanxi Province
Shaanxi History Museum, Xi'an

62. **Plate in the shape of two
peach halves with design of
two foxes**
TANG DYNASTY (618–907)
Silver with gilding; h. 1.5 x
max. width 22.5 cm
Unearthed in 1970 at Hejia
village, Xi'an, Shaanxi Province
Shaanxi History Museum, Xi'an

63. **Censer found with figure
of Ganesha**
TANG DYNASTY (618–907)
Silver with gilding; h. 41.8 cm,
diam. of mouth 24.5 cm
Discovered in 1987 in
underground chamber of the
Famen Temple Pagoda, Fufeng
county, Shaanxi Province
Famen Temple Museum,
Shaanxi Province

64. **Storage container with
bird designs for holding
brick tea**
TANG DYNASTY (618–907)
Silver with gilding; h. 17.8 cm,
diam. 16.1 cm
Discovered in 1987 in
underground chamber of the
Famen Temple Pagoda, Fufeng
county, Shaanxi Province
Famen Temple Museum,
Shaanxi Province

65. **Jar with design of figures
in a landscape**
TANG DYNASTY (618–907)
Silver with gilding; h. 24.7 cm,
diam. of jar 12.3 cm,
diam. of foot 12.6 cm
Discovered in 1987 in
underground chamber of the
Famen Temple Pagoda, Fufeng
county, Shaanxi Province
Famen Temple Museum,
Shaanxi Province

66. **Vessel based on bronze *hu*
vessel**
WESTERN HAN DYNASTY
(206 BCE–8 CE)
Wood-core lacquer; h. 57 cm,
diam. of mouth 18.1 cm, diam.
of foot 20 cm
Unearthed in 1972 from
Mawangdui tomb No. 1,
Changsha, Hunan Province
Hunan Provincial Museum,
Changsha

67. **Set of eight cups**
WESTERN HAN DYNASTY
(206 BCE–8 CE)
Wood-core lacquer; h. 12.2 cm,
w. 16–19 cm
Unearthed in 1972 from
Mawangdui tomb No. 1,
Changsha, Hunan Province
Hunan Provincial Museum,
Changsha

68. **Rectangular box with
cloud designs**
WESTERN HAN DYNASTY
(206 BCE–8 CE)
Wood-core lacquer; h. 21 x
l. 48.5 x w. 25.5 cm
Unearthed in 1972 from
Mawangdui tomb No. 3,
Changsha, Hunan Province
Hunan Provincial Museum,
Changsha

69. **Round tray with scroll
designs**
WESTERN HAN DYNASTY
(206 BCE–8 CE)
Wood-core lacquer; h. 4.5 cm,
diam. 53.7 cm
Unearthed in 1972 from
Mawangdui tomb No. 1,
Changsha, Hunan Province
Hunan Provincial Museum,
Changsha

70. **Rectangular tray with
scroll designs**
WESTERN HAN DYNASTY
(206 BCE–8 CE)
Wood-core lacquer; l. 75.6 cm
Unearthed in 1972 from
Mawangdui tomb No. 1,
Changsha, Hunan Province
Hunan Provincial Museum,
Changsha

71. **Round box with painted
and incised designs**
WESTERN HAN DYNASTY
(206 BCE–8 CE)
Wood-core lacquer; h. 18 cm,
diam. 32 cm
Unearthed in 1972 from
Mawangdui tomb No. 3,
Changsha, Hunan Province
Hunan Provincial Museum,
Changsha

72. **Reliquary with Buddhist
figures**
NORTHERN SONG DYNASTY
(960–1127)
Wood-core lacquer with seed
pearls; h. 41.2 x w. 24.5 cm
Unearthed in 1966 at the
Huiguang Pagoda site, Rui'an,
Zhejiang Province
Zhejiang Provincial Museum,
Hangzhou

73. **Sutra boxes with Buddhist
figures**
NORTHERN SONG DYNASTY
(960–1127)
Wood-core lacquer with seed
pearls; (outside box) h. 16 x
l. 40 x w. 18 cm, (inside box)
h. 11.5 x l. 33.8 x w. 11 cm
Unearthed in 1966 at the
Huiguang Pagoda site, Rui'an,
Zhejiang Province
Zhejiang Provincial Museum,
Hangzhou

74. **Round covered box with
aged scholar and servant**
Dated to 1351
YUAN DYNASTY (1279–1368)
Carved lacquer on a fabric-
covered wood core;
diam. 12.1 cm
Unearthed in 1953 from the
tomb of the Ren family,
Qingpu county, Shanghai
Shanghai Museum

75. **Round covered box with
figures viewing a waterfall,
inscribed**
MING DYNASTY, YONGLE MARK
AND PERIOD (1403–1424)
Carved lacquer on a fabric-
covered wood core; h. 7.7 cm,
diam. of mouth 22 cm
Palace Museum, Beijing

TEXTILES

76. **Potpourri bag**
WESTERN HAN DYNASTY
(206 BCE–8 CE)
Chain-stitch embroidery on
patterned silk; l. 48 cm
Unearthed in 1972 from
Mawangdui tomb No. 1,
Changsha, Hunan Province
Hunan Provincial Museum,
Changsha

77. **Gauze with patterns of
pine-bark lozenges, signifying
longevity**
WESTERN HAN DYNASTY
(206 BCE–8 CE)
Silk gauze; l. 75 x w. 48 cm
Unearthed in 1972 from
Mawangdui tomb No. 1,
Changsha, Hunan Province
Hunan Provincial Museum,
Changsha

78. **Embroidered silk with
designs signifying longevity**
WESTERN HAN DYNASTY
(206 BCE–8 CE)
Chain-stitch embroidery on
silk tabby; l. 23 x w. 16 cm
Unearthed in 1972 from
Mawangdui tomb No. 1,
Changsha, Hunan Province
Hunan Provincial Museum,
Changsha

79. **Printed silk with small
scroll motifs**
WESTERN HAN DYNASTY
(206 BCE–8 CE)
Silk tabby with printed and
drawn designs; l. 48 x w. 53 cm
Unearthed in 1972 from
Mawangdui tomb No. 1,
Changsha, Hunan Province
Hunan Provincial Museum,
Changsha

80. **Embroidered textile with
cloud design**
WESTERN HAN DYNASTY
(206 BCE–8 CE)
Chain-stitch embroidery on
silk tabby; l. 17 x w. 14.5 cm
Unearthed in 1972 from
Mawangdui tomb No. 1,
Changsha, Hunan Province
Hunan Provincial Museum,
Changsha

81. **Coverlet with dragon
design**
LIAO DYNASTY (916–1125)
Silk tapestry (*kesi*) with gold
threads; h. 90 x w. 56.5 cm
Unearthed in 1974 at Yemaotai,
Faku county,
Liaoning Province
Liaoning Provincial Museum,
Shenyang

82. **Zhu Kerou
Camellias**
SOUTHERN SONG DYNASTY
(1127–1279)
Silk tapestry (*kesi*), mounted as
album leaf; 25.6 x 25.3 cm
Liaoning Provincial Museum,
Shenyang

83. **Garden rocks with
chrysanthemum, high
mallow, and begonia, after a
painting by Cui Bai**
(act. ca. 1060–1085)
SOUTHERN SONG DYNASTY
(1127–1279)
Silk tapestry (*kesi*); 102.5 x 43.6
cm
Liaoning Provincial Museum,
Shenyang

84. **Heavenly King of the
West**
YUAN DYNASTY (1279–1368)
Silk embroidery; 250.8 x
247.7 cm
Donated in 1949 by Mr. Fei
Zhenshan
National Museum of Chinese
History, Beijing

85. **King of Bright Wisdom
Budong**
YUAN DYNASTY (1279–1368)
Silk tapestry (*kesi*); 90 x 56 cm
Administrative Office of Norbu
Linka, Lhasa,
Autonomous Region of Tibet

86. **Śākyamuni Buddha**
QING DYNASTY (1644–1911)
Silk tapestry (*kesi*); 182.7 x 77.6
cm
Liaoning Provincial Museum,
Shenyang

87. **Li Bai's "Evening in the
Peach and Plum Garden"**
QING DYNASTY (1644–1911)
Silk tapestry (*kesi*); 135.5 x
70.2 cm
Liaoning Provincial Museum,
Shenyang

88. General
QIN DYNASTY (221–207 BCE)
Terra-cotta; h. 196 cm
Unearthed in 1977 from the
Qin Shihuangdi tomb,
pit No. 1, Lintong county,
Shaanxi Province
Museum of Terra-cotta
Warriors and Horses of Qin
Shihuangdi, Xi'an

89. Military officer
QIN DYNASTY (221–207 BCE)
Terra-cotta; h. 198 cm
Unearthed in 1977 from the
Qin Shihuangdi tomb,
pit No. 1, Lintong county,
Shaanxi Province
Museum of Terra-cotta
Warriors and Horses of Qin
Shihuangdi, Xi'an

90. Military officer
QIN DYNASTY (221–207 BCE)
Terra-cotta; h. 192 cm
Unearthed in 1977 from the
Qin Shihuangdi tomb,
pit No. 1, Lintong county,
Shaanxi Province
Museum of Terra-cotta
Warriors and Horses of Qin
Shihuangdi, Xi'an

91. Soldier
QIN DYNASTY (221–207 BCE)
Terra-cotta; h. 185 cm
Unearthed in 1977 from the
Qin Shihuangdi tomb,
pit No. 1, Lintong county,
Shaanxi Province
Museum of Terra-cotta
Warriors and Horses of Qin
Shihuangdi, Xi'an

92. Chariot horse
QIN DYNASTY (221–207 BCE)
Terra-cotta; h. 163 x l. 200 cm
Unearthed in 1977 from the
Qin Shihuangdi tomb,
pit No. 1, Lintong county,
Shaanxi Province
Museum of Terra-cotta
Warriors and Horses of Qin
Shihuangdi, Xi'an

93. Chimera (bixie)
EASTERN HAN DYNASTY
(25–220)
Stone; h. 114 x l. 175 x
w. 45 cm
Unearthed in Yichuan county,
Henan Province
Guanlin Museum of Stone
Sculpture, Luoyang

94. Five kneeling musicians
WESTERN HAN DYNASTY
(206 BCE–8 CE)
Painted wood; h. 32.5–38 cm
Unearthed in 1972 from
Mawangdui tomb No. 1,
Changsha, Hunan Province
Hunan Provincial Museum,
Changsha

95. Standing figure
WESTERN HAN DYNASTY
(206 BCE–8 CE)
Painted wood; h. 47 cm
Unearthed in 1972 from
Mawangdui tomb No. 1,
Changsha, Hunan Province
Hunan Provincial Museum,
Changsha

**96. Standing performer with
a drum**
EASTERN HAN DYNASTY
(25–220)
Earthenware with pigment;
h. 66.5 cm
Unearthed in 1963 in Pi
county, Sichuan Province
Sichuan Provincial Museum,
Chengdu

**97. Squatting performer with
a drum**
EASTERN HAN DYNASTY
(25–220)
Earthenware with pigment;
h. 48 cm
Unearthed in 1982 from
Majiashan tomb No. 23,
Sanhexiang, Xindu county,
Sichuan Province
Administrative Office for
Cultural Relics, Xindu county,
Sichuan Province

**98. Tomb guardian holding
an ax and a snake**
EASTERN HAN DYNASTY
(25–220)
Earthenware; h. 87.2 cm
Unearthed in 1957 from the
Huangshui Xiang'ai tomb,
Shuangliu county, Sichuan
Province
Sichuan Provincial Museum,
Chengdu

**99. Kneeling woman holding
a mirror**
EASTERN HAN DYNASTY
(25–220)
Earthenware with red
pigments; h. 61.4 cm
Unearthed in 1963 in Pi
county, Sichuan Province
Sichuan Provincial Museum,
Chengdu

**100. Model of tower and
pond with animals**
EASTERN HAN DYNASTY
(25–220)
Glazed earthenware; h. 45 cm,
diam. of basin 55 cm
Unearthed in 1964 in Xichuan
county, Henan Province
Henan Provincial Museum,
Zhengzhou

101. Recumbent dog
EASTERN HAN DYNASTY
(25–220)
Glazed earthenware; h. 47 x
l. 44 x w. 20 cm
Unearthed at Nanyang, Henan
Province
Nanyang Municipal Museum

102. Tower
HAN DYNASTY (206 BCE–
220 CE)
Earthenware; h. 147 cm
Unearthed in 1952 at
Jiunüzhong, Huaiyang county,
Henan Province
Henan Provincial Museum,
Zhengzhou

**103. Tomb tile with scenes of
hunting and harvesting**
EASTERN HAN DYNASTY
(25–220)
Earthenware; l. 44.5 x
w. 39.6 x d. 6.5 cm
Unearthed in 1972 at Anren
village, Dayi county,
Sichuan Province
Sichuan Provincial Museum,
Chengdu

**104. Tomb tile with carriage
and horses**
EASTERN HAN DYNASTY
(25–220)
Earthenware; l. 45 x w. 39.5 x
d. 6.5 cm
Unearthed in 1955 from
Qingbaixiang tomb No. 1,
Xinfan county, Sichuan
Province
Sichuan Provincial Museum,
Chengdu

**105. Three aristocratic
women**
TANG DYNASTY (618–907)
Earthenware with pigment;
h. 73–83 cm
Unearthed in 1985 at
Hansenzhai, Xi'an, Shaanxi
Province
Institute for the Protection of
Cultural Relics, Xi'an

106. Horse
TANG DYNASTY (618–907)
Earthenware with pigment;
h. 87 x l. 93 cm
Unearthed in Luoyang, Henan
Province
Henan Provincial Museum,
Zhengzhou

107. Camel
TANG DYNASTY (618–907)
Earthenware with sancai
("three-color") glaze;
h. 81 x l. 68 cm
Unearthed in 1973 at Guanlin,
Luoyang, Henan Province
Luoyang Cultural Relics Work
Team, Henan Province

**108. Set of twelve calendrical
animals**
TANG DYNASTY (618–907)
Earthenware with pigment;
h. 38.5–41.5 cm
Unearthed in 1955 in the
suburbs of Xi'an,
Shaanxi Province
Shaanxi History Museum,
Xi'an

109. Civil official
TANG DYNASTY (618–907)
Earthenware with sancai
("three-color") glaze; h. 107 cm
Unearthed at Guanlin,
Luoyang, Henan Province
Luoyang Municipal Museum

110. Tomb guardian
TANG DYNASTY (618–907)
Earthenware with sancai
("three-color") glaze;
h. 103.5 cm
Unearthed in 1981 from the
tomb of An Pu at Longmen,
Luoyang, Henan Province
Luoyang Cultural Relics Work
Team, Henan Province

111. Heavenly king
TANG DYNASTY (618–907)
Earthenware with sancai
("three-color") glaze; h. 113 cm
Unearthed at Guanlin,
Luoyang, Henan Province
Luoyang Municipal Museum

**112. Four brick reliefs with
figures**
YUAN DYNASTY (1279–1368)
Earthenware; (1) h. 35 x
l. 35.8 x w. 21 cm (2) h. 34 x
l. 29 x w. 22.5 cm (3) h. 34 x
l. 31 x w. 19.5 cm (4) h. 35 x
l. 19.5 x w. 10 cm
Unearthed in 1973 at
Xifengfeng village, Jiaozuo,
Henan Province
Henan Provincial Museum,
Zhengzhou

**113. Bowl with stylized floral
or leaf designs**
NEOLITHIC PERIOD, YANGSHAO
CULTURE, MIAODIGOU TYPE
(4th millennium BCE)
Red earthenware with black
pigment;
h. 23 cm, max. diam. 36 cm
Unearthed in 1979 in Fangshan
county, Shanxi Province
Shanxi Provincial Institute of
Archaeology, Taiyuan

**114. Basin with human head
and fish designs**
NEOLITHIC PERIOD, YANGSHAO
CULTURE, BANPO TYPE
(late 6th–5th millennium BCE)
Red earthenware with black
pigment; h. 15.5 cm,
diam. of mouth 39.5 cm
Unearthed in 1955 at Banpo
village, near Xi'an,
Shaanxi Province
National Museum of Chinese
History, Beijing

**115. Vessel in the shape of
an owl**
NEOLITHIC PERIOD, YANGSHAO
CULTURE, MIAODIGOU TYPE
(4th millennium BCE)
Black earthenware; h. 35.8 cm
Unearthed in 1959 at Taiping
village, Hua county,
Shaanxi Province
National Museum of Chinese
History, Beijing

**116. Bottle in the shape of
a bird or dolphin**
NEOLITHIC PERIOD, LIANGZHU
CULTURE
(ca. 3600–ca. 2000 BCE)
Gray earthenware; l. 32.4 x
w. 11.7 cm
Unearthed in 1960 at Meiyan,
Wujiang county,
Jiangsu Province
Nanjing Museum

**117. Jar with incised animal
mask designs**
SHANG PERIOD (ca. 1600–
ca. 1100 BCE)
White earthenware; h. 22.1 cm,
diam. of mouth 9.1 cm, diam.
of foot 8.9 cm
Unearthed at Anyang, Henan
Province
Palace Museum, Beijing

**118. Jar (zun) with mat
impressions**
SHANG PERIOD (ca. 1600–
ca. 1100 BCE)
Ash-glazed stoneware
(protoporcelain); h. 27 cm,
diam. of mouth 27 cm
Unearthed in 1965 at
Zhengzhou, Henan Province
Zhengzhou Municipal
Museum

119. **Candleholder in the shape of a man riding a mythical beast**
WESTERN JIN DYNASTY (265–316)
Green-glazed stoneware (Celadon), Yue kilns; h. 27.7 cm
Palace Museum, Beijing

120. **Basin with applied Buddha figure**
WESTERN JIN DYNASTY (265–316)
Green-glazed stoneware (Celadon), Yue kilns; h. 7.5 cm, diam. of mouth 19.4, diam. of foot 10 cm
National Museum of Chinese History, Beijing

121. **Jar with six lugs and incised bird and tree motifs**
NORTHERN QI DYNASTY (550–577)
Green-glazed stoneware (Celadon); h. 28.5 cm, max. diam. of mouth 18.5 cm
Unearthed in 1958 from the tomb of Li Yun, Puyang county, Henan Province
Henan Provincial Museum, Zhengzhou

122. **Chicken-headed ewer with dragon handle**
NORTHERN QI DYNASTY (550–577)
Green-glazed stoneware (Celadon); h. 48.2 cm, max. diam. 32.5 cm
Unearthed in 1978 from the tomb of Lou Rui, Taiyuan, Shanxi Province
Shanxi Provincial Institute of Archaeology, Taiyuan

123. **Octagonal bottle**
TANG DYNASTY (618–907)
Green-glazed stoneware (Celadon), Yue kilns; h. 21.7 cm, diam. of mouth 2.3, diam. of foot 7.8 cm
Palace Museum, Beijing

124. **Bowl**
TANG DYNASTY (618–907)
Green-glazed stoneware (Celadon), Yue kilns; h. 6.8 cm, diam. of mouth 22.4 cm
Discovered in 1987 in underground chamber of the Famen Temple Pagoda, Fufeng county, Shaanxi Province
Shaanxi History Museum, Xi'an

125. **Octagonal bottle**
TANG DYNASTY (618–907)
Green-glazed stoneware (Celadon), Yue kilns; h. 21.5 cm, diam. of mouth 2.2, diam. of foot 8 cm
Discovered in 1987 in underground chamber of the Famen Temple Pagoda, Fufeng county, Shaanxi Province
Famen Temple Museum, Shaanxi Province

126. **Dish in the shape of a five-petaled blossom, base inscribed with character *guan* ("official")**
TANG DYNASTY (618–907)
White stoneware with transparent glaze, Xing or Ding kilns; h. 3.5 cm, diam. of mouth 13.8 cm, diam. of foot 6.45 cm
Unearthed in 1985 at Huoshaobi, Xi'an, Shaanxi Province
Institute for the Protection of Cultural Relics, Xi'an

127. **Dish in the shape of a three-petaled blossom, base inscribed with character *guan* ("official")**
TANG DYNASTY (618–907)
White stoneware with transparent glaze, Xing or Ding kilns; h. 2.3 x w. 11.7 cm, diam. of foot 5.9 cm
Unearthed in 1985 at Huoshaobi, Xi'an, Shaanxi Province
Institute for the Protection of Cultural Relics, Xi'an

128. **Covered jar with four lugs**
FIVE DYNASTIES (907–960)
White stoneware with transparent glaze, Xing or Ding kilns; h. 26.2 cm, diam. of mouth 10.4 cm, diam. of foot 9.1 cm
Donated by Mr. Zhou Rui
Shanghai Museum

129. **Bowl inscribed with characters *yang ding* ("glorious Ding")**
FIVE DYNASTIES (907–960)
White stoneware with transparent glaze, Ding kilns; h. 6.3 cm, diam. of mouth 19.9 cm, diam. of foot 7.5 cm
Donated by Mr. Huang Zhaoxi
Shanghai Museum

130. **Bottle with carved and combed peony designs**
NORTHERN SONG DYNASTY (960–1127)
Green-glazed stoneware, Yaozhou kilns; h. 19.9 cm, diam. of mouth 6.9 cm, diam. of foot 7.8 cm
Palace Museum, Beijing

131. **Bowl with incised ducks and water weeds**
NORTHERN SONG DYNASTY (960–1127)
White stoneware with transparent glaze and bronze rim band, Ding kilns; h. 6.4 cm, diam. of mouth 23.5 cm, diam. of foot 7.3 cm
Shanghai Museum

132. **Tripod vessel in the shape of an archaic bronze *lian* or *zun* vessel**
NORTHERN SONG DYNASTY (960–1127)
Pale blue-green–glazed stoneware, Ru kilns; h. 12.9 cm, diam. of mouth 18 cm
Palace Museum, Beijing

133. **Mallow-shaped bowl**
SOUTHERN SONG DYNASTY (1127–1279)
Crackled pale blue-green–glazed stoneware, Hangzhou *Guan* ("official") kilns; h. 4.2 cm, diam. of mouth 17.3 cm, diam. of foot 9.9 cm
Palace Museum, Beijing

134. **Vase with dish-shaped mouth and raised ribs**
SOUTHERN SONG DYNASTY (1127–1279)
Crackled pale blue-green–glazed stoneware, Longquan kilns; h. 31 cm, diam. of mouth 10.4 cm, diam. of foot 11.3 cm
Palace Museum, Beijing

135. **Jar with incised floral designs**
NORTHERN SONG DYNASTY (960–1127)
Bluish–glazed white stoneware (*qingbai*), Jingdezhen kilns; h. 26.6 cm, diam. of mouth 5 cm, diam. of foot 8.5 cm
Palace Museum, Beijing

136. **Vase with carved peony designs**
NORTHERN SONG DYNASTY (960–1127)
Cizhou-type stoneware with white slip and transparent glaze; h. 34 cm, diam. of mouth 6 cm
Unearthed in 1959 in Tangyin county, Henan Province
Henan Provincial Museum, Zhengzhou

137. **Pillow with painted design of a hawk chasing a rabbit among reeds**
JIN DYNASTY (1115–1234)
Cizhou-type stoneware with white slip, black pigment, and transparent glaze; h. 9.7 x l. 24.7 x w. 17 cm
Henan Provincial Museum, Zhengzhou

138. **Vase with two leopards incised on a ring-matted ground**
NORTHERN SONG DYNASTY (960–1127)
Stoneware with white slip and transparent glaze, Dengfeng kilns; h. 32.1 cm, diam. of mouth 7.1 cm, diam. of foot 9.9 cm
Palace Museum, Beijing

139. **Covered jar with floral designs in painted applied openwork**
YUAN DYNASTY (1279–1368)
Porcelain with underglaze cobalt blue and copper red painted and applied decoration, Jingdezhen kilns; h. 42.3 cm, diam. of mouth 15.2 cm, diam. of foot 18.5 cm
Unearthed in 1964 from a Yuan dynasty hoard at Baoding, Hebei Province
Palace Museum, Beijing

140. **Covered jar with three lugs**
MING DYNASTY, YONGLE PERIOD (1403–1424)
Pale green-glazed porcelain, Jingdezhen kilns; h. 10.4 cm, diam. of mouth 9.9 cm, diam. of foot 14.1 cm
Palace Museum, Beijing

141. **Flower-shaped brush washer**
MING DYNASTY, XUANDE MARK AND PERIOD (1426–1435)
Copper red-glazed porcelain, Jingdezhen kilns; h. 3.8 cm, width of mouth 15.9 cm, diam. of foot 13 cm
Palace Museum, Beijing

142. **Moon flask with dragons among lotus scrolls**
MING DYNASTY, YONGLE PERIOD (1403–1424)
Porcelain with underglaze cobalt blue decoration, Jingdezhen kilns; h. 44 cm, diam. of mouth 8 cm, diam. of foot 14.5 cm
Palace Museum, Beijing

143. **Jar with flowering plum, bamboo, and pine**
MING DYNASTY, YONGLE PERIOD (1403–1424)
Porcelain with underglaze cobalt blue decoration, Jingdezhen kilns; h. 36 cm, diam. of mouth 6.7 cm, diam. of foot 13.9 cm
Palace Museum, Beijing

144. **Stem bowl with scenes of ladies in a garden**
MING DYNASTY, XUANDE MARK AND PERIOD (1426–1435)
Porcelain with underglaze cobalt blue decoration, Jingdezhen kilns; h. 10.2 cm, diam. of mouth 15.5 cm, diam. of foot 4.5 cm
Palace Museum, Beijing

145. **Vase with flower and bird designs**
QING DYNASTY, KANGXI PERIOD (1662–1722)
Porcelain with *wucai* ("five color") decoration, Jingdezhen kilns; h. 46.4 cm, diam. of mouth 11.2 cm, diam. of foot 14.7 cm
Palace Museum, Beijing

146. **Vase with flower designs**
QING DYNASTY, YONGZHENG MARK AND PERIOD (1723–1735)
Porcelain with *doucai* ("clashing" or "matched color") decoration, Jingdezhen kilns; h. 26 cm, diam. of mouth 5.2 cm, diam. of foot 11.8 cm
Palace Museum, Beijing

147. **Stele with Maitreya**
Dated to 471
NORTHERN WEI DYNASTY
(386–534)
Sandstone; h. 86.9 x w. 55 cm
Unearthed in Xingping
county, Shaanxi Province
Forest of Steles Museum, Xi'an

148. **Śākyamuni on lion throne**
Dated to 502
NORTHERN WEI DYNASTY
(386–534)
Sandstone; h. 48.5 x w. 27.7 cm
Found in 1952
Forest of Steles Museum, Xi'an

149. **Stele with Śākyamuni and bodhisattvas**
NORTHERN WEI DYNASTY
(386–534)
Stone; h. 96 x w. 43.5 cm
Unearthed in 1974 in Qi
county, Henan Province
Henan Provincial Museum,
Zhengzhou

150. **Stele with Śākyamuni and attendants**
Dated to 523
LIANG DYNASTY (502–557)
Sandstone; h. 35.8 x w. 30.3 x
d. 20 cm
Unearthed in 1954 at the
Wanfo Temple site, Chengdu,
Sichuan Province
Sichuan Provincial Museum,
Chengdu

151. **Stele: (obverse) bodhisattvas; (reverse) lower tier, figures, animals, and buildings in mountainous landscape; middle panel, lotus pond; upper tier, Buddha preaching to monks in garden setting**
LIANG DYNASTY (502–557)
Sandstone; h. 121 x w. 60 x
d. 24.5 cm
Unearthed in 1954 at the
Wanfo Temple site, Chengdu,
Sichuan Province
Sichuan Provincial Museum,
Chengdu

152. **Engraved panel with Buddha beneath canopy**
Dated to 524
NORTHERN WEI DYNASTY
(386–534)
Stone; h. 39.5 x l. 144 x
w. 14 cm
Unearthed in the late 19th
century in Luoyang,
Henan Province
Henan Provincial Museum,
Zhengzhou

153. **Pillar base with mountains, dragons, and figures**
NORTHERN WEI DYNASTY
(386–534)
Stone; h. 16.5 x w. 32 cm
Unearthed in 1966 from the
Sima Jinlong tomb, Shijiazhai,
Datong city, Shanxi Province
Shanxi Provincial Museum,
Taiyuan

154. **Stele with Śākyamuni and Maitreya**
Dated to 532
NORTHERN WEI DYNASTY
(386–534)
Sandstone; h. 90 x w. 46 x
d. 14 cm
Institute for the Protection of
Cultural Relics, Xi'an

155. **Stele: (obverse) Śākyamuni and attendants; (reverse) Maitreya**
WESTERN WEI DYNASTY
(535–557)
Sandstone; h. 48.2 x w. 21.5 x
d. 12.1 cm
Institute for the Protection of
Cultural Relics, Xi'an

156. **Śākyamuni**
Dated to 540
EASTERN WEI DYNASTY
(534–550)
Sandstone; h. 35 cm
Unearthed in 1954 at the
Huata Temple site, Taiyuan,
Shanxi Province
Shanxi Provincial Museum,
Taiyuan

157. **Stele with enthroned Buddhas and attendant bodhisattvas and monks**
Dated to 559
NORTHERN QI DYNASTY
(550–577)
Limestone; h. 110 x w. 58.5 x
d. 10 cm
Unearthed in 1963 in
Xiangcheng county, Henan
Province
Henan Provincial Museum,
Zhengzhou

158. **Stele: (obverse) Śākyamuni and attendants; (reverse) myriad Buddhas**
Dated to 565
NORTHERN ZHOU DYNASTY
(557–581)
Stone; h. 259 x w. 73.4 x
d. 19.5 cm
Unearthed in 1963 in Luoning
county, Henan Province
Henan Provincial Museum,
Zhengzhou

159. **Stele with Buddhist trinity**
NORTHERN ZHOU DYNASTY
(557–581)
Marble; h. 40 x w. 28 x
d. 8.5 cm
Unearthed in 1975 at Caotan
in the northern suburb of
Xi'an, Shaanxi Province
Institute for the Protection of
Cultural Relics, Xi'an

160. **Amitābha altar**
Dated to 584
SUI DYNASTY (581–618)
Gilt bronze; h. 41 cm, l. of altar
stand 24.3 cm, w. of altar stand
24 cm
Unearthed in 1974 at Bali
village, Xi'an, Shaanxi Province
Institute for the Protection of
Cultural Relics, Xi'an

161. **Stele with Śākyamuni and attendants**
NORTHERN QI DYNASTY
(550–577)
Sandstone with polychrome;
h. 46 x w. 27 cm
Unearthed in 1954 at the
Huata Temple site, Taiyuan,
Shanxi Province
Shanxi Provincial Museum

162. **Seated Buddha**
SUI DYNASTY (581–618)
Marble with pigments;
h. 100.7 x w. 74.7 cm
Palace Museum, Beijing

163. **Head of a bodhisattva**
TANG DYNASTY (618–907)
Sandstone; h. 36 cm
Unearthed in 1954 at the
Wanfo Temple site, Chengdu,
Sichuan Province
Sichuan Provincial Museum,
Chengdu

164. **Head of Eleven-Headed Avalokiteśvara**
TANG DYNASTY (618–907)
Marble; h. 25.5 cm
Unearthed in 1983 in the
western suburb of Xi'an,
Shaanxi Province
Forest of Steles Museum, Xi'an

165. **Torso of a bodhisattva**
TANG DYNASTY (618–907)
Marble; h. 110 x w. 35 cm
Unearthed in 1959 in the
precincts of the Daminggong, a
Tang dynasty imperial palace in
Xi'an, Shaanxi Province
Forest of Steles Museum, Xi'an

166. **Head of a bodhisattva**
TANG DYNASTY (618–907)
Marble with gold; h. 15.7 cm
Unearthed in 1959 at the
Anguo Temple site, Xi'an,
Shaanxi Province
Forest of Steles Museum, Xi'an

167. **Torso of a guardian king**
TANG DYNASTY (618–907)
Marble; h. 100 cm
Forest of Steles Museum, Xi'an

168. **Torso of a vajrasattva (a type of bodhisattva)**
TANG DYNASTY (618–907)
Sandstone; h. 86 cm
Unearthed in 1954 at the
Wanfo Temple site, Chengdu,
Sichuan Province
Sichuan Provincial Museum,
Chengdu

169. **Heavenly King**
TANG DYNASTY (618–907)
Gilt bronze; h. 65 cm
Unearthed in Baoji, Shaanxi
Province
Baoji Municipal Museum

170. **Trailokyavijaya (conqueror of greed, hatred, and delusion)**
TANG DYNASTY (618–907)
Marble; h. 71 x w. 42 cm
Unearthed in 1959 at the
Anguo Temple site, Xi'an,
Shaanxi Province
Forest of Steles Museum, Xi'an

171. **Ratnasaṃbhava**
TANG DYNASTY (618–907)
Marble with traces of gold;
h. 67.5 cm
Unearthed in 1959 at the
Anguo Temple site, Xi'an,
Shaanxi Province
Forest of Steles Museum, Xi'an

172. **Mañjuśri**
TANG DYNASTY (618–907)
Marble; h. 75 cm
Unearthed in 1959 at the
Anguo Temple site, Xi'an,
Shaanxi Province
Forest of Steles Museum, Xi'an

173. **Head of a bodhisattva**
TANG DYNASTY (618–907)
Sandstone; h. 30 x w. 19 cm
Unearthed in 1957 at
Nannieshui village, Qin
county, Shanxi Province
Shanxi Provincial Museum,
Taiyuan

174. **Standing bodhisattva**
TANG DYNASTY (618–907)
Sandstone with gold; h. 60 cm
Unearthed in 1954 at the
Huata Temple site, Taiyuan,
Shanxi Province
Shanxi Provincial Museum,
Taiyuan

175. **Torso of a bodhisattva**
TANG DYNASTY (618–907)
Sandstone; h. 112 cm
Unearthed at the Guanghua
Temple site, Baicheng village,
Taigu county, Shanxi Province
Shanxi Provincial Museum,
Taiyuan

176. **Head of Avalokiteśvara**
TANG DYNASTY (618–907)
Sandstone; h. 41 cm
Unearthed in 1954 at the
Wanfo Temple site, Chengdu,
Sichuan Province
Sichuan Provincial Museum,
Chengdu

177. **Two arhats, one with dragon, the other with tiger**
NORTHERN SONG DYNASTY
(960–1127)
Stone; (1) h. 38 cm
(2) h. 38 cm
Discovered in 1980 at the
Boshan Temple site, Fu county,
Shaanxi Province
Shaanxi History Museum,
Xi'an

CALLIGRAPHY

178. **Ink stone**
NORTHERN WEI DYNASTY
(386–534)
Stone; h. 8.5 x l. 21.2 x
w. 21 cm
Unearthed in 1970 near
Datong, Shanxi Province
Shanxi Provincial Museum,
Taiyuan

179. **Zhu Yunming** (1461–1527)
"The Terrace of Ode to the
Wind" and other poems
composed by Zhu Yunming,
written in wild cursive script
(*kuangcao*)
Dated to 1523
MING DYNASTY (1368–1644)
Handscroll, ink on paper;
24.6 x 655.6 cm
Palace Museum, Beijing

180. **Zhang Ruitu** (1570–1641)
Transcription of Wang Wei's
"Song of the Aged General,"
written in cursive script
(*caoshu*)
MING DYNASTY (1368–1644)
Handscroll, ink on silk; 29.5 x
629.5 cm
Palace Museum, Beijing

181. **Wang Duo** (1592–1652)
Transcription of Wang Wei's
"Enjoying a Repast at the
Home of Elder Zhao in
Qizhou" and "Passing by the
Herbal Garden of Master
Hesui in Spring," written in
standard script (*kaishu*)
Dated to 1643
MING DYNASTY (1368–1644)
Handscroll, ink on satin; 21.2 x
165.5 cm
Palace Museum, Beijing

182. **Zhang Zhao** (1691–1745)
Transcription of "Seventh
Month" from the *Odes of Bin*,
written in standard script
(*kaishu*)
QING DYNASTY (1644–1911)
Hanging scroll, ink on paper;
176 x 92 cm
Palace Museum, Beijing

183. **Deng Shiru** (1743–1805)
Couplet in seven-character
lines, written in clerical script
(*lishu*)
QING DYNASTY (1644–1911)
Hanging scrolls, ink on gold-
flecked paper; 130.1 x 27.6 cm
Palace Museum, Beijing

PAINTING

184. **Wang Shen**
(ca. 1048–after 1104)
Misty River and Layered Hills
NORTHERN SONG DYNASTY
(960–1127)
Handscroll, ink and color on
silk; 45.2 x 166 cm
Shanghai Museum

185. **Zhao Kui** (1185–1266)
In the Spirit of Poems by Du Fu
SOUTHERN SONG DYNASTY
(1127–1279)
Handscroll, ink on silk; 24.7 x
212.2 cm
Shanghai Museum

186. **Anonymous**
Snowy Landscape
SOUTHERN SONG DYNASTY
(1127–1279)
Handscroll, ink and light color
on paper; 24 x 48.2 cm
Shanghai Museum

187. **Song Boren**
(act. mid-13th c.)
Album of Plum Blossom Portraits
1238; reprint, 1261
SOUTHERN SONG DYNASTY
(1127–1279)
Woodblock print book; each
leaf 23.1 x 28.6 cm
Shanghai Museum

188. **Ni Zan** (1306[?]–1374)
Six Gentlemen
Dated to 1345
YUAN DYNASTY (1279–1368)
Hanging scroll, ink on paper;
61.9 x 33.3 cm
Shanghai Museum

189. **Wang Meng**
(ca. 1308–1385)
*Dwelling in the Qingbian
Mountains*
Dated to 1366
YUAN DYNASTY (1279–1368)
Hanging scroll, ink on paper;
140.6 x 42.2 cm
Shanghai Museum

190. **Shang Xi**
(act. ca. 2nd quarter of 15th c.)
*The Xuande Emperor on an
Outing*
MING DYNASTY (1368–1644)
Hanging scroll, ink and color
on paper; 211 x 353 cm
Palace Museum, Beijing

191. **Xie Huan** (act. 1426–1452)
*The Literary Gathering in the
Apricot Garden*
Ca. 1437
MING DYNASTY (1368–1644)
Handscroll, ink and color on
silk; h. 37 cm
Zhenjiang Municipal Museum

192. **Dai Jin** (1388–1462)
*Landscape in the Manner of Yan
Wengui*
MING DYNASTY (1368–1644)
Hanging scroll, ink on paper;
98.2 x 45.8 cm
Shanghai Museum

193. **Wu Wei** (1459–1508)
Fishermen on a Snowy River
MING DYNASTY (1368–1644)
Hanging scroll, ink on silk;
245 x 156 cm
Hubei Provincial Museum,
Wuhan

194. **Zhou Chen**
(ca. 1455–after 1536)
Peach Blossom Spring
Dated to 1533
MING DYNASTY (1368–1644)
Hanging scroll, ink and color
on silk; 161.5 x 102.5 cm
Suzhou Municipal Museum

195. **Qiu Ying** (ca. 1495–1552)
*Playing the Flute by Pine and
Stream*
MING DYNASTY (1368–1644)
Hanging scroll, ink and color
on silk; 116.4 x 65.8 cm
Nanjing Museum

196. **Shen Zhou** (1427–1509)
Eastern Villa
MING DYNASTY (1368–1644)
Album, ink and color on paper;
each leaf 28.6 x 33 cm
Nanjing Museum

197. **Wen Zhengming**
(1470–1559)
Studio of True Appreciation
Dated to 1549
MING DYNASTY (1368–1644)
Handscroll, ink and color on
paper; 36 x 107.8 cm
Shanghai Museum

198. **Xu Wei** (1521–1593)
*Peonies, Banana Plant, and
Rock*
MING DYNASTY (1368–1644)
Hanging scroll, ink on paper;
120.6 x 58.4 cm
Shanghai Museum

199. **Chen Hongshou**
(1598–1652)
The Pleasures of He Tianzhang
MING DYNASTY (1368–1644)
Handscroll, ink and color on
silk; 25.3 x 163.2 cm
Suzhou Municipal Museum

200. **Dong Qichang**
(1555–1636)
*Poetic Feeling at Qixia
Monastery*
Dated to 1626
MING DYNASTY (1368–1644)
Hanging scroll, ink on paper;
133.1 x 52.5 cm
Shanghai Museum

201. **Ten Bamboo Studio
Manual of Calligraphy
and Painting**
Published 1627–1633 by Hu
Zhengyan (1584–1674)
MING DYNASTY (1368–1644)
Woodblock print book; each
leaf 25.8 x 31 cm
Palace Museum, Beijing

202. **Ten Bamboo Studio
Letter Papers**
Published 1644 by Hu
Zhengyan (1584–1674)
MING DYNASTY (1368–1644)
Woodblock print book; each
leaf 21 x 13.6 cm
Palace Museum, Beijing

203. *Album of a Hundred
Flowers*, after paintings by
Zhang Chaoxiang (act. 19th c.)
QING DYNASTY, TONGZHI PERIOD
(1862–1874)
Woodblock print book; each
leaf 24.2 x 16.8 cm
Palace Museum, Beijing

204. **Wang Yuanqi** (1642–1715)
*Complete in Soul, Sufficient in
Spirit*
Dated to 1708
QING DYNASTY (1644–1911)
Hanging scroll, ink on paper;
137.2 x 71.5 cm
Palace Museum, Beijing

205. **Wu Li** (1632–1718)
*Reading "The Book of
Changes" in a Streamside
Pavilion*
Dated to 1678
QING DYNASTY (1644–1911)
Hanging scroll, ink on paper;
211.7 x 78.7 cm
Shanghai Museum

206. **Kuncan** (1612–ca. 1674)
Clear Sky over Verdant Hills
Dated to 1660
QING DYNASTY (1644–1911)
Hanging scroll, ink and color
on silk; 85 x 40.5 cm
Nanjing Museum

207. **Hongren** (1610–1664)
Peaks and Ravines at Jiuqi
QING DYNASTY (1644–1911)
Hanging scroll, ink on paper;
110.6 x 58.9 cm
Shanghai Museum

208. **Yuanji** (Shitao; 1642–1707)
*Pure Sounds of Hills and
Streams*
QING DYNASTY (1644–1911)
Hanging scroll, ink on paper;
102.5 x 42.4 cm
Shanghai Museum

209. **Gong Xian** (1618–1689)
Summer Mountains after Rain
QING DYNASTY (1644–1911)
Hanging scroll, ink on silk;
141.7 x 57.8 cm
Nanjing Museum

210. **Bada Shanren**
(1626–1705)
Ducks and Lotuses
Dated to 1696
QING DYNASTY (1644–1911)
Hanging scroll, ink on paper;
166 x 76.3 cm
Shanghai Museum

211. **Yuanji** (Shitao; 1642–1707)
Clear Autumn in Huaiyang
QING DYNASTY (1644–1911)
Hanging scroll, ink and color
on paper; 89 x 57.1 cm
Nanjing Museum

212. **Zou Zhe** (1636–ca. 1708)
Album of Landscapes
QING DYNASTY (1644–1911)
Album, ink and color on paper;
three leaves each
12.6 x 28.6 cm, remaining
leaves each 12.6 x 14 cm
Nanjing Museum

213. **Yuan Jiang**
(act. ca. 1690–ca. 1746)
Garden for Gazing
QING DYNASTY (1644–1911)
Handscroll, ink and light color
on silk; 51.5 x 254.5 cm
Tianjin Municipal History
Museum

214. **Gao Cen**
(act. ca. 1645–1689)
The Temple on Jinshan
QING DYNASTY (1644–1911)
Hanging scroll, ink and color
on silk; 180.8 x 95.1 cm
Nanjing Museum

215. **Gao Xiang** (1688–1754)
Finger-Snap Pavilion
QING DYNASTY (1644–1911)
Hanging scroll, ink on paper;
69 x 38 cm
Yangzhou Municipal Museum

216. **Huang Shen**
(1687–after 1768)
Willows and Egrets
QING DYNASTY (1644–1911)
Hanging scroll, ink and color
on paper; 113.7 x 57.7 cm
Shanghai Museum

217. **Li Shan** (1686–after 1760)
Pine, Wisteria, and Peonies
Dated to 1755
QING DYNASTY (1644–1911)
Hanging scroll, ink and color
on paper; 238 x 118.2 cm
Shanghai Museum

218. **Jin Nong** (1687–1764)
*Album of Landscapes and
Figures*
Dated to 1759
QING DYNASTY (1644–1911)
Album, ink and color on paper;
each leaf 26.1 x 34.9 cm
Shanghai Museum

219. **Hua Yan** (1682–1756)
The Golden Valley Garden
Dated to 1732
QING DYNASTY (1644–1911)
Hanging scroll, ink and color
on paper; 178.9 x 94.1 cm
Shanghai Museum

THE SOLOMON R. GUGGENHEIM FOUNDATION